Civil Society in Democratization

Editors

PETER BURNELL
PETER CALVERT

FRANK CASS
LONDON • PORTLAND, OR

First published in 2004 in Great Britain by
FRANK CASS AND COMPANY LIMITED
A Member of the Taylor & Francis Group
Crown House, 47 Chase Side, Southgate
London N14 5BP, England

and in the United States of America by
FRANK CASS
ISBS, 920 NE 58th Avenue, Suite 300
Portland, Oregon 97213-3786

Copyright © 2004 Taylor & Francis Ltd

Website: www.frankcass.com

British Library Cataloguing in Publication Data

Civil society in democratization
1. Civil society 2. Democratization
I. Burnell, Peter J., 1947– II. Calvert, Peter
321.8

ISBN 0 7146 5589 9 (cloth)
ISBN 0 7146 8474 0 (paper)
[ISSN 1465–4601]

Library of Congress Cataloging-in-Publication Data

Civil society in democratization / edited by Peter Burnell and Peter
Calvert.
    p. cm.
Includes index.
    ISBN 0-7146-5589-9 (cloth) – ISBN 0-7146-8474-0 (pbk.)
    1. Civil society. 2. Democratization. I. Burnell, Peter J.
II. Calvert, Peter. III. Title.
    JC337.C5635 2003
    300 – dc21
                                            2003015391

Printed in Great Britain by Antony Rowe Ltd, Chippenham, Wilts.

CIVIL SOCIETY IN DEMOCRATIZATION

Of Related Interest

CIVIL SOCIETY
Democratic Perspectives
edited by Robert Fine and Shirin Rai

THE RESILIENCE OF DEMOCRACY
Persistent Practice, Durable Idea
edited by Peter Burnell and Peter Calvert

DEMOCRACY ASSISTANCE
International Co-operation for Democratization
edited by Peter Burnell

THE INTERNET, DEMOCRACY AND DEMOCRATIZATION
edited by Peter Ferdinand

DEMOCRATIZATION AND THE MEDIA
edited by Vicky Randall

FACTIONAL POLITICS AND DEMOCRATIZATION
edited by Richard Gillespie, Michael Waller and Lourdes López Nieto

Contents

Sources

Civil Society, Democratization and Development: Clearing the Analytical Ground by Gordon White (late Professorial Fellow at the Institute of Development Studies, University of Sussex) originally published in *Democratization* Volume 1, No. 3 (1994).

Bowling in the Bronx: The Uncivil Interstices between Civil and Political Society by Laurence Whitehead (Official Fellow, Nuffield College, University of Oxford) originally published in *Democratization* Volume 4, No. 1 (1997).

The Taming of the Idea of Civil Society by Gideon Baker (Lecturer in Politics, University of Salford) originally published in *Democratization* Volume 6, No. 3 (1999).

Civil Society: Market Economy and Democratic Polity by David Beetham (Professor Emeritus, Department of Politics, University of Leeds) originally published in *Democratization* Volume 4, No. 1 (1997).

Civil Society, the Market and Democracy in Latin America by Jenny Pearce (Professor of Latin American Politics, Department of Peace Studies, University of Bradford) originally published in *Democratization* Volume 4, No. 2 (1997).

Civil Society, the State and Democracy in Africa by Nelson Kasfir (Professor of Politics, Dartmouth College, New Hampshire, USA) originally published in *Commonwealth and Comparative Politics* Volume 36, No. 2 (1998).

The 'Civil' and the 'Political' in Civil Society: The Case of India by Neera Chandhoke (Professor of Political Science, Department of Political Science, Delhi University, India) originally published in *Democratization* Volume 8, No. 2 (2001).

Die Lehrjahre sind vorbei! Re-forming Democratic Interest Groups in the East German Länder by Joyce Mushaben (Professor of Comparative Politics, Department of Political Science, University of Missouri at St Louis) originally published in *Democratization* Volume 8, No. 4 (2001).

Civil Society and Transnational Non-Governmental Organizations in the Euro-Mediterranean Partnership by Annette Jünemann (Associate Professor, University of Kassel) originally published in *Democratization* Volume 9, No. 1 (2002).

Democratization in Bosnia: The Limits of Civil Society Building Strategies by David Chandler (Senior Lecturer in International Relations, Centre for the Study of Democracy, University of Westminster) originally published in *Democratization* Volume 5, No. 4 (1998).

Building Civil Societies in East Central Europe: The Effects of American NGOs on Women's Groups by Patrice McMahon (Assistant Professor, Department of Political Science, University of Nebraska at Lincoln) originally published in *Democratization* Volume 8, No. 2 (2001).

Civil Society in Democratization

PETER BURNELL and PETER CALVERT

'Civil society as the source of influence and control of representative
political institutions is the heart of a liberal democracy.'
(Jean Louise Cohen, in *Encyclopedia of Democratic Thought*)[1]

Probably the only proposition about civil society that few would contest is
that over the last ten to fifteen years interest in the subject has been
enormous and the literature about it has grown exponentially. Here is not the
place to attempt a comprehensive survey, or pretend to provide a
representative summary of the discourse. Rather this brief preface serves
only to identify the flavour of the collection of studies in this book, showing
what it offers readers at different levels – from specialists engaged in the
analysis of democratization to students of world politics and sociology who
may be approaching the subject of civil society for the very first time. The
book's coverage does not extend to civil society's place in the history of
political and social thought before it was rediscovered in the 1970s and
1980s in the context of popular protest movements in Latin America and
Central and Eastern Europe. But Whitehead's piece includes a concise
resumé; and there are complementary volumes that focus on the
philosophical treatment of civil society down the ages.[2]

The structure of the collection falls broadly into three parts. The first
third examines conceptual and theoretical issues surrounding civil society,
closely interrogating the meaning of this highly contested term. Both
Whitehead and Chandhoke are right: as the former remarks, we still lack a
single, unified meaning of the term, and as the latter observes, in becoming
a 'consensual' (or over-stretched) concept, civil society becomes
essentially-contested – that is, a concept on which, by definition, agreement
is impossible.[3] However, endorsement of the view that 'civil society' has
been used in a confusing variety of ways (tending, in White's words, to
become a 'muddled political slogan') is in itself no argument for rejecting
it, especially now that we have the benefit of White's pioneering efforts to
inject greater clarity. Pearce too confronts scepticism about the worth of the
term and asks whether it provides any added value, and argues that it can
indeed be a useful analytical tool. The moral is we should go on to try to
establish empirically what difference civil society makes to processes of

change, and so long as we employ it with due rigour and sensitivity we may be able to confirm that Pearce is right.

The middle part of the book contains studies that, while strongly grounded theoretically and conceptually refined, provide in addition more empirically-oriented applications. We find these in both new and established democracies, and worldwide in Latin America, India, Europe, and Africa both north and south of the Sahara. The final third comprises case studies of the efforts by various organizations in the 'international community' to help build civil society in emerging and prospective democracies, as part of a broader commitment to promote democratization and construct durable peace in formerly troubled societies. The concluding case takes as its exclusive interest gender initiatives and womens' groups specifically.

As can be seen, the reach of the idea of civil society knows no regional or geopolitical boundaries. It is a part of the remit of how we study countries, as much in the North as in the South. The bias in this collection towards the countries of the developing and post-communist worlds owes more to the interest in investigating connections between civil society and dramatic processes of political change than to any snub to the so-called mature democracies. And far from being something that is largely internal to countries or to distinct sub-national groups, civic associations have very much become a focus of international relations too. The proposition that we are now seeing the emergence of a global civil society provides a yet further dimension. But while that lies largely beyond the scope of this book, Jünemann's evaluation of the performance of *transnational* non-governmental organizations within the European Union–North Africa partnership arrangements does give a glimpse of what the future might look like.

The studies here include several that have come to be regularly cited in the contemporary literature on civil society and democratization because of the distinctive contributions they make to advancing our understanding. They are all equally accessible to a wide range of inquiries and, moreover, contain a good many cross-references. Yet the studies all share a common, unifying element: they are all strongly critical, even those with a relatively greater policy orientation or fieldwork basis. Crucial questions dealt with include: what kind of civil society? who are the constituent members? civil society for what purpose or to what end? These three are running threads tying the different accounts together, and yet give rise to varied and complex answers. Taken as a whole these perspectives, whether they originate in Europe, North America or further afield, both identify critical issues and suggest agendas for further research. Overall they explore many of the most controversial and problematic features of civil society as idea, theory and practice, not least by highlighting the contrasts between the rhetoric and the reality, in a rich variety of cultural and social environments.

Among the more specific questions that are addressed are the following. What are the boundaries between civil society and the other realms or domains in isolation from which it may not be possible even to distinguish civil society in the first place? And how certain are those boundaries and are they fluid and flexible, open or closed? Chandhoke gives reasons for doubting the vaunted autonomy that is sometimes claimed of actually existing civil society especially in regards to the state. She says the two are 'organically linked' through structures of power; White's pluralist account of civil society's relationship to the state approaches the relationship from the other side, and is complementary. Civil society it seems is unevenly distributed across space and develops unevenly over time, but patterns of change follow their own logic – and as Whitehead proceeds to point out, the logic does not necessarily coincide with the progress of state formation. Attempts to create new and inclusionary political societies that are democratically organized may not even comport with the pre-existing maps of dense associational life.

The next set of questions concerns civil society's analytical separateness from, and relations with, not just elements of political society other than the state such as political parties, but the market economy and organizations that speak for big business. The difference from non-governmental development organizations and the welfare service providing bodies of the 'third sector' offers a further set of boundary issues for resolution. Beetham's approach to those thinkers who doubt whether civil society's ambit truly extends to the market is to invite us to address a different conundrum first, namely the market economy's relationship to democracy, and he explains why this relationship is highly ambivalent and the implications. However it is Baker who most sharply delineates the conflict between two sets of ideas of civil society. There are those that envisage it as a site for struggle over the very meaning of democracy and a domain for democratic participation in its own right. And on the other side lies the domestication of civil society where it is viewed as an instrument for the service of a non-radical project of liberal democracy.

Baker's own normative standpoint is quite evident but is not unique. His concern about the 'taming of the idea of civil society' and the disagreements concerning precisely what kind of democratic contribution civil society should be expected to make after the downfall of authoritarian regimes resonate in Pearce's interpretation of trends in Latin America, for instance. But it is not only in Latin America that controversies over the 'demobilization of an idea that only a decade ago was oriented towards change' (Baker) are still ripe for debate. Their significance anywhere for

theories of democratization is difficult to underestimate. But perhaps they
have a special resonance in places like eastern Germany, where events
leading to the fall of the Berlin wall contributed materially to civil society's
rebirth as a potent idea. The former German Democratic Republic is
revisited here by Mushaben. More so than some other writers she makes the
connections between civil society and the nature and extent of social capital
and civic culture quite explicit. Her finding that citizens who cultivate
subjective ties to emerging intermediary organizations are more likely not
simply to internalize democratic values but to establish effective channels
for advancing their own interests within the new power structures, is,
perhaps, just what one would expect. But such is the significance of the
finding that it is precisely the sort of proposition that has to be robustly
tested in the field, in the way this case study demonstrates, and not left to be
taken for granted as self-evident truth.

The relationship between ideas of civil society as composed of civic
associations and, on the one side social movements and on the other side
'uncivil' social actors is an issue that taxes many who write about the
subject, none more so that Whitehead and Kasfir, who present very different
positions. The possibilities range from less to more inclusionary notions of
civil society. Thus for example Kasfir warns us that in Africa to exclude
possibly 'aggressive' and 'anti-democratic' ethnic and fundamentalist
religious organizations would be 'myopic'. In India, Chandhoke warns, far
from being unambiguously 'the realm of solidarity and warm personalized
interaction' civil society can be (and is) fragmented, divided and
hierarchically structured. The dilemma created by confining civil society to
those contemporary manifestations most familiar in the West is summed up
thus: how can the process of establishing democracy depend on the
exclusion of many, perhaps most, members of the society? For good
measure Kasfir proceeds to reason that civil society's attempts to propel
political reform by curbing state power could end up doing harm to
democracy's chances, by reducing the state's ability to regulate civil society
and its capacity to perform as much-needed balancer and reconciler of
competing interests in society.

It is only right that close concern should be devoted to the matter of how
authentic civic associations can be and to how sustainable they are likely to
become under the impact of democracy promotion activities directed from
outside. For as well as those external well-meaning actors whose strategies
for supporting civil society appear to be not always well thought out
(Chandler; McMahon), there are the more diffuse forces such as
globalization and its corollary marketization, whose potentially negative
consequences for civil society have been remarked by many. Beetham
expressly warns of the consequences of market economies' proclivity to

fashion market societies, where all relationships are conducted as relations of exchange for private advantage. Chandler, on the Organization for Security and Co-operation Europe (OSCE), and McMahon writing about women's groups, both expose strategic weaknesses in the western agencies' (official and non-governmental) endeavours to promote civil society, within a European context. There are echoes here of the profound scepticism that Kasfir evinces in regard to international attempts to understand civil society in Africa generally and attempts to transfer inappropriate western models more specifically. The researches by Chandler and McMahon both uncover grounds for saying that the endeavours may actually be counterproductive.

Finally, moving on from 'civil society construction in one country' Mushaben's revelation about the competition state-subsidized civic organizations from western Germany pose to non-subsidized indigenous associations in eastern Germany offers in microcosm what observers such as Jünemann detect happening at the international level. But while she too, like McMahon, notes external assistance's tendency to divorce local civil associations from their own social context or 'roots', she also draws attention to additional dilemmas for actors like the European Union. The desire to maintain good relations with governments such as in Morocco and Tunisia comes into conflict with those same governments' wariness of 'pressure from below'. For they understand all too well that civil society can still sometimes if not everywhere operate as a force for political change and might threaten their *status quo*.

NOTES

1. J.L. Cohen, 'Civil Society', in P.B. Clarke and J. Foweraker (eds.), *Encyclopedia of Democratic Thought* (London and New York: Routledge, 2001), p.71.
2. For example R. Fine and S. Rai (eds.), *Civil Society: Democratic Perspectives* (London: Frank Cass, 1997).
3. W.B. Gallie, 'Essentially-contested Concepts', *Proceedings of the Aristotelian Society*, Vol.56 (1955-56), pp.167–98.

Civil Society, Democratization and Development: Clearing the Analytical Ground

GORDON WHITE

This is the first section of a two-part article investigating the relationship between civil society and the recent wave of democratization in developing countries. It highlights the ambiguity of the term 'civil society' and proposes a definition which may prove serviceable in discovering the political role played by civil society in facilitating or impeding democratization. In addition to the conventional distinction between civil society and the state, the article makes further distinctions between 'civil society', 'political society' and 'society'. It specifies several commonly held expectations about the potential political influence exerted by civil society on the character of political regimes and the behaviour of the state, and generates certain historically rooted hypotheses about these relationships. These concepts and hypotheses are intended as an analytical framework to be applied to specific country case-studies.

Together with the market and democracy, 'civil society' is one of the 'magic trio' of developmental panaceas which emerged in the 1980s and now dominate conventional prescriptions for the ills of the 1990s. As the third element of a comprehensive reaction against the developmental states of the 1960s and 1970s, civil society is a sociological counterpart of the market in the economic sphere and to democracy in the political sphere. As such, it is a valuable analytical complement to the tired old 'state–market' dichotomy.

While each of these three ideas reflects central historical processes and embodies potentially powerful solutions to the central problems of development, they are commonly used in vague, simplistic or tendentious ways. This encourages wishful thinking and blunts their practical utility. No more so than with the idea of civil society, an idea which has a long, distinguished but highly ambiguous history in Western political theory.[2] Over the past decade it has been dusted off and deodorized to suit a variety of ideological, intellectual and practical needs. The result is that, though there is now a 'paradigm' of thought and a terrain of discussion about the developmental implications of 'civil society', the term means different things to different people and often degenerates into a muddled political slogan. The resultant intellectual confusion could well wreak havoc on the real world given the fact that the 'civil societies' of developing countries have now been recognised as a legitimate area of external intervention by aid donors as part of an ever-deepening process of international social engineering.

This piece will attempt to clarify the notion of 'civil society' with the aim of making it analytically more precise and empirically more useful in discussing the problems of developing nations. It will also seek to specify the links between civil society and democracy/democratization and generate some hypotheses about those links which can be investigated empirically. A related piece (*Democratization*, Vol.2, No.2 (1995), pp.56–84) tests these hypotheses through case studies of selected Third World nations and expands the framework of analysis by exploring the triadic relations between civil society, democratization and development. This involves an investigation into the political implications of civil society not merely for a transition to democracy, but also for the ability of democratic regimes to tackle effectively the key problems of development – poverty, exploitation and inequality and the 'social murder' they cause, ecological deterioration, structural unemployment, socio-political instability, and the lack of national sovereignty.

I. THE MEANING OF 'CIVIL SOCIETY'

The rehabilitation of 'civil society' as a term of political and social scientific discourse can be traced to its role in explaining the crisis of the developmental state, providing an intellectual rationale for attacks on state power and identifying the political forces leading these struggles. The term came to prominence in the context of the rise of social movements against communist states in Eastern Europe in the late 1970s and early 1980s, most notably Solidarity in Poland and a variety of oppositional groups in Hungary, Czechoslovakia and Yugoslavia.

To the extent that the task of redressing the political balance between overbearing states and repressed societies was an important priority for political forces elsewhere, 'civil society' has been a useful intellectual tool in contexts as far apart as South America, sub-Saharan Africa and Taiwan. The idea became embroiled in a demonology of the state, functioning often as an idealised counter-image, an embodiment of social virtue confronting political vice: the realm of freedom versus the realm of coercion, of participation versus hierarchy, pluralism versus conformity, spontaneity versus manipulation, purity versus corruption.[3] While this kind of apotheosis helps make the term serviceable as a rationale for political struggle, it reduces its value as a social scientific concept.

Despite the growth of a cottage industry among political theorists bent on tracing the roots of the concept and providing a definitive reading of its meaning, the precise meaning of 'civil society' remains elusive. It is used in a variety of ways for a variety of purposes, functioning as a pragmatic rather than a theoretical concept. It is often used loosely to mean either society as opposed to the state or, more precisely, as an intermediate sphere of social organization or association between the basic units of society – families and firms – and the state.[4] This usage could include decidedly 'uncivil' entities like the Mafia, 'primordial' nationalist, ethnic or religious fundamentalist organizations, as well as 'modem' entities such as trade unions, chambers of commerce and professional associations.

Faced with this social farrago, some authors try to give the term a more precise meaning to simplify empirical analysis. For instance, Lise Rakner restricts the term to organizations which actually interact with the state, as opposed, for example, to 'remote community organisations, kinship groups, some religious societies and self-help groups located in rural communities' which 'stand apart from the state and shun all contact with it'.[5] Jean-François Bayart links 'civil society' with the notion of antagonism between state and society, restricting the term to those social organizations which embody 'society in its relations with the state insofar as it is in confrontation with the state'.[6]

While such attempts at greater precision may reflect particular regional experience or a desire for empirical convenience, others have reflected divergent intellectual and political traditions. For example, Hugh Roberts equates civil society with 'political society' in the sense of a particular relationship between state and society based on the principles of citizenship, rights, representation and the rule of law.'[7] As such it becomes virtually indistinguishable from a standard conception of a liberal democratic political system and probably should be described as such.

Marxists may equate it with 'bourgeois society' on the grounds that historically the rise of 'civil society' has accompanied the rise of capitalism and, in Marx's writing, the term *bürgerlich* can be translated as both, 'bourgeois' and 'civil'.[8] Others such as Rakner work (in most cases implicitly) within the paradigm of 'modernization theory' by limiting civil society to 'modern' organizations such as trade-unions, Christian groups, business or professional associations, converting 'civil' into a virtual synonym of 'modern'. Analysts in the US tradition of pluralist political analysis tend to see 'civil society' in terms of conventional interest group analysis, often resting on a more or less explicit notion of the political process as a market and political outcomes as representing equilibria resulting from the interplay of social actors in 'civil society'.[9]

The term 'civil society' has also been hijacked in pursuit of various developmental or political projects, each with its own preferred sector of associational life. Neo-populist development theorists and practitioners extol the virtues of grass-roots NGOs as paradigms of social participation and the potential building blocks of democracy; economic liberals bolster their case for deregulation and privatization by emphasizing how these measures contribute to the emergence of a business class to counterbalance and discipline wayward states; treasury based cost-cutters see devolution of governmental functions to voluntary organizations as an ideologically palatable way of reducing state expenditure; conservative thinkers see it as a way of preserving traditional social solidarities in the face of the disruptions caused by markets; and radical socialists zero in on the potential role of social organizations based on community, group or issue in transforming society or providing an alternative form of social governance.

Can we disperse this ambiguity and come up with a serviceable notion of 'civil society' which will enable us to explore its implications for the establishment and maintenance of a democratic political system? One is tempted to throw up one's hands in despair since the idea is so systematically ambiguous, embodying as it does such widely varying intellectual and ideological traditions. Surely a concept with this degree of elusiveness should be sent back to its coffin in the crypt of the great church of political theory? For instance, the kind of issues it raises could be described in a more systematic and sophisticated way in the context of a framework which analyzes the changing forms and dynamics of state–society relations. In this framework, 'civil society' could be viewed as but one particular form of the political relationship between state and society along the lines suggested by those who equate 'civil society' with the liberal notion of 'political society'. In looking at particular societies, therefore, one would be seeking to identify and explain of the emergence of the social forces which play a political role in establishing this relationship.

But this kind of selective approach would probably involve the espousal of one or other of the intellectual paradigms mentioned earlier: civil society as referring to modern forms of association, or to those institutions which accept the principles of liberal democracy, or to the organizational repercussions of the growth of capitalism. Each approach would select a particular group of social organizations as 'truly civil', the rest being presumably 'uncivil', 'non-civil' or 'pre-civil' because they are traditional, authoritarian or pre-capitalist. Each of these approaches carries with it the characteristic problems and limitations of the particular paradigm and each runs the risk of pressing analysis into a manichean evaluative mould, with 'civil society' taking on distinct and usually favourable moral connotations.

However, if the analyst is aware of these limitations, each of these approaches to civil society – which link its growth with the growth of liberal democracy – can be converted into a potentially productive empirical exercise. The latter would establish a set of 'democratic' benchmarks against which specific social organizations are assessed to see whether or not they merit the term 'civil' and then proceed to investigate the historical interactions between their growth and the emergence and strengthening of democratic political institutions.

However, the term is used in a far broader sense in conventional development discourse to denote a much more complex social universe. Rather than trying to solve the problem of clarity by adopting a restrictive notion of 'civil society', it may make more practical sense to adopt an approach which tries to come to terms with this breadth rather than defining it away. The main idea which is common to most current uses of the term is that of *an intermediate associational realm between state and family populated by organisations which are separate from the state, enjoy autonomy in relation to the state and are formed voluntarily by members of society to protect or extend their interests or values.*[10] Accepting this, it is then perhaps sensible to agree with Jean-François Bayart when he says that 'there is no teleological virtue in the notion of civil society' and maintains that an inclusive definition – which recognizes 'actually existing civil societies' as opposed to a normative model of 'civil society' – is more appropriate to the hybrid character of developing societies and can better capture the consequent diversity of their associational life.[11]

It would also give us a more complete picture of the social forces which obstruct as well as facilitate democratization. We would then need to make distinctions between different types or sectors of civil society: for example, between 'modern' interest groups such as trade unions or professional associations and 'traditional' ascriptive organizations based on kinship, ethnicity, culture or region; between formal organizations and informal social networks based on patrimonial or clientelistic allegiances; between those institutions with specifically political roles as pressure or advocacy groups and those whose activities remain largely outside the political system; between legal or open associations and secret or illegal organizations such as the Freemasons, the Mafia or the Triads; between associations which accept the political status quo or those who seek to transform it by changing the political regime (such as a guerrilla movement or a reactionary religious organization) or redefining the nation (as in former Yugoslavia).

These distinctions are important when it comes to investigating the relationships between civil society and democracy because one would expect systematic differences between different categories of organization in their attitude to the reality or the prospect of democratic politics. One would be seeking to identify the specific constellations of social forces which underpin a process of political democratization, guided by an eclectic set of hypotheses. Depending on context, some elements of civil society would be politically uninvolved, some tolerant or supportive of authoritarian rule, some working towards an alternative conception of democracy radically different from the liberal version, and some 'progressive' in the sense that they favour and foster a liberal democratic polity. Thus any statement to the effect that a 'strong' civil society is more conducive to democratization would be meaningless unless one went further to investigate the precise content of this constellation of social forces.

As Bayart has argued in the African context: 'The advance of a civil society which does not necessarily contain the democratic ideal does not in itself ensure the democratization of the political system'.[12] Conversely, the statement that a 'weak' civil society is not conducive to democratization would be equally suspect: witness the case of the former Soviet Union where the main thrust towards democratization came from within the Party/state apparatus and not from the pressure of civil society: Since we are primarily interested in the role which civil society plays in the fostering of democracy, we are led to concentrate on that particular sector of civil society which can be described as 'democratic', but our analysis would have to be situated within the wider context of a civil society which may contain anti-democratic, undemocratic and non-political entities.

If we choose to identify civil society as a distinct, but broadly defined, sphere of intermediate social associations, we should, before proceeding, clarify its relationship to the state on one side and society on the other. Although the conventional *dichotomy between state and civil society* is important in understanding the political character of the latter – as an entity separate from and independent from the former and reflecting the voluntary association of social actors outside the state, it is an oversimplification of the relationship.

It is important here to introduce a distinction between on the one side civil society as an ideal type concept which embodies the qualities of separation, autonomy and voluntary association in their pure form, and on the other side the empirical world of civil society which includes associations which embody these principles to varying degrees. In this latter world, the boundaries between state and civil society are often blurred: states may play an important role in shaping civil society as well as vice-versa; the two organizational spheres may overlap to varying degrees (for example, the case of public sector unions and professional associations, or intermediate 'quangos' embodying representation from both sides); individuals may play roles in both sectors; the principle of voluntary association may be infringed through political pressure or legal regulation;

and the autonomy of civil society organizations is highly variable, a question of degree rather than either–or.

Turning to *the relationship between civil society and society more generally,* civil society derives much of its specific political character from the deeper socio-economic structure and the distribution of interests, social norms and power resources which society embodies. But note two aspects of this relationship. First, as a separate and distinct sphere of social relations, civil society itself embodies a specific source of social power based on a (differential) capacity for association which is a key path to social empowerment. Second, we cannot 'read off' civil society from the socio-economic structure because the degree of organizational representation of different sectors is different; there is associational slippage.

As the theorists of collective action constantly remind us, the capacity for collective action is affected by factors such as diseconomies of numerical scale, or the resources available to potential actors (for example, it is usually easier for a small group of large landowners to organize and exert influence than a large number of small tenants). The sad paradox is that those with greater access to socio-economic resources find it easier to organize effectively and vice versa. Although this may tend to reinforce unequal social relations, it is subject to contestation through strategies aimed at the empowerment of relatively deprived groups through a strategy of association-building. In this context, the question is not merely one of building up civil society against the state, but one sector of civil society against another, as for example, the clash between unionized rural workers and merchant cartels in parts of rural India.[13]

Moreover, when discussing the relationships between civil society and political systems, it is useful to make a further *distinction between civil society, political society and the state.* Drawing on Stepan, one can distinguish between the state, which refers to the apparatus of administrative, judicial, legislative and military organizations,[14] and political society which refers to a range of institutions and actors which mediate and channel the relationships between civil society and the state. Two crucial elements of political society are political parties and political leaders, which can act to strengthen or weaken the democratic or authoritarian potential of a given configuration of civil society. For example, parties may be integrative mechanisms in that they are able to group together disparate or conflictual elements of civil society into broad and stable political coalitions; alternatively, they may act to articulate or intensify the inherent schisms of civil society. Political leaders may play similarly varying roles. Even detractors of the former president of Zambia, Kenneth Kaunda, admit that he was very skilled in mitigating potential ethnic antagonisms, whereas the president of Kenya has been accused of fomenting ethnic conflict in order to stay in power. More broadly, Claude Ake argues that the main political problem in Africa derives not from ethnic conflict but from bad political leadership.[15] Clearly the specific character of political society is a crucial element in any discussion of the relationship between civil society and the impetus towards democratization and of the broader triadic relationship between democracy, civil society and the developmental capacity of the state.

II. THE RELATIONSHIP BETWEEN CIVIL SOCIETY AND DEMOCRATIZATION

(i) Expectations About the Role of Civil Society in Democratization

The idea of civil society is central to any discussion of democratization since it raises central issues about the role of social forces in defining, controlling and legitimating state power. In development debates, it is argued that the growth of civil society, in its 'modern' form at least, can play a crucial political role not merely by undermining authoritarian governments and contributing to the establishment and maintenance of a democratic polity, but also by improving the quality of governance within that polity.

We can identify four ways in which this might come about. First, a growing civil society can alter the *balance of power* between state and society in favour of the latter, thereby contributing to the kind of 'balanced opposition' held to be characteristic of established democratic regimes. In the context of the authoritarian developmentalist states which pervaded the developing world from the 1960s to the 1980s, this implies a gradually increasing ability of organized social forces to weaken the capacity of states which have sought, to a greater or lesser extent, 'to administer society, even against itself, and to order it according to the explicit canons of modernity'.[16]

The balance of power between states and civil societies varies widely. There are totalistic state socialist regimes where the state is all-pervasive and civil society is either non-existent or marooned on embattled islands. There are authoritarian regimes such as those current in much of Latin America and East Asia until recently where the writ of the state was extensive, but certain organised forces of civil society, notably churches and business interests, enjoyed considerable freedom of action and oppositional organizations were harassed but not necessarily repressed. The situation in many African countries is that the state might have been the dominant institution in society, but was itself weak and eroded by the invasions of particularistic social pressures, a 'Leviathan with feet of clay',[17] with the result that the state and the formally organized sector of civil society were both weak. These variations are obviously crucial when it comes to looking at the role of civil society in fostering and maintaining democracy in specific national contexts.

②Second, it is argued a strong civil society can play a *disciplinary role in relation to the state* by enforcing standards of public morality and performance and improving the accountability of both politicians and administrators. This rests on a version of Lord Acton's motto that power corrupts and absolute power corrupts absolutely, so that a change in the balance of power away from a hegemonic state to civil society will place the denizens of the former under greater pressure to use their power more responsibly. The argument can also be put historically. In the African context, for example, Wraith and Simpkins made this case by drawing on the experience of changes in the character of public institutions in Britain from the seventeenth to the nineteenth century.[18]

Of course, the validity of this argument depends on which particular sector of organized civil society one is talking about. In the British case, the key groups in question were the new entrepreneurs and professional groups of the bourgeois order. However, if a currently emerging civil society involves, say, ethnic associations seeking sectional advantage or business groups bent on buying political influence, the result could be forms of public behaviour and political accountability which most advocates of this argument might find distasteful. Again, we return to the more or less implicit argument that only certain types of civil society can perform this role, namely those that emerge from a process of modernization (if you happen to be a modernization theorist) or those that emerge from the spread of private entrepreneurs or the bourgeoisie if one is a (liberal or Marxist) political economist. This ties the question of the variable political functions of civil society to a basic theory of socioeconomic transformation, which in Hyden's terms promotes the growth of new social forces which undermine the clan politics of the economy of affection.[19] It also implies some fairly optimistic assumptions about the moral and political character of civil society in advanced capitalist countries.

Third, civil society plays a potentially crucial role as *an intermediary or (two-way) transmission-belt between state and society*, in ways which condition the relationship between individual citizens and the formal political system. In an optimistic scenario, an active civil society can serve to improve the performance of democratic polities by transmitting the demands and articulating the interests of sectors of the population. Civil society can facilitate political communication between state and society, functioning thereby as an alternative principle of representation complementary to periodic elections and as an additional mechanism for strengthening democratic accountability. It can also economize, as it were, on the transaction costs of democracy by identifying, 'packaging' and relaying political demands which otherwise might remain dormant or be expressed in fragmentary or ineffective ways.

By so doing, it may exert *a disciplinary effect on society* by channelling and processing disparate demands and contributing thereby to ameliorating the fundamental contradiction between the state as a (more or less) unitary institution and the citizenry as a collection of atomized individuals. This aspect is emphasized by those elitist theories of democracy which stress the important role played by the leaders of civil society organizations in underpinning the stability and effectiveness of democratic regimes. In the various forms of corporatism, moreover, this intermediary role takes on an institutionalized form. In a more pessimistic scenario, civil society may act to increase pressures on the state beyond tolerable limits, contributing thereby to a crisis of governability; it may also polarize conflicts between social interests and contribute thereby to political instability and decay, a phenomenon to which we shall return below in discussing the issues of 'social mobilization' and 'hypermobilization'.

Fourth, civil society can play a *constitutive role by redefining the rules of the political game along democratic lines*. This can be conceived of in pragmatic terms, in the sense that certain organizations of civil society see it in their interest to observe a set of rules of the political game character- istic of competitive liberal democracy and can therefore agree among themselves to perpetuate those rules even though there may be an irreducible degree of uncertainty about their specific outcomes and implications for each particular group. Adam Przeworski argues along these lines when he says that 'democracy is consolidated when compliance – acting within the institutional framework – constitutes the equilibrium of the decentralised strategies of all the relevant political forces'.[20] There is a slight tautological tinge to this approach, for it tends to rely too heavily on a rather simplistic notion of market equilibrium drawn from economics and it probably begs far more questions than it answers; but it contains an obvious political truth.

While Przeworski tends to discount the normative factor, other authors have argued that the constitutive role of civil society goes beyond organizational interest into the normative sphere, that is that civil society creates and sustains a set of new democratic norms which regulate the behaviour of the state and the character of political relations between state and the 'public sphere' of society and individual citizens. As Dwayne Woods argues, 'the public in many African countries is attempting to articulate a principle of political accountability that is binding on the state elite',[21] a principle characteristic of that found in established Western democracies and radically contradictory to previous forms of accountability based on ethnic, regional or patrimonial principles. Bayart is making a similar point when he refers to the need for a 'new cultural fabric' and a 'conceptual challenge' in the African context.[22] Thus different sectors of civil society can be expected to have different sets of norms about the political relationship between state and society and the yea or nay of democracy would depend on the interaction between these sectors. For our purposes, it would be sensible to consider both the pragmatic and normative dimensions of the political impact of civil society.

But there is a third element, power, which is lacking in both these approaches. On the pragmatic side, different sectors of civil society have different power resources at their disposal and notions of democratic consensus based on market equilibria tend to marginalize these. Just as real markets contain inequalities and exploitation, so civil societies contain inequalities and domination and the resolution of any competitive game between components of civil society depends heavily on its internal balance of power. In the words of Samuel Bowles and Herbert Gintis, heterogeneous social power 'gives rise to a multiplicity of distinct structures of dominance and subordinacy in social life'.[23]

Similarly, the capacity of different systems of norms to define political arrangements depends on the power embodied in or lying behind each system. Dietrich Rueschemeyer and his colleagues make this point forcefully when they argue that 'it is power relations that most importantly determine whether democracy can emerge, stabilise and then maintain itself even in the face of adverse conditions'.[24] Similarly, Michael Bratton defines the transitions to democracy, of which we have seen so many over recent years, as embodying 'a struggle between incumbent and opposition political interests over both the rules of the political game and the resources with which it is played'.[25] Understanding these power dimensions in turn requires that civil society must again be considered in terms of its relationship to the broader socio-economic structure in which it is embedded.

Thus, the constitution or otherwise of democracy is not merely a contest between state and civil society, but also depends on patterns of conflict and co-operation in these three aspects – interests, norms and power – between the constituent parts of civil society. Moreover, when assessing the process of and prospects for democratization in any country, the specific cluster of power, interests and norms embedded in civil society/society must be identified as only *one among three clusters,* the others being the political forces embedded in the international environment and in the state itself. In any given context of democratization (or its reverse), therefore, the 'civil society factor' may be more or less influential depending on the current and evolving balance of power between these three clusters.

(ii)   Hypotheses about the Historical Relationship between Civil Society and Democratization

In the Pollyannaish days of post-colonialism in the 1960s, it was felt by many that a combination of wise institutional bequests by the colonizers and gradual socio-economic improvement would lead to the consolidation of democracy in the Third World. However, the pervasive experience of de-democratization, buttressed by sobering scholarly studies of the ambiguous relationships between socio-economic and political levels of development, led to a new orthodoxy, crystallized in the seminal work of Samuel Huntington on *Political Order in Changing Societies* (1968). The central thrust of this view was that the excessive political pressures exerted on states in developing countries, resulting from social mobilization in pursuit of rapid improvements in material welfare, would lead to a crisis of governability.

In consequence, strong and probably authoritarian states were needed to provide the institutional capacity to control and process these pressures. If we rephrase this argument in the language of the 'civil society' paradigm, the rapidly growing strength of the latter would pose political problems – not, as today, solutions – since it would intensify the barrage of social demands raining down on hard-pressed states. For example, this kind of 'hyper-mobilization' resulting from a rapid explosion of demands from previously excluded social groups has been adduced as an explanation for the breakdown of Chilean democracy in 1973.[26]

However, the current paradigm of 'civil society' has returned, albeit in different and usually less systematic ways, to the ideas of the 1960s. It rests on historical arguments about the character and political repercussions of socio-economic development. A similar story can be told in different analytical languages. In the discourse of modernization theory, the process of modernization leads to greater structural differentiation which is the potential basis of socio-political pluralism; to higher levels of education and awareness which leads to greater popular expectations from government and greater ability to comprehend and participate in national-level politics; to a spread of specialized expertise which creates powerful elites increasingly able to enforce their claims in the political arena; and to the diffusion of the kind of secular and universalistic values which are conducive to the operations of modern bureaucracies and democratic polities. These changes provide the underlying conditions for, and impetus towards, liberal democracy which is the unchallenged institutional embodiment of political modernity.

Liberal and Marxist political economists, in their different ways, portray a similar great transformation, which identifies certain momentous social repercussions of the rise of the bourgeoisie which provide the political impetus first for liberalization and then for democratization: the pluralization of social power and the separation of the public and private spheres; the links between the assertion of private ownership rights and the demand for political rights and freedoms; the force of the market in undermining concentrated state power; the desire of the dominant classes to tame the state and transform it into an efficient instrument to further their own interests; and the democratizing political influence of the other groups brought into existence through successful capitalist development (the professional middle strata and the industrial working class).

The traditions differ in their view of the political end-point. On the liberal side, the political end of history is represented by the global triumph of liberal democracy, defined primarily in terms of a set of institutionalized procedures and political guarantees. On the Marxist socialist side, the feasibility of a radically different political model, embodied in the theory and practice of state socialism and the notion of 'socialist democracy' which it laid claim to, has been dealt an apparently mortal blow by the collapse of communism. Yet radical socialists, Marxist or not, define the nature of democracy and thus the process of democratization in terms which go well beyond the liberal model, stressing the need to democratize society as well as the state.

As Przeworski argues: 'Democracy restricted to the political realm has historically coexisted with exploitation at the workplace, within the schools, within bureaucracies, and within families'.[27] Yet, though these two traditions differ in their definitions of democracy, they both agree to some extent about the role of civil society organizations themselves as potential microcosms of democracy, practising in their internal relations the kind of 'organizational citizenship' which makes each of them a basic building block in the edifice of a national-level democratic system. For example, in the socialist tradition Claus Offe and Ulrich Preuss argue that a 'civilised democratic polity' should be based on a continual process of micropolitical learning within the organizations of civil society.[28] However, in the real world of civil society, the degree of democratic participation within associations varies widely and thus the contribution of the microcosms to the consolidation of a democratic macro-political system would depend on the specific configuration of different types of association.

To a considerable extent, the current language of 'civil society' represents an eclectic, and often highly confused and undigested, amalgam of these ideas used to address currently pressing political and develop-mental purposes. Implicitly or explicitly, there is an *underlying historical hypothesis:* of a transition from a previous political situation characterized by state dominance and 'traditional' social relations (pre-modern or pre-capitalist) to an emergent or established situation in which new forms of civil society, reflecting a new pattern of socio-economic relations and institutions, serve to transform the state and their relations with it. If we apply this to any given society, we would need to investigate the extent to which its particular level and pattern of development has led, first, to a shift in the balance of power between the state and emergent socio-economic forces; second, to a basic change in the social character of the associational forms through which these forces articulate and impel their interests in the social and political arenas; and third, to an increasing desire by the latter to consolidate and extend their new-found influence by redesigning the political system along democratic lines. One would expect, for instance, that the shift in the balance of power between state and society, the transformation of civil society itself and the impetus towards democratization would be more pronounced in societies which have undergone a relatively successful process of industrialization. One would also expect, *ceteris paribus*, that the degree of heterogeneity of a given society not only reflects the extent to which civil society has been transformed (along 'modern' or 'bourgeois' lines), but also affects the likelihood of civil society being able to develop the 'organisation principle', in Bayart's words,[29] which would enable it to create and sustain a viable democratic regime.

By way of conclusion, we have set out in the above analysis to achieve greater clarity on the major concepts involved in discussing the relationship between civil society and democratization and to identify some central hypotheses about the nature of this relationship.[30]

NOTES

1. For a critique of the conventional conception of 'the market' in current development discourse, see Gordon White, 'Towards a Political Analysis of Markets', *IDS Bulletin*, Vol.24, No.3(1993), pp.4–11.
2. For an excellent review of the term's intellectual heritage, see John Keane (ed.), *Civil Society and the State: New European Perspectives* (London: Versa, 1988).
3. On Taiwan see Michael Hsin-Huang Hsiao, Social Movements and the Rise of a Demanding Civil Society in Taiwan', *The Australian Journal of Chinese Affairs*, No.27 (1990), pp.163–80. A different example is Ahn Chung-si, 'Economic Development and Democratization in South Korea – An Examination of Economic Change and Empowerment of Civil Society', *Korea and World Affairs*, Vol.15, No.4 (1991), pp.740–54.
4. For example, David Booth refers to civil society as 'socio-economic life as distinct from the state', in 'Alternatives in the Restructuring of State–Society Relations: Research Issues for Tropical Africa', *IDS Bulletin*, Vol.18, No.4 (1987), p.23. Uses of the term also vary in respect of their degree of abstraction: for some, civil society is a public space, distinct from and autonomous of the state, which is occupied by associational activity; for others, civil society is a wide-ranging *behavioural* phenomenon which not only includes the activity of organizations, but also such 'spontaneous' phenomena as riots, protest demonstrations and parallel markets. Most commonly, however, the term is used to refer to the activity of

organized associations of a voluntary character.

5. Lise Rakner, *Trade Unions in Processes of Democratization: A Study of Party Labour Relations in Zambia* (Bergen: Chr. Michelsen Institute, Department of Social Science and Development, 1992), p.47.

6. Jean-François Bayart, 'Civil Society in Africa', in Patrick Chabal (ed.), *Political Domination in Africa* (Cambridge: Cambridge University Press, 1986).

7. Hugh Roberts, 'Editorial', in *IDS Bulletin*, Vol.18, No.4 (1987), p.4.

8. For a critical evaluation of Man's analysis of civil society, see Alvin Gouldner, *The Two Marxisms* (London: Macmillan, 1980); far a discussion of current Marxist uses of the term, see Ellen Meiksins Wood, 'The Uses and Abuses of Civil Society', in Ralph Miliband *et al.* (eds.), *The Socialist Regisier 1990* (London: Merlin Press, 1990), pp.60–84.

9. For example, see Harry Blair, 'Defining, Promoting and Sustaining Democracy: Formulating an AID Strategy for Development Assistance and Evaluation', *USA ID* (23 Sept. 1992).

10. This conventional use of 'civil society' usually excludes firms as well as families, but it could be argued that economic institutions, as key matrices of social organization, should also be included within the definition. In my view, this would stretch the term beyond the bounds of analytical utility. Rather one can identify a society's economic institutions and patterns of economic interaction as a distinct realm, akin to civil society', which could be dubbed 'economic society' or simply 'economic system', a realm which constitutes one of the basis foundations of 'civil society' in any social system.

11. Bayart, p.118. The term 'actually existing civil societies' refers to the now fading distinction made by Rudolf Bahro in describing communist Eastern Europe between ideal 'socialist' societies and the actual social form taken on by state socialism in the Soviet bloc, in Babro, *The Alternative in Eastern Europe* (London: New Left Books, 1978).

12. Bayart, p.118.

13. See Barbara Harris-White, 'Collective Politics of Foodgrains Markets in South Asia', *IDS Bulletin*, Vol.24, No.3 (1993), p.57.

14. Alfred Stepan, *Rethinking Military Politics: Brazil and the Southern Cone* (Princeton, NJ: Princeton University Press, 1988), pp.3–4. While Stepan would include legislatures and electoral systems under the heading of 'political society', I would prefer to see them as part of the institutional patterning of the state. For further discussion of the idea of 'political society', see Dietrich Ruescbemeyer, Evelyne Huber Stephens and John D. Stephens, *Capitalist Development and Democracy* (Cambridge: Polity Press, 1992), p.287. Just as political society mediates the relationship between civil society and the state, so the institutional patterning of the state (such as the distribution of power between its institutional segments, or the nature of the electoral system) structures the pattern of interaction between civil society and the state.

15. Claude Ake, 'Rethinking African Democracy', *Journal of Democracy*, Vol.2, No.1 (1991), p.34.

16. Bayart, p.113.

17. Chabal, p.15. For a fascinating analysis of the Algerian bureaucracy in these terms, see Hugh Roberts, 'The Algerian Bureaucracy', in Talal Asad and Roger Owen (eds.), *Sociology of 'Developing Societies': the Middle East* (New York: Monthly Review Press, 1983), pp.95–114.

18. Ronald Wraith and Edgar Simpkins, *Corruption in Developing Countries* (London: Allen & Unwin, 1963).

19. Goran Hyden, *No Shortcuts to Progress:African Development Management in Perspective* (London: Heinemann, 1980).

20. Adam Przeworski, *Democracy and the Market: Political and Economic Reforms in Eastern Europe and Latin America* (Cambridge: Cambridge University Press, 1991), p.26.

21. Dwayne Woods, 'Civil Society in Europe and Africa: Limiting State Power through a Public Sphere', *African Studies Review*, Vol.35, No.2 (1992), p.95.

22. Bayart,p.120.

23. Samuel Bowles and Herbert Gintis, *Democracy and Capitalism: Property, Community and the Contradictions of Modern Social Thought* (New York: Basic Books, 1987), p.32.

24. Rueschemeyer et al., p.5.

25. Michael Bratton, 'Zambia Starts Over', *Journal of Democracy,* Vol.3, No.2 (1992), p.82.
26. The original argument was by Henry A. Landsberger and Tim McDaniel, 'Hyper-mobilization in Chile, 1970–1973', *World Politics,* Vol.28, No.4 (1976), pp.502–41. For a critical response, see Rueschemeyer *et al,* p.332, fn.65.
27. Adam Przeworski in Guillermo O'Donnell, Philippe C. Schmitter and Laurence Whitehead (eds.), *Transitions from Authoritarian Rule: Prospects for Democracy* (Baltimore, MD: Johns Hopkins University Press, 1986), Vol.3, p.63.
28. Claus Offe and Ulrich K. Preuss, 'Democratic Institutions and Moral Resources', in David Held (ed.), *Political Theory Today* (Cambridge: Polity Press), pp.143–71.
29. Bayart, p.117.
30. The framework outlined here is applied to the cases of South Korea and Zambia, *see* 'Civil Society, Democratization and Development (II): Two Country Cases', *Democratization,* Vol.2, No.2 (1995), pp.56–84.

Bowling in the Bronx:
The Uncivil Interstices between Civil
and Political Society

LAURENCE WHITEHEAD

After contrasting the inclusive, universal character of democratic notions of political citizenship (within the relevant jurisdiction) with the exclusivity that necessarily marks civil society the essay argues that the interstices between these two forms will favour the production of multiple variants of 'incivility'. The category of 'uncivil citizens' is defined as those who enjoy political rights but are not constrained by the norms of civil society: anti-social individuals and groups whose recognizable shorthand can be found in the term 'mafia'. The essay then focuses on whether the greatest threat to civil society may come neither from intrusive statism nor from unthinking tradition, but from the 'insecurity, rootlessness, arbitrariness, and perhaps even the social cannibalism' that have come to be associated with many post-transition liberalized societies.

I. INTRODUCTION

What do we understand by the term 'civil society'? How does it arise? How is it related to pluralism, democracy, and democratization? If it has a tendency towards disintegration or self-destruction, does that threaten the consolidation of democratic regimes, or does it merely exacerbate anxieties about the quality of our 'really existing' democracies (polyarchies)? If it develops a capacity for self-preservation, does that necessarily reinforce the deepening of political democracy, or could it come at the expense of the universalism and non-discrimination required for democratic authenticity?

This contribution offers a very general – and provisional – overview of these issues. Its point of departure is the discrepancy between our inclusive view of citizenship and our tacitly more restrictive view of the requirements of civil society.

Modern liberal constitutionalism extends the scope of citizenship (formal political rights) to virtually all adults within the relevant jurisdiction. In a world of territorial states the exceptions to this rule are at a grave disadvantage. Typically, therefore, such exceptions (for example, the incarcerated, the certifiably insane or incompetent, refugees and asylum seekers) are narrowly defined and carefully delimited. If it were otherwise and categories of exception were loosely defined or easily extendible, then broad segments of the political community might feel their citizenship rights to be potentially under threat and might therefore become mobilized to defend an extended franchise. Historically, after all, the present almost universal and inclusionary conception of citizenship rights was only brought about through pressure and agitation by and on behalf of those who were initially excluded or marginalized from the territorial political community. The result is that nowadays the overwhelming majority of contemporary representative polities are strongly biased towards universality. In other words, they contain a strong presumption against the withdrawal of citizenship rights. This is true both of long-established democracies (polyarchies), and also of the many fragile and newly established constitutionally and potentially democratic regimes (neo-democracies).

However, although modern citizenship may assume the guise of universality, the same cannot be said for membership of 'civil society'. That, at least, is the claim upon which this analysis is based. The distinction between an inclusionary conception of citizenship (and therefore of 'political society'), and a more selective or restrictive view of what constitutes civil society will of course depend upon how the second category is defined. The discussion therefore begins with a brief review of the competing possibilities, all of which imply something narrower than universal citizenship. All of which, in other words, admit a third category of 'uncivil citizens', or persons enjoying political rights, but not submitting themselves to the constraints imposed by 'civil society'. Since there appears to be no single consensual definition of our second category there are alternative views of what form these constraints may take, but in some form or other they must surely include a requirement of 'civility'. The study therefore proposes a working definition which incorporates this requirement. It then proceeds to consider the implications of incivility, both for our understanding of 'civil society' and for our theorizing about the relationship between civil society and democratization.

The underlying assumption is that whether or not this particular working definition is adopted, on any reasonable account there will necessarily remain a substantial gap between universalistic conceptions of modern political society, and more restrictive or exacting notions of civil society. The interstices between these two social forms will favour the production of multiple variants of 'incivility' (a residual category derived from the notion of civil society, which may therefore need to be disaggregated and deconstructed). The discussion concludes that the quality and stability of both contemporary neo-democracies – and indeed of long-standing 'polyarchies' – is likely to be materially affected by the solidity and structure of civil society, and that these characteristics in turn will be heavily conditioned by the nature and strength of the challenges arising from the 'uncivil interstices'.

The weaknesses of civil society, and the dangers posed by various forms of 'incivility' are particularly evident in many neo-democracies. In both the post-authoritarian and the post-communist experiences efforts at democratization are frequently overshadowed by the emergence or proliferation of anti-social forms of individualism and group organization that substitute for, or even seek to subvert, the forms of civil associationalism celebrated by theorists of 'civil society'. An internationally recognizable shorthand for this flourishing of incivility can be found in the term 'mafia'. Were this a straightforward matter of criminality it would be of limited significance to students of politics, however difficult it might be for the police to handle. But it becomes of central concern when the requirements of democratization include the extension of political and citizenship rights to large sectors of the population who not only may have no prior experience of democratic politics, but also have few resources to escape mafia-type networks of political co-optation and control. It is also of central concern where uncivil forms of association are left over from the disintegration of the *ancien régime*, or arise in the course of political struggle between groups who are 'disloyal' to the prevailing (if fragile) constitutional order. The incentives to organize intolerant and uncivil forms of associationalism are particularly strong where claims to privilege and property are politically contestable; where servants of the old regime still seek impunity for past misdeeds, and fear revenge; and where the present justice system seems incapable of upholding a broad and impartial rule of law. These are all, of course, characteristic conditions to be found in many neo-democracies.

However, the discussion is not directed solely, or even mainly, to the travails of the many societies currently attempting to consolidate their fragile new democracies. The long-established polyarchies of the OECD area also manifest sharp disjunctions between the scope of their civil and political societies. Italy, as the original home of the mafia, has recently manifested the destabilizing macro-political potential of the uncivil interstices in a particularly dramatic form.[1] But such incivility takes many forms and appears in most polyarchies. For example, in France one of the most sensitive issues has become the spread of street violence through the *banlieux* of almost all the large urban centres, particularly where youth unemployment and islamic traditions coincide. The French police now keep monthly records of the incidents they deal with in the 1,017 *quartiers* which have been classified as *'sensitifs'*. July 1995 was a record month with 955 such incidents – the norm is around 500.[2] Nor is Britain exempt,[3] nor even the United States, particularly in some derelict inner city wastelands.

Indeed, the title of this chapter has been chosen to highlight the weaknesses of civil associationalism in parts of America not foreseen by Tocqueville.[4] The Bronx has been singled out in the hope of avoiding the exoticism that would arise from situating discussions of civil society in the context of such stereotypical 'Third World' locations as El Alto (La Paz), the Baixada Fluminense (Rio), or Guguletu (Cape Town). The assumption is that once we have gone bowling in the Bronx we are most of the way to understanding the relationship between civil society and democracy in Bolivia, Brazil, and South Africa as well.

II. THE MANY MEANINGS OF 'CIVIL SOCIETY'

When Hobbes referred to 'civil society' he equated the term with 'city' or 'union'.[5] It was differentiated from the notion of 'multitude' by the presumption that the respective individuals had entered into some form of compact or contract, by which they agreed to subordinate their separate wills into a unified common will: if for no other purpose than at least for the maintenance of peace and for common defence. But Hobbes did not believe that the creation of a civil society could ever abolish the underlying fears and dangers he associated with the state of nature. Although it could suspend their operation, the process of political life would always be reversible. The freedom and sociality made possible by civil society would perpetually be at risk from the possibility of regression into a non-social community. Indeed fear of such regression was probably the spur always needed to sustain the artificial construct that was civil society.

By contrast Hegel's version of 'civil society' was derived not from man's fear of death, but from his material needs as articulated through the division of labour. Neither family nor religious or political association fell within this rubric, which was restricted to the domain of instrumental and individualist rationality. However, both Hobbes and Hegel saw a radical antagonism between civil society and lawless criminality. Individuals in civil society (which for Hegel was heavily structured into guilds, corporations, and communities – compulsory rather than voluntary associations) would pursue their self-interest within a framework of mutually recognized rights and obligations regulated by public authority. This notion of civil society implied a reliable and impartial system of justice.

Hegel, following the Scottish political economists, was also concerned about the potentially self-dissolving properties of a civil society unconstrained by any higher normative principles. The unfettered development of the division of labour could be expected to generate a section of society that was both materially and spiritually impoverished by the narrowness and monotony of its work. But this sector would tend to lose its self-respect and thus its identification with the whole community. 'It hence becomes apparent that despite an excess of wealth civil society is not rich enough, i.e. its own resources are insufficient to check excessive poverty and the creation of a penurious rabble.'[6] Only the incorporation of civil society into a higher (that is, for Hegel a *political*) community could contain this self-destructive potential. But of course neither in Hegel nor in Hobbes was there any suggestion that the political authority required to regulate civil society should be democratic.

Marx, of course, preserved the framework of Hegel's theory, while inverting the mechanism. In the starkest form of this version the division of labour and the resulting 'bourgeois' civil society became the motor of historical change, while the political, ideological and normative realms became subordinate consequences of it. Moreover, the self-dissolving characteristics of civil society spawned a dialectical theory of revolutionary progress, through which its 'bourgeois' form would inevitably be displaced by a more advanced socialist version. The consequent relationship between civil society and political democracy was therefore antagonistic. 'Real' democracy would have to await the socialist revolution; the bourgeoisie in its progressive phase might perhaps temporarily espouse formal democracy (as a weapon against the pre-bourgeois classes), but that epiphenomenal political commitment would be bound to fade as the working class grew in strength and self-consciousness, and challenged the political supremacy of the capitalist class. In the Marxist version, therefore, there could be no presumption of an inherent and super-historical congruence between civil society and the administration of justice, and no guaranteed antagonism between the bourgeoisie and the criminal classes.

Tocqueville was perhaps the first major theorist to present civil society as the indispensable counterpart to a stable and vital democracy, rather than as an alternative to it. But the voluntary associations which constituted the core of his notion of 'civil society' were quite distinct from the self-defence compacts envisaged by Hobbes, or the corporate enterprises envisioned by Hegel or the bourgeois class in Marx. Indeed, whereas the pursuit of material self-interest was what distinguished civil society in the minds of these two German theorists, it was the containment of such materialism within the confines of benevolent voluntary institutions (which could be viewed as extensions of the family, or as practical applications of religious faith) that inspired the French liberal. Contrary to some neo-Tocquevillean literature of recent years, the original Tocqueville was neither pre-political (the institutions of local government figures prominently in his account of the bases of American democracy) nor sentimental (his strictures against social and intellectual conformity in small-town New England contrast markedly with fashionable contemporary nostalgias).

According to his account, what critically underpinned America's democratic political institutions was her profusion of voluntary public associations which enabled isolated individuals to co-operate for collective purposes despite the absence of an aristocracy and the remoteness of the federal state. In this conception of civil society ('associations that are formed in civil life without reference to political objects')[7] commercial, educational and religious activities are all included. Indeed, in addition to the division of labour, he refers to 'associations of a thousand other kinds, religious, moral, serious, futile, general or restricted, enormous or diminutive ... to give entertainments, to found seminaries, to build inns, to construct churches, to diffuse books, to send missionaries to the antipodes'. He even adds (perhaps for Foucault's benefit) 'in this manner they found hospitals, prisons, and schools' (ibid.). This is why Putnam's *angst* about the decline of bowling as a recreational activity is thought to reflect a deep crisis in contemporary American democracy. Whereas for Hobbes civil society is the response to the perils of the state of nature, and for Hegel it reflects the growth of commerce as a sphere supposedly independent from politics, in Tocqueville it fills the void left by the absence of an aristocracy. So, in Tocqueville's conception, for the first time, civil society and democracy were viewed as inherently linked together, whereas for previous authors they were seen as disconnected and indeed as potentially antagonistic principles of social organization.

Each of these successive characterizations of civil society abstracted from a very distinct and specific social reality, therefore posited the inclusion (or exclusion) of different corporate and collective entities. For Hegel religion pertained to the higher realm of state action, for Tocqueville it was the voluntary expression of local self-organization. For Marx the association of workers into unions was a fundamental reality, for Tocqueville it was rather the local newspaper which brought scattered American settlers into closer association with each other. These differences in emphasis and conception not only reflected contrasting sociological reference points, but also varying theoretical positions concerning the bases of state organization and well-springs of collective action.

Since the mid-nineteenth century our theories of civil society have, of course, been greatly elaborated and further diversified, but it would exceed the purpose of this section to track such developments.[8] Suffice it to say that we are still without a single, unified and consensual, meaning for the term. To this day, most writers on 'civil society' leave me uncertain whether trade unions occupy a central or a marginal role in their conceptions; whether 'the media' are to be viewed as internal or external; whether the neutral rule of law is an essential precondition and support, or a utopian ideal that civil society activists should use to critique existing strictures of political manipulation; and whether political democracy sprouts from, coexists with, or threatens to pollute the dense associative principles of civil society.

Having raised these doubts about the many meanings of the term, it is only possible to proceed any further by the somewhat arbitrary selection of a working definition. What follows appropriates a recent formulation proposed by Philippe Schmitter, which has the merit of being distilled from a wide variety of contemporary social realities (i.e. it does not generalize too obviously from an ethnocentric core), and which is structured by Schmitter's underlying preoccupation with the requirements for the consolidation of modern democratic regimes (both old and neo-democracies). His definition reads as follows: 'a set or system of self-organized intermediary groups' that:

(1) are relatively independent of both public authorities *and* private units of production and reproduction, i.e. of firms and families;

(2) are capable of deliberating about and taking collective actions in defence/promotion of their interests or passions;

(3) but do *not* seek to replace either state agents or private (re)producers or to accept responsibility for governing the polity as a whole;

(4) but *do* agree to act within pre-established rules of a 'civil' or legal nature.

He adds that 'civil society, therefore, is not a simple but a compound property. It rests on four conditions or norms: (1) dual autonomy; (2) collective action; (3) non-usurpation; (4) civility'.[9] Like most definitions, this one can be read in a variety of ways, but seems to exclude mafia-type organizations (under both (3) and (4)) and indeed more generally the 'segmentary' types of organization that so troubled Gellner because he thought them oppressive of individualism.[10] This interpretation is based on the four conditions, or norms, listed at the end, which it can be argued collectively presuppose a 'modern' and/or 'individualist' form of social organization.

At the risk of definitional overload something must be added about the key term 'civility', to flesh out Schmitter's fourth norm. In addition to any commitment to act within the constraints of legal or pre-established rules, Collingwood's definition introduces a more intimate dimension of civility, based on interpersonal behaviour:

> Behaving 'civilly' to a man means respecting his feelings, abstaining from shocking him, annoying him, frightening him, or (briefly) arousing in him any passion or desire which might diminish his self-respect; that is threaten his consciousness of freedom by making him

feel that his power of choice is in danger of breaking down and the passion or desire likely to take charge.[11]

This may be regarded as an essential aspect of civility not covered by minimal conformity to pre-agreed rules. Otherwise 'obeying the letter but not the spirit' of an agreement would have to be regarded as 'civil' behaviour, as would obeying uncivil agreements.

III. THE LACK OF CONGRUENCE BETWEEN 'CIVIL' AND 'POLITICAL' SOCIETY

All the rival meanings just discussed, and certainly the working definition I have finally selected, point to forms of voluntary (or at least uncoerced) associative organizations that we are most unlikely to find distributed evenly across the geographical and social terrain covered by the modern territorial state (the 'polity'). Uneven development is more or less self-evident in the realm of commerce and the division of labour. It is also a virtually inescapable characteristic both of Hegel's corporations and of Tocqueville's newspaper co-ordinated local associations. The same is true if we regard church-sponsored collectivities as a crucial component of civil society; these are more densely concentrated in some areas, and in some social strata, than in others. Similarly, working class labour unions and forms of community organizations tend to be geographically concentrated. Equally, if we follow Parsons in stressing the centrality of educational institutions (especially universities), again we will encounter uneven social coverage. Schmitter's definition carries the same implication, in that the four conditions he specifies are more reliably fulfilled in some social settings than in others (especially 'civility', but also dual autonomy, etc.). Although some of these patterns of distribution may be offsetting (strong working class associations where higher educational coverage is weak, etc.) others are cumulative. In fact all these definitions seem to imply that civil society will be 'denser' in Hampstead than in Brixton, in Santa Monica than in East Los Angeles. For however we specify the precise components of civil society, some sections of the citizenry will be over-supplied with 'dense associative life', while others will be under-provided. (This is probably true even of Habermas's 'life-world of communicative interaction' though it is hard to be certain.)[12]

Neither the market nor the state can be relied upon to even out this uneven social distribution of voluntary associationalism. Not the market because it obeys consumer sovereignty, which is skewed towards high income earners. Not the state, because the sovereign assembly is also typically skewed towards the most articulate and best-organized groups in

the polity (indeed parliamentarism has not infrequently been both praised
and criticized as the best form of government for securing the ascendancy
of civil society over the republican will). More fundamentally, theorists of
associationalism who wish to preserve its voluntary and participatory
features therefore resist centrally imposed standardization, and see state
regulation as a threat to liberty.[13] But in that case what countervailing
mechanism can they point to, to even out the inequalities of civil society?
The hopeful assertion that since voluntary associations are beneficial, those
who lack them can be taught or encouraged to create them, seems to me a
flimsy counterweight.

As we know from countless studies of policing and the administration of
justice, even those legal rights which are formally uniform throughout the
modern polity are in practice somewhat selectively distributed. Poverty,
race, underprivileged family background and so forth provide virtually
universal negative markers even in the most consolidated and 'social
democratic' of nation-states. Robert Putnam has recently drawn attention to
the evidence of strong regional and local variations in the quality of civic
life in different parts of Italy, and Francis Fukuyama has sketched a
framework for making similar comparisons internationally.[14] In most neo-
democracies the main attributes of civil society tend to be highly
concentrated in specific sites; are often reserved to a minority of the
population; and are not infrequently derived from privileges conferred by a
pre-democratic structure of power. And in so far as the 'rule of law'
constitutes an essential component of civil society, publicly provided and
impartial justice is typically an aspiration rather than a realized achievement
across broad swathes of the social landscape in most 'really existing'
democracies. (As Cohen and Arato reluctantly admit, although
'fundamental rights must be seen as the *organizing principle* of a modern
civil society a civil society in formation ... [as in Eastern Europe recently]
may for a time have to do without a settled structure of rights'.)[15]

Not only is civil society unevenly distributed across social space at any
particular moment of time, it also develops unevenly, and according to a
logic that is distinct from that of state formation, over time. Obviously the
diverse definitions of civil society outlined above each embody a distinctive
implicit theory of historical causation, and indeed it is more than likely that
somewhat different processes were involved in the generation of north
Italian civic traditions from those that produced Tocqueville's small town
America, or the emerging civil society of post-communist Poland. All that
need concern us here is the conclusion that, whichever historical route may
have been followed, the resulting patterns of associative life and social
communication will be highly structured, with insiders, traditionally
favoured sectors, and marginal or excluded sectors. Depending on where

one is located in relation to this structure of privilege and opportunity, and how flexible and open it proves to be, one may either view the resulting civil society as the most authentic expression and durable guarantee of a political democracy or the most flagrant negation of its universalistic promise.[16]

In contrast to the incremental, organic, uneven, and perhaps reversible rhythms of development that characterize the growth of civil society, modern political regimes are frequently constituted at short notice, as coherent interdependent structures, and with pretensions to uniform coverage across their respective territorial jurisdictions. The 'new states' created in Europe after 1918, or in Africa and Asia after 1945, provide many recent illustrations of this thesis, but it applies also to many neo-democracies created in the wake of the Soviet collapse of 1989/91. In nearly all such cases the claims of uniform coverage and of formal political equality for all citizens within the new jurisdiction, were initially to some extent no more than aspirations, or legal fictions, for much of the subject population. Nevertheless these new political guidelines of territorial sovereignty and civic equality were in principle created at a specific moment (for example, through the writing of a constitution), after which they acquired instant universality. In the cases that concern us here, it was a full panoply of democratic political rights that were ostensibly conferred upon a newly created citizenry. Yet the sudden creation of new inclusionary political societies may well not coincide with any pre-existing maps of dense associative life. The obvious question therefore follows: how are the associative and communicative *practices* of 'civil society' related to the aspirational or juridical *fictions* of 'political society' in new democracies ? If there is more than one historical route to the establishment of a civil society, it would seem to follow that there could be more than one way in which civil society is related to the construction of a democratic political regime.

Evidently, there could be a slow growth of civil society which eventually creates the conditions for the eventual implantation of political democracy. (This is the Whig interpretation of British history; it also applies to one dominant view of the democratization of Spain.) But there could also be a reverse sequence, through which a formal political regime would first be implanted, and only subsequently would civil society – perhaps nurtured by a protective liberal state – gradually mature. (This would seem a standard western model for theorizing the democratization of many post-communist states; it could also apply to such 'protectorate' experiences as the democratization of Puerto Rico and Hawaii.) Other combinations are also theoretically possible – a civil society which attains a high level of development, without ever culminating in a democratic political regime (Hong Kong, for example); a civil society which develops on the basis that its freedoms and rights can only be secure if non-members are excluded from political participation (be they Tamils, Palestinians, Turkish Cypriots, Muslims, or 'bantus'). Where new political frontiers are incongruent with older maps of associative life, it is just as likely that peripheral or cross-border civil societies will be damaged as that core civil societies will be reinforced. Viewed in this broadly comparative manner, there seems no strong reason – either theoretical or empirical – for presuming the existence of only one strongly determinate relationship between civil society and political democracy. If the two are so readily separable, and in principle, incongruent, we need to examine more closely the instertices between them.

IV. 'UNCIVIL SOCIETY' AND POLITICAL DEMOCRACY

In those social locations where civil society is weak or absent the reverse of Schmitter's four conditions apply – namely (1) encroachments on dual autonomy; (2) which subvert the capacity for deliberation; and may encourage (3) usurpation; and (4) incivility. This abstract formulation embraces a great variety of more specific possibilities, since threats to civil society can come from many – and often multiple – sources, and can be driven by political, socio-economic, or even by technological processes.[17] Consider this quick listing of some of the most celebrated historical examples – the Nazi party's subversion of civil society in Weimar Germany; followed by the Socialist Unity Party (SED) in post-1945 East Germany; the mafia in republican Sicily; Catholic clerical conformism – in, say, rural Ireland; Islamic fundamentalism in the *bidonvilles* of the Maghreb; state-imposed conformity in Singapore; and some would add media-manipulated docility in Eisenhower's America, amoral familism in the Philippines, or caste-based exclusionisms in some parts of South Asia. This list should not be read as lumping all these diverse phenomena into an undifferentiated amalgam of 'threats to western liberty', nor should one lightly endorse all the specific historical and social judgements of responsibility that it implies. In a grounded analysis of any specific case we should expect to find multiple causation and some degree of structured determination, rather than just the will of a single illiberal agency. In the instances listed above about half were examples of encroachments from above (the state) and half from below (illiberal society). In general one should expect some interaction between these two sources of constraint.

There is also a range of unintentional, non-political, or 'structural' threats to civil society which are tediously familiar, but still require some listing – unemployment (which is hardly conducive to civility, or collective deliberation); criminality (which erodes dual autonomy, encourages usurpation); monopolistic systems of local social control (which regardless of political intent block off deliberation, foster intolerance, obscure the legitimacy of alternative viewpoints); the atomizing effects of market supremacy, and so forth. Again, the purpose of this list is not to amalgamate all these structures into an undifferentiated threat, nor to imply that they are either separately or conjointly determinate. On the contrary, the purpose is to demonstrate their heterogeneity and fragmentation. For this implies that civil society will always be under pressure from multiple sources, and that in any modern polity it is always likely to coexist with substantial and persisting sources of incivility. It is never likely to achieve uniformity of coverage throughout any full-scale nation-state; and therefore it will always require an organized capacity for self-defence and self-reproduction if it is to secure and preserve its political hegemony.

In a modern democracy these pockets or strata of incivility also possess political rights and are entitled to their share of representation in the making of public policy. Depending, therefore, on their size and their capacity for political articulation, they will help steer the course of democratic government. They may indeed shape the rules and affect the resources allocations that underpin the civil part of society. For example, if we regard 'autonomous deliberation' as one of the most essential ingredients of a robust civil society, political democracy may well empower political forces which have no interest in fostering such practices, but may instead view them as either wasteful or even threatening. Similarly, there can be no guarantee that electoral majorities will always favour the preservation of the 'civility' so dear to well-educated minorities. On the contrary one sector's 'autonomy and civility' can easily be reinterpreted by another sector of society as elitist privilege, needing to be levelled.

The recent reinstatement in office, via competitive elections, of no more than lightly 'reformed' communist parties in various East European neo-democracies, serves to highlight this persistent tension between the rival claims for our allegiance of civil society and political democracy. Eminent liberal theorists, such as Gray and Gellner, have all invoked visions of civil society as counterposed to communism, that can be read as delegitimizing such electoral outcomes.[18]

Similarly, in an analysis centred on capitalist democracy, although Schmitter tends to present civil society as normally and in the long run positive for democratic consolidation, he also acknowledges the separateness of the two processes, and the potential for friction between them. 'Civil society, however, is not an unmitigated blessing for democracy. It can affect the consolidation and subsequent functioning of democracy in a number of negative ways.' Among these he includes:

(2) It may build into the policy process a systematically biased distribution of influence ... .

(3) It tends to impose an elaborate and obscure process of compromise upon political life, the outcome of which can be policies which no-one wanted in the first place and with which no-one can subsequently identify ... .

(5) Most dangerously it 'may prove to be not one but several civil societies – all occupying the same territory and polity, but organizing interests and passions into communities that are ethnically, linguistically or culturally distinct – even exclusive'.[19]

The two foregoing paragraphs have presented strikingly counterposed normative images of the relationship between civil society and democracy. In the first, 'civil society' is the bearer of liberty, and is threatened by the mechanical application of majoritarian politics in a society with a still prevailing uncivil inheritance. In the second, the consolidation of political democracy is taken as the desirable goal, and 'civil society' can therefore be scrutinized and evaluated according to the quality of its potential contribution, which could be negative. On the first view, the stronger the civil society the better, even if it is inherently 'denser' in some social locations than in others. On the second view, only those forms of civil society that contribute to the consolidation of a high quality of political democracy are clearly desirable. Other forms may be too inegalitarian, too pushy and disorienting, or even too 'uncivil', to be desirable. Indeed sound democratization could require far-reaching reform, and perhaps even the weakening, of inherited systems of dense associative life.[20]

The first account makes the implicit assumption of an overbearing state. Civil society therefore needs strengthening against that source of threat to its 'dual autonomy'. In the second account, by contrast, the state is implicitly assumed to lack strong authority. It is therefore the capture of civil society by particularistic interests that presents the main threat to dual automony.

Since these two possibilities are both theoretically and empirically plausible, we may conclude that the moral significance we can assign to civil society is indeterminate (perhaps even 'essentially contested'), at this abstract level. A reasoned evaluation will depend in part on where the observer is located in the social structure, and on how a particular civil society functions and relates to the broader political system. Perhaps it would be better for US democracy if we all went out to bowling clubs together more often. But while on the Upper East Side of Manhattan a natural focus of community deliberation would be excessive tax burdens and wasteful social spending, in the Bronx a different form of civility might be more likely to emerge. The impediments to effective collective action would almost certainly prove quite different in the two cases as well.

One way to cope with this diversity is to say that any collective deliberations that are not subversive, and that do not fall outside the law, are as legitimate as any others. Of course, in order to achieve positive results within a liberal constitutional framework, it will be necessary to win over many diverse interests. Some forms of deliberation will therefore be more successful (because more persuasive, or more skilfully targeted) than others. But ineffective and unpersuasive forms of deliberation are also permitted, provided they do not infringe a small number of clearly defined legal prohibitions. In principle this is indeed the way democratic regimes should define the scope of tolerated deliberations. But can the same criterion serve to delimit the scope of debate within 'civil society'? Following the definition adopted in this discussion it would seem not.

On most definitions (including the one used here) it would be more plausible to say that some forms of discussion which are not illegal in a democracy are nevertheless 'uncivil', and threatening to such crucial norms as non-usurpation and interpersonal toleration. Thus various forms of religious fundamentalism may have to be tolerated within a democracy, but cannot be regarded as part of a modern liberal 'civil society'. A rich family can plot to buy up a newspaper, and then use it to discredit their enemies, and with care the whole operation may be carried out within the law, but this would involve no manifestation of dual automony, or of civility. Public officials can collude to withold information that the electorate 'ought' to know (in order to make well-founded political choices), and again this may be done within the limits of the law, but it could still be 'uncivil'. In fact, the very question of how rigorously the law will be enforced in various settings may also be subject to uncivil manipulation which remains within the bounds of constitutionally permitted action.

In short, in the realm of collective discourse, as much as in the realm of social structure, there is a gap between the narrow coverage that properly pertains to our various conceptions of 'civil society' and the broader coverage required of the democratic polity. On the other side of that gap we can identify 'uncivil' deliberations, and 'uncivil' social strata. The precise boundary between the civil and the uncivil may be hard to define even in principle, and all the more so in practice. Alliances of convenience can be expected from time to time, spanning that boundary (as when the least civil of media barons are courted by the most respected of liberal institutions on some issue of common interest, or when fundamentalists seek the protection of civil libertarians). But a boundary there must be, if 'civil society' is to carry any of the moral or sociological connotations assigned to it by its theorists. If so, then the activities which lie on the other side of that boundary – in what I have called the 'uncivil interstices between civil and political society' – may be of great significance for the quality and stability of the democracy as a whole. This section has attempted to illustrate the extent of such effects even in well-established western democracies. By extension one could argue that in neo-democracies such uncivil interstices occupy a much larger social space, often more than that occupied by the emerging civil society itself.[21] In order to analyse the scope for 'democratic consolidation' in such societies we therefore need to attend to the political manifestations of 'uncivil society' in emerging democracies. We also need to consider how the scale and power of this 'uncivil' society may affect the content and characteristics displayed by whatever form of civil society can accompany it. The final section of this contribution outlines some preliminary ideas on this issue.

V. CIVIL SOCIETY AND THE 'OTHER'

If civil society is characterized by its capacity for deliberation, and for collective action (within the limits set by non-usurpation and civility) then we must expect it both to deliberate and to act on perceived threats to its existence, or to its capacity for future development. Such threats might be attributed primarily to 'traditional society' and its habitual constraints, or to the 'modern state' with its rationalizing and atomizing propensities. But, particularly in neo-democracies, they might also be located in the 'uncivil' (but neither private-traditional nor public-bureaucratic) interstices of the new political community.

Each of these alternative diagnoses invokes an alternative model (or theory) and implies a particular strategy of self-perpetuation. In any particular instance these three rival conceptions may be found in contention within the councils of a given 'civil society'. When traditional family and particularist loyalties are defined as the central problem to be overcome, 'state strengthening' strategies may seem acceptable, particularly those that strengthen the 'public sphere' by guaranteeing impersonal civic rights and reinforcing the rule of law. But when (as in post-communist neo-democracies, and also in Latin American neo-liberal discourse) the overbearing state is regarded as a greater menace, then deregulation, privatization and state shrinking will be preferred. In principle these may also involve enhancement of some kind of 'public space' where autonomous agents can interact without manipulation, and so here too it could be said that impartial legality and rights are implied, but it makes a great difference that such rights are asserted *against* the state, rather than under its protection, and that the justice system is liable to be subjected to the same austerity and market testing as the rest of the state bureaucracy.[22]

For in these conditions the resulting 'rule of law' will be above all responsive to the requirements of commerce, rather than to those of state directed rationality.[23] In the language of Habermas, this would lead to cultural impoverishment and the 'colonization of the life-world' from which modern civil society is supposed to emerge.

As the norm of 'dual autonomy' makes clear, civil societies are always to some extent under pressure from both sides, from traditional particularism and from the intrusive state. The preservation and enlargement of an autonomous realm requires a steady flow of resources and recruits, directed with vigilance and continuity of purpose. Civil society consists of multiple self-perpetuating centres of association, competing as well as co-operating in order to promote their rival interests and to project their alternative conceptions of autonomy, civility and self-preservation. Some such centres will shrink from particularism but hope to benefit from enlightened state activism; others will firmly resist state direction, but see little harm in allying with aspects of social traditionalism. Within each civil society alternative perspectives and priorities will compete for ascendancy with fluctuating success as the external environment is perceived to change.

But what if, as in many neo-democracies, the major threat to civil society comes – or at least is perceived to come – neither from statism nor traditional particularism, but from a majoritarian incivility of the modern kind? This refers to such phenomena as the impersonal irresponsibility of modern commercialized mass media; the impulsiveness of an uprooted and disoriented electorate; the short-termism of speculative financial markets; and the insecurity generated by well-organized crime, typically lodged in such strategic sectors as arms trafficking, money laundering, and the narcotics trade? Norms of dual autonomy, rational deliberation, civility, and Cohen and Arato's 'universal fundamental rights' may all come under siege from potentially majoritarian incivilities of this kind, which cannot for the most part be attributed directly to either of the two long-standing sources of threat against which civil society has typically been organized. As stressed in this discussion, this third alternative challenge to civil society can now be found everywhere – even in the most secure and developed of liberal democracies. Some theorists emphasize the importance of global integration, and the erosion of the authority of the nation state, as the dominant new tendencies at work. That might help to account for *some* of the elements of majoritarian incivility listed above, but by no means all, in my opinion. Particularly in neo-democracies it is often the manner in which the authoritarian regime foundered, and the uncivil inheritances it left in its wake, that prove more critical than the erosion of the nation state as such.

In neo-democracies emerging civil societies are, by definition, incipient and untested. The norms of dual autonomy, independent deliberation, and civility were little cultivated under authoritarian rule (except perhaps among some very privileged minorities under what Linz termed 'limited pluralism'), and so they had to be promoted and upheld in the face of official repression. That often provided an intense learning experience for activist minorities, and often their social influence exploded when the authoritarian regime left power. But at best they were a select group, not all of them deeply socialized in the norms of civility, and the choices they faced during the helter-skelter of democratization dispersed them into widely scattered activities. (The virtual disintegration of the Solidarity bloc in Poland after 1989 seems a paradigmatic case.) Competing with them for influence in post-transition public life were many active groups schooled in less civil norms – pragmatists from the authoritarian power structure; revanchistes, chauvinists, and fundamentalists, from other sectors of the opposition; the new rich, often engaged in 'primitive accumulation'; carpet-bagging foreign advisers with no durable commitment to the local society; and so on. The list could be extended further, but the point is already clear. In such settings whatever 'civil society' may have been precariously established will be fragile and under siege from all sides. It will have to contend with a democratic polity mostly populated by actors whose commitment to civility is questionable or absent.

Long before this 'civil society' can be stabilized and entrenched, the polity will have produced a succession of foundational decisions that will heavily constrain subsequent patterns of political interaction. No doubt certain forms of constitutional engineering may improve the prospects of a viable civil society (for example, through a well-crafted bill of rights, or perhaps through parliamentarism or federalism). Similarly some strategies of economic modernization are likely to be more supportive than others (for example, law-based schemes of open regionalism, deregulation, some forms of privatization). But there is no single or guaranteed prescription applicable to all cases, nor should the health of civil society be the only point for consideration when choosing between these alternatives. In practice other considerations will usually prove decisive. There is equally no single unique way in which the leaders of an incipient civil society must necessarily respond to the internal contradictions and external constraints that they face, but the range of alternatives compatible with survival and eventual growth are sure to be limited and inhibiting. In some cases strong civil societies may nevertheless be erected over the longer term, but not under conditions of their own choosing. In Gellner's language, the conditions for a realistic civil society may not permit the realization of the civil society *ideal*.

Constitutional government based on universal suffrage would normally imply that those who wish to realize an ideal of public conduct should promote their cause through a political party or at least via the electoral process. But the norms of 'dual autonomy' and 'non-usurpation' that we have attributed to civil society imply that the term should not be extended to embrace political organizations that compete for public office. Moreover, in many neo-democracies some of the most effective vote-winning organizations lack a tradition of commitment to the norm of 'civility', and/or permit very little 'deliberation' over their internal affairs. There is therefore, in general, no particular reason to expect an 'elective affinity' between a vigorous civil society and electorally successful political parties. Certainly in various cases we may find that the emergence of a more broadly based civil society is followed by the establishment of democratic political parties which proceed to legislate in accordance with a civil society ideal. But two other models are equally plausible, namely (i) an antagonism between the architects of civil society and successful party leaders; or (ii) a compartmentalization of the two spheres.[24] The relationship between civil society and party politics clearly requires careful analysis, which has not been possible in this paper.[25] But we can at least warn against the error of reductionism here.

So what if the 'Other' against which the thinking heads of civil society can organize themselves is neither the coherently intrusive state, nor the inertia of unthinking tradition, but rather the insecurity, rootlessness, arbitrariness, and perhaps even the social cannibalism, that have come to be associated with many post-transition liberalized societies? What kind of civil society, based on what organizing principles, can survive and develop in the face of this modern anomic 'other? A Hobbesian 'city' perhaps united only by its fear of the surrounding war of all against all? Hegelian guilds? Or a Marxian bourgeoisie? A Tocquevillean network of local associations (and bowling clubs)? Or even Habermas's 'life-world of communicative interaction'? Each of these tends to privilege a particular sociological category – specialists in security, master craftsmen, capitalists, local journalists, intelligentsia, and so forth – and none of them seem self-evidently applicable to neo-democracies as a whole. Each may suggest a fragment of the potential whole, but none gives clear guidance as to the principles upon which it might be integrated. In practice different forms of civil society are likely to prove relatively viable in different neo-democracies. But in general it may be concluded that the most effective principles of integration are more likely to come from without, rather than from within. That is to say, those forms of civil society which can cope best with the pressures of uncivil majoritarianism have the best prospects. Whether they can also live up to the idealistic hopes vested in them by so many recent theorists is another matter.

NOTES

1. For a useful and up-to-date compilation of the intricacies, including institutional and regional disaggregation and a discussion of the Andreotti trials, see Luciano Violante (ed.), *Mafie e antimafia: Rapporto '96* (Rome: Laterza, 1996).
2. *Le Monde*, 30 Dec.1995, p.6.
3. Britain, like many long-established 'polyarchies', extends political rights (rights to vote and organize) to substantial communities that reject its constitutional authority and that consider it legitimate to practice 'uncivil' forms of political opposition. Sínn Féin, Heri Batasuna, and the Corsican nationalists all illustrate this pattern of incivility.
4. The title is also a reference to Robert Putnam 'Bowling Alone: Democracy in America at the End of the Twentieth Century', in D. Rueschemeyer (ed.), *Participation and Democracy: East and West* (forthcoming). Putnam concludes that in the USA
   participation has fallen (often sharply) in many types of civic associations, from religious groups to labor unions, from women's clubs to fraternal clubs, and from neighborhood gatherings to bowling leagues. Virtually all segments of society have been afflicted by this lessening in social connectedness ... (which) seems a likely contributor to many of the social and political ills now afflicting America, and perhaps to those besetting other advanced democracies, as well.
5. Thomas Hobbes, *Philosophicall Rudiments Concerning Government and Society* (1651), Part Two, Ch.5, paragraph 9.
6. *Hegel's Philosophy of Right* (trans. T.M. Knox), (Oxford: 1942), para. 245.
7. Alexis de Tocqueville, *Democracy in America*, Vol. II, Ch.V, para. 2.
8. For a recent and sophisticated exposition, conducted from within the German critical theory tradition, see Jean Cohen and Andrew Arato, *Civil Society and Political Theory* (Cambridge, MA: MIT Press, 1993). Among the major authors they evaluate, Arendt, Gramsci, Parsons, and – inevitably – Habermas receive particularly thorough attention. See Chapter Nine.
9. 'On Civil Society and the Consolidation of Democracy: Ten Propositions' (mimeo, Stanford Department of Political Science, July 1995). Note that this definition includes trade unions but excludes private firms. Where does this leave privately owned communications media, or established churches?
10. Ernest Gellner, *Conditions of Liberty: Civil Society and Its Rivals* (London: Allen Lane, 1994), pp.8, 10. However, those who find this strand of Gellner's argument troublingly eurocentric, could turn to Michael Carrithers, Steven Collins and Steven Lukes (eds.), *The Category of the Person: Anthropology, Philosophy and History* (Cambridge: Cambridge University Press, 1985), and to Jack Goody, *The East in the West* (Cambridge: Cambridge University Press, 1996) for partial correctives.
11. R.G. Collingwood, *The New Leviathan: On Man, Society, Civilization and Barbarism* (Oxford: Clarendon Press, 1992), para. 35–41, p.292. Does the norm of civility also apply to the treatment of outgroups, those not covered by pre-established rules, or not socialized into this conception of self-respect? Collingwood went to press at the darkest period of the Second World War (January 1942) and seems a little ambivalent over this crucial issue.
12. In his account of what he calls the 'structural transformation of the public sphere', Habermas views civil society as the arena in which pluralistic public opinion makes itself felt as an independent source of power. But of course some voices express themselves more loudly than others in the arena of public opinion, and not all the opinions expressed in an unconstrained public arena will be equally 'civil'; Jürgen Habermas, *Strukturwandel der Öffentlichkeit* (Frankfurt: Suhrkamp, 1993).
13. For a vigorous recent presentation of this case see Paul Hirst, *Associative Democracy: New Forms of Economic and Social Governance* (Massachusetts: University of Massachusetts Press, 1994).
14. Robert Putnam, *Making Democracy Work: Civic Traditions in Modern Italy* (Princeton, 1994) and Francis Fukuyama, *Trust: New Foundations of Global Prosperity* (London: Hamish Hamilton, 1995).

15. Jean L. Cohen and Andrew Arato, *Civil Society and Political Theory* (Cambridge, MA: MIT Press, 1992), pp.440-42.

16. On a recent visit to South Africa I was struck by the richness and stability of the civic society that had sheltered the whites – and even perhaps the coloureds of Cape province – under *apartheid*, while actively and energetically suppressing the possibilities of peaceful association for the none-white majority. Protestant Ulster probably displays a somewhat comparable polarity in civic provision, in this case legitimated by a universal suffrage that guaranteed Catholic subordination.

17. If Putnam's friends no longer go bowling, this is at least in part because so many rival entertainments are now supplied to them electronically and at home.

18. In his last book Ernest Gellner trenchantly sets out the two rival theoretical claims to validation, and asserts his clear choice:
    Theorists of democracy who operate in the abstract, without reference to concrete social conditions, end up with a vindication of democracy as a general ideal, but are then obliged to concede that in many societies the ideal is not realizable .... Is it not better to state the conditions that make the ideal feasible, or even mandatory, and start from that? Civil society is a more realistic notion, which specifies and includes its own conditions .... Because it highlights those institutional pre-conditions and the necessary historical context 'Civil Society' is probably a better more illuminating slogan than democracy; op. cit., pp.188–9.
    But Gellner's imprecise specifications relate only loosely to the ideals of democratic theory.

19. Mimeo, op. cit. p.14. Note that these negative potentialities tend to run counter to the positive attributes emphasized by Schmitter's initial definition. Here non-usurpation becomes policy bias; deliberation becomes opacity; and civility becomes tribalism. It is difficult to sustain an idealized image of civil society, while also reflecting its multiple and ambiguous manifestations and its lopsided impact on the workings of the larger polity.

20. Carlos M. Vilas provides some striking illustrations of this viewpoint, in an overview of the neo-democracies of Central America; 'Prospects for Democratisation in a Post-Revolutionary Setting: Central America', *Journal of Latin American Studies*, Vol.28, Part 2 (1996), pp.461–503. He portrays local oligarchies founded on tight inherited structures of social exclusivity that have learnt to parade the rhetoric of market democracy as a public discourse masking their continued supremacy, while their more intimate social practices perpetuate deeply undemocratic values. Compare E. Gyimah-Boadi on the weaknesses of civil society in Africa 'preliberal or antiliberal values ... tend also to pervade the modern and secular civil associations ... tendencies of some key civil associations ... to refuse to establish "rational" bureaucracies; to "anoint" rather than elect (including those involved in prodemocracy work) their executives; and to endow their leaders with "life" chairmanships', 'Civil Society in Africa', *Journal of Democracy*, Vol.7, No.2 (1996), p.129.

21. Giorgio Alberti of the University of Bologna has based his conception of *movimentismo* in Peru and Argentina on an analogous argument (see his '"Movimentismo" and Democracy: An Analytical Framework and the Peruvian Case Study (Mimeo, CESDE, Bologna, Oct. 1995). Guillermo O'Donnell coined the term 'brown areas' to refer to the large sectors of Latin American society where uncivil conditions prevail; 'On the State, Democratization and Some Conceptual Problems: A Latin American View with Glances at Some Postcommunist Countries', *World Development*, Vol 21, No.8 (1993), pp.1355–69.

22. Compare the Czech debate over 'civil society' in which President Havel tries to promote the concept as a corrective to excessive emphasis on purely market relationships, while Prime Minister Havel equates democracy with individual freedom, including freedom from social engineering in the name of civil society; Vaclav Havel, Vaclav Klaus and Petr Pithart, 'Rival Visions', *Journal of Democracy*, Vol.7, No.1 (1996), pp.18, 20.

23. Recall the liberal pluralism of Durkheim for whom it was the State which 'creates and organizes and makes a reality' of the individual's natural rights, indeed its 'essential function' was to 'liberate individual personalities', by offsetting the pressure on them of local domestic, ecclesiastical, occupational and other secondary groups (while the latter were also needed to offset the potential tyranny of the state); Steven Lukes, *Emile Durkheim* (London: Allen Lane, 1973), p.271.

24. These three alternatives have been elaborated by Carlos A. Forment, 'Civil Society and the Invention of Democracy in Nineteenth Century Cuba' (mimeo, Princeton, Sept. 1995).
25. My approach has been to exclude all political parties from 'civil society' on the grounds that they compete for national office. An alternative would be to include those political parties (and only those) who represent the interests of substantial sectors of civil society. This would involve making some invidious distinctions between political parties. Does the Italian Communist Party express the interests of a major element in civil society, or does it displace and suborn those interests? Is this stable over time, or variable? How do we prove one interpretation rather than the other?

The Taming of the Idea of Civil Society

GIDEON BAKER

Since 1989, civil society theory within the literature on democratization reflects the hold exerted by the model of actually existing liberal democracy over political studies. Thus civil society is viewed in largely instrumental terms – as a support structure for democracy at the state level – and earlier, more radical, models – which understood civil society to be a democratic end in itself – are forgotten. Liberal-democratic conceptualizations of civil society, therefore, remain largely unchallenged as to their normative assumptions; increasingly, the category civil society is seen as a neutral tool for social science analysis. This essay seeks to complicate this picture, and to expose the current civil society orthodoxy as rather less than value-free. It does this via a critical exploration of the boundaries of the new thinking, and by juxtaposing it with more substantive models from the 1970s and 1980s.

This essay offers a critique of conceptualizations of civil society which have emerged from two of the largest and most influential literatures on democratization of the 1990s: those relating to Central-Eastern Europe and Latin America. It is argued that the horizons of civil society theory within these two literatures are bounded by a liberal democratic perspective on the relationship between state and society. Establishing this is important, first, in charting the decline of earlier, and more radical, models of civil society that flourished briefly in both regions during the 1980s. Secondly, the wider picture that emerges is of a near-consensus amongst analysts of democratization that actually existing liberal democracy is the only form of democracy on offer. While it might come as no surprise that, post-1989, the tenets of liberal democracy are in the ascendant within political science, the story of civil society theory reveals that in some fields this ascendancy is more accurately described as hegemony. This spontaneous consent that liberal democratic 'civil society' is what it ought to be should cause considerable concern to opponents of discursive closure, whether or not they wish to advocate more radical alternatives. For what is at stake in this area of the debate about democratization is no less than a growing, and largely unchallenged, acceptance of a liberal democratic 'end of history'. With radicals increasingly abandoning the search for a form of democracy beyond that of the liberal, capitalist type also, it is necessary to redouble commitment to the theory of democracy – which requires, *inter alia*, an ongoing critique of the dominant ideology: liberal democratic thought. For the purposes of this essay, that means questioning just how axiomatic and value-free the new civil society orthodoxy really is.

CIVIL SOCIETY IN THE LITERATURE ON DEMOCRATIZATION IN CENTRAL-EASTERN EUROPE

For the opposition theorists of the 1970s and 1980s, civil society was an explicitly normative concept which held up the ideal of societal space, autonomous from the state, wherein self-management and democracy could be worked out.[1] That is, the idea of civil society was political and prescriptive, as, for example, in a series of lectures given in 1982 under the title *Power and Civil Society* by Leszek Nowak (a philosopher and Solidarity activist in Poland) to his Solidarity co-internees, where civil society is defined as 'the sphere of civil autonomy'.[2] Since 1989, by contrast, civil society has been used mostly as a term to describe various sets of non-state institutions[3] (though with implicit normative implications, as will become apparent below), or, where the concept is used more reflexively, as an analytical tool with which to account for democratization in the region and to explore the likelihood of democratic consolidation.[4] As Szakolczai and Horvath observe, in 'explaining the revolutionary changes that occurred in Eastern Europe during 1989, one often encounters a discourse centring upon the resurrection of civil society'.[5] Within this discourse, contra its earlier appearance as a ideal orientated towards political mobilization, civil society is now a putatively neutral social-scientific concept. Lewis, for example, is critical that '[w]ith reference to Eastern Europe during the 1980s, "civil society" became more of a slogan than an analytical concept'.[6] Frentzel-Zagorska similarly states that: 'I want to avoid [theoretical approaches to civil society], since I intend to use the concept ... as an analytical tool for the particular historical developments taking place in Eastern Europe'.[7] In short, within the domain of civil society theory, the positivist fallacy of a value-free science is at hand.

Why do commentators such as Lewis and Frentzel-Zagorska believe that they can circumvent the political theory of civil society for a 'scientific' theory of civil society? One reason, the implications of which shall now be explored in more detail, is that it is clear to these commentators what a concept of civil society should do; put simply, it should further our understanding of the conditions necessary for the transition to, and consolidation of, liberal democracy. Since these apparently indisputable ends are known, the means of civil society theory fall neatly into place.

The Instrumentalization of Civil Society for Liberal Democracy

For the radical oppositionists from the 1970s and 1980s in communist countries such as Poland, Hungary and Czechoslovakia, civil society was itself the seat of democratic legitimacy and practice:

> Hope ... lies ... [in] the realization of a social order in which the formalized and functionalized structure of society will be regulated and controlled by this 'newly discovered' spontaneous civic activity, which will be a *permanent and essential* source of social self-awareness.[8]

However, as a quote from Miller illustrates, civil society now denotes a very different kind of activity:

> The [opposition] model of civil society has been superseded. The idea of civil society has by no means been discarded as a consequence, however. On the contrary, it has become a virtual 'buzz-word' in the discourse of post-communist politics. But the tasks assigned to civil society are substantially different: its role is to be constitutive and preservative of the liberal-democratic political systems and free-market economies ... .[9]

Epitomizing the democratization genre here, Miller blatantly reifies the category civil society, since he moves from acknowledging its status as a concept to a description of its supposed character 'on the ground'. But the central change to the theory of civil society is that civil society is now seen as external to, though no doubt important for, democracy understood as a political mechanism for controlling the state. This is illustrated by Skapska's assertion that, '[a]s the post-communist experience indicates, the alternative forms of civil society flourishing before the collapse of communism prove to be dysfunctional in democratic society'.[10] Skapska is here referring to the negative impact upon the new institutions of political democracy that has ensued from the 'mistrust and hostility towards official institutions' engendered by the radical, autonomous and anti-statist model of civil society. Skapska may well be correct in this analysis, but the underlying assumption remains that the civil society project present before transition occurred could not, of itself, create a democratic society in the absence of 'official institutions' and 'legal rules of the game'.[11]

This shift in democratic theory, with the idea of civil society being similarly realigned, has been close to universal within the literature on democracy and civil society after 1989. Essentially, it involves the instrumentalization of civil society as now merely supportive of liberal democracy, rather than as *the* site for democratic participation which it mostly signified prior to 1989. Examples are numerous: Bibic and Graziano, for instance, write that the 'real or potential role of civil society with regard to democracy and democratization ... refers above all to political democratization and political democracy'.[12] Bernhard likewise begins his analysis of civil society and democratic transition in Central-Eastern Europe with the assertion that:

> Modern democracy ... ha[s] only existed in conjunction with a civil society. It constitutes the sphere of autonomy from which political forces representing constellations of interests in society have contested state power. Civil society has been a necessary condition for the existence of representative government including democracy.[13]

In his introduction, Bernhard also declares that he will question whether civil society 'can be more than this'. Yet from his conclusion it is clear that Bernhard's intention was never to examine the potentialities of civil society as a democratic end in itself, but merely to ponder whether, apart from its role in 'curtail[ing] state autonomy and as a basis for interest representation', civil society might also assist 'the process of democratic consolidation and the transition to a market economy'.[14] Clearly, the horizons of Bernhard's democratic theory do not enable him to imagine civil society as anything other than a support structure for liberal democracy as it is currently constituted. Effectively, this means limiting the horizons of civil society theory to the liberal agenda of separation of powers, control of power, and pluralist interest representation. The model of civil society emanating from the democratic opposition during the late 1970s and 1980s – from theorists such as Michnik and Kuron (Poland), Havel and Benda (Czechoslovakia), and Konrad and Kis and Bence (Hungary) – appears to have been forgotten entirely. *These* theorists, in addition to their calls for a more liberal politics of checks and balances, also saw civil society originally in the more positive, or socialist, terms of community and solidarity. Indeed, for many such theorists civil society indicated a movement towards post-statism; for control of power, while not unimportant, would be insufficient for the fundamental redistribution, or even negation, of power itself. If this was to be achieved, self-management in civil society was necessary. As Havel expressed it in 1979, 'the classic impotence of traditional democratic organizations' (which he elsewhere identified as parliamentary institutions) 'can only be overcome through the structures which 'naturally rise from below as a consequence of authentic self-organization'.[15] From a Hungarian perspective also, in the words of Konrad from the early 1980s:

> In Eastern Europe today, self-management is society's prime demand ... Workplace and local community self-government, based on personal contact, exercised daily, and always subject to correction, have greater attraction in our part of the world than multiparty representative democracy because, if they have their choice, people

are not content with voting once every four years ... When there is parliamentary democracy but no self-administration, the political class alone occupies the stage.[16]

Konrad's Polish contemporary, Michnik, although he appeared to hark back to a civil society from the past, also emphasized self-management as the core of civil society: 'The essence of the spontaneously growing independent and self-governing Solidarity lay in the restoration of social ties [and] self-organization ... For the first time in the history of communist rule in Poland 'civil society' was being restored ... .'[17]

Returning to the current debate about democratization, and to the starkly contrasting view of civil society which it contains, Ralf Dahrendorf, an influential commentator on the transitions of 1989, is another analyst for whom civil society is now redefined as merely strategic to liberal democracy.[18] He introduces civil society (which he notes only in passing had been an idea central to opposition thinking) as the key to pulling together 'the divergent time scales and dimensions of political and economic reform ... It is the ground in which both have to be anchored in order not to be blown away'.[19] Elsewhere, he has similarly written that 'civil society is the common denominator of a functioning democracy and an effective market economy. It is only if and when civil society has been created that political and economic reform can be said to have credence'.[20]

There are a number of reasons why Dahrendorf, Bernhard and others see civil society as basically outside of democracy and as only functional for liberal democracy. The first, as has been shown, is that they understand democracy as limited to institutional mechanisms for controlling the state. Secondly, they view civil society as simply associational life outside of the state. For these theorists, then, civil society does not constitute democratic space[s] for participation and self-management; instead, it is seen as representing interests in a functionalist fashion.[21] While civil society is indispensable to the presence of choice within both the economic and political spheres, there is nothing inherently democratic about it.[22] This is why many such commentators warn of the dangers of 'uncivil society' and of the non-democratic elements of civil society.[23] For the oppositionists, of course, if associations were not democratic (as they understood democracy in terms of popular self-management), then they were not part of civil society.

The Anti-Republican Model of Civil Society and the Fear of 'Excessive' Participation

In apparent agreement with the opposition theorists (Kuron, in this case) who originally coined the term 'self-limiting revolution', Bozoki and

Sukosd emphasize the importance of the self-limitation of popular movements, which they see as preserving human rights and as necessary because democracy is only possible if self-limitation becomes a '*collective experience* in society'.[24] Yet Bozoki and Sukosd go on to reveal that their enthusiasm for self-limitation is less an endorsement of non-violent politics (the realization that the violent 'revolution devours its own children'),[25] which was what the oppositionists had in mind, and more like antipathy to a mobilized citizenry *per se*, which was precisely what the oppositionists called for. 'The role of society in democratic transition', they write, 'is vital, nevertheless it is primarily symbolic ... there is no need for constant mass political mobilization'.[26] Reinforcing the impression of a basically elitist outlook, Bozoki and Sukosd ask: 'How could the masses that through the program of civil society had originally been mobilized ... be demobilized?' Although they concede that the demobilization of civil society and the rise of political society (political parties) has turned out 'only too well', Bozoki and Sukosd's preference for a civil society that encourages high levels of participation only prior to regime transition is already clear.[27]

Bozoki and Sukosd are not alone in this regard. Dahrendorf also wants to downplay the republican aspects of civil society which the oppositionists sought variously to encourage. For Dahrendorf:

> A civil society is civil, even civilized, and this requires men and women who respect others, but more important still, who are able and willing to go and do things themselves ... I do not particularly like notions like 'active citizenship', which seems to place all the emphasis on the obligations associated with membership of society ... civic virtues are indispensable but [so is] self-reliance.[28]

The perennial liberal fear of an 'over-mobilized' society that lurks behind Dahrendorf's statement here, is even more starkly present in Lewis's elitist account of the dangers of an unmediated civil society:

> ... the apparent victory of civil society over communist dictatorship might be construed as leading less to political democracy than to populism, referring to the direct political dominance of 'the people' with little regard to constitutional arrangements, the institutional mediation of power relations or any protection of minority rights. It is an outcome seen in societies not dissimilar to those of Eastern Europe where political processes have been, at least initially, relatively unconstrained ... The desires and aspirations of a greater fraction of society might indeed be better satisfied by the arrangements of such a political order – but this is not the same thing as the establishment of political democracy.[29]

Though differently from the orthodox liberal theory that those such as Dahrendorf and Lewis provide, even 'radical' theory has contributed to the widespread rejection of the republican or self-management vision of civil society which the oppositionists advocated. Central here is that hugely influential figure of the New Left, Habermas, who has claimed that 'the public opinion that is worked up via democratic procedures into communicative power cannot "rule" of itself, but can only point the use of administrative power in specific directions ...'.[30] Following Habermas in his hostility to a fully autonomous civil society, for example, is Miller, who understands 'self-restraint' in civil society not in the oppositionists' terms of non-violence, but as involving the recognition of 'the imperative of specialized expertise for the exercise of governmental policy-formation and regulation'.[31]

The Colonization of Civil Society Theory by the Model of Liberal Democracy

In the face of the oppositionists' earlier model of civil society as the locus for a 'third way' for democracy beyond that of East and West, state-socialism and liberal-capitalism,[32] civil society is now seen as the exclusive property of liberal democracy. Curry, for example, concludes her study of the 'realities of civil society in the light of postcommunist society' by asking:

> What are the necessary ... conditions making institutions of democracy/pluralism like 'civil society' work a la the Western model? ... How do local groupings build a base for and encourage the development of a national level 'civil society' that also works in the way Western democracies work?[33]

That the idea of civil society has now been adopted by theorists who see it as fully present only within liberal-democratic societies, is revealed also by an increasingly common cluster of assumptions about why Central-Eastern European countries apparently do not possess civil society after all. One such assumption, coming often from Central-Eastern European theorists themselves, is that civil society requires a pluralist political culture which is simply not present in the region. This is what Sztompka argues via the accusation of 'civilizational incompetence' on the part of post-communist countries;[34] which is an analysis similar to the one provided by Tarkowska and Tarkowski under the rubrics 'amoral familism' and 'privatized society'.[35] Indeed, in a recent edition of *Democratization*, Tempest refers to Hann's report into the 'ingrained apathy and suspicion of all outsiders' in rural Hungary, which Tempest sees as being 'in contradistinction to the pluralist civil society theme'.[36]

Questioning the analyses of these commentators – some of whom are anthropologists with vast experience of the societies within which they live and work – is not the important point here; and Tempest himself is critical of the implicit projection of 'civilizational competence' on to western society. However, quite apart from the minutiae of research findings is the impression given by these analysts that they are investigating whether it is possible for civil society to exist in the culture or not. Clearly, for them, civil society is about the sociology of liberal, pluralist polities, rather than that transhistorical political space for democratic action such as the opposition theorists of civil society had in mind.[37] This is revealed when Tempest, for example, talks of the crisis of 'civil society' also in the West: '[T]he middle class is in process of disintegration and [thus] *the principal social requisite for civil society* is in dissolution'.[38]

Lewis also questions whether the label 'civil society' is appropriate to Eastern Europe. His concern is that the earlier equation of civil society in the region with social movements obscures the following problematic:

> These [movements] were often not conducive either to general processes of democratization or to the development of the multi-party systems that are the prime institutional expression of modern representative democracy. They were, to varying degrees, inclusive and relatively undifferentiated forms of organization ... [and were] not so far removed from ... Marxist resistance to pluralism ... These movements were...not well suited to one of the core processes of modern democracy ... – that of interest representation.[39]

Lewis's proposition is that organizations such as Solidarity did not constitute 'a process of representation in any way related to the articulation and pursuit of interests observed in developed western democracies'.[40] With this analysis he reveals clearly that the only model of democracy that he has in mind is that built upon the liberal-democratic preference for the possibility of 'exit' over 'voice'. His unease with the contribution of movements such as Polish Solidarity is therefore unsurprising. For he does not hold, as participants in these movements generally did, that democracy rather privileges 'voice' – that is, publicity, participation and collective action – over the 'exit' possibilities opened up by pluralist interest representation and its provision of choice for the self-interested individual.[41]

Another common proposition concerning the liberal democratic model of civil society which would have sat uncomfortably with the radical opposition theorists – given their frequent calls for (socialist) self-management in the economic as well as political spheres[42] – is that civil society should not be understood as a realm of substantive, that is socio-economic, equality, but only of citizenship or political equality:

The vision of civil society that the anticommunist opposition in Central and Eastern Europe used in its fight for liberty has lost out as a social program. The moral civil society, an … anticapitalist … community, could endure as a viable ideal only so long as it remained unencumbered by the need to make real choices. Actual postcommunist civil society … is challenging the egalitarian outlook that numerous opinion surveys have shown to be deeply rooted in the minds of Central and East Europeans.[43]

Smolar goes on to argue that civil society is actually the basis of private property and of a market economy. Having stated that 'the major problem facing postcommunist societies is how to relegitimate private property and the open society with all the uncertainty that accompanies them', Smolar looks to civil society to provide 'the moral foundations of private property': 'The civic principle is not just a principle of equality; it also creates the normative basis for the integration of civil society as well as its integration with the political system'.[44]

The argument that civil society is a precondition of a successful market economy is also reversed in many accounts – in other words, it is claimed that marketization is itself a precondition of a mature civil society. An extreme version of this argument is made by Narojek, who sees the reconstruction of civil society as making necessary the exclusion of the option of going back on market-reform from the sphere of democratic decision-making![45] Morawski, though in a more moderate fashion, also sees the 'transformation into a mature civil society' as possible 'only when economic changes make marketization and property changes (towards the consolidation of private property) effective'.[46] Korbonski, too, is persuaded that 'in the absence of a private economic sphere or a competitive market economy, it makes little sense to talk about civil society, whose dependence on the market has been emphasized by many scholars'.[47]

A third component of the cluster of liberal democratic assumptions about civil society is that democracy is a process which occurs at the level of the state. This belief makes the legitimacy of the state an unquestioned aspect of the liberal-democratic approach to civil society theory. Bibic, for example, begins his work on democracy and civil society by first outlining Schumpeter and Lipset's proceduralist models of political democracy and, secondly, by concurring with O'Donnell and Schmitter that '[p]olitical democracy is the goal of the recent democratic revolutions and debates'.[48] By contrast, the earlier, radical, theorists of civil society characterized the mechanism of the state and democracy as in many ways antithetical to one another.[49] Of course, most such theorists conceded that a limited state was necessary to the prevention of anarchy and also because maximal self-management would lead to society becoming politicized all over again (Michnik in Poland and Kis and Bence in Hungary were especially aware of this threat);[50] but they were little able to recommend it as positive for the democratic ordering of society – which was why civil society became so central to their democratic theory. For most of the post-1989 literature on civil society in the region, however, the positive role of the state *vis-à-vis* civil society is emphasized repeatedly.[51] Indeed, the liberal state's legitimacy, contra earlier models and reflecting the influence of liberal contract theory, is apparently seen as prior to that of civil society itself:

> ... sovereign state power may be considered an indispensable condition for the democratization of civil society.[52]

> For [societal] agents to constitute a civil society they need the sanction of the state; the public space must be guaranteed as a realm of freedom from the state by the state itself ... Barring this, a liberated public space would be but an anarchy of competing interests.[53]

In fact, Bernhard uses this argument to support the notion that the Polish opposition, while establishing 'important landmarks in the self-liberation of civil society, ... fell short of a full reconstruction of civil society [itself] ... This was because the Polish party-state had still made no *de jure* recognition of the opposition, its right to exist, or the boundaries or of the public space it had carved out'.[54] On this reading, civil society only comes into being once political pluralism is enshrined by the state. In other words, it arises out of the legal framework established in the transition to liberal democracy, and cannot be said to have substance outside of this transition.[55] Needless to say, the radical oppositionists saw things very differently. For the (self-managing) civil society that they had in mind was often described as being no more present in the West than in the East.[56]

Finally, the liberal democratic model of civil society appears to have fundamentally influenced even those more radical theorists who, though they no longer stand by a 'third way' model of civil society, are still concerned with its radical potentialities. The evolution of Arato's work is instructive here.[57] For in his original analysis of the Polish model of civil society in 1981, Arato was optimistic about the possibilities for greater self-management in all spheres that the strategy of putting 'civil society first' held out. He was also convinced of the need for the western liberal democracies to be transformed through an encounter with a radical, republican civil society. Yet in a 1994 analysis of *The Rise, Decline and Reconstruction of the Concept of Civil Society and Directions for Future Research*, Arato ends up in a not dissimilar place to the theorists of democratization examined above. That is, his focus is now limited to the question of what civil society can do for liberal democracy in terms of extending its legitimacy and deepening its democratic practices. Arato concludes his study by highlighting a number of issues of importance for a theory of civil society. These include, first, the problem of democratic legitimacy: civil society is seen to make a contribution here in terms of widening the legitimacy of procedural, parliamentary politics through providing networks for participation. In addition, Arato calls for further exploration of the possible role of civil society in 'constitution making, in the stability of constitutions, and in the development of constitutional patriotism'.[58] He finishes by stating that: 'I certainly do not think that these ... areas of research are the only ones relevant to those who wish to turn the theory of civil society into a more differentiated set of analytical instruments, more intellectually plausible for the decades ahead.'[59]

Thus while Arato is more aware than liberal-democratic theorists of the possibilities presented by civil society for democratic deepening, in the final analysis he now turns to the concept as an analytical tool with which to explore how existing liberal democracy might be improved. This project is some distance removed from his original enthusiasm for a democracy of civil society that held out the prospect of a new form of politics altogether.

CIVIL SOCIETY IN THE LITERATURE ON DEMOCRATIZATION IN LATIN AMERICA[60]

The democratic transitions that swept away military regimes throughout Latin America in the 1980s caught academic observers by surprise. Previously, these observers had had to explain the failure of democracy in the region, rather than its apparent success.[61] Dominating the field, consequently, were a whole range of structuralist models which accounted for Latin America's authoritarian politics as variously due to: low levels of modernization in the region which therefore had a weak middle class;[62] authoritarian values inherited from Iberian colonialism and Catholicism;[63] excessive political demands from the popular forces in the absence of developed institutions;[64] and economic dependency between core and periphery.[65] When democratization occurred without any of these structural conditions changing to a significant degree, structuralist paradigms were at once robbed of their predictive power and also rendered obsolete for the new task of explanation.

The Transition Debate

The most widespread response to the breakdown of the structuralist paradigms in the mid-late 1980s was 'the retreat into voluntarism'.[66] Instead of trying to explain democratization in terms of long-term processes of change, this portion of the literature, particularly O'Donnell, Whitehead and Schmitter's seminal volume *Transitions from Authoritarian Rule* (1986), disavowed determinism in favour of an open-ended account of the role of 'key actors' during the transition period: '[Transition] is that terrain where the unpredictable combination of virtu on the part of leaders, and *fortuna* in the combination of circumstances, may make the crucial difference'.[67]

Within this largely voluntarist literature on Latin America's democratic transitions, there was little use found for the category civil society; of course, the sphere of civil society, however defined, was not of paramount importance to theorists with an elite-centric focus. Non-state actors, on such accounts, merely form the backdrop to transition, as can be seen when O'Donnell and Schmitter begin their chapter entitled 'Resurrecting Civil Society (and Restructuring Public Space)' by claiming:

> ... elite dispositions, calculations, and pacts ... largely determine whether or not an opening will occur at all and ... they set important perimeters on the extent of possible liberalization and eventual democratization. Once something has happened [within the elite] ... a generalized mobilization is likely to occur, which we choose to describe as the 'resurrection of civil society'.[68]

The understanding of civil society as a generalized mobilization which only appears after transition, began to be found everywhere in the literature on Latin American transitions. Stepan, for example, also wrote of 'the civil society that emerge[s] once liberalization beg[ins]'.[69] This sense of civil society as a 'popular upsurge', or as 'pressure from below', was an instrumentalist one. The associations and movements of civil society were not seen as important in themselves – for example as mini public spheres for popular participation – but only in as much as their 'heroic, exemplary actions' provided the conditions for elites (or rather for reformers within elite circles) to negotiate transitions to political democracy: 'The importance of civil society's resurrection cannot be exaggerated. This mobilization and the intense demands it places upon all political actors greatly strengthen the position of the democratic opposition'.[70]

The link between instrumentalist democratic theory (democracy as the means by which to control the state) and a similarly utilitarian view of civil society is clear. In another classic example of this approach, Linz and Stepan write:

> Democracy is about an open contest for state power by means of elections and the oversight and control of state power by the representatives of the people ... Therefore, by definition, civil society must consider how it can make a contribution to the democratic control of military, police, and intelligence systems.[71]

Understanding civil society's contribution as that of a 'popular upsurge' means that while it is heralded as vital to opposition, there are doubts expressed about its uses after transition. Analysts of the transition, like the elite-democrats who they mostly follow, fear that 'excessive' political mobilization by the popular classes would be damaging to the political stability of the new democracies:

> ... historical experience in Latin America underscores the importance of ... demobilization [of mass actors], given that 'no stable political democracy has resulted from regime transitions in which mass actors have gained control, even momentarily, over traditional ruling classes'. The double paradox that emerges from this pattern of mobilization is that the political significance of the popular sectors may actually be greater *prior* to the restoration of a democratic regime – and this may actually be good for democracy![72]

O'Donnell is another analyst who, for the sake of democratic 'consolidation', does not regret the 'demobilization of society' and the reemergence of parties 'as the main interlocutors of the government'.[73] Since O'Donnell does not see political parties as part of civil society, there is a sense in which the category of civil society ceases to be of any importance for him post-transition. In short, commentators on transition such as O'Donnell are interested more in the consolidation of liberal political institutions than in the general mobilization which is seen, by Huntington and the 'Political Development school' of writers, to have led to earlier breakdowns of parliamentary democracy.[74] According to this model, the only tangible contribution that civil society can make to democratic consolidation is by restraining its demands.[75]

A further implication of such a model is that the character of civil society groups themselves are of little or no interest to theorists of transition, so long as they can provide a 'general upsurge' during transition and acquiescence during consolidation. This is a purely strategic approach to civil society; its non-strategic potentialities: solidarity, association and communication, are overlooked.[76] Thus civil society is articulated as quite apart from democracy itself; and there appears to be no good reason why non-state associational life should be equated with 'civil society' in the first place, since quite uncivil groups can play the role adequately of providing a 'general upsurge'.[77] Such is the paradox of a consequentialist conceptualization of civil society.

Given their thesis that civil society only emerges 'once something happens' within the existing authoritarian elite, O'Donnell and Schmitter, typically of elite-centric theorists, actually have difficulty accounting for the origins of transitions at all. In a somewhat contradictory manner, O'Donnell and Schmitter attempt to get round this problem by pointing to the importance of civil society's role in eroding the normative and intellectual basis of authoritarian regimes.[78] In effect, they appear to admit the importance of regime legitimacy or, rather, its absence. But ultimately, as Przeworski observes, 'the "loss of legitimacy" theory is an "up" theory of regime transition', because it suggests that a regime's crisis of legitimacy occurs initially in civil society and that it is only when this crisis becomes apparent that the ruling bloc responds. In this case, mass unrest or non-compliance should be observable before liberalization begins.[79]

This is certainly a problem with O'Donnell and Schmitter's analysis of civil society, and it comes from their refusal to allow for instances where popular pressure itself leads directly to a process of liberalization. In arguing that civil society only resurrects 'once the government signals that it is lowering the costs for engaging in collective action and is permitting some contestation on issues previously declared off limits', civil society is portrayed as purely reactive.[80] The best that can be said for it is that it 'performs the role of pushing the transition further than it *would otherwise have gone*'.[81]

Essentially, the problem is one of the narrow focus – that of the transition period alone – that these theorists have. If civil society is primarily experienced as a 'popular upsurge', then it should be unsurprising that we find it taking place when the state begins to liberalize. But this is to ignore the fact that in at least some countries in the region (Chile, for example), the movements and associations which are recognized as carrying out the 'upsurge', were formed long before transition and indeed arose during the period of severest repression. It is the apparent indeterminacy of the transition period which encourages this exclusive focus on the *outcomes* of upsurges; exploring the conditions necessary for the emergence of groups and movements which actually carry them out would require the reintroduction of structural variables. Yet voluntarists, whether they know it or not, are dealing with structures, since they 'implicitly hold constant those structural features of the situation that do not actually change during the period of observation':

> It is for this reason that process-oriented historical studies – even if they transcend sheer narrative and are conducted with theoretical, explanatory intent – often emphasize the role of voluntary decision and tend to play down – by taking them as givens – structural constraints that limit some options of historical actors and encourage others.[82]

In the final analysis, the indeterminacy thesis has been dominant in accounts of Latin America's democratic transitions because theory-building has been thrown into crisis by these very transitions themselves. A harsh reading would be that the description of events as entirely undetermined is to all practical purposes an admission of theoretical inadequacy: 'We describe events as unpredictable, random, and idiosyncratic when we have no way of explaining them.'[83] In keeping with this paradigm crisis, civil society is not adequately theorized by the analysts of the transitions. For their inability to explain where the civil society that they identify came from is obscured by a pervasive elite-centrism that largely overlooks the category civil society in the first place.

The Debate on Democratic Consolidation

The more recent literature on democratic consolidation in Latin America engages with the concept of civil society to a greater degree than the literature on transition, dominated as the latter is by the elite-centric perspective. However, despite the increasing number of references to civil society, it is just as true of the literature on consolidation that civil society is seen as functional solely for liberal democracy.[84]

Diamond and Linz provide a typical example of how civil society is understood as having an important role to play in achieving democratic consolidation:

> Just as democracy requires an effective but limited state, so it needs a pluralistic, autonomously organized civil society to check the power of the state and give expression democratically to popular interests ... there is a strong correlation between the strength and autonomy of associational life and the presence and vitality of democracy.[85]

This positive view of civil society is echoed by Jelin, who argues that 'the hard task of demanding, persuading, prompting, and policing [the state] falls to the makers of civic society'.[86] Although civil society is afforded far more significance here than in transition literature, it is none the less pictured only in relation to the state. All of the strengths of civil society listed by Diamond, Linz and Jelin connect to its role in either balancing the state or increasing the state's efficacy in representing interests. In short, these authors are a long way from the self-management agenda of the democratic-socialist theorists of civil society from Latin America in the 1980s. They, like their Central-Eastern European counterparts, turned away from opposition directed at the state – and not just in its vanguardist forms – towards the democracy of autonomous self-organization in civil society:

> This radically democratic and collectivist attitude ... demonstrate(s) the emergence of the will to renewal on the part of civil society which rejects the notion that the 'political opening' remains at the level of

redemocratization, based on liberal-individualist principles which in the past safeguarded social injustice, class inequality, and traditional bourgeois domination.[87]

Moreover, the positive approach to civil society in the literature on consolidation, although it includes the call for civil society to police the state, implies strongly that civil society activity should not threaten the system. Valenzuela, for example, although he agrees with O'Donnell and Schmitter that restraint by civil society is useful for transition, does not call, as these authors do, for civil society effectively to be demobilized post-transition. On the contrary, he sees pressure from civil society as desirable for democratic consolidation. However, according to Valenzuela, this pressure should fall within the 'demand-processing-settlement' criteria. This constitutes: 'the establishment, expansion, or recreation of popular and other associations to voice demands and negotiate some resolution to them, with leaders who have the necessary legitimacy and support to be able to call off demonstrations and other collective actions'.[88] In other words, Valenzuela is willing to support demands coming from civil society, but only to the extent that these do not cause significant disruption to the status quo or call into question society's wider power structure. Indeed, Valenzuela continues by arguing that 'these settlements are most adequate to facilitate democratic consolidation when they are perceived by all those concerned to operate with a minimum of politicization'.[89] This anti-political model of civil society sees it as having a purely technical function. It is also elitist:

> In brief, democratic consolidation is favoured if social conflicts and demands are handled through predictable and broadly accepted procedures that are inclusive of all the relevant groups but are, at the same time, insulated within the narrowest possible boundaries in terms of the specificity of the issues and the state, political and social actors who are involved.[90]

The idea that the contribution of civil society is to further interest representation in the state is by far the dominant one in the literature on consolidation. Schmitter, in a recent collection on the consolidation of democracy in Latin America, doubts whether social movements have 'determined either the degree of consolidation or the type of democracy'. What he will allow, though, is that, 'nevertheless [these movements] have broadened and complicated the policy agenda of most new democracies'.[91] Schmitter believes further that many social movements will decline as their demands are met and also because they will 'have trouble focusing on subsequent issues'.[92] He seems to have missed the non-instrumental character of many new social movements established in the 1970s and 1980s – such as neighbourhood associations in the *favelas* and women's groups – which were not orientated towards the formal political sphere in the first place. Indeed, the self-understanding of many of these groups was that autonomy from statised politics (including political parties – even those on the left) was their very *raison d'être*.[93] Though the cooption of some social movements by political parties has been a feature of the 1990s, this is hardly the same thing as 'demand settlement'.

A striking feature of the instrumentalist view of civil society is that it overlooks the possibility, held up by the radical model, that civil society can provide spaces for participation and, indeed, itself constitutes the public sphere. As Weffort put it 1983, 'The discovery of the value of democracy is inseparable, within the opposition, from the discovery of civil society as a political space'.[94] The possibility, as outlined by Weffort and others, that publicity might be fed from the 'grass-roots' upwards escapes most contemporary theorists of consolidation. The editors of one volume, for example, wonder whether 'civil society is adequately connected through political parties and other channels of representation to the evolving political debates'.[95] The implication here is that publicity occurs in the state and that civil society, unless otherwise connected with this, the 'true' public space, is relatively apolitical.[96] Again, the assumptions of the radical model of civil society are here turned on their head and we see once again the statist bias so prevalent in mainstream political science.[97] From this perspective, non-state associations, given their relatively weak institutionalization and their 'micro' outlook, are simply not that important to an understanding of political processes. Such an academic focus systematically masks the many ways in which less institutionalized political movements are often both more effective and more legitimate as far as non-elites are concerned. Within the Latin American field, a good example here would once again be the many new social movements that arose in the 1980s, especially the neighbourhood groups. In terms of collective provision for basic needs and in providing opportunities for political participation, these movements succeeded where the state in Latin America – whether liberal-democratic or not – has almost always failed.

The Minimalist Approach to Democracy in the Literature on Democratization in Latin America

Why then do analysts of Latin American democratization processes have little time for civil society in their accounts of transition, and why do they offer a purely instrumentalist conception of civil society's role in democratic 'consolidation'? In their defence, it could be argued that these theorists have been influenced in restricting civil society's role by the theory of moderation, which has grown out of events in Latin America such as Chile in 1973, where unmoderated, radical popular action apparently provoked a reactionary backlash. Yet this is still a subjective reading of historical circumstances, rather than incontrovertible fact,[98] and it is actually necessary to look no further than these scholars' democratic theory in order to explain in large part their conceptualizations of civil society.

It has already become clear that little is now said about civil society as a democratic space in its own right due to the growing dominance of liberal democratic theory and the formal or institutional view of democracy that attends it. The one thing that most accounts of transition and consolidation have in common is a minimalist and highly tautological notion of democracy as a form of government constituted by institutions extant in western liberal-democracies. Of particular significance to these theorists is Dahl's notion of 'polyarchy'.[99] Defined by Dahl as the 'highest feasible attainment of the democratic process in the government of a country', polyarchy expects no more than that there be a universal spread of citizenship rights – these being identified narrowly as 'the right to oppose and vote out the highest officials in the government'.[100]

The degree of acceptance of Dahl's proceduralist or institutional model of democracy is remarkable. Diamond, Linz and Lipset, for example, use polyarchy as the bench-mark for the democracies studied in their volume on Latin American transitions.[101] Similarly, Whitehead, claiming that 'Dahl's observations apply with special force to Latin America', describes his 'litmus test' for democracy as being captured by the questions: 'How does a purportedly democratic regime treat those held in its prisons?' and 'Would we describe the regime as sufficiently democratic to qualify as a leading western democracy'.[102] In the same volume of works on Latin America, Huntington – announcing that the ultimate cynic of democratic theory, Schumpeter, 'has won' – celebrates 'the prevailing effort … to make democracy less of a hurrah word and more of a common sense word. Democracy has a useful meaning only when it is defined in institutional terms … The key institution [being] the selection of leaders through competitive elections'.[103]

Also in the literature on consolidation, we find, for example, a major collection which contains in its introduction the following: 'The essays in this book attach their conception of democratic consolidation to a minimal and procedural definition of democracy'.[104] Similarly, Valenzuela's work on 'Consolidation in Post Transition Settings', begins with a defence of Dahl's definition of democracy, arguing that: 'the notion of democratic consolidation should … be linked … to a minimalist, not a maximalist conception of democracy'. Drawing on Schumpeter's notion of competitive democracy, Valenzuela debunks 'participatory' models as simply 'inadequate'.[105] Mainwaring, in the same volume of works on consolidation, also accepts that Schumpeter's focus on electoral competition amongst political elites and parties has 'prevailed'. Mainwaring adds only universal suffrage to this Schumpeterian framework (which he terms the 'participation' element), arriving at Dahl's definition of polyarchy whereby democracy is defined less – if at all – in terms of its outcomes, and more – if not entirely – according to the rules governing politics.[106] An extreme version of this refusal to focus upon democratic outcomes as long as democratic procedures are in place is offered by Valenzuela: ' … without … formal democratic procedures at the nation-state level a democracy cannot be said to exist no matter how egalitarian the society, how progressive the social policies, how advanced the democratic procedures at the subnational level'.[107]

In keeping with these kinds of approaches to democracy, more substantive definitions are rejected in the democratization literature for applying democracy to spheres where it supposedly does not belong. 'Democratization', claims Stepan, 'refers fundamentally to the relationship between the State and civil society'.[108] For Pastor, democracy is 'impossible if the government exercises complete control over the economy'.[109] Diamond, Linz and Lipset also see democracy as 'political' in the narrowest sense of the word:

> We use the term 'democracy'… to signify a political system separate and apart from the economic and social system to which it is joined … Indeed, … [we] insist that issues of so-called economic and social democracy be separated from the question of governmental structure.[110]

Because of the emphasis on a strict separation of spheres, the vision of a 'grass-roots' democracy is viewed with suspicion: '[S]ubstantive views of democracy … often appear associated with more or less utopian conceptions of "participatory" democracy, aiming to replace or subordinate representation to a more "authentic" expression of the people's will'.[111]

At points, this antipathy to a more direct democracy manifests itself to extraordinary degrees. Mainwaring's anti-substantive notion of democracy is such that it comes much closer to liberal theory than democratic theory. Indeed, Mainwaring seems so concerned with protecting 'political expertise' and property, and with warding off the 'tyranny of the majority', that he basically ends up writing out majoritarian decision-making altogether from his vision of a democratic polity. Criticizing Przeworski's claim that democracy represents 'institutionalized uncertainty', Mainwaring raises the spectre of workers, for example, voting to nationalize the means of production:

However, even if workers did vote to nationalize the means of production, this fact in itself would have no legal effect ... in democratic regimes, because it is not generally workers who make this kind of decision, but rather executives and legislatures functioning in well-defined institutional and legal structures. Workers help elect those who decide, but modern mass democracy is representative democracy, not direct democracy.[112]

More typically, the issue of democracy at the grass-roots is simply deemed unimportant to political democracy: 'I do not [believe] that associations ... are models of participatory democracy. Nor do I believe that small-group democracy is necessary to maintain democratic politics on the national level'.[113]

What stands out in all of these accounts of democracy is that little significance is attached to those democratic practices which the radical model of civil society claimed as its own. The focus has shifted away from the practice of participatory democracy outside of the state and from the (socialist) orientation towards basic needs and social transformation.[114] Thus the model of civil society that Cardoso described as recently as 1983 seems already to belong to a different epoch:

[One] version of why Brazil is breaking with authoritarianism combines a radical vision of autonomy of civil society with a socialist critique of social domination ... *Real* democratization will arrive ... as it is crystallised in the spontaneous solidarity of the disinherited. It lives as *comunitas*, experiences of common hardship which form a collective we based on the same life experience that is transformed only when, through molecular changes, the simultaneous isolation of the State and the exploiters – which will perish at the same time – comes about.[115]

Effectively, civil society theory has been rewritten in order to assess its significance for formal political democracy rather than grass-roots democracy. While the radical vision of civil society may live on among some Latin American political activists and intellectuals, mainstream political science has almost entirely forgotten it. In its paradoxically ideological pursuit of a value-free science of the possible, elite-democracy and an effectively demobilized civil society are paraded as the only form of democracy and civil society on offer. Indeed, a field more saturated by the thesis of an 'end to history' would be hard to find

Finally, as with the contemporary discourse on civil society in relation to Central-Eastern Europe, even those more progressive conceptualizations of civil society that do exist in the literature on democratization in Latin America seem to have lost touch with earlier radical models. Przeworski, for example, adheres to the Gramscian notion that loss of legitimacy for the powers in the state only comes about through the organization of counter-hegemony ('collective projects for an alternative future').[116] Nevertheless, Przeworski still talks of civil society exclusively in terms of the 'transition game', never mentioning the model of civil society that looks to democracy outside of the state as an end in itself. In this sense, Przeworski retains an orthodox approach to Gramsci's categories in contrast to the radical theorists of civil society who reworked them.[117] That is, he focuses on how civil society can transform existing power in the state before influencing the state for its own ends, rather than on the organization of a popular and counter-hegemonic civil society that turns its back on the state permanently.

Huber is similar to Przeworski in adopting, by her own admission, a Gramscian definition of civil society as: 'the totality of social institutions and associations, both formal and informal, that are not strictly production-related nor governmental of familial in character'.[118] Yet although she is influenced by Gramsci's understanding of civil society, Huber is cut off from earlier radical models. This is because, despite viewing the density of civil society as reflecting the extent and degree of autonomy of the subordinate classes (any other form of civil society, for Huber, is just a 'conduit for the dominant ideology'),[119] Huber defines civil society only in relation to the state – that is, as deciding the extent to which these subordinate classes have power *vis-à-vis* the state. Thus Huber, like Przeworski, does not conceive of civil society as substantively autonomous; she continues with Gramsci's approach rather than, as with the earlier radicals, using Gramsci's political method (counter-hegemony in civil society) to move beyond Gramsci's more Marxist concern with achieving power in the state.

CONCLUSION

It should be clear by now that civil society theory within the democratization literature is not a value-free science. The normative backdrop is a liberal-democratic one, and there is a pervasive sense that civil society both can not and should not reach beyond its role as a support structure for actually existing democracy at the state level. This uncritical attachment to what is often no more than competitive elitism reflects both an implicit acceptance of Fukuyama's thesis that liberal democracy represents the 'end of history' and, further, Schumpeter-like cynicism regarding prospects for its improvement.[120] To put it bluntly, this is because many analysts are fearful of 'too much' democracy. Of course, this is not an uncommon standpoint; indeed from Plato onwards it has been the predominant view within academia.

Yet the democratization literature is obfuscatory about the other values and institutions, apart from those of democracy, with which it is also very much concerned. In analyzing conceptualizations of civil society within this democratization literature, these values are revealed more clearly. They include, first, a pervasive 'hierarchism' (defined by Blaug as the belief that effective political action requires 'a hierarchy of command, centralized control and the institutionalization of roles of expertise and leadership'),[121] which is seen in the exclusive focus upon the formal institutions of the state as the sphere of politics and democracy 'proper'. Second, there is close to universal acceptance of the broadly neo-liberal case for economic liberalization and an attendant concern with the institution of the free-market and the entrenchment of private property. Third, we find a widespread belief in the necessity of 'limited' politics, which results in calls for the demobilization of the popular sectors and for the routinization of politics in general.

Civil society is seen as crucial to these features of a 'mature' democracy, and is therefore defined, in a rather tautologous fashion, exclusively in terms of them. Taking the above examples in turn: 'hierarchism' is reflected in the notion of civil society as consisting of groups which arise functionally out of the division of labour, civil society being defined therefore as relatively insignificant or apolitical beyond its role in mediating between society and the state (the idea that civil society straightforwardly programmes the state in society's interests represents also a revival of idealized pluralist thinking). Far from being neutral, this instrumentalist approach is opposed to the more republican view that civil society, as an end in itself, refers to a nexus of active citizenship wherein some form of self-management occurs and by which interests emerge communicatively. Second, equating democracy with the negative liberty which is supported by free market capitalism means that civil society and the market, as has been shown, are often discussed as if they were coterminous, or at least mutually reinforcing. Little or no consideration is given to the ways in which the distribution of economic power might undermine or threaten civil society, even if formal political power has been democratized. In these instances, civil society theory again reflects the normative prioritization of the politics of the market over the politics of the forum, the valorization of choice for the consumer over public space for the citizen. Third, the wider concern for a de-radicalization of politics is echoed in the notion that civil society is made up of interests and allegiances that cross-cut one another, civil society thereby being presented as antithetical to the articulation of mass actors with shared interests and objectives, to 'the mob' that is.

However, all of these concerns, which amount to the call for the negative liberty of liberal democratic politics, particularly for the separation of powers, control of power and pluralist interest representation, were articulated quite adequately by liberals before the revival of the concept of civil society. Why then do they need it now? Indeed, it was the concern for a more substantive democracy than that already on offer which was part of the reason that radicals in Central-Eastern Europe and Latin America redeployed the concept of civil society in the first place. These theorists used the idea of civil society, which until then had been largely forgotten, because they wanted to say something new about the conditions necessary for democracy. *Their* model of civil society from the 1980s, far from returning only to liberalism with its focus on the need to control political power at the top, contained also a radical-democratic concern with participation and self-management, or the redistribution of power (both political *and* socio-economic) to the grass-roots. This gives the lie to the positivistic approach prevalent in the democratization literature of the 1990s, which apparently considers the relationship between word – civil society – and object – that which supposedly relates to civil society in the world – as entirely unproblematic. Clearly, the meaning of the concept, far from being fixed, has shifted considerably according to the wider political context.

Indeed, it was the loss of its status as an idea in opposition which arguably undermined the radical idea of civil society after 1989. Once democratization occurred in both Central-Eastern Europe and Latin America during the course of the 1980s, a contra-state, self-management discourse no longer seemed so necessary or relevant, now that the state was no longer the enemy as such. Thus the radical idea of civil society has largely not survived the changes to the political base that the so-called 'third wave' of democracy has brought to pass.[122] The explicitly transformative politics which informed the radical model has also led to it being overshadowed by the realism on offer from liberal-democratic theorists of civil society, who, indisputably, do a good job of telling us what democratization currently means in practice, though they conflate this with what democratization *ought* to mean. The normative content of the liberal-democratic model having been disguised in this way, alternatives to the *status quo* are scarcely considered; civil society is something that we already possess, not an ideal to which we should aspire. It is the loss of this critical edge to the theory of civil society in particular which should cause disquiet, for it represents the effective demobilization of an idea that, only a decade ago, was orientated towards change.

NOTES

1. For some of the many studies of opposition discourses on civil society see Andrew Arato, 'Civil Society Against the State: Poland 1980–81', *Telos*, No.47 (1981), pp.23–47; John Keane (ed.), *Civil Society and the State: New European Perspectives* (London: Verso, 1988); Gideon Baker, 'The Changing Idea of Civil Society: Models from the Polish Democratic Opposition', *Journal of Political Ideologies*, Vol.3, No.2 (1998), pp.125–47.

2. Leszek Nowak, *Power and Civil Society: Towards a Dynamic Theory of Real Socialism* (Westport, CT: Greenwood Press, 1991), p.29.

3. In these cases, knowledge of the earlier normative-political idea of civil society, or of the self-definition of movements such as Solidarity as 'civil society', often seems completely absent. The term civil society is used basically as a label for the 'popular upsurge' that took place immediately prior to transition. Splichal, for example, writes: 'Civil society was created in East-Central Europe in a very short period of time; almost overnight it succeeded in overthrowing the old regimes and inaugurating parliamentary democracy'. S. Splichal, 'Civil Society and Media Democratization in East-Central Europe', in A. Bibic and G. Graziano (eds.), *Civil Society, Political Society, Democracy* (Ljubljana: Slovenian Political Science Association, 1994), p.305.

4. Bibic and Graziano's introduction to their volume on civil society and democracy is a typical example here. They begin: 'Civil society has played a crucial role...in the transition from authoritarian regimes to political democracy ... A strong civil society is important in the consolidation of democracy in post-authoritarian regimes as well as in deepening democracy in already established liberal democracies'. See Bibic and Graziano, op. cit., p.i.

5. A. Szakolczai and A. Horvath, 'The Discourse of Civil Society and the Self-Elimination of the Party', in P.G. Lewis (ed.), *Democracy and Civil Society in Eastern Europe* (London: Macmillan, 1992), p.16.

6. P.G. Lewis, 'Democracy and its Future in Eastern Europe', in David Held (ed.), *Prospects for Democracy* (Cambridge: Polity, 1993), p.300.

7. Frentzel-Zagorska, 'Patterns of Transition from a One-Party State to Democracy in Poland and Hungary', in Robert. F. Miller (ed.), *The Development of Civil Society in Communist Systems* (Sydney: Allen and Unwin, 1992), pp.40–41.

8. R. Battek, 'Spiritual Values, Independent Initiatives and Politics', in Vaclav Havel *et al.*, *The Power of the Powerless: Citizens Against the State in Central-Eastern Europe* (London: Hutchinson, 1985), p.108: emphasis added. (The essays in this book are drawn from a collection written by signatories of Charter 77 – with Havel's 'The Power of the Powerless' forming the centre piece – which were published in 1979, in *samizdat*, under the title *On Freedom and Power*.) See Z.A. Pelczynski, 'Solidarity and the Rebirth of Civil Society', in Keane (ed.), op. cit., p.375; Adam Michnik, *Letters From Prison and other essays* (London: UCLA Press, 1985), p.148; J. Hajek, 'The Human Rights Movement and Social Progress', in Havel, *The Power of the Powerless*, p.138; L. Hejdanek, 'Prospects for Democracy and Socialism in Eastern Europe', in Havel, *The Power of the Powerless*, p.144.

9. Robert F. Miller, 'Civil Society in Communist Systems: An Introduction', in Miller (ed.), *The Development of Civil Society*, p.8.

10. G. Skapska, 'Learning to be a Citizen: Cognitive and Ethical Aspects of Post-Communist Society Transformation', *Democratization*, Vol.4, No.1 (1997), p.158.

11. Ibid., p.158.

12. Bibic and Graziano, op. cit., p.ii.

13. M. Bernhard, 'Civil Society and Democratic Transition in East Central Europe', *Political Science Quarterly*, Vol.108, No.2 (1993), p.307.

14. Ibid., p.326

15. Havel, *The Power of the Powerless*, p.93.

16. G. Konrad, Antipolitics (London: Quartet, 1984), p.137.

17. Michnik, *Letters from Prison*, p.124; cf. Arato, 'Civil Society Against the State', p.46; J. Kuron, 'Not to Lure the Wolves out of the Woods: An Interview with Jacek Kuron', *Telos*, No.47 (1981), pp.96–7; Battek, op. cit., p.108; Hegadus, 'Interview with Hungarian philosopher Hegedus', *Telos*, No.47 (1981), p.144.

18. Interestingly, Michnik, despite his earlier contribution to the Polish opposition's radical model of civil society, now follows Dahrendorf in claiming that the crucial issue is simply between those who prefer 'what Popper calls 'the open society', and those who prefer a closed society' (Adam Michnik, 'The Three Cards Game: An Interview with Adam Michnik', *Telos*, No.89 (1991), p.101). This illustrates that many earlier radicals now accept a liberal-democratic reading of the category of civil society as constituting a sphere of negative liberty: see Adam Michnik, 'The Presence of Liberal Values', *East European Reporter*, 4 (1991), p.70; 'Interview with Adam Michnik', *Constellations*, Vol.2, No.1 (1995), pp.8–10; G. Konrad, 'Chance Wanderings: Reflections of a Hungarian Writer', *Dissent*, No.37 (1990), p.189; G. Konrad, 'What is the Charter?', *East European Reporter*, 5 (1992), pp.36–7; J. Kis, 'Interview with Janos Kis', *Constellations*, Vol.2, No.1 (1995), p.18; Andrew Arato, 'The Rise, Decline and Reconstruction of the Concept of Civil Society, and Directions for Future Research', in Bibic and Graziano, op. cit., p.10.
19. R. Dahrendorf, *Reflections on the Revolution in Eastern Europe* (London: Chatto & Windus, 1990), p.93.
20. R. Dahrendorf, 'Roads to Freedom: Democratization and its Problems in East Central Europe', in P. Volten (ed.), *Uncertain Futures: Eastern Europe and Democracy* (New York: Institute for East-West Security Studies, 1990), p.15.
21. Examples abound of this functionalist approach: 'What makes [civil society] "civil" is the fact that it is the locus where citizens freely organize themselves into ... associations ... in order to pressurize the formal bodies of state authority into adopting policies consonant with their perceived interests' (Miller, op. cit., p.8). 'The basic function of civil society...is to link the goals of the activity of the state with those of the independently structured population through different mechanisms of mediation' (Frentzel-Zagorska, op. cit., p.41).
22. Dahrendorf, for example, writes: 'I prefer to think of civil society as providing the anchorage of liberty, including its economic ingredients'. Dahrendorf, *Reflections*, p.96.
23. See Dahrendorf, Reflections, p.96; Lewis, *Democracy and its Future*, p.302; P. Hirst, 'The State, Civil Society and the Collapse of Soviet Communism', *Economy and Society*, Vol.20 (1991), p.222.
24. A. Bozoki and M. Sukosd, 'Civil Society and Populism in the Eastern European Transitions', in *Praxis International*, Vol.13, No.3 (1993), p.228.
25. Nowak, op. cit., p.57.
26. Bozoki and Sukosd, op. cit., p.229.
27. Bozoki and Sukosd, op. cit., p.233.
28. Dahrendorf, *Reflections*, p.99.
29. Lewis, *Democracy and its Future*, pp.301–2.
30. J. Habermas, 'Three Normative Models of Democracy', *Constellations*, Vol.1, No.1 (1994), p.9.
31. Miller, op. cit., p.8.
32. See V. Havel, 'Anti-Political Politics', in Keane, p.397; Bernhard, op. cit., p.319; Konrad, *Antipolitics*, p.140.
33. J.L. Curry, 'A Reconsideration of the Realities of "Civil Society" in the Light of Postcommunist Society', in Bibic and Graziano, op. cit., p.247.
34. P. Sztompka, 'The Intangibles and Imponderables of the Transition to Democracy', *Studies in Comparative Communism*, Vol.XXIV, No.3, (1991), pp.295–311.
35. E. Tarkowska and J. Tarkowski, 'Social Disintegration in Poland: Civil Society or Amoral Familism?', *Telos*, No.89 (1991).
36. C. Tempest, 'Myths from Eastern Europe and the Legend of the West', *Democratization*, Vol.4, No.1 (1997), p.137; referring to C. Hann, 'Philosophers' Models on the Carpathian Lowlands', in J.A. Hall (ed.), *Civil Society: History, Theory, Comparison* (Cambridge: Polity, 1995).
37. See Havel, *Anti-Political Politics*, p.397; and Hegadus, op. cit., p.144.
38. Tempest, op. cit, p.139, emphasis added.
39. Lewis, *Democracy and its Future*, pp.302–3.
40. Ibid., p.303.
41. Lewis is reluctant to accord much, if any, democratic significance to movements such as Solidarity because of his agreement with elite-democrats such as Huntington that democratization comes more from 'the top' of society than from 'below'. Along with

theorists such as these, Lewis wants to emphasise the role of elite pacting. Ibid., pp.304–5.
42. See Arato, 'Civil Society and the State', p.46; J. Kuron, 'Interview with Helen Luczywo', in J. Rupnik, 'Totalitarianism Revisited', in Keane, p.285; Havel, *The Power of the Powerless*, p.94; Hejdanek, op. cit., p.142; Hajek, op. cit., p.140; Konrad, *Antipolitics*, p.137.
43. A. Smolar, 'From Opposition to Atomization', *Journal of Democracy*, Vol.7, No.1. (1996), p.37.
44. Ibid., pp.37–8; see M. Federowicz, 'The Actors and Mechanisms of Systemic Changes in the Economy', *Sisyphus*, Vol.9, No.2 (1993), p.98.
45. W. Narojek, 'The Making of Democratic Order and Market Economy: Social Engineering for Democratic Transformation', *Polish Sociological Review*, No.105, (1994), p.15.
46. W. Morawski, 'Economic Change and Civil Society in Poland', in Lewis, *Democracy and Civil Society*, p.110.
47. A. Korbonski, 'Civil Society and Democracy in Poland: Problems and Prospects', in Bibic and Graziano, op. cit., p.222.
48. A. Bibic, 'Democracy and Civil Society', in Bibic and Graziano, op. cit., p.45, with reference to G. O'Donnell and P. Schmitter, *Transitions from Authoritarian Rule: Tentative Conclusions about Uncertain Democracies* (London: Johns Hopkins University Press, 1986).
49. In their equation of civil society with self-management, radical theorists were close to philosophical anarchism in questioning whether the conditions necessary for ongoing democratic legitimacy could ever be met by the state, given the citizen body's only indirect control over it. Hejdanek, for example, claims that thoroughgoing democratization is impossible 'without the emancipation of the overwhelming majority of the lives of societies and individuals from the clutches of *dirigisme* and control by the machinery of the state'; this critique, it should be noted, is *not* directed only at state-socialism (Hejdanek, op. cit., p.150.). This thinking compares closely to Kuron's syndicalism (see Kuron, 'Not to Lure the Wolves', p.97.) and to Nowak's (neo-Marxist) utopian vision of the state as a mere administrator of things (see Nowak, op. cit., p.64). See also: Michnik, *Letters from Prison*, p.148; Konrad, *Antipolitics*, p.142; V. Benda, 'Catholicism and Politics', in Havel, *The Power of the Powerless*, p.122; P. Uhl, 'The Alternative Community as Revolutionary Avant-Garde', in Havel, *The Power of the Powerless*, p.195.
50. See Michnik, *Letters from Prison*, p.105; and, for Kis and Bence, see Arato, 'Civil Society Against the State', op. cit., p.31.
51. In some accounts, the democratization of the state is what actually constitutes civil society in the first place: 'Civil society is a society of citizens, and this notion is more or less equivalent to political democracy'. S. Ehrlich, 'Introductory Remarks', in Bibic and Graziano, op. cit., p.ix.
52. Lewis, *Democracy and its Future*, p.302.
53. Bernhard, op. cit., p.309.
54. Ibid., p.315.
55. Coming from a similar angle, Dahrendorf asks: 'Can one build a civil society ... ? ... Citizenship certainly can be built ... [it is] a matter of legislation and supporting policies'. Dahrendorf, *Reflections*, p.96.
56. See, for example, Hajek, op. cit., p.138; Hejdanek, op. cit., p.149-150; and Battek, op. cit., p.108.
57. I differentiate Arato here from the radical oppositionists – who have now gone largely silent on the subject of civil society – because Arato is still engaged in theorising civil society. Furthermore, Arato, unlike many of the one-time oppositionists, can still be thought of as radical.
58. Arato, 'The Rise, Decline and Reconstruction of the Concept of Civil Society', p.15.
59. Ibid., p.16.
60. The watershed of 1989 does not apply so neatly to the democratization literature on Latin America, for the simple reason that democratic transitions in the region began earlier in the 1980s. Yet as a heuristic device, by which to identify that the ascendancy of the liberal-democratic model of civil society is only a 1990s phenomenon, 1989 remains a useful marker. Indeed, in this section I look at just one work from prior to 1989, because it is only

since 1989 that the democratization literature on Latin America mentions civil society extensively.

61. K.L. Remmer, 'New Wine or Old Bottlenecks?', *Comparative Politics*, Vol.23, No.1 (1991), p.479.
62. See S. Lipset, *Political Man: The Social Basis of Conflict* (New York: Doubleday, 1959).
63. See A. Almond and S. Verba, *The Civic Culture: Political Attitudes and Democracy in Five Nations* (Princeton, NJ: Princeton University Press, 1963).
64. See S. Huntington, *Political Order in Changing Societies* (New Haven, CT: Yale University Press, 1968).
65. See T. Dos Santos, 'La Viabilidad de Capitalismo Dependiente y la Democracia', *América Latina: Estudios y Perspectivas*, Vol.1 (1979). Source: Remmer, op. cit., p.479.
66. Remmer, op. cit., p.483.
67. O'Donnell and Schmitter, *Tentative Conclusions about Uncertain Democracies*, p.17.
68. Ibid., p.49: emphasis added.
69. A. Stepan, 'Introduction', in A. Stepan (ed.), *Democratizing Brazil* (Oxford: Oxford University Press, 1989), p.vii.
70. G. O'Donnell, 'Transitions to Democracy: Some Navigation Instruments', in R.A. Pastor (ed.), *Democracy in the Americas: Stopping the Pendulum* (London: Holmes & Meier, 1989), p.67.
71. J. Linz and A. Stepan, 'Political Crafting of Democratic Consolidation or Destruction: European and South American Comparisons', in Pastor, op. cit., p.51.
72. P. Oxhorn, 'Where Did All the Protesters Go?: Popular Mobilization and the Transition to Democracy in Chile', *Latin American Perspectives*, Vol.21, No.3 (1994), p.50.
73. O'Donnell, *Transitions to Democracy*, p.72.
74. F. Hagopian, 'After Regime Change', *World Politics*, Vol.45, No.3 (1993), p.480.
75. J. Pearce, 'Civil Society, the Market and Democracy in Latin America', *Democratization*, Vol.4, No.2 (1997), p.60.
76. Ibid., p.61: after J.A. Cohen and A. Arato, *Civil Society and Political Theory* (Cambridge, MA: MIT Press, 1992), p.80.
77. Pearce, p.62.
78. O'Donnell and Schmitter, *Tentative Conclusions about Uncertain Democracies*, p.51.
79. A. Przeworski, 'Some Problems in the Study of the Transition to Democracy', in O'Donnell, Schmitter and Whitehead (eds.), *Transitions from Authoritarian Rule: Comparative Perspectives* (London: Johns Hopkins University Press, 1986), p.50.
80. O'Donnell and Schmitter, *Tentative Conclusions about Uncertain Democracies*, pp.47–9.
81. Ibid., p.56: emphasis added.
82. D. Rueschemeyer, E.H. Stephens and J.D. Stephens, *Capitalist Development and Democracy* (Cambridge: Polity, 1992), p.33.
83. Remmer, p.485.
84. In one sense the very term, 'consolidation', should alert us to continuity with the 'transition' approach, since the implication is that the task for democrats is merely to safeguard the establishment of formal democratic institutions in the state, rather than, say, to widen participation in the new regimes. The word consolidation implies that the desired ends have been achieved and that the sustainability of these ends is all that matters for the future. Here again, democracy is being identified as a set of institutions which we already have, rather than with a political value, or basket of values, which we will always fall short of realising.
85. L. Diamond and J. Linz, 'Introduction: Politics, Society, and Democratization in Latin America', in L. Diamond, J.J. Linz and S.M. Lipset (eds.), *Democracy in Developing Countries Volume Four: Latin America* (London: Lynne Rienner, 1989), p.35.
86. E. Jelin, 'Building Citizenship: A Balance Between Solidarity and Responsibility', in J.S. Tulchin (ed.), *The Consolidation of Democracy in Latin America* (London: Lynne Rienner, 1995), p.92.
87. F.H. Cardoso, 'Associated-Dependent Development and Democratic Theory', written in 1983 and translated in Stepan, op. cit., p. 323; see F. Weffort's 1983 essay, 'Why Democracy', translated in Stepan, ibid., particularly pp.329 and 345; S. Mainwaring and E. Viola, 'Political Culture and Democracy: Brazil and Argentina in the 1980s', *Telos*, No.61

(1984), p.28; M. Lowy, 'Mass Organizations, Party and State: Democracy in the Transition to Socialism', in R. Fagen *et al.* (eds.), *Transition and Development: Problems of Third World Socialism* (New York: Monthly Review Press, 1986), p.264; S. Mainwaring, 'Urban Popular Movements, Identity, and Democratization in Brazil', *Comparative Political Studies*, Vol.20, No.2 (1987), p.149; J. Villalobos, interviewed in J.G. Castaneda, *Utopia Unarmed* (New York: Vintage Books, 1994), p.201; Pearce, op. cit., p.63; S. Ellner, 'The Changing Status of the Latin American Left in the Recent Past', in B. Carr and S. Ellner (eds.), *The Latin American Left* (London: Latin America Bureau, 1993), p.11.

88. J. Valenzuela, 'Consolidation in Post-Transitional Settings', in Mainwaring, O'Donnell and Valenzuela (eds.), *Issues in Democratic Consolidation: The New South American Democracies in Comparative Perspective* (Indiana: University of Notre Dame Press, 1992), p.86.

89. Ibid., p.86.

90. Ibid., pp.86–7.

91. P.C. Schmitter, 'Transitology: The Science or the Art of Democratization', in Tulchin, op. cit., p.24.

92. Ibid., p.24.

93. See Mainwaring and Viola, op. cit.

94. Weffort, op. cit., p.345. For an extended discussion of the radical model of civil society in the Latin American context, see Gideon Baker, 'From Structuralism to Voluntarism: The Latin American Left and the Discourse on Civil Society and Democracy', *Contemporary Politics*, Vol.4, No.4 (Dec. 1998).

95. Mainwaring *et al.*, Issues in Democratic Consolidation, p.4.

96. Even where civil society is seen as a space for citizenship in the literature on consolidation, it is often defined, as by Reilly for example, as constituting only 'secondary citizenship'. Thus while, in a Toquevillian manner, 'opportunities for negotiation, competition, contained conflict and the search for consensus' (from Reilly, op. cit., p.264) are found in civil society, these experiences implicitly count only as a 'dry run' for politics proper at a state level. Here the emphasis is upon the contribution civil society can make to a democratic political culture, not to participation for its own sake. Put another way, civil society is to be supportive of citizenship, and is not seen as the space for citizenship in the first place (as with the radical model).

97. Regarding the anti-statism of earlier models of civil society, especially within the new social movement context, see T. Evers, 'Identity: the Hidden Side of New Social Movements in Latin America', in D. Slater (ed.), *New Social Movements and the State in Latin America* (Amsterdam: CEDLA, 1985), p.51; J.L. Coraggio, 'Social Movements and Revolution: the case of Nicaragua', in Slater, p.206; J. Quijano (interviewed in 1986), in A. Escobar and S. Alvarez (eds.), *The Making of Social Movements in Latin America* (Oxford: Westview, 1992), p.186; O.A. Borda, 'Social Movements and Political Power in Latin America', in Escobar and Alvarez, ibid., pp.311–13. Since these earlier theorists mostly saw genuine publicity as occurring in civil society alone, they were also suspicious of the party form, since political parties were just another method for turning politics towards the state, thereby alienating it from ordinary people's concerns and also from their control (on this see also N. Vink, 'Base Communities and Urban Social Movements – A Case Study of the Metal-Workers' strike 1980, Sao Bernardo, Brazil', in Slater, op. cit., p.117; and J.A. Hellman, 'The Study of New Social Movements in Latin America and the Question of Autonomy', in Escobar and Alvarez, op. cit., p.53). For liberal democratic theorists, of course, parties are crucial for articulating societal demands in a manageable way – they are therefore often included in the category civil society.

98. Bermeo argues that if theorists of the Latin American transitions had looked further afield to Portugal and Spain, they would have seen that transitions *can* survive radical pressures from below and even radical provisional governments. N. Bermeo, 'Myths of Moderation: Confrontation and Conflict During Democratic Transitions', *Comparative Politics*, Vol.29, No.3 (1997), pp.305–22.

99. Pearce, op. cit., p.59.

100. R.A. Dahl, *Democracy and its Critics* (London: Yale University Press, 1989), pp.220–22.

101. Diamond, Linz and Lipset, op. cit., p.xvi.

102. L. Whitehead, 'The Consolidation of Fragile Democracies', in Pastor, op. cit., p.77.
103. S. Huntington, 'The Modest Meaning of Democracy', in Pastor, op. cit., p.15.
104. Mainwaring *et al.*, Issues in Democratic Consolidation, p.5.
105. Valenzuela, op. cit., p.60.
106. S. Mainwaring, 'Transitions to Democracy and Democratic Consolidation: Theoretical and Comparative Issues', in Mainwaring *et al.*, *Issues in Democratic Consolidation*, p.297.
107. Valenzuela, op. cit., p.61.
108. Stepan, op. cit., p.ix.
109. Pastor, op. cit., p.18.
110. Diamond, Linz and Lipset, op. cit., p.xvi.
111. B. Lamounier, 'Brazil: Inequality Against Democracy', in Diamond, Linz and Lipset, op. cit., p.150.
112. Mainwaring, 'Transitions to Democracy and Democratic Consolidation', op. cit., p.313.
113. D.H. Levine, 'Venezuela: The Nature, Sources, and Future Prospects of Democracy', in Diamond, Linz and Lipset, op. cit., p.280.
114. As in Central-Eastern Europe, those theorists who initially engaged with the concept of civil society in Latin America were socialists of various persuasions. That is, their concern was with a substantive democracy, one in which political equality was matched by some form of socio-economic equality.
115. Cardoso, op. cit., p.313.
116. A. Przeworski, 'The Games of Transition', in Mainwaring, O'Donnell and Valenzuela, op. cit., p.107.
117. For the reworking of Gramscian categories within the radical model of civil society from the 1980s, see Baker, 'From Structuralism to Voluntarism', pp.395–9; R. Barros, 'The Left and Democracy: Recent Debates in Latin America', *Telos*, No.68 (1986), p.66; C.M. Villas, 'Popular Insurgency and Social Revolution in Central America', *Latin American Perspectives*, Vol.15, No.1 (1988), p.58; R.H. Chilcote, 'Post-Marxism: The Retreat from Class in Latin America', *Latin American Perspectives*, Vol.17, No.2 (1990), p.12; R. Munck, 'Farewell to Socialism?', *Latin American Perspectives*, Vol.17, No.2 (1990), p.118; Castaneda, op. cit., p.199.
118. E. Huber, 'Assessments of State Strength', in P.H. Smith (ed.), *Latin America in Comparative Perspective* (Oxford: Westview Press, 1995), p.172.
119. Ibid., p.173.
120. F. Fukuyama, 'The End of History?', *The National Interest*, Summer (1989).
121. R. Blaug, 'The Tyranny of the Visible: Problems in the Evaluation of Anti-Institutional Radicalism', unpublished paper presented to the University of Leeds Politics Department, Sept. 1998, p.4.
122. Another reason for the decline of the radical model of civil society, as I have argued elsewhere (Baker, 'The Changing Idea of Civil Society'), was its internal contradictions. Civil society understood as societal self-management ran up against the utopia of the withering away of the state, which most theorists of civil society, particularly in Central-Eastern Europe, condemned as threatening the politicization of society all over again. In other words, the desire for maximal self-management in civil society contradicted the call, made by the same theorists, for a separation of spheres between state and society in order to ward off 'totalising' politics.

Civil Society:
Market Economy and Democratic Polity

DAVID BEETHAM

This essay focuses on the relationship of the market to democracy and therefore to civil society. It problematizes the assumption of much of current work on this issue, that there is a congruence between a market economy and a democratic polity. It does this by setting out the case for and against the above proposition – that there is a correlation between market economy and political democracy – and concludes that the market is at once supportive and undermining of democracy. It concludes that the important issue is how to regulate, contain and supplement market forces so that the necessary *civility* of social relations in a democratic polity can be protected and enhanced, rather than to argue about whether the market should or should not be placed within the ambit of civil society.

Among the many current disagreements about the definition and use of the concept 'civil society', not the least is whether a market economy properly belongs to it or not. Those who wish to include it can point to the development of the civil society concept within eighteenth-century political economy, to designate a sphere of autonomous economic activity and social coordination independent of the state, which also formed an integral part of a liberal constitutional order.[1] For these theorists a market economy continues to form an essential element of the freely associative life which underpins democratic political institutions.[2] Those on the other hand who wish to exclude the market from civil society argue that the economic domain, involving the pursuit of essentially private, self-regarding interests in consumption and accumulation, should be distinguished from the sphere of public deliberation and collective organization concerning matters of the common interest, which is civil society proper; it is the latter form of associative life that is important, not only for the health of democratic institutions, but as a site for the exercise of democracy in its own right. Indeed, in idealized versions of this argument, civil society becomes the authentic sphere of democratic participation and debate, in contrast to the depersonalized logic of market forces on one side, and the bureaucratized state on the other.[3]

In part what is at issue here is a conceptual disagreement about how narrowly 'civil society' should be defined: whether to include all those features of society that are potentially supportive or facilitative of democracy, even if their consequences are indirect and unintended, or only those forms of association that are themselves inherently public or political in character. But there is also a substantive disagreement at issue about how far a market economy is actually supportive of democracy, and, if so, in what sense. Here debates about the conceptualization of civil society become the site for the replay of much older arguments between liberals and critical theorists about their respective assessments of market capitalism.

In my view it is this second, substantive issue that is the important one. Or rather, it is only when we have clarified the relation between market and democracy that we can decide the conceptual question of whether the former should be included in the concept of 'civil society', and what is at stake in doing so. Most of this essay, therefore, will be about the substantive question. At the end I shall return to look at the implications of my analysis for the theory of civil society itself.

The conventional wisdom in Anglo-American political science, it should be said straightaway, is that a market economy is a precondition for democratic political institutions, and that therefore economic liberalization and political democratization as *processes* go hand in hand. To be sure, the burgeoning literature on economic liberalization and democratization has now moved well beyond the simplistic formulations about the connection inspired by the collapse of Communism and Fukuyama's celebration of the triumph of liberalism in 'The End of History?'.[4] In a recent number of the *Journal of Democracy* devoted to the subject, various authors developed a number of differentiated typologies to help analyze the complexities of actual practice: the different time-scales and dynamics of economic liberalization and democratization respectively; the different stages of their respective institutionalization; the different order of priority in which they might occur; the differentiated effects that each has on the other; and so on.[5] Despite this increasing sense of complexity, however, they all subscribe to an assumption of much older provenance, that there is a fundamental congruence between a market economy and a democratic polity; that the two belong together.

This connection has often been expressed in the proposition that the market constitutes a 'necessary though not sufficient condition' for democracy; that is to say, although a market economy may not require a democratic regime to sustain it, yet the latter requires the former.[6] Thus Lindblom, in his survey of the relation between forms of economy and forms of political system, found many examples of 'market-oriented authoritarianism', whereas the category of non-market democracies was an 'empty box'.[7] The empty box idea was repeated in a recent article by Berger, who described the causal relation between the two as an 'asymmetrical' one. Although there have been numerous cases of *non*-democratic market economies, he writes, 'there has been no case of political democracy that has *not* been a market economy'.[8]

Now although this statement of the causal relationship is today widely accepted, the precise reasons for it are much less so. What exactly is it about a market economy that is supportive of, but not sufficient for, democracy, and within what limits? In addressing this question, I shall first distinguish a number of different arguments that are often confused in the literature. I shall show that the supposedly virtuous effects of the market for democracy are not in all respects equally straightforward or equally strong. I shall then consider some negative or less benign consequences of the market for democracy. I shall conclude that the common formula 'necessary but not sufficient' is a misleading characterization of the complex relations between market and democracy, and that we should do well to abandon it.

But what is 'the market' and what is 'democracy' for the purpose of this analysis? And why speak of a market economy and not capitalism *simpliciter*? There are a number of reasons we might have for preferring the former designation. First, most of the arguments about the favourable consequences of capitalism for democracy turn out to be arguments about the role of the free market, as the characterization of the process as 'economic liberalization' itself confirms. Secondly, capitalism can take, and has historically taken, forms in which the state rather than the market is the chief determinant of opportunities for private profit, and these are not typically democracy-supportive. Thirdly, we may wish to keep open the alternative of market *socialism* with dispersed forms of social ownership as at least a theoretical possibility, which might be as supportive of democracy as free market capitalism, and for similar reasons. However, none of these considerations is completely conclusive, and I would admit that in much of what follows market economy and capitalism could be used almost interchangeably.

A more serious objection to systematic theorizing about the relation between market and democracy is that there is no such thing as a market economy *tout court*, only a variety of different market economies, in different institutional contexts and conditions, and at different stages of development. Just as the effectiveness of a market economy as an agent of economic growth is dependent upon these institutional conditions, it could be argued, so might also be its propensity to support democracy. And since some of the institutional conditions are state-determined, might we not reasonably conclude that one way in which democratic polities maintain themselves is through the democracy-supportive types of institutional market framework (as also the types of civil society) that they tend to foster?

Establishing causal connections in the social sciences is always open to the charge of circularity; and it is for this reason, if no other, that it is necessary to define market and democracy in ideal-typical terms, and in abstraction from particular societal contexts, so that there can be no danger of overlap between the supposed cause and its effect. The usefulness of such an abstracted approach can only be judged by its results, not a priori. Without further ado, therefore, let me define a market economy for the present purpose as an economy based upon the free exchange of commodities under conditions of competition, together with the minimum necessary institutional framework to make exchange possible over time – a predictable system of law guaranteeing property rights and the security of contract. On the other side a democratic polity can be defined as a system of popular control over governmental decision-makers, based upon free expression and association, and free electoral choice under conditions of political equality.[9]

Two things stand out immediately from these definitions. First, if the minimum political condition for a market economy is the legal guarantee of property and contract, then it is clear why it does not require a democratic system to sustain it. Secondly, whatever causal relations are at work in the other direction, they must be complex ones, given the variety of elements involved in even these simplified concepts. Thus we might expect a market economy to have different implications for, say, political freedoms, electoral competition, and political equality, respectively. And it is not only the market *as such*, but which aspect of the market we consider, whether the consumer market which embodies individual choice, or the labour market which distributes employment opportunities and exclusions, or the market in international trade and investment which shapes regional and national economies, or the casino market in financial futures which can bring the whole lot crashing down about us. The range of complexity is considerable. In what follows I shall attempt to bring some order into the complexity by first distinguishing a number of different arguments for the positive connection between market and democracy. I shall set them out in the form of propositions to assist clarity of analysis.

(1) *The more extensive the state, the more difficult it is to subject it to public accountability or societal control.*

The argument for the market economy in this context is that, by making the arena of economic activity a matter of 'private' responsibility, it limits the scope of public decision making, and in principle allows for the separation of economic from political power. The market 'limits the sphere of politics by limiting the sphere of public authority' (Schumpeter); 'by removing the organisation of economic activity from the control of political authority, the market ... enables economic strength to be a check to political power rather than a reinforcement' (Friedman).[10] The proof of this proposition is generally demonstrated negatively, from the command economies of the

Soviet type, whose monolithic political apparatus was in principle unaccountable to, and uncontrollable by, the society it administered. This effect was not solely a function of single party rule, but derived from features inherent in a centrally administered economy: an enormous bureaucratic apparatus, capable of controlling individual behaviour across all spheres of life; the absorption of all talent by the state and its agencies; the exclusion of private property, such that access to the means of communication could be denied to any independent public opinion.

Here the argument about the virtuous effects of the market for democracy can readily become part of a wider argument about 'civil society'. If the distinctive, democracy-supportive feature of civil society is its capacity for self-organization independently of the state, and the variety and strength of its associational life, then a market economy could be held to be both an essential part of this, and a condition for its larger flourishing.[11] A market economy offers a paradigm of social relations constructed voluntarily and laterally, rather than compulsorily and hierarchically; of the dispersal of ownership and resources, rather than their concentration; of decentralized, rather than centralized, decision making. Although all these features may be qualified in practice, for example, through tendencies to oligopoly, yet the sheer extent and significance of economic life would suggest that its organization through functioning market relations constitutes a pivotal feature of any democracy-supporting civil society.

If the key aspect of the market economy for democracy here is the construction of social relations and the pursuit of social activity *independently* from the state and its tutelage, then this can provide us with a criterion for distinguishing between forms of state involvement in the economy (other than the command economy already considered) which may compromise a democratic political order, from those which are less likely to do so. Regulatory measures of all kinds, market-supporting interventions, temporary initiatives to foster new industries within the market, redistribution according to formal citizenship criteria – none of these need compromise independence in the sense used above.[12] On the other hand, the extension of state-owned industries, even if operating within a formal system of market relations, or the determination of private economic opportunities by the state rather than the market, for example, through government contracts, licences, quotas, etc. (what Max Weber called 'politically oriented capitalism')[13] – either of these will tend to compromise the independence of economic activity, and accumulate discretionary power in the hands of state officials. Although there may be legal and institutional ways in which this discretionary power can be limited, a surer method is to remove it altogether. Here the economic and political cases for liberalization tend clearly to converge.

This first argument, then, to the effect that the market economy serves both to limit the state and to underpin the independence of civil society, is a plausible one. However, like all arguments for the democracy-supportive character of civil society, it is subject to two substantial qualifications, which have been repeatedly rehearsed since Marx's time. First, the market is itself a structure of power relations, comprising financial and industrial hierarchies that are anything but internally democratic. While one strand of argument may assert that all that matters for democracy is that these institutions be pluralistic, independent and self-organizing, another insists that, where people are subject to authoritarian or paternalistic relations in their daily lives – in family, workplace, religion and so on – a citizen body that is active in the defence of democracy is unlikely to result. It is, in any case, a very attenuated conception of democracy which pays no attention to the democratic quality of the society to which an elected government is supposedly accountable.

Secondly, if the argument is that a market economy 'enables economic strength to be a check to political power rather than a reinforcement', to use Friedman's words, then this requires not only that the state keep at arm's length from economic activity, but that government should not be subordinate to dominant interests in the economy. In practice the separation of economic from political power in a market economy is often more apparent than real. Although it is possible to limit the impact of wealth and economic muscle on the political process, by restricting media ownership, regulating the financing of political parties and election campaigns, opening up procedures of government consultation to public inspection, and so on, it is impossible to eliminate it entirely. In these respects, then, there is a price to be paid in democratic terms for the necessary autonomy of civil society; and societal control of government is not coterminous with popular control.

(2) *The more that is at stake in the electoral contest, the greater the incentive for participants to compromise the process, or reject the outcome.*

This proposition could be seen as a variant of the first, about the necessary separation of the economic and political spheres for democracy. Here, however, the effect concerns the viability of electoral competition, rather than government accountability to society more generally. It is a truism of political science that the stakes in electoral competition should be significant, but also limited. If too little is at issue, the electorate will not bother to vote; if too much, then political elites will have an incentive to undermine the elections, or refuse to accept the outcome. What counts as 'too much' is naturally a matter of judgement and context. But the stakes are raised enormously if elected office brings not only control over public policy, but key access to private economic opportunities for the contestants and their following, whether through appointments to the state apparatus, control of parastatals, or discretion over government contracts and licences. The cost of electoral defeat is heavily compounded for the losers if it brings exclusion from economic advancement as well as loss of political office.

Now of course any incentive to frustrate the electoral process is also dependent on the strength of the normative and political constraints that typically accrue from a long history of electoral replacement of office holders, and the recognition that elections constitute 'the only game in town'. Democratic sustainability in this context involves a ratio between the solidity of the underlying structure and the force of the pressures to which it is subject.[14] Long established democracies can withstand much greater divisiveness of electoral competition than recent ones. For the latter, then, it is particularly relevant that the route to economic advancement should not be dependent on electoral outcomes, and that it should be determined by market rather than political criteria. Here again, the economic and political arguments for liberalization converge.

(3) *Market freedoms and political freedoms are mutually supportive.*

This proposition is based in part on the apparently self-evident connection between the freedoms of movement, exchange and property in the economic sphere, and the freedoms of movement, expression and association at the political level. Are such freedoms not indivisible? Are they not inspired by the same desire on the part of individuals not to be obstructed by unnecessary legal restrictions on their activity?[15] The apparent naturalness of this connection is reinforced by the observation that the bourgeoisie were the historical 'bearers' of economic and political freedom simultaneously, whether in the independent trading cities of the early modern period, or in struggles against absolutist rule and mercantilist economic policies in the eighteenth and early nineteenth centuries. 'In our time the connection between the market and the particular liberties prized in the liberal tradition is still intimate,' concludes Lindblom.[16]

However, the connection between economic and political freedoms has not always proved so secure in practice. As Marx, for example, argued in his theory of the Bonapartist state, when the freedoms of speech and association exercised by the propertyless came to threaten property and profits, capitalists would be only too ready to abandon free political institutions for ones that could more readily guarantee order and property, even if this meant leaving their own parliamentary representatives in the lurch.[17] Freedom of profit for the few was not necessarily consistent with political freedoms for the many, as many examples from the twentieth

century have subsequently confirmed. Even a liberal such as Max Weber
was compelled to admit that there was little similarity between the small
scale competitive capitalism of the classical bourgeois period, and the
cartellized, bureaucratized systems of production and labour control of his
own day, at least in respect of their implications for political freedom. 'It is
ridiculous in the extreme', he wrote in his 1905 study of the prospects for
bourgeois democracy in Russia, 'to ascribe to modern advanced capitalism
.... any affinity with "democracy" or even "freedom" (in *any* sense of the
word). All the forms of development are excluded which in the West put the
strong *economic* interests of the possessing classes in the service of the
movement for bourgeois liberty.'[18]

Conditions of course change. The intensity of class struggle may for the
moment have abated, and the structure of capitalism is continually being
transformed. Yet the sociological point that both Marx and Weber were in
different ways making is still pertinent: that the connections between
economics and politics are mediated through social *agency*. And the
question therefore is whose economic conditions of life, whose economic
interests, require political freedoms of expression and association to realize,
and who therefore can be expected to be active in their defence? Neo-
Marxists have a straightforward answer: it is the working class, in alliance
with all those other disadvantaged groups whose economic interests can
only be protected or advanced by collective rather than individual action,
and to whom therefore the political freedoms of movement, expression and
association are essential rather than an optional extra.[19] Neo-Weberians, if
they may be so called, have a different answer: it is all those technical and
professional strata, in education, science, the media and elsewhere, whose
work gives them a consistent interest in the free flow of information, and
who play an increasingly weighty role in the 'information society'.

Both answers have their plausibility, and we do not have to choose
between them. The important thing is the question, since the answers must
depend upon the context. Once economic and political freedoms have been
shown to constitute no seamless web, then the issue becomes one of
identifying which economic agents in a market system (and of course other
social agents as well) have a settled interest in political freedoms that
derives from their basic situation and activity.

(4) *Both market and democracy require the rule of law; to ensure it for the
one is to do so for the other.*

This proposition is different from the previous ones, in that the causal chain
does not run from the market to democracy, but from a third factor that is
seen as necessary to both. Just as a market economy requires the rule of law
– a predictable system of legal interpretation, adjudication and enforcement

by courts that are independent of the executive – to ensure the security of property and contract, so democracy requires it to ensure that government officials only act within competences approved by parliament, and that citizens have access to legal redress in the event of maladministration or the abuse of power. Providing an effective system of independent courts to facilitate economic exchange will thereby also facilitate the legal accountability of the executive and its officials.

Although at first sight plausible, this proposition suffers from the same drawback as the previous one in that, as with the concept 'freedom', the connection established between the economy and polity by the 'rule of law' may be merely terminological rather than actual. There is nothing impossible or even contradictory in practice in a market system being subject to law in the interest of economic predictability, while a government acts oppressively towards its citizens. The judiciary may be independent in matters of commercial law, but be subordinate where matters of vital interest to the government are concerned, say in questions of administrative or electoral law. Or the executive may so dominate the legislature that the rule of law at the political level is merely formalistic, since the government can change the law at will, or rule through legally endorsed discretion. Or a system of commercial courts may be well developed and resourced, while legal avenues for citizen redress or protection against the abuse of power may be undeveloped. Or it may simply be that only powerful and wealthy economic agents and corporations can actually afford access to the law rather than ordinary citizens. In all these ways the rule of law may be effective in the one sphere but not in the other.

In so far as there are any crossover effects here from economics to politics, it may once again be through the medium of social agency rather than merely impersonal causes. In the modern period lawyers have played an important role in struggles to limit the arbitrary powers of an oppressive state, whether in the French revolutionary era, or the human rights campaigning of our own time. While there is nothing in the specialism of commercial law to generate such a concern, the more extensive the body of trained lawyers, we may suppose, and the wider their training in legal principles and comparative law, the more likely the emergence of individuals with a commitment to a defence of the rule of law in the service of public accountability as well as the predictability of economic transactions.

(5) *The sovereignty of the consumer and the voter alike rests on the same anti-paternalist principle.*

The close parallel has often been pointed out between the individual as consumer in the economic market and the individual as voter in an electoral democracy, and between the open competition among firms for market share, and the open competition among parties for a share of the vote.[20] In each case similar processes can be observed at work: that of *open competition*, whether between firms or parties, with access for new entrants who can identify an unsatisfied segment of the market or of electoral opinion; the expectation that the *rewards* of success – whether it be profits or political office – will be dependent on the ability to attract support, whether of customers or voters, for the particular product or policy/leadership package that is on offer; the assumption, therefore, that ultimately the individual, whether as consumer or as voter, is *sovereign*. Democracy, in other words, empowers the voter, in exactly the same way as the market empowers the consumer, by making the expressed preferences of the individual, and the ability to satisfy them, the fundamental condition for political as much as economic success.

Of course in neither case is competition perfect, due to high entry costs, and the preferences of consumers and voters alike are subject to manipulation from above through advertising and propaganda. Yet this does not alter the fact of the link between the two spheres, whose parallelism is no mere coincidence, since it rests on a basic anti-paternalist principle of liberalism that is common to both.[21] Both consumer and voter sovereignty are underpinned by the idea that individuals are the best judges of their own interests. People's conceptions of their interests may be revisable, improvable with greater knowledge or more education, certainly; but at the end of the day they must be the judges of what is good for themselves, and collectively what is good for society. On this view it was no coincidence, therefore, that the peoples under former communist rule should demand a market economy alongside political democracy, since in each case what they were reacting against, whether in the authoritarian political order or the planned economy, was the same paternalist claim that their needs could be best known or defined by higher authority.

Now once more the connection may not be as secure as it looks at first sight. Against it can be urged that, while individuals may be the best judge of their interests in private affairs and individual choices, decisions about the societal good require special knowledge, experience or judgement that is not available to all. Paternalism at the political level may thus coexist with the principle of individual choice in the economic sphere. Indeed there are many who argue that it *should* do so, and not only the outright opponents of democracy such as Lee Kuan Yew, but those false friends of democracy who urge that, for the sake of democratic stability, the masses should be kept at arm's length from the political process. Yet we may also doubt whether the legitimacy of a paternalist regime is secure over time, when it coexists with a market economy; whether assumptions about the individual's capacity for responsibility and self-determination can be successfully confined to the economic sphere; and whether decisions about the collective good can be entirely separated from the individual goods of which people are assumed in market transactions to be the best judge. The point, then, is not that a market economy is inconsistent with all authoritarianisms, which we know to be untrue; but that over time it erodes the *legitimacy* of political orders based on avowedly paternalist principles.

(6) *A market economy is necessary for long-term economic growth.*

After the philosophizing of the previous proposition, here is an argument that appeals to the purse rather than to principle. For many the key point of connection between market and democracy is the simple one of economic growth. This is a two-staged argument: democracies need economic growth to meet the expectations of voters, and to reduce the intensity of distributional conflicts; only market economies can deliver long term growth, now that the closed economies of the Soviet type have been exposed as unsustainable. We may note that this proposition says nothing about any given level of economic *development* (whether Huntington's $500–1000 per capita GNP, or some other) as being necessary for democracy.[22] Nor does it commit us to taking sides in the seemingly unresolvable argument about whether democracies are superior to authoritarian regimes in fostering economic development, and at what stage(s), since the causal link lies in the opposite direction. In these respects the claims of the proposition are relatively modest.

Even so, however, the proposition requires careful qualification, in both its parts. Because a market economy may be necessary for sustainable growth does not mean that it will guarantee it, much less that the more the market, the more growth we can expect. As the history of the past two decades has shown, policies of market deregulation do not necessarily improve growth in relatively weak economies, either in the developed or the less developed world. And there is a good deal of evidence that they serve to intensify rather than ameliorate economic inequalities even where growth does take place. So the idea that economic growth as such is democracy-supportive also needs careful qualification.

Let us take stock of the argument so far. The claim that a market economy constitutes a necessary but not sufficient condition for a democratic polity entails that the market has certain characteristics that are supportive of democracy, that democracies are not sustainable without these, and that other conditions (unspecified) are also required. The strength of the claim lies in the range of potentially positive effects that can be seen to follow from a market system for widely different aspects of democratic life: for societal control over government, for electoral competition, for civil freedoms, for the rule of law, for the principle of self-determination, for economic growth. This range of potentially virtuous effects is impressive, covering as it does most of the elements identified in the earlier definition of democracy.

Against this, however, have to be set three substantial qualifications. First, in so far as the positive effects work, they do so through a set of mediating factors or intermediate causes, whether of structure or agency. That is to say, the effects are indirect rather than direct. It is never $x > z$ (market > democracy), but $x > y > z$, or $x > y' > y'' > z$, or $y > x$ and z, where y is a third element or set of elements linking the two, or common to both. The more indirect the connection, the more dependent it is upon other conditions for its virtuous effects.

Secondly, it does not follow from the existence of positive effects for democracy from a market economy, that the *more* an economy is marketized (liberalized, deregulated, exposed to competition and so on), the more secure or pronounced these effects will be. This is in part because it depends upon the character of government intervention in the economy, whether through discretionary power fostering political dependency, or regulation as such. It is in part because, thirdly, the market also has negative consequences for democracy. Some of these have already been touched on, but it is time now to examine them more systematically. I shall concentrate on three, which are the direct counterpart of positive propositions already considered. The analysis will show that these negative effects of the market for democracy are not incidental, but are the very consequence of its virtues, as the reverse side of the coin is inseparable from its face. As before, I shall set them out in propositional form.

(1) *The independence of the market from the state makes the economy difficult to subject to democratic control.*

Democratic control over government (through elections, public opinion, organized pressure and so forth) is valueless if the government for its part is incapable of controlling anything. Yet one of the key advantages of the market from a democratic point of view was precisely that it removed the central arena of economic activity from political control, in the interest of limited government. It follows that key issues affecting the wellbeing of society and the public interest, such as the level and pattern of investment and employment, the variation in the business cycle, the distribution of profits and wages, and so on, are surrendered to private decision, or to the unintended outcome of a multiplicity of private decisions. Pre-1945 socialists termed this the 'anarchy' of the market, which they sought to eradicate by placing the economy under conscious collective control. Today we know that this is not the answer; but equally that the 'invisible hand' cannot ensure the public interest by itself. Keynesianism was an attempt to square this circle by expanding the steering capacity of the state, without extending its power over the institutions of civil society; but it seems to be generally agreed that it can no longer work in one country alone.

At this point the tension between market and democracy is experienced as an acute disjuncture between the different levels at which each operates: between the international reach of market forces, and the restriction of democratic government to the level of the nation state. It is perhaps not surprising that a widespread loss of confidence in the democratic process should result, when people perceive that the forces shaping their economic well-being are beyond their control, and elected governments are reduced to tinkering at the margin, or to managing appearances, as they take credit for economic sunshine while abjuring responsibility for drought or flood. To be sure, there is considerable difference in the degree to which different political economies are able to consolidate domestic advantages so as to benefit from international trade and investment. But no one sets the overall terms on which international competition is conducted, and the process itself therefore eludes any democratic control.

(2) *Free market competition intensifies economic and social inequalities.*

This is a two-stage argument in reverse, and forms the counterpart to claims about the virtues of economic freedom for democracy. Left to itself, the market intensifies the inequalities of financial and social capital people bring to it; the sharper the inequalities, and the wider the economic exclusions, the more they undermine equality of political citizenship and compromise democratic institutions themselves.

That market processes systematically generate and reinforce economic inequalities has always been insisted on by the Left, but it is accepted by many on the Right as well. Apologists for the market such as Nozick or Friedman do not deny its unequal outcomes; they only insist that they are justifiable, whether as the product of the fair exchange of legitimate holdings, as indicators of socially recognized value, or as the inevitable price of freedom.[23] Of course markets are open systems, allowing new entrants the possibility of success. But competition necessarily entails losers as well as winners. Economists of Left and Right may currently debate whether the losers could price themselves back into work at a level of wages sufficient to subsist on, and how far the social security system prevents them from doing so. But the simple fact is that processes of competition and the requirements of profitability in the present market order are inseparable from insecurity and unemployment for substantial numbers of the workforce in developing and developed economies alike.

It would be mistaken to imagine that the consequences which follow from economic inequality and exclusion are uniform for democracies everywhere. Yet it is possible to distinguish two different kinds of negative effect. One is its consequence for the impoverished and excluded themselves: social alienation, loss of effective civil and political rights, criminalization. The other is the consequence of this in turn for the wider democratic process: extension of the surveillance state, intensification of repressive apparatuses, both public and private, the expansion of populist and exclusionary political movements. As with the positive effects of the market, so here the causal process is indirect, and therefore subject to the same qualification. Yet the direction in which it tends is clear.

(3) *Market dispositions undermine the integrity of the democratic public sphere.*

This proposition is the counterpart of the positive connection drawn between consumer and voter sovereignty. Although the same liberal anti-paternalist principle serves to validate both economic and political choice, yet the preoccupation with its exercise in the market, and its assumption there as paradigmatic, serves to diminish rather than enhance democracy, in two respects. First, market choices come to preempt political ones, as individual decisions are prioritized over collective ones, and citizens themselves come to be defined as consumers. Secondly, the logic of private self-interest tends to colonize the public sphere, and to corrode the formation of a distinctive public interest, and the ethos of public service.

As to the first of these effects, it is evident from the recent market penetration of the public sphere in the UK that the more we emphasize individual choice – in health, education, transport and so on – the more we abandon any collective control over the consequences of these choices, and the shape and distribution of provision between different sections of the population.[24] And the more we construct the citizen as consumer in the public sphere, the more we undermine the distinctive republican conception of that sphere as 'forum' rather than 'market', as a place for debate and discussion between citizens about collective choices, from the most local to the national level.[25] It may be objected that these were always elite choices, to which ordinary citizens had no access. But this observation only serves to highlight the contrast between strategies for empowerment through democratization, and through a market model which preempts collective choice.

As to the second aspect of the proposition, it has been a repeated criticism of the market since the early nineteenth century that its logic of self-interest maximization comes to undermine the very conditions on which the operation of the market itself depends – including trust in

economic relations, the conditions of social cohesion, and the integrity of
public officials. The tendency of market economies is to become market
societies, in which all transactions and relationships come to be conducted
as relations of exchange for private advantage. The effectiveness of
government, on the other hand, depends in part on fostering and protecting
those features that distinguish it from the market: its ability to construct a
public interest independently of private interests, and to develop a culture of
disinterested public service. This distinctiveness is vulnerable to penetration
by the market, to the treatment of government as a branch of private
management, or to the contracting out of its functions to private enterprise.
Its erosion is particularly damaging to democratic polities, where trust
between citizens and public officials is important for continued popular
support.

    Now it could be argued that the negative effects identified here are not
the product of the market as such, but of market *ideology*, which mistakenly
treats the consumer (using 'exit' rather than 'voice') and the model of
private management (prioritizing financial accountancy) as paradigmatic
for the public sphere. However, the distinction between market forces and
market ideology is not altogether easy to draw, when the same economic
agents are the instruments of both. In other words, a characteristic feature of
market economies is both the production and fertile reception of an
ideological tendency which pushes market processes and the
commodification of social activity to their extreme.

There are a number of conclusions to be drawn from the above analysis,
which bear on the issues raised at the outset of the essay. First, the thesis that
a market economy constitutes a necessary but not sufficient condition for a
democratic polity turns out to be a misleading account of the relationship. It
invites us to conclude that the effects of the market on democracy are
wholly beneficent, and that the causes of the absence, erosion or failure of
democracy are to be sought in factors that are extraneous to the market itself
(compare 'water is a necessary but not sufficient condition for life'). Yet, as
we have seen, the market is at once supportive and undermining of
democracy, in a number of different respects, and the accurate
characterization of their relationship is therefore one of *ambivalence*.

    Secondly, if this characterization is correct, as I would argue that it is,
then the complexities and contradictions in the relation between economic
liberalization and democratization as *processes* do not stem primarily from
the factors identified in the literature that was mentioned towards the
beginning of the discussion. That is to say, it is not a question of their
respective order, their differential speed, their specific stages, or whatever.

It is a consequence of the inherent ambivalence in the relation between market and democracy, considered abstractly or ideal-typically, as I have done here.

Thirdly, if any strategy for democratic consolidation or deepening therefore requires modifying the negative effects of the market as well as encouraging the positive ones, then we should discourage the current habit of linking liberalization and democratization in the same breath. A democracy-supportive agenda will include neo-Keynesian policies at an international level, strengthening the protection of economic and social rights alongside civil and political ones, re-forming (not just curtailing) the welfare state, as well as strengthening the ethos of public service and protecting the integrity of the public sphere. Of course striking a balance between these and policies of liberalization may involve a difficult matter of judgement in contexts where they conflict. However, the above should no longer be viewed as merely a partisan Left or social-democratic agenda, but as much supportive of democratization as liberalization itself.

Finally, if the relation between market economy and democratic polity is one of ambivalence, as I have suggested, then this would help explain some of the disagreement between theorists about whether the market properly belongs to civil society or not, depending on whether they choose to emphasize its positive or negative features, from a democratic point of view. Part of the point of the concept 'civil society', after all, is to identify those aspects of social life that have a positive contribution to make to the consolidation or persistence of democracy. Yet, as Philippe Schmitter most recently has pointed out, such features also have their negative effects.[26] In this respect my conclusion about the ambivalence of a market economy for democracy is not very different from analyses of civil society more widely. Whether we take the further step and say that the market is itself a part of civil society, or only a facilitative condition for it, or only in some respects, seems to me fairly arbitrary, and only of secondary importance in comparison with the substantive issue of how to so regulate, contain and supplement market forces that the necessary *civility* of social relations in a democratic polity can be protected and enhanced.

NOTES

1.   For a discussion of Adam Ferguson, see   John Varty, 'Civil or Commercial? Adam Ferguson's Concept of Civil Society', *Democratization*, Vol.4, No.1 (1997), pp.29–48.
2.   For example, Ernest Gellner, *Conditions of Liberty: Civil Society and its Rivals* (London: Hamish Hamilton, 1994); Victor M. Perez-Diaz, *The Return of Civil Society* (Cambridge, MA: Harvard University Press, 1993).
3.   Jean Cohen and Andrew Arato, *Civil Society and Political Theory* (Cambridge, Mass.: MIT Press, 1992); Andrew Arato, 'The Rise, Decline and Reconstruction of the Concept of Civil

Society, and Directions for Future Research', in Adolf Bibic and Gigi Graziano (eds.), *Civil Society, Political Society, Democracy* (Ljubljana: Slovenian Political Science Association, 1994); Jürgen Habermas, *The Structural Transformation of the Public Sphere* (Cambridge, MA: MIT Press, 1989).

4. Francis Fukuyama, 'The End of History?', *The National Interest*, No.16 (Summer 1989), pp.3–18.

5. *Journal of Democracy*, Vol.5, No.4 (Oct. 1994), Special Issue on 'Economic Reform and Democracy'. See especially Moises Naim, 'Latin America: The Second Stage of Reform', pp.32–48; Joan M. Nelson, 'Linkages between Politics and Economics', pp.49–62; Minxin Pei, 'The Puzzle of East Asian Exceptionalism', pp.90–103. See also Adam Przeworski, *Democracy and the Market* (Cambridge: Cambridge University Press, 1991); Iain McLean, 'Democratization and Economic Liberalization: Which is the Chicken and Which is the Egg?', *Democratization*, Vol.1, No.1 (Spring 1994), pp.27–40; Padma Desai, 'Beyond Shock Therapy', *Journal of Democracy*, Vol.6, No.2 (April 1995), pp.102–12.

6. For an early formulation of this proposition, see Milton Friedman, *Capitalism and Freedom* (Chicago, IL: Chicago University Press, 1962), p.10; for a recent one, see Jagdish Bhagwati, 'Democracy and Development', *Journal of Democracy*, Vol.3, No.3 (July 1992), p.40.

7. Charles E. Lindblom, *Politics and Markets* (New York: Basic Books, 1977), pp.16–2.

8. Peter L. Berger, 'The Uncertain Triumph of Democratic Capitalism', *Journal of Democracy*, Vol.3, No.3 (July 1992), p.9.

9. For a fuller discussion of the definition of democracy, its key principles and their realization in institutional form, see my chapter 'Key Principles and Indices for a Democratic Audit', in David Beetham (ed.), *Defining and Measuring Democracy* (London: Sage Publications, 1994), pp.25–43.

10. Joseph Schumpeter, *Capitalism, Socialism and Democracy* (London: Allen & Unwin, 5th edn., 1952), p.297; Friedman, op. cit., p.15.

11. See, for example, Gellner: 'Civil society is based on the separation of the polity from economic and social life ... The autonomy of the economy is needed so as to provide pluralism with a social base which it cannot any longer find anywhere else', Ernest Gellner, *Conditions of Liberty* (London: Hamish Hamilton, 1994), p.212.

12. 'Independence' should not be confused with 'freedom', as a consideration of their opposites will make clear: restriction or obstruction vs. dependency.

13. Max Weber, *Economy and Society* (Berkeley, CA: University of California Press, 1978), pp.164–6.

14. For a fuller discussion, see David Beetham, 'Conditions for Democratic Consolidation', *Review of African Political Economy*, No.60 (1994), pp.157–72.

15. See Friedman, op. cit., Ch.1, 'The Relation between Economic Freedom and Political Freedom'.

16. Lindblom, op. cit., p.164.

17. 'The bourgeoisie correctly understood that all the so-called bourgeois liberties and organs of progress were attacking and threatening its own *class rule* ... and that its political power must be broken in order to preserve its social power intact.' Karl Marx, 'Eighteenth Brumaire of Louis Bonaparte', in *Political Writings*, Vol.2 (ed. David Fernbach) (Harmondsworth: Penguin Books, 1973), pp.189–90.

18. Quoted in David Beetham, *Max Weber and the Theory of Modern Politics* (Cambridge: Polity Press, 1984), pp.46–7.

19. See, for example, Dietrich Rueschemeyer, Evelyne Huber Stephens and John D. Stephens, *Capitalist Development and Democracy* (Cambridge: Polity Press, 1992), p.98: 'The working class, not the middle class, was the driving force behind democracy.'

20. Most famously by Anthony Downs in *An Economic Theory of Democracy* (New York: Harper & Row, 1957).

21. The connection is particularly evident in Benthamite utilitarianism; see Jeremy Bentham, 'Constitutional Code', in *Collected Works*, Vol.9 (ed. Bowring) (Edinburgh: William Tate, 1843).

22. Samuel P. Huntington, *The Third Wave: Democratization in the Late Twentieth Century* (Norman, OK: University of Oklahoma Press, 1991).

23. Robert Nozick, *Anarchy, State and Utopia* (Oxford: Blackwell, 1974); Friedman, op. cit.,

Ch.10.
24. Diane Elson, 'choice in the small does not provide choice in the large', quoted in Adam Przeworski, 'The Neoliberal Fallacy', *Journal of Democracy*, Vol.3, No.3 (July 1992), p.53.
25. See Jon Elster, 'The Market and the Forum', in J. Elster and A. Hylland (eds.), *The Foundations of Social Choice Theory* (Cambridge: Cambridge University Press, 1986), pp.103–32.
26. Philippe C. Schmitter, *Some Propositions about Civil Society and the Consolidation of Democracy* (Vienna: Institute for Advanced Studies Political Science Series 10, 1993).

Civil Society, the Market and Democracy in Latin America

JENNY PEARCE

'Civil society' has been used in a confusing variety of ways in Latin America by academics, policy-makers, non-governmental organizations and activists. This article explores the ambiguities in the usages of the concept over the last decade in a bid to rescue it from the danger of abandonment for having become all things to all people. If used rigorously, the concept remains a useful analytical tool for exploring the process and progress of democratization and capitalist development in Latin America. It encourages us to ask what *difference* a vibrant associational life can make to building more inclusive and sustainable democracies in Latin America. The case of Chile is used as an example of how 'civil society' opens up new questions for research in a country which many hail as the most successful example of economic and political liberalization in Latin America.

The three concepts in the title of this article have been frequently linked together by academics and policy-makers in recent debates about Latin American political and economic development. There is an assumption, at times implicit at others overt, that the three elements constitute a 'package' which could mark a turning point in the region's history. Such a turning point, it is felt, would end the 'pendulum'[1] or 'cycles' of Latin American political history, between 'populist inclusion and authoritarian exclusion', creating dynamic economies, establishing the rule of law and consolidating fairly elected and accountable civilian governments.

A review of the literature and usages of 'civil society' in Latin America by scholars, policy-makers, NGOs and social/political activists, however, reveals that an extraordinary variety of often conflicting assumptions and meanings have been attached to the term since the mid-1980s. This article explores these different meanings and usages over the last decade, and suggests that a more serious debate is needed about precisely how this concept should be used in studies of contemporary Latin American processes of economic and political liberalization.

There is a considerable theoretical literature on 'civil society' today and this is not the place to engage with that literature.[2] This article will suggest, however, that the debate on the usefulness and relevance of the concept to Latin American democratization processes must at least distinguish in the way Robert Fine has suggested, between 'civil society' as a concept and 'civil society theory'.[3] The former derives from the political economy tradition and the unwilled, non-purposive arena of human interaction. Associational life emerges from the interactions of individuals as they pursue their private interests. It rests on negative liberty, that is, freedom from interference and assumes no positive content to that freedom. It reflects the eighteenth-century philosophical engagement with the emergence of the market economy and the self-regulating impetus of bourgeois, commercial society; as Michael Ignatieff has expressed it: 'the idea of the invisible hand sought to capture what was distinctively self-acting and self-correcting about market and society alike'.[4]

Civil society theory, on the other hand, is about willed action, agency, creativity and resistance. It reflects the efforts of the progressive movements and organizations of Latin America to forge a theoretical tool for political action and change in the wake of the collapse of communism. It is about the search for new subjects and agents of history. The movements of the 1980s which helped bring down communist and non-communist dictatorships gave impetus to the theoretical enquiry, which has sought inspiration in the work of Gramsci and more recently in that of Habermas.

These two distinct approaches to 'civil society' are apparent in the literature surveyed below, but they are often confused with each other. Both are of great interest, but must be treated as distinct projects. At the same time, failure to acknowledge that the dominant discourse derives from the political economy tradition, can lead to dangerous voluntarism amongst movements that derive their impetus from a critique of the market as well as the state. It is no coincidence that contemporary efforts to modernize capitalism in Latin America hark back to ideas associated with the emergence of capitalist modernity in Europe. Many of the social movements and popular organizations of Latin America, on the other hand, are expressions of class, ethnic and gender-based challenges to core elements of this project or at least its failure to deliver satisfaction to all sectors of society.

In identifying the variety of usages of 'civil society' with respect to Latin America, it is hoped to rescue the concept before it is abandoned for having become all things to all people. While the search for a theory of 'civil society' remains an interesting and important enterprise, a more modest objective is proposed here. 'Civil society', it is argued, is particularly useful as an analytical tool for exploring the practice and meaning of democratization processes in Latin America today. In this sense, it is relevant to modernizers and their critics, a means of assessing the meaning and impact of those processes on society as a whole.

First, it allows us to focus on how and in what circumstances what happens *within* society impacts on political processes. This contrasts with approaches to democratization which focus only on the state, parties and elites. It also contrasts with approaches which focus only on social movements and which concentrate on the way those movements redefine the realm of the 'political' rather than their relationship to existing political structures and institutions. Civil society presupposes a relationship between individuals in their collectivities and the state. Secondly, it can be empirically tested. We can ask the question of any democratization process, to what extent does a vibrant 'civil society' make a *difference* to the process of political change and how can we research and measure that difference? Thirdly, it draws our attention to the factors which foster and hinder the growth of associational life. In the Latin American context the latter range from state repression and state cooption on the one hand to ineffective states and criminal violence on the other. They include the problem of weak judiciaries, party manipulation and clientelism. And they also encompass the impact of inequalities generated by the operations of the market and which strengthen some associations (for example, business groups) while undermining others (such as labour unions).

The first part of this article analyzes the literature on 'civil society' in Latin America over the last decade; this literature is grouped under four headings: Civil Society and Democratic Transition, Civil Society and the Inclusionary Project, Civil Society and Economic Liberalization and Civil Society and Democratic Consolidation. The second part of the article offers a case study of Chile. Widely regarded as the most successful example of economic and political liberalization in Latin America today, it is suggested that focusing on 'civil society' enables us to ask new questions about the character of Chilean democratization.

CIVIL SOCIETY AND DEMOCRATIC TRANSITION

'Civil society' emerged as a significant concern of Latin American scholars in the mid-1980s about the same time as the concept was revived in Eastern Europe; it was probably influenced by that revival. Academics incorporated it into the debate of the time: the prospects for and sustainability of democratic transition in Latin America.

The mainstream political scientists studying transitions (or 'transitologists') were particularly concerned with the mode of transition and how it affected the prospects for democracy.[5] The major question was whether the transition would succeed in bringing about a return to civilian rule and a sustainable democratic order. The definition of the latter was heavily influenced by Robert Dahl's concept of 'polyarchy', considered to be the 'highest feasible attainment of the democratic process in the government of a country'.[6] Democracy as the achievement of a 'procedural minimum' guided the literature. Its emphasis was on the role of political actors and the strategic choices they made, in particular those by the military and civilian elites involved in the transition. Bargains and pacts between these elites were a major focus of analysis, as were the degree to which the former power-holders were able to impose conditions on the transition process and subsequent political order. The ultimate goal was for all major actors to agree to the 'procedural minimum' and no longer use resources outside those sanctioned by the rules of the democratic game.

While political scientists concerned themselves with the role of political actors in the transitions, sociologists were focusing on the role of social actors and movements. The years of what Marcelo Cavarozzi refers to as the 'state-centred matrix' in Latin American development, from the 1930s to the late 1970s, also saw an expansion of what he calls 'civil society', in particular the emergence and strengthening of the organizations of workers, the urban poor and to a lesser extent peasants.[7] The mechanisms of inclusion and control with respect to these sectors varied greatly according to such factors as the nature of political parties, character of constitutional norms and institutions, and the political role of the military. The years 1960 to 1980 in particular, were years of unprecedented contestation by such sectors. It was only under the extreme authoritarianism of military dictatorship, US-inspired counter-insurgency programmes or parastatal violence that much of this contestation was finally defeated, often with direct US assistance. Bureaucratic-authoritarian states emerged in the Southern Cone as this contestation was pacified, while the military kept a significant influence over politics or counter-insurgency efforts elsewhere in the region. The result was the suppression everywhere of precisely those kinds of organizations that had grown up during the 'state-centred matrix'.

Authoritarian government, however, itself gave rise to various counter-movements. These often involved new social actors in that they were spearheaded by those not tied to the organizations and parties suppressed by the authoritarian governments and involved women, young people, radical or liberal clergy, and in the case of Brazil a new labour movement. Sociologists called these 'new social movements'; political scientists of the transition called them 'civil society'. But Cardoso points out how in Brazil: '... everything which was an organized fragment which escaped the immediate control of the authoritarian order was being designated *civil society*. Not rigorously, but effectively, the whole opposition ... was being described as if it were the movement of Civil Society.'[8]

The 'transitologists' were swept along with the tide to some extent. O'Donnell and Schmitter in their influential work on the democratic transition entitle a chapter of their book 'the resurrection of civil society'.[9] The authors argue that one of the key moments in pushing the democratization process forward was when the associations of 'civil society' mobilized in a 'popular upsurge' against the authoritarian regime, taking advantage of internal splits in the regime and its underlying crisis of legitimacy. But they are clear that while 'civil society' recovers and is resurrected and takes on a politicized character during the struggle for democracy, this would only create problems if sustained under the fragile new regimes.

'Civil society' is defined by O'Donnell and Schmitter as the network of groups and associations which mediate between individual and the state/political society. Alfred Stepan, on the other hand, makes a distinction between 'civil society', 'political society' and the state:

> By 'civil society' I mean that arena where manifold social movements ... and civic organizations from all classes attempt to constitute themselves in an ensemble of arrangements so that they can express themselves and advance their interests. By 'political society' in a democratizing setting I mean that arena in which the polity specifically arranges itself for political contestation to gain control over public power and the state apparatus. At best, civil society can destroy an authoritarian regime. However, a full democratic transition must involve political society, and the composition and consolidation of a democratic polity must entail serious thought and action about those core institutions of a democratic political society ... through which civil society can constitute itself politically to select and monitor democratic government.[10]

In their important study of 'Civil Society and Political Theory', Cohen and Arato have made some astute observations about the implications of these different conceptualizations of 'civil society' and 'political society' in the transition literature.[11] O'Donnell and Schmitter conceptualize an undifferentiated civil society counterposed to the state/political society; Stepan, above, differentiates 'civil' from 'political society' and both from the state.[12]

In the first formulation, however, the fate of 'civil society' after it has dutifully demobilized and accepted the elite negotiated transition remains undefined. Cohen and Arato ask: 'The question is whether there is anything left of a "resurrected civil society" after selective repression, co-optation, manipulation, internal conflicts, fatigue, disillusionment, and the channelling of opposition into the party and electoral systems take their toll and demobilize "the popular upsurge"?'[13] There is no indication about how a demobilized, depoliticized 'civil society' could actually contribute to democratic consolidation except by restraining its demands. Stepan's distinction between 'civil' and 'political society', on the other hand, is fruitful in that it 'establishes the priority of nonstrategic domains of solidarity, association and communication'[14] and distinguishes them clearly from 'political society' *per se*. But there is still the danger that 'civil society' will be unable to define its role *vis-à-vis* 'political society' or the state. While the actors of 'civil society' may be able to learn through their failures that they need 'political society' to achieve their aims, this is not true of political elites, who are under no impetus to build and strengthen the organizations of the civil sphere .[15]

Ultimately neither version is truly interested in the sphere of 'civil society' itself, except in so far as it has played an historic role in the struggle against dictatorship, or in Stepan's version, accepts that only 'political society' can guarantee the stability of the post transition democratic polity. 'Civil society' is not conceptualized in relationship to democracy itself, as in any sense necessary to it, and there is no apparent reason why associational, organizational and movement life amongst the population should be conceptualized as 'civil society' at all. Its use merely reflects the general fashion of the time, which had been required to recognize the role of organized citizens in the demise of dictatorial and totalitarian regimes in various parts of the world.

Yet, the importance of clarifying these conceptual ambiguities has been underscored by the actual outcomes of a number of transitions. Chile is the paradigm case; here the elan of the social protests against the Pinochet dictatorship was quickly dissipated as 'political society' took over the negotiation of the transition process and political parties reoccupied the public space initially opened up by the social organizations. The social organizations expressing the needs of the poorer sectors of Chilean society and those who suffered most under the military dictatorship have not yet recovered that space. The relevance of this to Chilean democratization will be discussed later.

If the political science literature of the transition is inadequate in its use of 'civil society', the social movement literature of the period was also unable to articulate the social organizational impetus to the political processes taking place at the same time. This literature proclaimed the eruption of new social movements, rather like political scientists declared the 'resurrection of civil society'. But it could not explain the collapse of many of these movements in the wake of the transitions or how they could impact on the post-transition democratization. Unlike the political science literature, the social movement literature concerned itself primarily with the arena of social organization and collective action per se and the way it was redefining the nature of what is 'political'. For many writers, this redefinition was significant in itself. David Slater suggested that the role of the 'new social movements' was to: 'subvert the traditional "given" of the "political" – state power, political parties and so forth ... their role has been that of revealing the political essence of the social'.[16]

Some of this literature grew out of an anti-party discourse and one which rejected the historic left emphasis on seizing state power. But the search for new subjectivities led to the 'overpoliticization' of the social arena itself. 'Civil society' became the source of a new politics, and political parties were even subsumed under its umbrella. A typical example can be seen in Francisco Weffort's article in Stepan's volume on *Democratizing Brazil* where 'civil society' is treated not as a mediating arena but as an end in itself.[17]

This view of 'civil society' reflected the influence of Gramsci on the Latin American left of the 1980s. 'Civil society' articulated a new strategic vision for a left which was still searching for a transformatory project but facing the defeat or collapse of old paradigms. Activists began to use the term as interchangeable with NGOs and popular movements in the course of the democratization struggles of the 1980s. Gramsci had conceptualized a terrain of contestation, a counter-hegemonic struggle that could take place through a 'civil society' independent of the state but also not reducible to the economy. Gramsci believed that such a struggle would ultimately be aimed at the overthrow of capitalism; for the left the essential point was that it offered a new rationale for a more multi-faceted struggle against dictatorship and militarism rather than capitalism as a whole. For many, this paved the way for an abandonment of Marxism. For others it was a means to hang onto some utopian social project, and 'civil society' became in this way an expression of a voluntaristic ideal. Carlos Castañeda has put this very concisely in his sharp and critical analysis of the Latin American left, *Utopia Unarmed*:

> While Latin Americans were reinventing 'civil society', many bolder Europeans were arguing that, as a separate entity from the state, it had never really existed. But there were political reasons for the region's theoretical untimeliness ... the struggle against the dictatorships took place, by definition, outside previously existing 'state' structures, and multiple new forms of grass roots organizations and movements were sweeping Latin America. Second, the defeat of the Chilean experience in particular, and, more broadly, the setbacks suffered in the struggle for 'state power' led several Latin American analysts on the left to hypostatize the importance of the grass roots. They were suddenly seen as a substitute for political parties, traditional unions, armed groups, etc. Both the armed left, since Che Guevara's death, and the peaceful, reformist left – since Allende's – had been defeated in their respective quests for power; perhaps a new left it was thought,

emanating from the plural, proliferating popular movements could succeed where others had failed.[18]

Out of the social movement literature, however, has at least come some recognition of subaltern politics in Latin America, of the importance of popular culture and social action, and the values and beliefs of non-state actors. A new range of literature has emerged around these themes which has challenged the elitist focus of much of the mainstream political science literature on Latin America; in particular, serious attention has been given to gender exclusions. But the two literatures still seem to operate along separate, parallel tracks.

There were two authors writing during the period of the transitions who suggest possible ways of synthesizing the approaches. They suggest that 'civil society' could be conceptualized as making a positive and even necessary contribution to liberal democracy. Alain Touraine wrote in 1987 about the difference between the European and Latin American experiences of social organization. Latin America, he argued, had never experienced the clear separation between social actors, representative political forces and the state, the former have lacked an autonomous identity outside their political status. A democratic political system, he suggests, 'does not presuppose only the representativity of political forces and the freedom of representation; it rests equally on the existence of autonomous social actors, representable, that is, conscious and organized, in a direct manner and not only through political agents'.[19]

The second author is the Brazilian sociologist and later President of his country, Fernando Henrique Cardoso. Cardoso writing in the late 1980s suggested that the 'possessive individualism' of Western liberalism was a weak basis for the democratization process in Brazil's 'associated dependent society'. He suggests social inequality and the 'fragility of the individual before business and bureaucracy' calls for the legitimation of the 'collective' historical subject, that is, the union, the community, the movement and even the party.[20] Out of the 'collective we' comes a democratizing impulse, distrustful of delegation and leaders. While evidently not sharing the Weffort conceptualization of a democracy 'of civil society', Cardoso also distinguishes himself from the anxieties of the 'transitologists' with respect to collective social action and the values it represents, and argues:

> It would be wrong not to recognize that in spite of the problems that such values pose for the institutionalization of democratic life, they have a positive side ... There is an embryonic democratic thought which is not restricted to accepting the party-parliamentary game ... as a form of justifying the democratic world view. Without greater

transparency of information and of the decision making process in the firm (whether private or State) and in the bureaucracy (idem, ibidem), and without evolving mechanisms for participation and control both through parties and directly by the interested publics, the democratization process will be crippled and meet with little reception in a society in which the 'private' in the strict sense of the word, is weak in relation to the organized, corporate, and State interest.[21]

Cardoso's suggestion is that the collective interactions of 'civil society' could be an essential mechanism to counteract the centralizing, elitist and bureaucratic tendencies of Latin American polities and bring them closer to democratic principles.

CIVIL SOCIETY AND THE INCLUSIONARY PROJECT

In the early 1990s the academic interest in 'civil society' as such waned, not withstanding some notable exceptions. Where it persisted, there was some effort to clarify the role it could play, but no serious efforts at conceptual clarification. Rueschemeyer, Stephens and Stephens, gave 'civil society' a prominent place in their important study of democracy and capitalist development published in 1992 and in which Latin America is a significant case-study: 'Capitalist development' they argued 'furthers the growth of civil society .... strengthening the organization and organizational capacity of the working and middle classes serves to empower those classes and thus to change the balance of class power'.[22] Their book nevertheless pays most attention to class-based organizations, the pressures for inclusion they generate and their contribution to democratization. There is no great theoretical advance on why we should use 'civil society' to describe these pressures for inclusion, as opposed to merely narrating the growth in organizational capacity of certain classes.

Philip Oxhorn writing in 1994 tried to look in more detail at the problematic nature of 'civil society' in Latin America. The concept itself is not treated as problematic, but Oxhorn makes some important points about its historic weakness in Latin America.[23] He questions the 'naive optimism' of the 1980s social movement literature, although he is concerned with the same social actors within his understanding of 'civil society' and the extent to which they are able to create more inclusionary, democratic societies in Latin America. Ultimately, Oxhorn's main concern is to draw attention to the way Latin America's traditional political parties undermine the emergent 'civil society'. Without a new type of party, he argues, Latin America's democracies will be founded on new forms of controlled inclusion.

This is an important observation, very much confirmed by the Chilean transition. However, it does not take us much further in terms of understanding what difference it makes to use the concept of 'civil society' in these circumstances rather than popular organizations, given that the two are virtually equated by the author.

Yet, the early 1990s did at least confirm that the concept was not going to go away. If the academic literature did not make any conceptual leaps in this period and indeed, many academics seemed to lose interest in the term, political activists, social organizers and NGO professionals seized on it, proclaimed it and asserted themselves to be the major actors in it.

The Zapatistas in Mexico made it clear that they considered themselves a 'civil society organization'; in Guatemala, the 'Civil Society Assembly' (Asamblea de la Sociedad Civil) brought together many organizations trying to influence the peace process in that country. The concept is mentioned in nearly all the literature emanating from these and many popular organizations and NGOs working throughout Central and South America in these years. There is little clarity or even uniformity in the usage of the term in this literature. In Guatemala, the 'civil' element had particular weight in the context of the anti-militarist agenda of the Assembly; in Mexico it refers rather to the movement against the ruling party, the PRI (Institutionalized Revolutionary Party), and its domination of Mexican political life. In Peru, the interest in 'civil society' is growing as political parties have collapsed and the state has shown increasingly authoritarian tendencies under President Fujimori. The strengthening of associational life is conceptualized as the only potential defence of society against the state.

At the grass-roots level and amongst middle-class reformers, 'civil society' had taken root by the early 1990s in much of Latin America as an expression of an inclusionary rather than a revolutionary project. How could the economically poor and marginalized access the institutions and structures of newly democratized polities and make them work for them?

CIVIL SOCIETY AND ECONOMIC LIBERALIZATION

In the meantime, interest in 'civil society' in Latin America was growing at a totally different level and with rather different assumptions and aspirations. International financial and development agencies were beginning to take the concept seriously in their new policy agendas for the 1990s. In the forefront of the initiatives has been the Inter-American Development Bank (IDB), under the imaginative leadership of Enrique Iglesias. The policy proposal around 'Strengthening Civil Society' in Latin America, became part of the agenda of the IDB at the meeting of governors of the Bank in Guadalajara in April 1994. It grew partly out of the preoccupation with growing inequity and marginalization in Latin America despite the renewed economic growth in much of the region. A strategy of 'Strengthening Civil Society' was seen as being at the heart of a strategy for overcoming marginalization and poverty and a means to encourage the participation of excluded groups in the process of capitalist modernization. Enrique Iglesias himself spoke at the meeting and declared:

> The modernization of the State and the participation of civil society in the solution to social problems are complex challenges for the Institution ... Together with the need to redefine the relationship of the State with civil society, we believe that the new strategy of development which is integral, competitive and based on solidarity, requires at the same time, a programmed effort to ensure the participation of and the strengthening of civil society in bringing it about, as a basis of sustainable development and school for training responsible citizens committed to economic growth and the maintaining of democracy.[24]

Subsequently, the IDB organized a conference in Washington in September 1994 on the 'Strengthening of Civil Society' and held a regional Central American workshop in San José in November 1995 on the same theme. In the latter, Edmundo Jarquín, head of the State and Civil Society Unit of the IADB, reiterated concern for the fragility of the processes of economic and political change in Latin America. He drew attention to the connection being made by IADB policy-makers between the sustainability of the process of economic liberalization and state modernization and democratization through a strengthened civil society:

> ... the encouraging survival of a democratic panorama in the region does not conceal the weakness of the democratic institutions in terms of their effectiveness and credibility. The political, institutional and normative environment manifests fragilities and obsolescencies which limit the participation of citizens and the exercise of their rights, at the same time as it inhibits saving, investment and growth.[25]

The IDB initiative is paralleled in the discourses of other multilateral agencies, such as the United Nations Development Programme (UNDP), which is also emphasizing the importance of 'civil society', in particular of work with NGOs, in more participatory, grass-roots-oriented development strategies. Once again, there is no conceptualization offered of 'civil society' or argument about why the term should be used rather than just associations, NGOs or pressure groups. Little evidence is offered to support the claim that a stronger 'civil society' will in turn strengthen democracy, increase the effectiveness of the state and concomitantly the sustainability of the model of economic development. Along with the popular organizations and the NGOs, the use by the funding agencies of 'civil society' reflects a hope, an aspiration. It is believed that somehow traditional elites, corrupt state officials, old-style party bosses and conservative economic forces will wither if 'civil society' is stronger.

The principal aspiration of the poor and those working closely with them is ultimately for a better standard of living, a secure means to life and its reproduction and a capacity to resist/challenge the abuse of power by the state and the unregulated logic of the market. For the banks and funding agencies, it is to bring about a more effective and more equitable capitalist modernization. The problem remains, however, that economic liberalization in Latin America is simultaneously weakening those sectors of 'civil society' most in need of stronger organizational capacity, while strengthening those with a competitive advantage already, such as business and professional associations. Nor is it clear that the power of traditional elites has been sufficiently weakened to force them to accept stronger organizational capacity amongst the poor and disadvantaged. International funding agencies may, however, be able to use their financial leverage to encourage these elites to accept greater participation of, for instance, the middle class reformers in the NGOs. The capacity of the middle class to win inclusion in response to the fear of ruling elites that the alternative is to encourage an alliance between the middle class and the poor, has been an historic feature of some of the inclusionary struggles in Latin America this century.

CIVIL SOCIETY AND DEMOCRATIC CONSOLIDATION

Academics began to engage once again with 'civil society' as the focus of the literature shifted in the mid-1990s from democratic transition to democratic consolidation. Within Latin America and outside, social scientists have tried to look more critically at the concept and tease out both its potential contribution and relationship to democracy as well as some of its ambiguities.

Norberto Lechner, for instance, has tried to show why 'civil society' is not just the concern of the left in Latin America.[26] For the left it is related to a critique of the meaning of formal democracies and a 'strengthened civil society' becomes a means of ensuring the full exercise of citizenship rights. But for public choice theorists, it suggests a transference of the rational calculation of interests and preferences amongst individuals in the market place to the sphere of democracy. Strengthening 'civil society' involves individual citizens shaping a collective will in accordance with each one's rational calculation of individual interest rather than allow that will to be appropriated and defined by the state and political elites.

In a thorough conceptual exploration of the term, Ana Maria Bejarano writing in Colombia, concludes in a way reminiscent of de Tocqueville, that 'civil society' does have an important and necessary role to play in any democracy:

> In the first place, since it constitutes the source par excellence of resistance against authoritarianism, the space for the recreation of the social fabric, of the formation and socialization of citizens, in sum of the generation of a democratic culture. In the second place, since it can develop independently of the state, its own mechanisms for the peaceful and efficient management of its conflicts, instead of ignoring them or delegating all power over their resolution to state institutions.[27]

In North America, Larry Diamond has come up with a checklist of the democratic functions of 'civil society'.[28] He makes a clear statement of the relationship between 'civil society' and 'political society'. The mainstream literature was apparently moving into exploring actual problems between the two and giving content and meaning to each sphere. Diamond maintains 'civil society' must be independent of 'political society' in order to perform certain 'unique mediating and democracy-building functions'. Indeed, civil society:

> can, and typically must, play a significant role in building and consolidating democracy ... the more active, pluralist, resourceful, institutionalized, and democratic is civil society, and the more effectively it balances the tensions in its relations with the state – between autonomy and cooperation, vigilance and loyalty, skepticism and trust, assertiveness and civility – the more likely it is that democracy will emerge and endure.[29]

Diamond's contribution is important in that he offers some challenge to that influential literature on Latin America which emphasizes the institutional and procedural factors most conducive to democracy; essentially he is saying that what happens within society matters as much as whether there is a presidential or parliamentary form of government. But Diamond's article is still at a level of abstraction which cannot be totally convincing without some empirical support. Nor, once again, does he offer any conceptualization of 'civil society' which would enable us to be sure why the term is being used rather than any other term for a diverse associational life, like pluralism or interest group politics. Diamond is concerned to point out that not all 'civil society' organizations contribute to democracy building. But his understanding of the role and function of those that do recalls pluralist theory and the idea that institutionalized pressure group politics and the diffusion of power within society are a means to ensure stability and predictability in the political system.

Like the IDB, Diamond assumes there is no contradiction between economic liberalization, a strengthened 'civil society' and the goals of political and social equality. Indeed his article explores how such liberalization can be assisted and made sustainable by coalitions of modernizing and reforming groups within 'civil society'. There is more than a hint here that Diamond is as much concerned with reconciling economic change and political order in Latin America as with democracy. His emphasis on an 'institutionalized civil society' is suggestive of such an agenda. Struggles for justice and equity which might bring about 'more democracy' would be destabilizing and polarizing. Such a view is a leitmotif of the consolidation literature, as it was in the transition literature.

In a 1996 article, 'Towards Consolidated Democracy', Juan Linz and Alfred Stepan put forward six conditions for a democracy to be consolidated, amongst them are a 'free and lively civil society' and a 'relatively autonomous political society'.[30] Taking up Stepan's earlier theme of distinguishing between 'civil' and 'political society', they argue the importance of understanding the difference between the two as well as their complementarity. While a 'robust civil society' can help consolidate and deepen democracy, the authors are concerned at the tendency among its leaders to view with suspicion the compromises and 'institutional routinization' which are key to the process of consolidation and an 'indispensable practice of political society in a consolidated democracy'.[31]

These kinds of conclusion are a reflection of the limited set of problems the authors are concerned with, namely the parameters that ensure democracy works. This is understood to be when the 'complex system of institutions, rules and patterned incentives and disincentives' which constitute democracy have become 'the only game in town'.[32] The concerns are with the stability, sustainability and legitimacy of the political order. The associations of 'civil society' can positively contribute to these as long as they accept the limits of their role as well as the fact that the health of the entire order demands the aggregation and channelling of their interests by political parties. Associational life, by implication, will disrupt rather than deepen democracy if it retains the overpoliticized role which helped it bring down non-democratic governments.

When compared to Rueschemeyer *et al.*'s discussion of precisely how the struggles of class-based organizations in the twentieth century have contributed to an – as yet incomplete – pursuit of political equality in Latin America, this analysis seems unconvincingly ahistorical. These struggles have been about extending the parameters and boundaries imposed by elites on who can and cannot influence the process of decision-making. Who defines the boundaries of the 'rules of the democratic' game is not an uncontestable issue in Latin America, despite the transition to elected civilian governments; the 'procedural minimum' still reflects class, gender and ethnic exclusions and lack of representation in the real world of politics. In Colombia, the M19 guerrilla movement grew out of political exclusion by the dominant two parties. While they gave up their arms in 1990 and accepted the procedural minimum as the only 'game in town', few observers of Colombian politics would accept that the political system has been seriously opened up to free and fair contestation. The important question for political scientists is not whether compromise has brought into the democratic game a group which had rejected it, but whether or not the rules of that game have changed sufficiently to ensure fair political competitition and representation. A first step in Colombia might be the establishment of the rule of law which protected the lives of social activists and organizers from state police and security forces and paramilitary groups.[33]

The Stepan/Linz analysis has accepted that 'civil society' has something to contribute to the health of democracy, but only if it abides by the necessary rules. There is something which borders on the functionalist about this approach to democracy and 'civil society'. It is a view which takes no account of the fact that 'political society' in Latin America has hitherto felt no obligation to nurture and encourage an independent 'civil society' able to hold it and the state accountable. If the problem is defined as one of order, stability and legitimacy, it is a truism to say that democracy is about the compromises and procedures that make that possible. If the problem is defined as the achievement of greater political equality and mechanisms of redress when formal rules and rights are flouted in the practice of politics – as is still true for much of Latin America – the emphasis is on the dynamics of associational and political life and whether or not they contribute to further democratization. The former approach offers only a limited research agenda, the latter, it is argued here, opens up a richer and more important research agenda.

Lawrence Whitehead takes the discussion forward in a more helpful way. He problematizes the relationship between 'civil society' and democracy and critically dissects the many voluntaristic and unsustainable assumptions in the literature.[34] He points to the geographical and social unevenness of associational life, the inequalities within civil society that make it possible for a dense associational life to exist at one end of the class spectrum and not at the other. He also points to the threat from the 'uncivil' elements which are rife and powerful in many of the new democracies in particular, where they are often ignored by those who reify rather than analyse the concept of 'civil society'. Well-organized crime is one such uncivil element, which cannot be ignored in much of Latin America today (not to mention Eastern Europe, the former Soviet Union and elsewhere).

Whitehead raises some very important issues; but the thrust of his critique is really against that unreflective, voluntaristic and reifying literature. Any conceptualization of 'civil society' which cannot take on board Whitehead's critique is evidently partial and unhelpful. The particular problem is when 'civil society' is conceptualized normatively and teleologically, as an essentially 'good thing' which can only include pro-democratic and 'civil' associations, and this is then confused with empirical and observable reality. It is possible, however, to treat 'civil society' as a conceptual tool, which may indeed contain normative assumptions about the desirablity of an associational life which is pro-democratic and civilizing, but which does not assume that this is empirically necessarily the case. Such an approach can incorporate Whitehead's critique. 'Civil society' can then be seen as an arena of contestation, a space which reflects the social divisions of society as a whole. To what extent the 'civil' or democratizing groups gain strength *vis-à-vis* opposing forces, is part of the dynamics of history, to be researched and explained, not assumed.

There is another literature which has begun to emerge in the mid-1990s and has attempted to move beyond the level of abstraction and generality in much current usage. It has sought ways of exploring empirically the extent to which associational life in any given context is able to impact on political structures.

Some examples of this literature are Stephen Ellner's study of neighbourhood associations in urban Venezuela, Jonathon Fox's work on rural Mexico and Anthony Pereira on the north-east of Brazil.[35] Ellner is interested in the political shifts that have taken place in Venezuela since the late 1970s when 'civil society was still very weak'. He concludes that the neighbourhood associations which have grown up since then have forced changes on both political parties and the state. Important services have been transferred to municipal government and party machines have been challenged. An obstacle to further changes was the ongoing tension between the autonomous organizational capacity of the associations and the efforts of political parties to control and influence them. He shows that associations in the wealthier districts achieved greater autonomy than those in the poorer districts, where the conditions of daily life are so much more difficult and a 'quick fix' through a party contact becomes a more attractive option. The ability of middle-class associations to access the media enables them to present themselves nationally as *the* neighbourhood movement, and its aspiration to be free of party control becomes *the* concern of that movement. In reality however, they are far outnumbered by the associations of the poor districts which operate in a very different way and under very different constraints.

Jonathon Fox is concerned to look beyond some of the procedural terms in which democracy is measured and to 'develop a framework for explaining progress toward *another* necessary condition for democratization: respect for associational autonomy … interests and identities without fear of external intervention or punishment'.[36] His analysis is particularly pertinent for countries such as Mexico, Brazil and Colombia where formally democratic national electoral systems coexist with clientelism, local authoritarian enclaves and corrupt political machines. Fox asks how in these circumstances do regimes come to accept the *right* of citizens to pursue their goals autonomously? He argues that this happens in the course of repeated cycles of conflict between autonomous social movements, authoritarian elites attempting to hang on to power and reformist state managers. Over time, these cycles gradually increase official acceptance of autonomous organization. Authoritarian elites split over the use of coercion or concessions and reformists manage to challenge the hardliners. This encourages a shift to reliance on semi-clientelist mechanisms while at the same time social movements gradually occupy and widen the fissures that open up. New 'enclaves of pluralist tolerance' open up alongside 'semi-clientelism', along a continuum of authoritarian-clientelist combinations. These grow, as organizations of 'civil society' broaden and deepen their roots.

Fox explores these ideas in relationship to rural development reform in Mexico. He shows how in the case of the Mexican Regional Solidarity Funds, two decades of 'ebb and flow of protest and mobilization' had enabled some of the weakest sectors of Mexican society – organized indigenous small-holders – to gain both autonomy from entrenched regional political and economic elites and access to resources.

Anthony Pereira's study of the sugar-growing region of the Brazilian north east, explores how the weakness of civil society in this impoverished region of Brazil impacts upon the possibilities of democratization. Not only is associational life weak here, characterized mostly by the struggles of the rural workers unions, but state institutions are also unable or unwilling to enforce legal equality and the right of free assocation. This is because of the highly concentrated nature of landownership in this mono-crop region and the political power which goes with it. Despite the formal end to military rule in Brazil in 1985 and Brazil's reputation for a strong 'civil society', the situation in the agrarian north-east is very different to that of the industrialized south east of the country. Here the weakness of 'civil society' has meant that the return to electoral democracy has been characterized by an imbalance between civil and political society. The electoral arena dominates and voluntary associations are used a vehicles for politicians and parties. This has serious implications for the ability of the rural poor to improve their lives in the region. Pereira concludes that strengthening the state is as important as strengthening 'civil society' in the region as a counterweight to the overwhelming power of the landed class.

The character of 'civil society' in particular socio-economic contexts is thus an important research question if its contribution to democratization is to be seriously assessed. Pereira's study suggests that in some poor regions of Latin America and despite democratic transitions on the continent as a whole, the weakness of civil society and the weakness of state institutions act to preclude the extension of full citizenship rights to the majority of the population.

These three examples of attempts to explore what difference 'civil society' might make to democratization processes are an important advance in the literature. They are not just concerned with the procedures, rules and institutions of democracy, nor with the contribution of 'political' and 'civil society' to these. They are also concerned with precisely how democracy can be made meaningful for poor and marginalized sectors of the population (a significant majority of most Latin American countries), how there can be 'more democracy', and whether the relationship between 'political' and 'civil society' facilitates or blocks the extension and broadening of democratic practices.

In the second part of this article a case study of Chile similarly uses 'civil society' to explore the process of democratization. First, however, the term 'democratization' will be briefly analysed in order to clarify its usage in the case study. 'Civil society' offers a rich set of research questions and a means of opening up the discussion on the prospects for democracy. It enables us to explore the everyday dynamics of democratization in one of Latin America's most successful market economies and the specific contribution of associational life to reconciling the many tensions between political and economic liberalization in the region.

'CIVIL SOCIETY', DEMOCRACY AND THE MARKET: THE CASE OF CHILE

There is a big difference between those who see democracy in terms of Dahl's polyarchy with its attempt to marry vision and 'feasibility', and those who see democracy as truly the rule of the people. For the former, we have seen that 'civil society' is considered important to sustaining a democracy built on compromise, bargains and elite pacts. For the latter, the associationalism of 'civil society' is a mechanism of politicization and empowerment of those excluded through class, gender and ethnic inequalities from any direct influence over political decision-making. The literature on social movements has evidently been sobered by the events of the 1980s, when many of the movements that had erupted so strongly against dictatorship, failed to find a place in the new democratic order and subsequently collapsed in demoralization. 'The politics of emancipation' wrote David Slater in 1994, 'is a far more complex and perilous project than was often initially supposed'.[37] Yet, behind the popular left discourses of civil society, the hope persists that the associationalism and activism of Latin America's grass-roots may still constitute the embryo of an alternative, both to the dominant economic model and also to the persistent elitism and exclusions of the liberal democratic model.

Are we simply stuck between, in John Dunn's words, 'the two distinct and developed democratic theories loose in the world today – one dismally ideological and the other fairly blatantly utopian'?[38] The former appeals to the realists, as a practical and workable form of government, ensuring some accountability of the governors to the governed; the latter inspires but ultimately demobilizes today, given the post-communist collapse of the socialist ideal and uncertainty about what a transformatory project might look like.

David Beetham offers a third approach, however, which, while it does not reconcile these irreconcilable approaches, at least puts forward a view of democracy as something which can be improved through the actions and interactions of the associations of a 'civil society' which is neither 'overpoliticized' nor 'depoliticized'. He takes the core and fundamentally uncontested elements of the concept of democracy, namely political equality and popular control, and suggests there is a spectrum along which most democracies can be placed in accordance with their degree of both.[39] Democracy here is not the 'end state' of the procedural minimum as it is in much of the literature on democratic transition and consolidation. It is a process which can only become meaningful to the majority of the population if they feel they can access its institutions, redress the abuse of rights, ensure the rule of law, influence decision-making and ensure that it does not just serve the needs of an educated and wealthy elite.

These objectives have not yet been met by the transitions in Latin America. Some 'transitologists' have begun to accept that the transitions in Latin America have not reproduced the 'Northwestern' model of liberal democracy in the way that was initially hoped. While accepting the Dahlian democratic model, Guillermo O'Donnell has challenged some of the assumptions of the transition literature and its consolidationist successors. He has acknowledged that the former had 'little predictive power' and that the transitions have given rise to hybrid political orders, such as 'delegative democracies'.[40] His more recent article, 'Illusions about Consolidation', points to the way particularisms have continued to exist in 'uneasy tension with the formal rules and institutions'.[41]

These particularisms include time-honoured political practices, many of them built upon the exclusionary dynamics of urban and rural poverty, such as clientelism. But there is reluctance to accept that the collectivist rather than liberal-individualist impetus within society might be the mechanism to challenge these. During the momentum of the transition, only Cardoso saw the potential of this impetus in terms of 'the emergence of a will to renewal on the part of civil society which rejects the notion that the "political opening" remains at the level of a *re*-democratization, based on liberal-individualist principles which in the past safeguarded social injustice, class inequality, and traditional bourgeois domination'.[42]

Even without recourse to theories of 'civil society' and their search for the new subjectivities for progressive change, it is possible to identify a collectivist impetus amongst those unsuccessful in the market place. Associationalism has a new legitimacy in Latin America, given its links with individuals and markets. Even in countries which have never known free and public debate and where associational rights and freedoms have been severely restricted, Latin American governments find it difficult today to deny the universalism implicit in liberal discourse. International financial agencies and Northern donors have even made human rights an issue of aid conditionality.

There is a today an opportunity to develop a universally accessible 'public sphere' in most Latin American countries, a sphere of discursive and social interaction which could provide a firmer base for extending the democratization process than at any point in the past.[43] Latin America's socially and economically marginalised populations, could *potentially* make use of this 'public sphere' to transform the white, male and elitist domination of politics, just as workers, women and black peoples did in the struggles to democratize the liberal state in Western Europe. Whether they are able to do so, however, depends on many contingent factors.

Neoliberalism has evidently strengthened some socio-economic groups over others. Popular/social movements have not been able to respond very rapidly to the new circumstances. The collapse of mobilizing and unifying ideals has left a demoralizing vacuum for many. They have been badly weakened in some countries by the continued dominance of political parties and their unwillingness to accept the value of an autonomous but not depoliticized civil society. In other countries, the weakness or collapse of political parties has resulted in a fragmented associational life, which has no means of articulating its concerns before the state. The impact of neoliberalism and the uneven access to market power, has debilitated many sectors of the population confronted with a relentless struggle for survival in a region of the world notable for its extreme inequality in wealth distribution.

The case of Chile illustrates these difficulties in extending and deepening the impact of democratization where 'civil society' remains ill-balanced between the social sectors and genders, where party machines have historically dominated social as well as political organizations and associations and where a flourishing market economy is raising living standards but differentially across the social spectrum. Despite its tradition of contestatory civilian politics prior to the Pinochet dictatorship – one which should have advantaged the democratization process compared to other Latin American countries – the elitism of Chilean political life remains unchallenged even today. The process of democratization has been compromised as a result.

The initial years of the return to civilian rule led to an optimistic, congratulatory literature which emphasized the importance of the 'textbook' elite-negotiated transition, a result of a compromise between military and civilian elites which ensured a stable return to democratically elected civilian government. However, in the wake of the second democratic transfer of power in 1993, questions began to be asked about the Chilean transition and the nature of the democracy emerging from it..

Fieldwork in Chile during the first years of the democratic transition suggested two parallel phenomena. On the one hand there was evidence of a shift in the state–private sector relationship. While the latter maintained close relations with government through its strong associations, the relationship was based on a new understanding of the specific competence of each.[44] State-centred economic development and a private sector oriented to favours and patronage from the state, were gone. In their place have emerged a reduced but effective state sector which does not assume economic agency, and strong entrepreneurial associations reflecting a dynamic private sector able to articulate its interests within the democratic order.

On the other hand, other sectors of society have seen their capacity to influence government weakened. Many non-governmental organizations which played a role during the Pinochet years in facilitating and supporting anti-authoritarian social movements, joined the elected centre-left government in 1990 and allowed themselves to be absorbed into the agenda of the state. Those NGOs that did not wish to accept such a relationship with the state found themselves marginalized and under-resourced. This removed an important catalyst and support for grass-roots movements.

But the latter have also been weakened by the re-establishment of political parties into their dominant position in Chilean political life. Many of the left-wing activists of these parties, influenced by exile in Europe, look to West European social democratic models of party organization. They are little concerned with the need for roots in 'civil society' and the mobilization of people by committed party activists. They now seek to make direct appeals to the electorate, through their leaders and the media. Associational life is not valued as an autonomous arena which enables people through their social interaction and discursive engagement to develop opinions and capacities to hold elected representatives accountable. It is the means to secure votes and a potential instrument of party influence if not control. Such an approach builds on time-honoured traditions of Chilean politics, where the instrumentalization of associational life by party elites has been a noteworthy feature.

The gap between a strong 'political' society and a weak 'civil society' has grown in the years of democratic transition in Chile, except where wealth and power give access to resources and some measure of autonomy can be asserted. Chilean 'transitologists' who have hitherto looked rather uncritically at the Chilean democratic transition have begun to explore the implications of this gap. Manuel Antonio Garreton, for example, has noted:

> True there is freedom, and social indicators are improving, but social actors are extremely weak, whether older ones like unions and peasant movements, or newer ones like local environmental or youth movements. The only actors with an important presence are business and some professional organizations. Because the centre-left *concertación* has been so successful in administering the government, some emerging conflicts and actors in society have found it hard to find political channels of expression. For example, old social actors like national unions no longer feel fully represented by the political parties to which their leaders belong, and newer issues regarding the environment, local and regional interests, poverty and modernization seem unable to find organized social or political actors to express and represent them.[45]

Opinion polls show that political parties remain the prime articulators of political opinions, but they 'no longer serve as the unique expressions of social aspirations and programs'.[46] The tendency of the 'modernizers' in the political system to ignore the 'social arena' may enable autonomous leaderships to emerge over time. It is also possible that the process of decentralization and municipalization will open up new local public spaces for a more diverse range of social actors and their associations. But there is always the danger that as social organizations gain strength, the parties will make efforts to control and co-opt them.

The fate of the women's movement in Chile and its efforts to penetrate the male-dominated sphere of politics, is indicative of the problems facing Chilean democratization. Women remain very under-represented in government and legislature, while the Women's Ministry, SERNAM, has implemented a very limited agenda in terms of extending women's rights. This contrasts with the hopes that emerged in the 1980s when grass-roots and middle-class women played a protagonistic role in the struggles against the Pinochet dictatorhsip. Such movements failed to sustain an agenda to influence elected civilian government while some women put party interests before gender ones. Many observers have noted the disarticulation of the grass-roots women's movements, with arguably only a handful of project-oriented women's NGOs continuing to keep the feminist agenda alive. Ann Matear has concluded, for instance:

> Women's voices in all their diversity are missing from a wide range of political debates, not only on gender issues. Compared to the levels of female mobilization during the military regime, the circle has narrowed considerably leaving working class women and the popular organizations on the periphery of the political debate.[47]

⁹ Another factor that has weakened the building of a stronger, more representative 'civil society' in Chile has been the impact of the free market. An individualist and consumerist culture is being fostered in a society where a good third of the population still lack many basic amenities, and a good percentage of the rest operate in a flexible, insecure labour market with few rights and little labour protection. Alienation and disenchantment with democracy are evident in the shanty towns of Santiago. Public opinion polls indicate a declining interest in politics in a country renowned in Latin America for its former levels of political mobilization. But a leading member of the *Concertación* government told the author in an interview in 1991 that this was a strategic objective of the centre-left in Chile: to create a society in which people looked upon politics like they look upon their football team. In other words, they go to the match every Sunday but take no interest during the week.

The Chilean political elite believe that a depoliticized, disarticulated population is more likely to guarantee democracy than the highly mobilized population of the pre-Pinochet period. The political elite has created a flourishing economy offering seductive visions of a developed consumerist life-style, a depoliticized citizenry willing to entrust their interests to them and a political right with a guaranteed stake in the political order. But it might equally be argued that the further atomization of society under the impact of market liberalization coupled with a weak autonomous associational life debilitates rather than strengthens democracy.

In his study of the 1993 elections, Gerardo Munck concluded that the political right is still a problem for Chilean democracy.[48] Demobilization and apathy amongst a population which at one point felt there was something at stake from its engagement in politics, has deprived Chile of a potential force to check the power of the right and rid Chile of the authoritarian enclaves which limit its democracy. An atomized, politically disinterested society with no mechanisms for formulating opinions outside those handed down by media and politicians does not create the means to make the state accountable. It will not ensure full respect for civil, political and human rights in a country where these were suspended for so long and so recently. The power of the armed forces in Chile today, and their capacity to operate above and beyond the law, are a reminder to the poorest in Chilean society of what happened when they organized in support of an alternative, egalitarian vision of society. International human rights organizations continue to express concern about the impunity enjoyed by perpetrators of past abuses and the persistence of cases of torture and ill-treatment by security forces of the state, although by no means on the scale of the past.[49]

Also it is feasible that the Chilean right will find a ripe terrain of alienation and frustration amongst the excluded individuals on the periphery of the economic success story. Their ability to tap into that frustration will derive from the weakening of the associational life amongst the poor, of that social solidarity promoted first in the 1960s by the Christian Democrats, subsequently by the left and sustained under the dictatorship, thanks to Church protection. It was from here that the first steps against Pinochet were taken in the street protests of the 1980s. In other words, the first bid to defend the notion of civilian government and democratic rights came not from the political elite, but from the poor, whose self-organization and collective solidarity had grown in the midst of state repression and in the absence of political parties.

The weakness of civil society in Chile on the one hand, therefore, limits the potential for deepening democracy in the country and extending its reach to excluded social groups, such as women and the urban poor. On the other, it limits the impetus to assert the full rule of law and civilian authority over the military and the civilian right. This in turn impedes the emergence of a 'denser' and more vibrant civil society. The Chilean case illustrates that a focus on associational life poses questions that would not be raised if Chilean democracy was seen through the lens of its political institutions and elites only.

CONCLUSION

The concept of 'civil society' remains a useful and relevant tool for analyzing democratization processes in Latin America, despite the multiplicity of meanings invested in it in the literature. For some its usefulness lies in its historic roots in the rise of the market economy and liberalism in Western Europe. As such it holds the promise of a network of self-regulating and mutually restraining associations that can guarantee the freedom to pursue private interests. Such an ideal, it is thought, might transform Latin America's political culture and poor economic performance.

But, just as liberalism could never remain the exclusive ideology of the bourgeoisie, so the concept of 'civil society' has meaning also for social organization amongst the excluded and marginalized of a region where inequitable wealth distribution is acknowledged to be amongst the most extreme in the world today. It legitimizes their efforts to access the new or revived democratic structures at national and local level, to make party machines accountable, and to emphasize 'civility' in political life for a region more accustomed to the barrel of a gun.

For scholars interested in the process and progress of Latin American democratization, the concept of 'civil society' encourages us to ask what difference a more diverse associational life can in fact make to the development of a rights-based state in the region. We can explore the *extent* to which the inequalities of the market place can be reconciled with the political equality premised in the concept of 'democracy', and whether associational life can contribute to such a reconciliation by re-shaping the political arena in ways that make it accountable to and representative of wider social groups.

On the periphery of capitalism, the problems inherent in such a reconciliation are even more complex than elsewhere. Much of the transition and consolidation literature is essentially an acknowledgement of the fragility of such a project. How to institutionalize social organization and encourage groups with opposed interests to accept the compromises which limit but stabilize democratic politics is one of its central preoccupations.

But those who aim simply to end the 'pendulum' at the point where elected civilian government is no longer challenged, cannot ignore the politics 'from below' which reflect the lived experience of those still excluded from the core sources of social, economic and political power. Fernando Henrique Cardoso has drawn our attention to the possibility that Latin America's collectivist impulse might inject a more egalitarian and socially responsible ethic into Latin America's political processes. How far Latin American civilian and military elites will accept a renewed growth of associationalism amongst the socially and economically excluded remains to be seen; its historical record is very poor and much may depend on whether economic growth can outstrip the pace of demands for equity. The real test for the processes of democratization in Latin America has not yet taken place.

NOTES

1. Robert A. Pastor (ed.), *Democracy in the Americas: Stopping the Pendulum* (New York: Holmes & Meier,1989).
2. See, for example: J. Cohen and A. Arato, *Civil Society and Political Theory* (Cambridge, MA: Massachusetts Institute of Technology, 1992); E. Gellner, *Conditions of Liberty, Civil Society and its Rivals* (London: Hamish Hamilton, 1994); K. Kumar, 'Civil Society: An Inquiry into the Usefulness of an Historical Term', *British Journal of Sociology*, Vol.35, No.1 (1993), pp.1–41. More modestly, I have undertaken my own ground-clearing exercise in J. Pearce, 'How Useful is "Civil Society" to the Conceptualisation of Democratisation Processes? With Reference to Latin America', in Lee-Anne Broadhead (ed.), *Issues in Peace Research*, 1995–96, (Bradford: Department of Peace Studies, University of Bradford, 1996), pp. 137–65.
3. R. Fine, 'Civil Society Theory, Enlightenment and Critique', *Democratization*, Vol.4, No.1 (1997) (Special Issue), pp.7–28.
4. M. Ignatieff, 'On Civil Society', *Foreign Affairs*, March/April 1995, p.129.
5. For a good review of this literature, see G. Munck, 'Democratic Transitions in Comparative Perspective', *Comparative Politics*, Vol 26, No. 3 (1994), pp. 355–75.
6. Robert Dahl, *Democracy and Its Critics* (New Haven, CT and London:Yale University Press, 1989), p.222. This is Dahl's most recent contribution, although the concept of 'polyarchy' dates from much earlier writings. In this book, Dahl identifies seven institutions necessary to the 'highest feasible form of government': elected officials, free and fair elections, inclusive suffrage, right to run for office, freedom of expression, alternative information, associational autonomy. Ibid, p.221.
7. Marcello Cavarozzi, 'Beyond Transitions to Democracy in Latin America', *Journal of Latin American Studies*, Vol.24 (1992), pp.665–84.
8. Fernando Henrique Cardoso, 'Associated-Dependent Development and Democratic Theory', in A. Stepan (ed.), *Democratizing Brazil* (New York and Oxford: Oxford University Press, 1989), p.319.
9. Guillermo O'Donnell and Philippe Schmitter, *Transitions from Authoritarian Rule:Tentative Conclusions about Uncertain Democracies* (Baltimore, MD: John Hopkins University Press, 1986).
10. Alfred Stepan, *Rethinking Military Politics, Brazil and the Southern Cone* (Princeton, NJ: Princeton University Press,1988), p.4.
11. Cohen and Arato, *Civil Society … .*
12. Ibid., Ch.1, pp.48–58.
13. Ibid., p.56.
14. Ibid., p.80.
15. Ibid., p.80.
16. David Slater, 'Power and Social Movements in the Other Occident:Latin America in an International Context', paper presented at the CEDLA/CERLAC joint workshop, 13–15 Nov., 1991, Amsterdam, mimeo.
17. F. Weffort, 'Why Democracy?', in Stepan (ed.), *Democratizing Brazil*, pp.327–50.
18. C. Castañeda, *Utopia Unarmed* (New York: Vintage Books, 1994), p.200.
19. Alain Touraine, *Actores Sociales y Sistemas Politicas en America Latina* (Santiago: PREALC, 1987), p.13.
20. Cardoso, 'Associated-Dependent Development', p.323.
21. Ibid., p.324.
22. D. Rueschemeyer, J. Stephens and E. Huber, *Capitalist Development and Democracy* (Cambridge: Polity Press, 1992), p.6.
23. P. Oxhorn, 'Controlled Inclusion to Coerced Marginalisation', in John A. Hall (ed.), *Civil Society, Theory History Comparison* (Cambridge: Polity Press, 1994), pp.250–73.
24. 'Exposicion del señor Enrique V. Iglesias, Presidente del Banco Interamericano de Desarrollo y del Directorio de la Corporación Interamericana de Inversiones, en la Sesion Inaugural de la Reunión Anual de las Asambleas de Gobernadores', Guadalajara, Mexico, 11 April 1994, mimeo.

25. Jarquin, E. 'El BID, La Modernizacion del Estado y el Fortalecimiento de la Sociedad Civil', Exposicion en la Conferencia sobre el Fortalecimiento de la Sociedad Civil en Centroamerica y Republica Dominicana, San Jose, Costa Rica, 27–29 Nov. 1995, mimeo.
26. Norberto Lechner, 'La Problematica Invocacion de La Sociedad Civil', *Revista Foro*, Bogota, Colombia, No. 28, (1996), pp.24–33.
27. Ana Maria Bejarano, 'Para Repensar las Relaciones Estado, Sociedad Civil y Regimen Politico. Una Nueva Mirada Conceptual', *Controversia*, Bogota, Colombia, No.167, Oct.–Nov. 1995, p.30.
28. L. Diamond, 'Toward Democratic Consolidation', *Journal of Democracy*, Vol.5, No.3 (1994), pp.4–17.
29. Ibid, p.16
30. Juan Linz and Alfred Stepan, 'Towards Consolidated Democracy', *Journal of Democracy*, Vol.7, No.2 (1996), p.17.
31. Ibid., p.17.
32. Ibid., p.15.
33. J. Pearce, *Colombia: Inside the Labyrinth* (London: Latin America Bureau, 1990). The tendency in the mainstream literature to see Colombia as a problem of 'order' rather than a problem of 'democracy and democratization', has meant that thousands of people have been killed over the last decades without this being viewed as a problem originating in the very heart of the Colombian political system.
34. Lawrence Whitehead, 'Bowling in the Bronx: The Uncivil Interstices between Civil and Political Society', *Democratization*, Vol.4, No.1 (1997) (Special Issue), pp.94–114.
35. Stephen Ellner, 'The Deepening of Democracy in a Crisis Setting: Political Reform and the Electoral Process in Venezuela', *Journal of Interamerican Studies and World Affairs*, Vol.35, No.1, pp.1–41; Jonathon Fox, 'From Clientelism to Citizenship: Lesson from Mexico', *World Politics*, Vol.46 (1994), pp.151–84; Anthony Pereira, 'Economic Underdevelopment, Democracy and Civil Society: The North-East Brazilian Case', *Third World Quarterly*, Vol.14, No.2 (1993), pp.365–80.
36. J. Fox (1994), op. cit., pp.151–2.
37. David Slater, 'Introduction: Social Movements and Political Change in Latin America', *Latin American Perspectives*, Vol.21, No. 2 (1994), p.6.
38. John Dunn, quoted in Susan Mendus, 'Losing the Faith, Feminism and Democracy', in John Dunn (ed.), *Democracy, the Unfinished Journey, 508 BC to AD 1993* (Oxford: Oxford University Press, 1992), p.208.
39. David Beetham, 'Key Principles and Indices for a Democratic Audit', in David Beetham (ed.), *Defining and Measuring Democracy* (London: Sage Publications, 1994).
40. Guillermo O'Donnell, 'On the State, Democratisation and Some Conceptual Problems: A Latin American View with Glances at Some Postcommunist Countries', *World Development*, Vol.21, No.8 (1993), pp.1355–69.
41. Guillermo O'Donnell, 'Illusions about Consolidation', *Journal of Democracy*, Vol.7, No 2 (1996), pp. 34–51.
42. Cardoso 'Associated-Dependent Development', p.323.
43. For a discussion of the emergence of the 'Public Sphere' in Western Europe, see J. Habermas, *The Structural Transformation of the Public Sphere*, (Cambridge: Polity Press, 1989).
44. This is discussed in detail in J. Pearce, 'Democracy and Development in a Divided Society', in A. Leftwich (ed.), *Democracy and Development* (Cambridge: Polity Press, 1996).
45. Manuel Antonio Garreton, 'Redemocratisation in Chile', *Journal of Democracy*, Vol.1 (1995), p.153.
46. Ibid., p.156.
47. A. Matear, 'Desde la protesta a la propuesta: Gender Politics in Transition in Chile', *Democratization*, Vol.3, No.3 (1996), p.262.
48. Gerardo Munck, 'Democratic Stability and its Limits: An Analysis of Chile's 1993 elections', *Journal of Inter-American Studies*, Vol.36, No.2 (1994), pp.1–38.
49. See, for example, the report to the UN Human Rights Commission, of the *Relator Especial a Chile*, 4 Jan. 1996, mimeo.

Civil Society, the State and Democracy in Africa

NELSON KASFIR

The importance of new civil society organizations for creating and maintaining democracy in Africa has been greatly overstated. Scholars and donors holding the conventional view claim that new autonomous, interest-specific and rule-respecting associations can liberalize authoritarian states and sustain democratic governance. But they idealize the Western practices from which they borrow and overlook the defects in the outdated pluralist argument they urge on Africa, particularly its inequalities of access, difficulties in responding to problems of collective action and lack of local finance. However, because of the paradoxical position of the state in civil society, the problem of creating civil society organizations that are powerful enough to force the state into democratic reform might also weaken it severely. Excluding aggressive organizations, such as ethnic or religious associations, on the ground that they are uncivic is myopic. If associations that are both strong and democratically oriented are created, they would challenge the capacity of state institutions to reconcile interests. A broader strategy of governance that takes into account both building civil society and assisting political institutions is more likely to contribute to democracy.

How robust is the relationship between civil society and democracy in Africa? Conventional proponents of civil society, both academics and donors, claim that strengthening civil society promotes democracy. They argue that civil society actors, particularly newly formed organizations, initiated the recent wave of democratic reforms and are participating significantly in their consolidation. One writer concludes that 'civil society has played a crucial role in building pressure for democratic transition and pushing it through to completion'.[1] Another suggests that 'the nature and strength of Africa's fledgling civil societies will also help to determine the prospects for democratic consolidation'.[2] Donors often take a stronger position. At the outer limit, civil society is claimed to be a necessary condition for democracy. One of USAID's 'Guidelines for Strategic Plans' states that 'vibrant civil society is an essential component of a democratic polity'.[3] Both writers and donors seem to agree that 'the road to a democratic and just order must pass through the coalescence of civil society'.[4]

What kind of civil society and what kind of democracy do proponents have in mind when they argue that the two are causally related and that civil society is the independent variable? They insist on what amounts to a new civil society, consisting primarily not of the organizations that represent the interests of existing social groups, but of non-state organizations that promote new relationships between state and society. For example, 'to be considered part of civil society an organization must simultaneously contain state power and legitimate state authority (civil rights groups provide one obvious example)'.[5] How realistic for contemporary situations in Africa are the assumptions they make about the operation of a democracy populated and secured by vigorous new civil associations?

The short answer is that their premises are not especially realistic, nor particularly robust – which is *not* to suggest there is no relationship at all. Africa has long been rich in associational life but poor in democracy. Those who see democratic potential coming from civil society insist that a different sort of association is needed. Donors have lavished much effort and finance during the 1990s to organize new civil associations with explicit objectives to protect democratic advances already gained and to campaign aggressively for more.

But less than a decade after the initiation of democratization in Africa, there is much less confidence that African states are becoming democracies.[6] With few exceptions, those states that initiated transitions, and even those that replaced their rulers by election, have entered an uncertain limbo in which their regimes reflect a contradictory combination of characteristics of democracy, authoritarianism and inherited practices of neopatrimonialism. To a significant extent, this unwieldy combination results from well-known factors – weakly institutionalized states, a political economy greatly dependent on patronage and ethnically mobilized societies, particularly where democratic competition has been re-introduced. Though it may be too soon to tell, lowered expectations for the consolidation, or even the continuation, of democracy call for a closer examination of what sort of linkage can exist between either newly created civil associations or the older 'front-line' organizations, such as the churches, and the consolidation of democracy.

Both sides of this linkage bear examination, not just the impact of organizations on the effectiveness of democracy. The kind of democracy that is created will surely influence which organizations form and flourish. This effect is masked by the ubiquity of liberal democratic doctrine. Current efforts to create democracy all over the world are equated with multi-party liberal democracy as practised either in the USA or in Europe.[7] For USAID 'there is little mystery about the model of democracy upon which the basic strategy of democracy assistance is based. It is what might be called the conventional western model of liberal democracy, or … in some ways a quite US-specific blueprint'.[8] Once this equation has been made, the anticipated function that civil society organizations should serve seems to follow logically: thus, 'the growth of social associations constitutes the organizational foundation for multiparty politics'.[9]

But there are other ways to organize democracy. The multi-party liberal version is only one of many shapes that democracy can assume.[10] Participatory democracy is the classic alternative. In place of the emphasis on leadership, and thus elites, in the competitive multi-party approach, the driving force in participatory democracy is control by the masses from below.[11] Each alternative presents different opportunities, as well as costs, for African countries.[12] These differences are likely to result in significant variations in the composition of civil society. Since elite democracy typically favours the wealthy, it advantages the organizations they form. Participatory democracy, on the other hand, is often expressed through popular councils, which can benefit poor and marginalized groups with few resources for creating independent organizations to express their interests. As significant as this difference in the type of democracy appears to be for civil society, most recent writers are far more interested in whether civil society helps achieve democracy. Thus, the rest of this discussion will focus on the plausibility of explanations of democracy that take civil society as the independent variable.

If new objectives or new organizations are necessary before civil society can strengthen democracy, then there are two ways to examine their relationship. One approach is to examine the ideas and strategies through which scholars and donors propose that changes in civil society will contribute to democracy. How are the new organizations supposed to promote democracy? The other is to consider the consequences for politics of introducing and strengthening civil associations. How will the political order respond to more effective civil society actors? For both topics, we need to keep firmly in mind the social conditions that regularly produced past African authoritarian regimes. It would be difficult to argue that the underlying structures of African society have changed dramatically in the few years since the new democratic initiative began in 1989.

The better claim may be that civil society will reflect both divisions in the larger society and the needs and demands of state actors. If that is so, civil society organizations will have limited capacity to cause authoritarian states to become more democratic. Deeply divided societies have great difficulty in uniting over rules that permit democratic changes in governments as well as continuing protection for rights of free communication and association. Patronage-based political economies produce incentives for civil society actors to organize platforms for gaining power rather than creating reform. Habituated by many years of extensive interference, and little effective capacity to implement policies, state officials both threaten and infiltrate organizations in order to deflect initiatives for reform.

The difficulty is not that proponents of a leading role for civil society hope that African countries will adopt democratic reforms. Instead, the problem lies in the restricted notion of civil society which they adopt and the mechanism they imagine will carry forward these desirable changes. Using a normative concept of civil society to analyse African politics is likely to obscure more than it clarifies. Non-state organizational actors in African civil society may be capable of no more than modest, tentative and often reversible contributions to democratization. Assessing whether these actors strengthen democracy requires a notion of civil society which evaluates what is happening, not what ought to happen.

IDEAS AND STRATEGIES OF SCHOLARS AND DONORS

While there is much dispute over the different meanings of civil society, particularly in the philosophic literature, there seems to be relatively broad agreement about the constituent elements in the conventional notion of civil society in discussions of democratization in low income countries. In general, donors and scholars think of civil society as non-state associational activity acting on the basis of certain normative criteria. In a carefully elaborated definition of civil society, Philippe Schmitter specifies the significant characteristics held by most users of this notion. They are 'the set' of 'self-organized intermediary groups' characterised by (1) autonomy from both social interests and state, (2) capacity for collective action promoting interests or passions, (3) absence of an intention to govern the polity, and (4) agreement to act within civil rules 'conveying mutual respect'.[13]

Thus, civil society incorporates organizations whose formal rules insulate them from demands from above and below. These organizations can act independently of state actors as well as their constituents. They form for specific, preferably narrow, purposes that do not include seeking state power.[14] They follow a code of conduct that contemplates listening to opponents, pursuing political compromise and engaging in transparent behaviour. In short, they accept the rules they attempt to force on the state. This schematic should be qualified by recognizing that different stages of political transition may impose different requirements on civil society actors.[15] Nevertheless, the point of this concept of civil society is to create a political system that will help to sustain democracy after it has been conceded by a formerly reluctant authoritarian state. So, the ultimate objective is to adapt or create civil associations that are willing to work within the system rather than shape organizations intending to do combat with the state.[16]

It is striking how little of African politics this concept of civil society captures. Much associational life and all unorganized protest or demands must occur outside civil society. Direct participation by ethnic or religious social forces, however momentous for political decisions, is not part of civil society.[17] Neopatrimonial relations to the state, that is the transactions through which loyalty is exchanged for material reward, are also excluded from civil society. Each of these factors – lack of organized protest, sectarian identities and the importance of state patronage – significantly shapes contemporary African politics. Given the overwhelming political importance of all three, it seems reasonable to suppose that the proportion of political issues presently settled through civil society interactions in contemporary African polities will be small, particularly in comparison with the role played by civil society in high income Western democracies. In this sense, civil society is an artefact pointing to the future of African politics, not to its present.

Thus, considerable reform will be essential if civil society is to become the basis for conducting democratic politics in Africa, an outcome proponents of the conventional notion consider highly desirable. For example, building directly from his definition, Schmitter infers that 'the more these efforts [interactions between the state and individuals, firms and clans] are channeled through intermediary organisations, the greater is the degree of civil society and, by implication, the easier it will be, *ceteris paribus*, to consolidate democracy'.[18] By almost identical reasoning from a similar definition of civil society to democratic reform, Diamond explains how 'civil society ... may contribute to democratic consolidation'.[19] Where a logic leads to a 'good' outcome and support for it can easily be found, considerable momentum for change is likely to follow.

So the ideas of scholars often become the strategies of donors. In the process of operationalizing them, however, earlier qualifications sometimes disappear. Virtues become necessities. In this case, for example, a 1996 USAID report insists that 'sustaining newly emerging democracies *will depend* on building autonomous centers of social and economic power that promote accountable and participatory governance'.[20] In any case, both scholars and donors taking this approach enthusiastically support broad intervention to create a new civil society that will consolidate democracy.

In arguing the case for democracy, writers on civil society focus on one of two broad areas. Either they stress how civil associations inculcate democratic habits among their members and thus build a culture supporting democracy, or they emphasize how interest and advocacy organizations compete with each other to influence government officials to adopt positions supporting their members and to follow formal rules facilitating open, free and fair political debate and decisions.[21] The former approach focuses on creating social capital by developing knowledge of co-operation within an organization and thus trust.[22] In turn, these characteristics strengthen individual democratic behaviour in relations with government at all times, but especially during elections. It is, therefore, an indirect approach that depends first on the creation of new habits and then on generalizing their application to encounters with governments, though it is often attempted directly through civic education during political campaigns preceding elections.

The latter concentrates on building organizations that can act independently and are willing to confront the government, either to hold it to account or to influence a policy. Both approaches command serious inquiry, but for the past several years scholars and donors have paid more attention to the latter approach, emphasizing organizations rather than individuals.[23] For that reason, the organizational approach to building democracy will be the subject of the remainder of this article.

The starting point for strengthening civil society in Africa, according to proponents of the conventional approach, is to increase participation – in the numbers of appropriate organizations and in the members active within them.[24] The presumption is that since civil society plays an important role in enriching Western democracies, it would have the same effect in Africa. But, the notion of civil society that both donors and scholars consider desirable seems to be an idealized version, rather than an application of what is actually happening in the countries they take as their models. It is difficult to argue that Western practice provides a useful guide for organizing the new civil societies of Africa when participation in Western civil societies, particularly in America, has been declining for some time. Since the causal logic suggests that an active civil society would increase the willingness of citizens to vote, the persistent decline over the past generation in voting turnout in Great Britain and the USA raises disturbing questions about civic engagement.

Participation is also falling in many voluntary associations in Western countries. 'Increasingly', Walzer laments, 'associational life in the "advanced" capitalist and social democratic countries seems at risk.'[25] Robert Putnam presents a wide array of data to demonstrate 'that the vibrancy of American civil society has notably declined over the past several decades'.[26] Attendance in church, at school and town meetings, membership in labour unions, women's groups, the PTA, Boy Scouts, Red Cross volunteers and fraternal groups have all fallen by a quarter or more during the past two or three decades.[27] Putnam dismisses the civic contribution of the new social-movement groups that have proliferated in recent years, such as the Sierra Club, Common Cause and Amnesty International, because they demand little of their members beyond writing cheques for worthy causes.[28]

His critics retort that these new groups have created large numbers of grassroots chapters engaged in communal life that help replace the decline in civic activity by members of longer established associations.[29] But, as Putnam points out, they do not fill the gap, since overall associational membership in America has 'declined significantly between 1967 and 1993'.[30] In any event, the continuing fall in civic activity in the USA should give serious pause to scholars and donors who use the American model as the rationale for expanding civil society in Africa.

Proponents of the conventional approach to civil society frequently have a version of pluralism in mind when they consider how organizations in civil society should relate to both state and society in low income countries. For example, 'the more pluralistic civil society can become without fragmenting, the more democracy will benefit. Some degree of pluralism is necessary by definition for civil society'.[31] In the 1950s and the first part of the 1960s, the pluralist model was the dominant interpretation of American politics.[32] Strong hints of this model are apparent in proposing

> voluntary associations as the building blocks of liberal government in Africa, suggesting that they play a leading role in pluralizing the institutional environment, in giving voice to popular demands, and in promoting a popular culture. To many political scientists, the growth of social associations constitutes the organizational foundation for multiparty politics.[33]

A recent USAID report argues the case for pluralism as a significant dimension relating civil society to democracy, because it 'deepens policy accountability'.[34] So does the Danish aid agency: 'A pluralistic civil society plays an important role in bringing about democratic changes and is an important actor when it comes to consolidating democratic gains.'[35] Nevertheless, the implications of pluralist thinking have not been carefully articulated in discussions of civil society in African politics, at least partly because the logical requisites of pluralism are largely ignored.

The pluralist argument presents a democratic theory of representation and responsive government. Civil society is not a term frequently used by the writers who have applied a pluralist approach to American politics. But, the importance they place on the political activities of non-state organizations in shaping government policies has obvious attractions for those who would reform African governments in which state officials regularly make decisions without much regard for local concerns.

In the 'classic' pluralist approach elaborated in American political science, the number of different interests in the society grows as economic and social interests diversify.[36] Since formal organizations can focus more governmental attention on policies affecting the interests they represent than unorganized interests can elicit, social groups will be motivated to create organizations to represent them along the lines of the interests they feel most intensely. Emanating from social groups, these organizations are more or less independent from the state and controlled to some extent by their members.

The scarcity of resources in the society drives these organizations to compete with each other to influence government policy in directions favourable to their members. As more groups form organizations to promote their interests, competition will produce more 'efficient' policy outcomes, because government officials will receive greater information. Organizations representing groups that stand to lose more will fight harder to make the government adopt or maintain policies protecting them. In the battle over influence, intensity of preference can help interest groups to make up for differences in the wealth or social status at their disposal. On any issue, stakes, and therefore intensities of preference, will be unequal. Where the costs to other interests are limited, they may not oppose control over a particular policy area by a group which feels it has a lot at stake.

Organizations will tend to promote the narrow and specialized interests of their constituents, because making broad demands would increase the number of organizations likely to perceive a threat to the interests of their own members and cause them to mobilize in opposition. On the other hand, a large coalition composed of a variety of interests is unlikely to dominate policy making, and thus exclude weaker interests from affecting government decisions, because it will find it difficult to maintain internal agreement over many issues for very long.

In addition, elected officials have an incentive to be responsive to intensely felt interests in order to avoid punishment at the next election. Finally, if interest groups compete with each other to influence government officials, a premium is placed on bargaining to resolve conflicts. Presumably, this will cause organizations to moderate their demands in order to find compromises.[37] Thus, in theory, organizational competition over influencing government policy can achieve an equilibrium once each interest is represented. If that point could be reached, pluralists argue that government outcomes would represent social interests as successfully as is possible.

The emergence of pluralist analysis from the study of American politics is not at all surprising. American government is built on checks and balances that play off one institution against another. Consequently, there are innumerable nooks and crannies in which the application of pressure by even a small interest group could dramatically affect policy, typically by preventing change. The founders of government in the United States believed that 'by so contriving the interior structure of the government ... its several constituent parts may, by their mutual relations, be the means of keeping each other in their proper places'.[38] Pitting one part of the government against another, Madison reasoned, would allow the brisk competition of interests to support a responsive democracy. Factional activity would be harnessed to support the public interest.

As a result, the American founders multiplied the sites involved in making any government decision, which has motivated groups to form organizations entirely independent of the state to protect and advance their interests. By contrast, European political systems follow a more corporatist pattern, because the governments, which are more unitary in structure than in America, encourage the hierarchical organization of social interests and often formally incorporate them into government policy making.[39]

For various reasons, all instructive when applied to Africa, pluralist arguments are no longer so highly regarded as explanations of American policy making. Writers attacking pluralism question its, often implicit, assumptions that access is equally open to all interests, that it is social groups that cause governments to change their policies rather than the other way around and that negotiations will necessarily lead to compromise. Several arguments have been put forward to support these challenges.

First, there is the collective action problem. Organizations need incentives to keep members' support, even if they are clearly acting for objectives which members hold with high intensity. If the membership is large enough to make the contribution of a single member imperceptible, no rational member will give it support.[40] Instead, they will choose to be free riders, unless the organization provides them with selective, that is, individual, usually material benefits. For many organizations these selective benefits replace the collective benefit as the main focus of the organization's activity. Since individuals join the American Association of Retired Persons for car and hotel discounts rather than for its pursuit of legislation protecting the elderly, this organization puts much of its energy and budget into serving travellers.

In addition, the logic of collective action dictates that groups whose strength is in large numbers will find it more difficult to organize than groups in which the few envision the prospect of sharing the benefits accruing from organizational activity. Farmworkers and women, for example, will find it harder to organize than corporations selling the same product. Finally, in the case of forming public interest organizations to protect civil liberties or lobby for reforms to campaign finance or government accountability, the hurdles posed by collective action are even higher because there are no material benefits, that is, private interests, to attract members.

Second, if the collective action dilemma prevents constituents who share a common interest from contributing to the formation of a new organization, the necessary resources may have to come from outsiders – in American politics foundations, government agencies, economic associations or large firms often make the difference.[41] Third, organizational skills are unevenly distributed and available mainly to those with greater resources. Some interests may not gain access to the government because they were either unable to form organizations or lacked the skills to sustain them. Fourth, pluralists may have got the causal relationship backwards. The policies government officials put forward may stimulate interest groups to form and to respond rather than the other way around.[42] Since state officials can usually choose among a broad range of policies and shape them to the advantage of one group rather than another, they can significantly affect the competition among groups.

Fifth, the pluralist assumption that all interests can be reconciled through compromise may turn out to depend more on the legitimacy of particular government structures than on the effects of pluralist competition. That is, the impetus to bargain over differences may owe more to the insistence of official agencies than to rivalry among interest groups. Compromise is also more likely where disputes are fought over narrow issues involving divisible benefits. The more the institutional structure of government stimulates the organization of interests on a narrow basis, the more likely it is to work out compromises. But where the interests in dispute are intrinsic and not easily divisible, such as questions of morality and identity, there will be fewer opportunities for compromise.

Though these challenges were originally developed to demonstrate that pluralism did not explain American politics well, each of them applies with far greater force to politics in Africa. Consider the implicit assumptions behind pluralism discussed above. Access to policymakers is much more skewed in favour of the educated and wealthy in Africa and the state is far more powerful in shaping interests there than in the USA. Unlike Madison's scheme, African states were designed by European colonial powers to be unitary governments and have largely remained so despite constitutional tinkering. The practice of neopatrimonial politics, where a single ruler possesses a monopoly over patronage, strongly reinforces unitary government.[43]

The paradox of collective action applies with special force in Africa. Most of the population, particularly those in the countryside are unorganized and have no direct incentives to change that situation. It is far harder to organize in Africa than it is in the United States. Since fewer interests have emerged, leaving most of the population unorganized, the organized enjoy far greater access to policymakers by comparison with their counterparts in America. That is, on any given policy there simply is no welter of competing interests to whom an African policymaker needs to listen.

Given the exceptional difficulties posed by collective action especially in African circumstances, current support for 'civic advocacy' organizations among donors and writers is most puzzling. 'The single most favoured area of US civil society assistance is that of advocacy NGOs, such as human rights groups, election monitoring organizations, and environmental organizations.'[44] The logic is straightforward. If strong organizations without ties to the state promote democratic rules and human rights, the prospects for holding the state accountable and consolidating democracy are that much better. Since donors wish to avoid appearing to favour one interest or political view over another, the idea of supporting non-partisan advocacy is particularly attractive.

But the case for using civil advocacy organizations to build civil society rather than merely providing cannon fodder to force democratic concessions from reluctant states is more difficult to maintain. These are organizations whose purposes are not only to promote public rather than private interests, but public interests which are new to African polities and for which there does not exist a domestic constituency. They exist because donors want them to and are willing to put finance and organizational training into them that could not possibly be found locally. The reason is not hard to understand. Donors support reform and have short-term horizons. They want to see results and they are willing to pay for them. So they provide the organizational resources. As a recent USAID report put it: '*The art and craft of the democracy strategist, then, lies in building and supporting coalitions of associations that are proreform at a particular historical moment in the democratic path.*'[45]

The collective action problem focuses attention squarely on whether outsiders can help create the kind of organizations needed for the new civil society. From within African societies, the 'outsider' most capable and most likely to stimulate organizational activity is, of course, the state, even taking into account the tentative steps to clip its wings through privatization and liberalization.[46] These changes do little to remove the strong neopatrimonial motives the state has for limiting autonomous organizational activity as much as possible. State officials organize followers in order to ensure loyalty, not autonomy. Where they have the discretion, they are far more likely to shape policy to help groups with which they sympathize – typically either for their own profit or to create a clientele. State action to crush threatening organizations is one of the best established propositions in the literature on African politics.

The only other significant alternative source for new organizational activity is, of course, the donors. They deploy far larger sums to help new organizations form and persist than state officials would ever consider. In the two fiscal years 1991–93 roughly $156 millions, about 22 per cent of all

USAID expenditure on democracy, was spent on civil society projects.[47] Organizations, whether new or old, are likely to make a political impact when resources of a completely different magnitude than that available from within the society are poured into them. In fact, for a time they may contribute to the appearance of a vigorous civil society. But donors rarely create autonomous organizations.[48] Indeed, an aid-created independent civil organization comes close to being an oxymoron. Furthermore, donors have no expectation of helping them forever. Unless the new externally funded African organizations can develop effective social roots and local resources of their own, they will die on the vine as soon as their foreign patrons depart or lose interest.

Finally, one simply has to ask whether the new organizations that writers call for and donors create can change the foundations of African political struggle at all. Contingent though ethnic identities may be, when they are mobilized in Africa the cleavages they create are often difficult for politicians to reconcile. One important reason is that state officials frequently depend on ethnic mobilization to maintain their positions. If patronage continues to be solicited on an ethnic basis by politicians solidifying their hold on state office, a widely accepted view of how politics works throughout sub-Saharan Africa, newly formed civil society organizations can amount to little more than a sideshow.[49] If they would like to see a pluralist model of politics take root in Africa, proponents of civil society – donors and scholars alike – have their work cut out for them.

SUCCESSFUL CIVIL SOCIETY ACTORS AND THE STATE

Now suppose instead that the conventional approach does manage to create successful civil society organizations despite its narrow, unrealistic assumptions and the weak rationale it uses to establish a causal link to democracy. Assume a population of adequately funded, capably staffed and locally supported public interest and advocacy organizations ready to confront the government for its misdeeds and willing to present the voices of their constituents at critical junctures in policy making. If such organizations were created, would not African civil society then strengthen democracy?

Unfortunately, the answer is: not necessarily. First, many of the most active African ethnic and fundamentalist religious organizations are excluded from civil society by definition. The conventional wisdom holds that they are anti-democratic and will not help to consolidate democracy. Then, too, aggressive civil society organizations may cripple democracy rather than sustain it. Whether they do so depends on how effectively the state can incorporate and respond to their demands. Left to their own devices, civic associations will not choose to limit the demands they pursue just because they harm the interests of others. It is the state that is supposed to play that role. In addition, civic advocacy groups may insist on constraints on government that interfere with its capacity to carry out functions that are unique to the state.

Whether or not organizations succeed in accomplishing private or public interests, they will not pay much attention to the sustained capacity of the state to develop and consistently apply policies based on informed consideration and choice among interests. Taking account of state capacity would only deflect interest groups from the purpose for which they were organized. The state is the one association in civil society whose task it is to form policies by deciding among opposing interests.

The contradiction in being simultaneously part of civil society and outside it gives rise to what Walzer calls 'the paradox of the civil society argument': the state 'both frames civil society and occupies space within it'.[50] For this reason, it plays a different role from all other civic associations. 'For civil society, left to itself', he points out, 'generates radically unequal power relationships, which only state power can challenge.'[51] And, even more fundamentally, as the plight of stateless Somalia reminds us, the state is almost always the supplier of the public order that enables civil society to exist.

Thus, civil society organizations confront the state, but must also be regulated by the state. That leads Walzer to the unsatisfactory conclusion, at least for purposes of this analysis, that 'only a democratic state can create a democratic civil society; only a democratic civil society can sustain a democratic state'.[52] His suggestions for achieving both at once emphasize communal policies based on decentralizing the state, maintaining public control over some aspects of the market and dampening nationalism. Whether or not these policies are good ideas, he can only feel comfortable in suggesting them because the Western democracies in which the existence of a shared normative framework for legitimising state action can be taken for granted form the context for his analysis.

But then, one may ask, how can *democratization* be possible? By definition, the starting point is not a democratic state, and rarely anything approaching a democratic civil society. How does one get inside this circle in which state and civil society each act as prior conditions for the other? Even though Walzer does not consider this problem, his paradox leads inexorably to it. Since proponents of the conventional approach insist that democratization must grow, at least in part, from civil society, and since, on their terms, the present existence of civil society in African countries is both marginal and, from the state's perspective, unwelcome, their problem is to decide how powerful civil society organizations must become in order to be effective. Presumably, the answer requires making them strong enough to force the state to change in a democratic direction. But what impact will so strengthening these organizations have on the capacity of the state to maintain political order?

Introducing more enterprising civil society organizations is problematic for democracy because the legitimacy of states all over Africa is already in question. Indeed, the whole point of democratization is to deny legitimacy to existing governments. In the logic of proponents of the conventional approach, more vigorous civil society organizations are needed to democratize the state. Without bringing pressure to bear on them, authoritarian governments will not allow open political activity, particularly where they face the prospect of losing power.

But that does not necessarily mean that the more aggressive the civil society, the more likely the democracy. Aggressive organizations may seek power to destroy democracy or exclude others from it. Effective organizations have promoted the causes of the Nazis, anti-immigrant groups throughout Europe, and apartheid in South Africa and the American South.[53] In Africa, the male-dominated and gerontocratic character of most organizations, in addition to the ubiquity and strong loyalties characterizing ethnic and fundamentalist religious associations, suggest that increasing organizational effectiveness may not make democratization more likely.[54] Thus, Michael W. Foley and Bob Edwards ask a good question: 'If civil society is a beachhead secure enough to be of use in thwarting tyrannical regimes, what prevents it from being used to undermine democratic governments?'[55]

If the causal relationship between civil society and democracy is to be preserved, this question must be answered. The conventional solution is to categorize organizations according to whether they are civic or uncivic and then define civil society so as to exclude the latter. Doing so follows logically from accepting as part of the definition of civil society the norm that its members act respectfully towards one another by limiting their demands and remaining open to compromise. What this means in practice, however, is ruling out one kind of aggressive civil society organization while tolerating another. Uncompromising and even disrespectful political activity may be appropriate, for example, if organizations are attempting to force openings for democracy, a point elaborated below.

Identifying those organizations within civil society that encourage democracy is a distinct improvement over the argument that civil society as a whole promotes democracy. But, insistence on identifying civic behaviour with democracy makes circular reasoning almost irresistible. If those organizations that seek democracy are civic and those that do not are uncivic, it is tautologous to insist that civil society promotes democracy.[56] But even when proponents of the conventional approach are careful to separate the definition of cause from that of its effect, use of this normative criterion still gets them into great difficulties.

In Africa, ethnic and fundamentalist religious organizations are typically excluded as uncivic while new reform-minded non-governmental organizations are included as civic. So, to demonstrate the weakness of civil society in Africa, E. Gyimah-Boadi asserts that 'civil society has ... failed to transcend ethnoregional, religious and other cleavages in any lasting way', even though he knows perfectly well that ethnic and religious organizations commonly promote political objectives throughout Africa.[57] Michael Bratton supplies the conventional argument: 'While familial affection can be a consolidating glue for small organizations, it can create internal cleavage and factional conflict in larger structures.'[58] That is what makes them 'uncivic'.

The hidden premise here, that ethnic and fundamentalist religious intensity cannot be politically domesticated, means these organizations must be barred from civil society. But is their exclusion analytically useful? While politicians who use state resources to build ethnic clienteles do generate demands that the state finds peculiarly difficult to resolve, as discussed above, there are many other ethnic associations that present issues of their own. Not all ethnic or fundamentalist religious interests are so intense that their promoters are unwilling to accept procedural rules, compromises and democratic decisions. If leaders of ethnic or fundamentalist religious organizations perceive that the design of political structures in which they must act are open, that is, will provide them and their constituents with opportunities for rewards in the future, they are much more likely to compromise current claims, even those that involve the identities of their followers.[59] In some cases, therefore, the causal arrow is reversed: the level of ethnic intensity will be a function of the capacity of the political order to reconcile interests. In order to think clearly about how organizations representing social interests support or undermine democratization, it is essential to stop considering ethnic and fundamentalist religious associations as invariably uncivic.

Indeed, considering that these associations form such a large proportion of all the organizations that have established deep social roots in Africa, it is almost a contradiction in terms to insist that they cannot be considered part of the struggle for democracy. How can the process of establishing democracy depend on the exclusion of most members of that society? Worse, to leave the shaping of democracy to new public interest advocacy groups is likely to focus the content of any reforms adopted on the interests of members of those groups rather than those preferred by members of ethnic and fundamentalist religious organizations, particularly those living in the countryside. For the most part, the former are part of the educated urban elite who shaped policy since independence and were largely responsible for the erosion of earlier attempts to establish democracy.

Instead, it would be far more helpful to expand the space for civil society in Africa by including both new and old associations. Peter Ekeh correctly suggests that a much richer and more analytically useful concept of civil society would be found in Africa, if it were based on a 'primordial public realm' instead of a 'civic public realm'.[60] But that merely cures one problem while creating another. Surely, the new civic advocacy organizations also play an important role in promoting greater democratization. If the point of the concept of civil society is to understand the variegated impact of organizational activity on democracy, there is no reason to leave out either realm.

On the other hand, the relationship between democracy and those organizations that conventional proponents define as civic is also problematic. Not all associations that are incontestably civic choose to promote democracy. Organizations frequently have complex goals, particularly where the promotion of democracy is not their formal objective. Taking on authoritarian governments will be costly in achieving their other purposes. Some non-governmental organizations will challenge their governments to be more democratic while others will decide they can achieve their formal objectives more successfully by quietly acquiescing in government injustices, even within their own field of operations. Stephen N. Ndegwa's carefully researched case study comparing the Green Belt Movement and the Undugu Society, both squarely within the civic category, illustrates this difference in public response.[61]

Making the conventional norm of civic behaviour part of the definition of civil society organizations poses a more serious problem. Whether organizations confronting dictatorial governments must also observe the civic restraints which they would be expected to follow in fully consolidated democracies is a dilemma inherent in democratization. A daring violation of the law, disrespectful of state officials, may force concessions from a reluctant leader. Should organizations be classified as civic no matter how aggressively they act, so long as they struggle for democracy? After all, authoritarian regimes have enormous resources available to threaten or destroy those pressing for fundamental change. It is difficult to know when respect for procedure and the willingness to compromise, the hallmarks of civic behaviour, should be cast aside in order to bring down a tyrant. But it seems clear that the answer cannot be 'always' or 'never'.

Nevertheless, the unrelenting pursuit of democracy and governmental accountability is not only praised, but highly rewarded by donors. Among the associations promoting public goods, there has been a tendency to treat those groups that advocate governmental reform as the core of civil society, singling them out from all other non-governmental organizations pursuing development or providing social services.[62] The Green Belt Movement of

Kenya, which has vociferously and successfully fought its national government on a variety of environmental and democratic issues – and inspired many citizens to support democratic reform, is the quintessential example of a 'civic' civil society organization. Yet, ethnic associations opposing the government just as vigorously are considered uncivic. By what standard of civic behaviour can aggressive organizational behaviour in the name of democracy be acceptable, if it is regarded as fatally damaging to democracy when promoting ethnic objectives?

One resolution of this dilemma is to take the civic requirement seriously – the other is to expand the political space in civil society by dropping it entirely. Whitehead makes the case for applying it seriously by refusing to accept highly aggressive organizations as part of civil society, whether they pursue democratic goals or not. He goes even further by expanding the notion of 'civic' to mean agreement with the spirit, not just the letter, of the rules and then openly faces the consequences that follow for democratization.[63]

By his logic, civil society organisations are justified only if they contribute to democratic consolidation. Some associations, he insists, 'may be too inegalitarian, too pushy and disorienting, or even too "uncivil" to be desirable. Indeed, sound democratization could require far-reaching reform and perhaps even the weakening of inherited systems of dense associative life'.[64] But then what would Whitehead make of discernible steps toward greater democratisation taken by pushy elite organisations to force concessions from a reluctant ruler? It was hard to imagine Kenyan President Daniel arap Moi paying the slightest heed to non-governmental organizations that not only followed the letter of the laws created by a parliament the majority of whose members owed their allegiance to his patronage powers, but their spirit as well.

The alternative is to eliminate the normative element from the definition, that is, understanding civicness as respect for the rules, in order to examine fully the conditions under which organizations promote democratization. That greatly widens the field of organizations whose potential contribution to democracy must be seriously considered, particularly in Africa. It forces empirical examination of what organizations are actually doing rather than arbitrarily ruling the larger number irrelevant to the question of democracy. In doing so, it makes the question of the state's effectiveness in reconciling interests far more pertinent than it seemed when so few organizations were regarded as capable of promoting democracy. Since stronger civil society actors can seek their own interests more effectively, they may weaken the state's ability to listen, balance and respond to issues.

Under what circumstances, then, would the attempt by civil society to achieve democratic reform by curbing the power of the state result in undermining the state's ability to regulate civil society, or even democracy itself? This question poses a dilemma ignored by proponents of the conventional approach to civil society – one which reflects another consequence of applying Walzer's paradox to the problem of democratization. On the one hand, without determined and courageous political pressure for democratic reform, authoritarian governments will not yield. Unbridled civic activity for a good cause may be essential to remove authoritarian government. But, on the other, these pressures may take their toll on the state procedures that perform the function of reconciling interests. The attack on the state needed to achieve democracy may seriously weaken its capacity to make democracy work afterwards.

Consider, for example, the Limuru proposal made in April 1997 by the Kenyan opposition, which came together as the National Convention Assembly, a civic advocacy group. It demanded the creation of a transitional consultative council that would equally represent the government, opposition and civil society and would possess the authority to make decisions binding on the government to effect the transition to a new regime.[65] The members of this group are probably correct in thinking that only a clean start in which both elected and self-selected representatives hammer out a new constitution can achieve meaningful change in Kenya. But the precedent such a council would create would be likely to weaken severely the future capacity of the state to reconcile intensely felt interests.

Each new government would know that the possibility of a fresh group constituting itself and arrogating the same powers assumed by the National Convention Assembly would depend on the government's decisions on politically charged issues. It would constantly be looking over its shoulder instead of deciding issues in terms of competing interests – or their merits. In the case of a democracy in which the legitimacy of state authority was widely shared, one might argue that the prospect of a citizen-generated constitutional council would provide a desirable prospective democratic influence on government action. But that shared legitimacy is not present for either the current Kenyan (arap Moi's presidency), any other African government, or, most likely, for the government that would have emerged from the process the National Convention Assembly proposed.

The destruction of German democracy in the 1930s provides a useful case in which to examine the darker possibilities raised by this dilemma between achieving reform and preserving state capacity to reconcile interests. In Sheri Berman's view, the Nazis positioned themselves to seize power not through the absence of civil society in the Weimar Republic, but by taking advantage of its dense associational networks.[66] The inability of older German parties to attract followers led to an efflorescence of civil society actors organized within rather than across group boundaries.[67] This reinforcement of social cleavages combined with the vigour of associational activity amplified widespread discontent with political structures.

The Nazis plunged into associational life in the 1920s, creating local party chapters whose members also belonged to occupational, sports and fraternal groups.[68] In addition, the party developed an explicit strategy to infiltrate other groups, particularly agricultural organizations, which provided channels to spread Nazi political views widely.[69] Given the foothold that associational life made possible, and the 'political vacuum' at the top, the Nazis became a credible alternative to the other parties. Thus, she concludes, contrary to the conventional civil society argument, 'associationism and the prospects for democratic stability can actually be inversely related'.[70]

Her argument blaming the downfall of democracy on aggressive civil society activity rests heavily, as she recognizes, on Samuel P. Huntington's insight that the absence of shared legitimacy prevents political structures from containing conflicts among easily mobilized groups.[71] On this point, Huntington observes that if 'groups gain entry into politics without becoming identified with the established political organizations or acquiescing in the established political procedures', they weaken the capacity of parties or governments to keep the loyalties of others.[72] Perhaps the most extreme African case in point is the destruction of the national state in Somalia by competing armed groups organized on ethnic lines and refusing to recognize any higher authority.

For Berman and, of course, Huntington, political institutionalization must precede civil society activity – the reverse of the conventional civil society approach.[73] Berman thus introduces an important qualification into Putnam's sweeping argument that effective states emerge where civil society is dense – as he puts it, 'strong society, strong state'.[74] Instead, she demonstrates that a strong civil society will sometimes overwhelm a state. It depends on how institutionalized existing political structures are. Thus, the better proposition is that aggressive civil society organizations can sustain democracy where political institutions are strong, but may destroy it where they are weak.

However, the causal connections in Berman's explanation of the rise of the Nazis are difficult to identify. The most explicit claim she makes is that reinforcement of social cleavages by weak and unresponsive political institutions prepares the way for aggressive civil society activity. Precisely how Weimar political institutions failed to respond is not explained. Nor is it clear whether she thinks it was German parties or government bodies that could not keep civil society organizations within bounds. Notice, by the way, that if the fault lay with the parties rather than the state, it may be possible to escape Walzer's paradox. Finally, it is not obvious why the weakness of political institutions should have cleared the way for the Nazis to eclipse all pre-existing social groups, particularly when these other groups had apparently also formed strong associations for their defence.[75]

Even if its precise connections to the German case remain opaque, her work focuses attention, as conventional civil society arguments do not, on the threat in certain situations that civil society can pose to the political order. Analyzing the responsiveness of state institutions to multiple and conflicting demands means looking at how procedures are used to listen, to channel and to mediate.[76] Realistic evaluation explaining how civil society may best promote democracy in Africa, then, requires the analyst – and the donor – to balance the absorptive capacity in existing state political structures against the support available for pro-reform coalitions of organizations – instead of simply making the latter the centrepiece of its strategy, as a USAID report has recently proposed.[77] The establishment and maintenance of democracy depends on the responsiveness of state institutions at least as much as it does on civil society.

CONCLUSION

The core of the problem with the conventional argument that civil society makes a critical contribution to democracy is the separation of the organizations which the concept privileges from the society which they are supposed to reform. Since the success of democratization ultimately depends on broad acceptance or acquiescence in the distribution of social power reflected in the new political settlement, the organizations that promote it must themselves be connected to the social roots of the society. They must be engaged in the issues that matter. Authoritarian rulers resist democracy because they represent the interests of social forces that benefit from their regimes. Societies are not fundamentally changed by groups which are created primarily to correct the flaws of government, however much those flaws may need correcting.

With notable exceptions, the African organizations specified by conventional civil society notions are new, lack social roots, have objectives unrelated to ongoing political conflicts and are heavily financed by outside donors. Indeed, Schmitter's broadly shared definition creates a civil society of actors with little purchase on the substantive politics of the larger society they inhabit – particularly in Africa. Though his intention is to identify a category of organizations, his definition tends to isolate them from politics. The autonomy these organizations must manifest from both social interests and the state, their lack of an intention to rule and their willingness to act 'civilly', combine to make them peculiarly non-political. I am not suggesting they are irrelevant to politics. When provided with sufficient resources, these civil society organizations will have a substantial political impact and can even make a dictator falter or give way. But that does not suggest they are capable of creating a viable democracy.

Perhaps it is the absence of embeddedness of civil society organizations, particularly those engaged in civil advocacy, that makes them so attractive to proponents of the conventional approach. If democracy in Africa has been conspicuous mostly by its absence, then new initiatives by new organizations may strike these analysts and donors as the best way to bring it into being. Since they regard multi-party democracy combined with respect for human rights, tolerance of different views and densely populated civil societies as a fixture in Western countries, these new civil society organizations become their vehicle for importing democracy into Africa. But it is an idealized version not the actual practice of civil society in Western countries that they wish to import. One of the puzzling features of their enthusiasm is that participation in civil society organizations in many Western countries, particularly America, has been declining for more than a generation. Either civil society has less to do with democracy in the West than these civil society analysts and donors think, or the nature of Western democracy is changing in ways that make it less desirable as a model for Africa.

Because they support strong civil societies as the means to achieve democracy, it is not surprising that they exhume a functional notion of pluralism based on competing interest groups that had its heyday in American political science a generation ago. The empirical problems that caused its demise in America are far more serious in contemporary Africa. Pluralist system analysis depends on relative equality of access to policy makers, of organizational skills and the presence of the material resources that help organizations overcome the problem of collective action. Pluralists presume that all interests can be reconciled through compromises achieved by competition of groups for the attention of decision makers. Unequal distribution of organizational access, resources and skills is manifestly greater in Africa than in America. So are the difficulties of reconciling divergent interests, especially those based on identity.

Given the explicit support of scholars and donors holding the conventional view for citizen participation through civil society and their reliance on pluralist analysis as a basis for achieving democracy, it is simply wrong to insist that 'the model of democratization embodied in US democracy assistance is not drawn from the domestic political experience of the United States or other established democracies. Neither is it borrowed from the world of academic theory'.[78] In fact, it is drawn from both, but inappropriately. Carothers is correct in thinking that 'practitioners have a low tolerance for the political science jargon frequently found in academic analyses of democratization'.[79] But whether they recognize it or not, their analyses of democratization and how their interventions can promote it are deeply influenced by the ideas of political science. Unless these links are recognized, donors will continue to apply discredited ideas likely to undercut their purposes.

But even if conventional civil society adherents were capable of creating effective and energetic civil associations, they may harm rather than promote the democratization process by making it more difficult for African states, whose legitimacy has never been secure, to reconcile competing interests. This problem grows out of the ambivalent role of the state as both part of and guarantor of civil society – Walzer's paradox of civil society. The paradox is heightened by the process of democratization which necessarily weakens state authority, though perhaps only temporarily.

The conventional civil society approach is to encourage more enterprising and more effective activities by organizations promoting democracy while excluding ethnic and fundamentalist religious organizations as uncivic. In addition to the problem of tautology this sort of analysis invites, it seems foolish to exclude ethnic associations, possibly the greater part of Africa's existing associations, from any analytically useful explanation of the struggle for democracy. On the other hand, insisting that conventional civil society organizations adhere carefully to standards of civility would make it unlikely that they could force authoritarian regimes to concede power. The better approach is to consider civil society as consisting of non-state organizational activity whether or not the organizations within it conform to the norm of civility. That will facilitate assessment of the negative as well as the positive contributions of organizations to democratization.

Enabling civil society organizations to become more aggressive makes it harder for the state to mediate among competing interest groups. In addition, allowing aggressive organizational activity against the state in the promotion of democracy creates a precedent that will make it difficult for the state, even if it is democratically reformed, to regain sufficient authority to be able to settle disputes among interest groups without losers resorting to further aggressive acts to reverse their losses. Scholars and donors, then, need to rethink the assumptions on which they expect civil society to contribute to democracy. In the process, they ought to pay at least as much attention to political institutions as to civil society.

NOTES

1. Larry Diamond, 'Introduction: In Search of Consolidation', in Larry Diamond, Marc F. Plattner, Yun-han Chu and Hung-mao Tien (eds.), *Consolidating the Third Wave Democracies: Themes and Perspectives* (Baltimore, MD: Johns Hopkins University Press, 1997), p.xxx.

2. Michael Bratton, 'Civil Society and Political Transitions in Africa', in John W. Harbeson, Donald Rothchild and Naomi Chazan (eds.), *Civil Society and the State in Africa* (Boulder, CO: Lynne Rienner, 1994), p.76. More recently, Bratton appears to have qualified his position. See Michael Bratton and Nicolas van de Walle, *Democratic Experiments in Africa: Regime Transitions in Comparative Perspective* (Cambridge: Cambridge University Press, 1997), p.255.

3. Quoted in Gary Hansen, 'Constituencies for Reform: Strategic Approaches for Donor-Supported Civic Advocacy Programs', USAID Program and Operations Assessment Report No. 12 (Washington, DC, February 1996), p.1. For similar views of other donors, see Mark Robinson, 'Strengthening Civil Society Through Foreign Political Aid', ESCOR Research Report, R 6234, Institute of Development Studies, University of Sussex (Falmer, Brighton, UK, September 1996), pp.6–7.

4. Naomi Chazan, 'Africa's Democratic Challenge', *World Policy Journal*, Vol.9, No.2 (Spring 1992), p.302. Also, 'the emergence of a civil society does not guarantee the development of a democracy; however, it is highly unlikely that a viable democracy can survive without a civil society'. Dwayne Woods, 'Civil Society in Europe and Africa: Limiting State Power through a Public Sphere', *African Studies Review*, Vol.35, No.2 (Sept. 1992), p.94.

5. Chazan, 'Africa's Democratic Challenge', p.283. She immediately adds that 'parochial associations … are outside the bounds of civil society'.

6. Bratton and van de Walle, *Democratic Experiments in Africa*, pp.3–9, pp.233–4.

7. Philippe C. Schmitter, 'More Liberal, Preliberal, or Postliberal?', *Journal of Democracy*, Vol.6, No.1 (Jan. 1995), p.15. The thrust of his article is to question this equation not so much for the Third World as for the First. But if, as he speculates, the 'established liberal democracies' are evolving toward a 'postliberal' democracy in which individuals place much less value on political participation and voluntary contributions, these states may no longer provide good models of liberal democracy for others to emulate. See pp.20–21.

8. Thomas Carothers, 'Democracy Assistance: The Question of Strategy,' *Democratization*, Vol.4, No.3 (Autumn 1997), p.115. European donors, he adds, base their democratic aid on the pattern of liberal democracy in their countries, pp.121–22.

9. Chazan, 'Africa's Democratic Challenge', p.282.

10. See, for example, the different types identified in David Held, *Models of Democracy* (Stanford, CA: Stanford University Press, 1987).

11. Joseph Schumpeter provides the classic rationale that democracy requires competition by leaders in *Capitalism, Socialism, and Democracy* (New York: Harper Brothers, 1950), pp.269–83. Carole Pateman makes the argument for control from below in *Participation and Democratic Theory* (Cambridge: Cambridge University Press, 1970).

12. Nelson Kasfir, 'Popular Sovereignty and Popular Participation: Mixed Constitutional Democracy in the Third World', *Third World Quarterly*, Vol.13, No.4 (1992).

13. Philippe C. Schmitter, 'Civil Society East and West', in Diamond *et al.* (eds.), *Consolidating the Third Wave Democracies* (Baltimore, MD: Johns Hopkins University Press, 1997), p.240. On the following page he uses 'intermediary organizations' as the equivalent of 'intermediary groups'. While there is considerable controversy in philosophic discussions over the meaning of civil society, there is broad agreement by those who apply it in reform efforts. Virtually identical definitions are adopted by Bratton, Chazan, and Woods cited above, as well as by Michael Walzer, 'The Idea of Civil Society: A Path to Social Reconstruction', *Dissent*, Vol.38, No.2 (Spring 1991), p.293, and Laurence Whitehead, 'Bowling in the Bronx: The Uncivil Interstices between Civil and Political Society', in Robert Fine and Shirin Rai (eds.), *Civil Society: Democratic Perspectives* (London: Frank Cass, 1997), pp.100–101.

14. On this definition, it is unclear whether civil society would include the national conferences which claimed sovereign power to reshape the constitutions of many Francophone African

countries in the early 1990s or the National Convention Assembly which was formed in 1997 to demand that it be allowed to organize a new constituent assembly in Kenya.

15. Bratton and van de Walle, *Democratic Experiments in Africa*, pp.253–5.

16. There is a profound difference between this use of civil society and the application of the term to the establishment of a moral community in opposition to the state in the Communist countries of eastern Europe – what Vaclav Havel called 'living in truth'. The unexpected collapse of these states left an organizational void not the triumph of civil society: 'a civil society whose essence was radical opposition to the communist state could not survive the disappearance of that state'. Aleksander Smolar, 'From Opposition to Atomization', in Larry Diamond, Marc F. Plattner, Yun-han Chu and Hung-mao Tien (eds.), *Consolidating the Third Wave Democracies: Themes and Perspectives* (Baltimore, MD: Johns Hopkins University Press, 1997), p.267. Only after the establishment of post-Communist societies was it possible to contemplate civil associations that could work within the system.

17. By broadening the objectives of civil society organisations to include 'passions' as well as 'interests', Schmitter may be willing to include the ethnic organisations other writers rule out, but only so long as they are not overwhelmed by their followers, respect civil rules and do not threaten to take over government. Most ethnic 'passion', it is safe to say, will still remain outside civil society.

18. Schmitter, 'Civil Society East and West', p.241.

19. Diamond, 'Introduction: In Search of Consolidation', p.xxx. His list of contributions includes 'stabilising expectations and social bargaining, generating a more civic normative environment, bringing actors closer to the political process, reducing the burdens of governance, and checking potential abuses of power'.

20. Gary Hansen, 'Constituencies for Reform: Strategic Approaches for Donor-Supported Civic Advocacy Programs', Assessment Report No. 12, Center for Development Information and Evaluation, United States Agency for International Development (February 1996), p.v (italics added).

21. This distinction between the internal effects on members and the external effects on policymaking overlaps but is not identical with the two versions identified in Michael W. Foley and Bob Edwards, 'The Paradox of Civil Society', *Journal of Democracy*, Vol.7, No.3 (July 1996), p.39. Their external approach, drawn from the conception of civil society in eastern Europe under Communist rule, focuses on resistance to authoritarian rule, rather than support for a functioning democracy.

22. Robert Putnam, *Making Democracy Work: Civic Traditions in Modern Italy* (Princeton, NJ: Princeton University Press, 1993).

23. For donors, see Mark Robinson, 'Strengthening Civil Society Through Foreign Political Aid', p.4.

24. Not so long ago, American political scientists were warning us that too much participation endangers democratic stability. See Carole Pateman's critical analysis of empirical democratic theory of the 1950s and 1960s in *Participation and Democratic Theory*, pp.1–17.

25. 'The Idea of Civil Society', p.293. See also Whitehead, 'Bowling in the Bronx', p.109, and Clive Tempest, 'Myths from Eastern Europe and the Legend of the West', in Fine and Rai (eds.), *Civil Society: Democratic Perspectives*, p.139.

26. Putnam, 'Bowling Alone: America's Declining Social Capital', *Journal of Democracy*, Vol.6, No.1 (Jan. 1995), p.65.

27. Ibid., pp.67–70.

28. Ibid., pp.70–72.

29. Foley and Edwards, 'The Paradox of Civil Society', pp.43–4.

30. Putnam, 'Bowling Alone', p.72.

31. Larry Diamond, 'Toward Democratic Consolidation', *Journal of Democracy*, Vol.5, No.3 (July 1994), p.12. Or, the claim that 'a serious pluralist connection linking civil society and the state' may be emerging in Botswana. Patrick Molutsi and John D. Holm, 'Developing Democracy When Civil Society is Weak: The Case of Botswana', *African Affairs*, Vol.89, No.356 (July 1990), p.338.

32. William Crotty, 'Interest Representation and Interest Groups: Promise and Potentialities', in Crotty, Mildred A. Schwartz and John C. Green (eds.), *Representing Interests and Interest Group Representation* (Lanham, MD: University Press of America, 1994), p.1. Three of the

leading texts shaping pluralist analysis are V.O. Key, *Parties, Politics and Pressure Groups* (New York, 1947); David Truman, *The Governmental Process* (New York, 1951); and Robert Dahl, *Who Governs?* (New Haven, CT: Yale University Press, 1961).

33. Chazan, 'Africa's Democratic Challenge', p.282. She cites Michael Bratton for this view. Later, she relates stock characteristics of pluralism – 'multiple membership' and 'associational diversity' – to 'the strong pluralist tradition inherited from (mostly British) colonial rule'. 'Africa's Democratic Challenge', p.291.

34. Harry Blair *et al.*, 'Civil Society and Democratic Development: A CDIE Evaluation Design Paper', USAID Working Paper No. 211, Center for Development Information and Evaluation, USAID (Washington, February 1994), p.9. In suggesting how US pluralism might apply to civil society in low income countries engaged in democratic transitions, Blair notes two familiar aspects of the logic of pluralist analysis: first, the 'constant flow of citizen inputs to the state, which, being continually reminded of what its citizens want, finds it difficult to wander too far from those wishes;' and second, 'fostering pluralist competition by encouraging all groups to press their agendas on the state, which accordingly discovers itself having to accommodate conflicting voices in such ways that it cannot surrender to any one voice or small coterie of voices'. Blair, 'Civil Society and Democratic Development', pp.9–10.

35. DANIDA, 'Support for Civil Society', Ministry of Foreign Affairs, Copenhagen (1995), p.2, quoted in Mark Robinson, 'Strengthening Civil Society Through Foreign Political Aid', p.7.

36. Several points in this sketch of 'classic' pluralism are taken from Clarence N. Stone, 'Group Politics Reexamined: From Pluralism to Political Economy', in Lawrence C. Dodd and Calvin Jillson (eds.), *The Dynamics of American Politics* (Boulder, CO: Westview Press, 1992), pp.277–79.

37. Joseph R. Gusfield, 'Mass Society and Extremist Politics', *American Sociological Review*, Vol.27, No.1 (Feb. 1962), p.22.

38. James Madison, 'Federalist Number 51', in James Madison, Alexander Hamilton, John Jay and Isaac Kramnick (eds.), *The Federalist Papers* (Harmondsworth: Penguin, 1987), pp.318–19.

39. Philippe C. Schmitter, 'The Consolidation of Democracy and Representation of Social Groups', *American Behavioral Scientist*, Vol.35, Nos 4 & 5 (March & June, 1992), pp.434–5.

40. Mancur Olson, *The Logic of Collective Action* (Cambridge, MA: Harvard University Press, 1965). Further work developing the implications is discussed in Stone, 'Group Politics Reexamined', p.280.

41. Stone, 'Group Politics Reexamined', p.281.

42. Theodore Lowi, 'American Business, Public Policy, Case Studies and Political Theory', *World Politics* No.16 (1964) discussed in Stone, 'Group Politics Reexamined', pp.280–81.

43. Bratton and van de Walle, *Democratic Experiments in Africa*, pp.61–8.

44. Carothers, 'Democracy Assistance, p.114.

45. Hansen, 'Constituencies for Reform', p.3 (italics in original).

46. For a discussion of the slow rate of progress toward privatization in Africa, see Roger Tangri, 'The Politics of Africa's Public and Private Enterprise', *Journal of Commonwealth and Comparative Politics*, Vol.33, No.2 (July 1995), pp.173–5.

47. Blair, 'Civil Society and Democratic Development', p.2.

48. For a description of the negative consequences on recipient organizations of the withdrawal of foreign financing from civil society even in a relatively wealthy African country, see John D. Holm, Patrick P. Molutsi and Gloria Somolekae, 'The Development of Civil Society in a Democratic State: The Botswana Model', *African Studies Review*, Vol.39, No.2 (Sept. 1966), pp.54–5.

49. For the explicit linkage of political patronage and ethnicity see Richard A. Joseph, *Democracy and Prebendal Politics in Nigeria: The Rise and Fall of the Second Republic* (Cambridge: Cambridge University Press, 1987), pp.58–63.

50. 'The Idea of Civil Society', pp.301–2.

51. Ibid., p.302.

52. Ibid., p.302.

53. Sheri Berman, 'Civil Society and Political Institutionalization,' *American Behavioral Scientist*, Vol.40, No.5 (March/April 1997), p.565.

54. Eboe Hutchful, 'The Civil Society Debate in Africa', *International Journal*, 51 (Winter 1995–96), pp.66–7.
55. 'The Paradox of Civil Society', *Journal of Democracy,* Vol.7, No.3 (July 1996), p.46.
56. For example, 'civil society can contribute to democratic consolidation only if other institutions are also favorable, and if actors in civil society behave in a "civil" way, respecting the law and other social and political actors while accepting and not seeking to usurp or conquer democratic political authority'. Diamond, 'Introduction: In Search of Consolidation', p.xxxi.
57. 'Civil Society in Africa', in Larry Diamond, Marc F. Plattner, Yun-han Chu and Hung-mao Tien (eds.), *Consolidating the Third Wave Democracies: Themes and Perspectives* (Baltimore, MD: Johns Hopkins University Press, 1997), p.280.
58. 'Beyond the State: Civil Society and Associational Life in Africa', *World Politics*, Vol.41, No.3 (April 1989), p.415.
59. Adam Przeworski *et al.*, *Sustainable Democracy* (Cambridge: Cambridge University Press, 1995), pp.20–21.
60. 'The Constitution of Civil Society in African History and Politics', in B. Caron, A. Gboyega and E. Osaghae (eds.), *Democratic Transition in Africa* (Ibadan: University of Ibadan Press, 1992) as discussed in Hutchful, 'The Civil Society Debate in Africa', p.61, see also p.71.
61. *The Two Faces of Civil Society: NGOs and Politics in Africa* (West Hartford, CT: Kumarian Press, 1996).
62. See Blair *et al.*, 'Civil Society and Democratic Development', pp.4–10 and Hansen, 'Constituencies for Reform', especially p.3 quoted in the text at footnote 45 above.
63. Whitehead, 'Bowling in the Bronx', pp.100–101.
64. Ibid., p.106. On this basis he rejects religious fundamentalist organizations and wealthy families controlling newspapers to discredit their political enemies, p.107.
65. Wachira Maina, 'Taking Stock of the Reforms', *The CGD Reforms Digest* (Nov. 1997), p.5.
66. Sheri Berman, 'Civil Society and the Collapse of the Weimar Republic', *World Politics*, Vol.49, No.3 (April 1997).
67. Berman, 'Civil Society and the Collapse of the Weimar Republic', p.411, p.414: 'civil society institutions often catered to member of a particular group: socialists, Catholics, and bourgeois Protestants each joined their own choral societies and bird-watching clubs', p.426.
68. Ibid., pp.419–21.
69. Ibid., pp.421–4.
70. Ibid., p.426.
71. Berman develops her use of Huntington more fully in 'Civil Society and Political Institutionalization', pp.567–70.
72. *Political Order in Changing Societies* (New Haven, CT: Yale University Press, 1968), p.21.
73. 'It is logically prior and historically more important', she says, citing Huntington. Berman, 'Civil Society and the Collapse of the Weimar Republic', p.402. One could also possibly argue that the two proceed reciprocally. For example, Holm, Molutsi and Somolokae suggest that civil society and democracy in Botswana are developing in parallel, but their data indicates that the process has not gone very far, and they do not analyse how the development of the two might depend on each other. 'The Development of Civil Society in a Democratic State', pp.63–6.
74. *Making Democracy Work*, p.176.
75. The other causal link she highlights is even more mystifying – that 'civil society activity may become an alternative to politics, increasingly absorbing citizens' energies and satisfying their basic needs' where political structures are weak or illegitimate. Berman, 'Civil Society and the Collapse of the Weimar Republic', p.427. It may be more 'satisfying', but on what basis does she think individuals lost interest in the policy making process through which the Weimar government allocated benefits that could affect their pocketbooks?
76. Foley and Edwards, 'The Paradox of Civil Society', p.49.
77. Hansen, 'Constituencies for Reform', p.3.
78. Carothers, 'Democracy Assistance', p.117.
79. Ibid., p.118.

The 'Civil' and the 'Political' in Civil Society: The Case of India

NEERA CHANDHOKE

The main objective of this article is to interrogate some of the dominant conceptualizations that have come to cluster around the concept of civil society in recent theory. Due to a variety of historical factors, these conceptualizations have romanticized the concept to a large extent. In the process, any meaningful or politically relevant discussion of civil society has often been obfuscated. The article problematizes the notion of civil society as the 'third sphere' in recent theory, and illustrates the argument with recent examples from India, with the intention of restoring some of the important insights that should logically attend any serious understanding of the concept.

INTRODUCTION

We have, since the 1980s, witnessed alongside the resurgence of civil society, a somewhat uncritical celebration of the concept to such an extent that it has become a *consensual* concept. But when concepts become consensual they become problematic. Indeed, if a variety of dissimilar groups such as international funding agencies, non-governmental organizations (NGOs), and institutions of the state on the one hand, and left-leaning liberals, trade unions, and social movements on the other, subscribe equally to the validity of the concept, it is time to worry. It is time to worry for if groups who should otherwise be disagreeing on the concept come to agree on it, the concept must have been *flattened* out to such an alarming extent that it loses its credibility. In other words, the concept of civil society may have, through consensus, become slack.

In effect, just because a concept acquires widespread acclaim all over the world, this does not by any means either indicate or ensure that it possesses either analytical rigour or conceptual clarity in contemporary theorization. And when concepts lack these attributes, their value as well as their validity as intellectually relevant and politically worthwhile categories diminishes considerably. The first section of this article outlines the reasons for the flattening out of civil society. The subsequent sections argue that civil society is part of a constitutive complex of other concepts and that it cannot be seen as independent of the constitutive complex. This recognition may help to alter our understanding of civil society to some extent.

CIVIL SOCIETY: THE POWER OF AN IDEA

The reasons for the widespread consensus that civil society has come to command in recent times are by now well known. In the 1970s and the 1980s, East European intellectuals, political activists, and trade union leaders mounted a sustained challenge to the power of 'Stalinist' states by invoking the concept of civil society.[1] The power of the idea revealed itself rather starkly in 1989, when so many awesome states collapsed like the proverbial houses of cards, helpless before a people determined to gain or recover political and civil freedoms in a space they called civil society. In this space peopled by self-help organizations, and marked by solidarity and civility, it was hoped that ordinary men and women would be able to associate and express their sentiments in freedom and without fear, under the protection of the rule of law. They would simply be able to make their own histories collectively, howsoever ineptly they made them.

The invocation of civil society in eastern Europe came to embody three, possibly even more than three, historical meanings, all of which led to some sensational consequences. First, the civil society argument sought to limit formerly untrammelled power of the state by the institutionalization of political, but more importantly, civil rights and the rule of law. Second, and correspondingly, the argument sought to carve out a domain that would function independently of state regulation. Here people, free from state inspired *diktat*, could engage in projects of all kinds. Third, the civil society argument propelled an important issue onto the political agenda. It simply asserted that the active engagement of ordinary men and women in groups that were smaller than the state, namely family and kinship groups, neighbourhoods, professional and social associations, and voluntary agencies, was a good thing in itself.

Note the main planks of the civil society argument: freedom guaranteed by civil rights and the rule of law, publicity, accessibility, property rights, and the free market. In retrospect, it is more than clear that the East Europeans in the 1980s practically re-enacted the bourgeois revolution, which more than 200 years ago had positioned itself against absolutist state power in countries such as England. Indeed John Locke (1632–1704), the quintessential liberal thinker, may well have authored the civil society script in this part of the world.

Correspondingly, even as political activists concentrated on crystallizing a project of social autonomy in a sphere free from state power, they in effect declared an end to the revolutionary vision. Traditionally, radical theory has focused on harnessing political passions to the cause of social and political transformation, now these very same political passions were to be yoked to the liberal democratic project. *Civil society began where revolution ended.*

It is true that in the historical conditions prevailing in that part of the world in the 1980s, even these self-limiting imaginations led to some incredible consequences. As the idea spiralled through time, the invocation of civil society quickly outstripped its own boundaries. By the last year of the 1980s, this purportedly self-limiting social revolution transformed itself into a highly charged political movement.[2] The *civil public* had dramatically transformed itself into the *political public,* asserting its right not only to hold state power accountable, but its right to dismiss states that failed to respond to the political aspirations of their people. A fourth dimension had been added to the civil society argument: notably that people had the competence to chart out a *political* discourse on the kind of polity they wanted to live in. The balance of power in those heady last years of the 1980s perceptibly shifted from the state to civil society.

The spectacle of the transformation of the *civil public* to a *political public* concerned with the shape and content of the polity carries an important lesson for states and societies. The lesson simply is that wherever and whenever states pulverize domains of collective action, the assertion of civil society against the state can prove to be politically explosive. Witness how the 1989 'velvet revolutions' were to demonstrate the power of what can be called the 'pressure cooker' effect, merely substantiating what Gramsci had told us, namely, that states without civil societies are tremendously fragile compared to states that possess civil societies.[3]

It is not surprising that the argument proved immensely attractive for political activists struggling to free the people from the stultifying grip of the state. In South America, Africa, and Asia in the 1970s and the 1980s the idea of civil society became an important plank in the struggle of urban-based professional groups, intellectuals and political activists, both against military regimes and non-responsive political parties. The recent spectacular success of the mobilization of civil society against the regime led by President Suharto in Indonesia bears testimony to the power of this idea. In effect, the sight of the civil society argument winning some spectacular victories against tyrannical elites has sent an important, albeit a tautological message – the desirability of civil society.

CIVIL SOCIETY AS THE THIRD SPHERE

The spectacle of so many people out there on the streets in 1989 in eastern Europe, and later in other countries, interrogating states, clamouring for an end to arbitrary power, carving out with astonishing rapidity domains of collective action within the interstices of monopolistic and coercive bureaucracies, and simply connecting in webs of solidarity and fraternity, has proved enormously stimulating to democratic political imaginations. After all, what could be more seductive than the promise that it is possible for people to create their own histories together, independently of the state, howsoever badly they may create these histories? What could be more sparkling than the promise that arbitrary states can be controlled, even dismantled, by the exercise of the popular will? What could be more enticing than the notion that it is not the state with its bureaucratic and legal language of power, not the market with its language of materiality, but the people and their languages of solidarity who lay down the limits of what is politically permissible?

Equally, what could be more delightful than the imagery conjured up by Michael Walzer when he speaks of civil society as the space of uncoerced human association? 'The picture here', he writes,

> is of people freely associating and communicating with one another, forming and reforming groups of all sorts, not for the sake of any particular formation – family, tribe, nation, religion, commune, brotherhood or sisterhood, interest group or ideological movement – but for the sake of sociability itself. For we are by nature social, before we are political or economic beings.[4]

Civil society, suggests Walzer, is the 'setting of setting', here people associate with each other on various grounds but notably for the sake of realizing their natures as social beings.

Given promises of a sphere that just brings together people in meshes of solidarity, as opposed to the meshes of power, is not surprising that in time civil society came to be slotted in the Tocquevillian (after Alexis de Tocqueville) mode as the 'third sphere'.[5] It simply came to be juxtaposed to both the state and the market by virtue of its radically different nature. Here social associations bringing people together in networks of solidarity cultivate the art of empathy, perform functions of pedagogy and socialization, and in general, help citizens to connect. They thus offset what in another context Jürgen Habermas has called the instrumental rationality of the state and of the market.

It is not surprising that the idea of the 'third sphere' came quickly to represent a distinct, even an autonomous sphere of collective life. Charles Taylor, for instance, argues that civil society comprises 'those dimensions of social life which cannot be confounded with, or swallowed up in, the state'.[6] Axel Honneth conceptualizes civil society as 'all civil institutions and organisations which are prior to the state'. Issac speaks of civil society as 'those human networks that exist independently of, if not anterior to, the political state'.[7]

And Cohen and Arato in a, by now well-known, definition, refer to a 'third realm' differentiated from the economy and the state as civil society.[8] Civil society as the space for associational life is, on the face of it, neither contaminated by the logic of politics nor that of economics. For both logics have been found wanting, mired as they are in the politics of conflict, on the one hand, and the politics of competition, on the other. Civil society in the hands of these two authors becomes a normative model of a societal realm different from the state and the economy and having the following components: (1) plurality: families, informal groups, and voluntary associations whose plurality and autonomy allow for a variety of forms of life; (2) publicity: institutions of culture and communication; (3) privacy: a domain of individual self-development and moral choice; and (4) legality: structures of general laws and basic rights needed to demarcate plurality, privacy and publicity from at least the state and, what may appear more tendentious, from the economy too.[9]

Let us now in the course of an exploration of civil society overturn this assumption by raising the following questions. Can we assume that civil society possesses a distinct logic of its own, which is in sharp contrast to that of the state or the market? Can we correspondingly assume that it is quite as autonomous of other spheres as much as we would like it to be? These questions are significant because the answers may hold important implications for our comprehension of what civil society is and for the way we think of civil society as a *political project*. In effect, what is being suggested here is that our *normative expectations* about the sphere of civil society should not derange our analysis of *actually existing civil societies*. We should in other words learn to problematize the sphere exactly as Hegel, Marx, and Gramsci had done, even if the results of our investigation may not prove to be entirely satisfactory for our political or indeed academic concerns. But, on the other hand, we cannot allow our political passions and normative concerns to obfuscate our understanding of this sphere, for that may lead us into tediously repetitive dead ends.

Admittedly, the idea of civil society as an autonomous third sphere, with its attending imagery of solidarity, empathy, and self-organization is immensely attractive. For only if we accept this as our basic premise, can we proceed to assume that atomized and impersonal societies can be emancipated from the alienation that besets them. It is only then that we can hope that warm, perhaps intimate, relationships among people can be restored. Indeed, the concept of civil society seems peculiarly apt when it comes to realizing the project associated with Habermas: of rescuing and regenerating the life world. What makes it attractive, writes Adam

Seligman, is 'its assumed synthesis of private and public "good" and of individual and social desiderata. The idea of civil society thus embodies for many an ethical ideal of the social order, one that, if not overcomes, at least harmonizes the conflicting demands of individual interest and social good.'[10] As we shall see, the shadow of Adam Smith and his *Theory of Moral Sentiments* (1759) looms large over these conceptualizations.

But howsoever attractive and seductive the idea of civil society as a third sphere of human interaction may be, howsoever radically novel in its conceptualization and design it may appear, howsoever much it may seem to provide an answer to our pressing and intractable problems, the idea itself is deeply problematic. For it brings up not only the problem of boundary maintenance between spheres, it also throws up the additional problem of how overlapping boundaries can possibly contain separate and discrete logics. In the subsequent section, I argue that this kind of separation between spheres of individual and collective life is both misplaced and confusing. In effect, it can blur our grasp of civil society to a large extent.

THE CONSTITUTIVENESS OF CIVIL SOCIETY

The question that we need to ask at this stage of the argument is simply the following: can we think of *any* sphere of human activity as either autonomous or as marked by a different logic? The assumptions behind the 'third sphere' argument presumably is that whereas people once they are out of the household enter into transactions with other members in civil society, these interactions will not be marked by either conflict, mediation, or compromise that is the stuff of politics. Nor will they be characterized by competition over scarce resources, which is the stuff of economics. This kind of bounding off of civil society leads to some confusion, for we will have to presuppose that each and every sphere of human action is marked by a different sectoral and organizational logic. And it is precisely this that is reiterated by Cohen and Arato when they write that 'economic activities in the substantive sense are (at least in part) included in civil society, but economy as a formal process is outside of it'.[11]

They go on to suggest that while the borders between the economy and civil society are not sealed off, the economy can be differentiated from civil society. This really means that at some point, and at some site, civil society may be engaged in economic transactions, but this is not a *general* feature of civil society, it may be, however, an *occasional* one. What is important is that the ethos of the market does not constitute civil society. Further confusion piles up when they suggest that we should separate the political, that is, non-state society from civil society. Not only is civil society not political, the domain of politics does not affect it. Besides, we now have another site of human association added to the three spheres: the public sphere that is the non-state sphere of politics. In this fourfold classification of collective life, civil society as the realm of warm, sociable and personalized associational life is markedly different from the economy, the public sphere and the state, though on occasion members of civil society may execute activities that spill over into the other domains.

Other conceptualizations of civil society fill in the 'third sector' with voluntary groups and refer to it as the 'voluntary sector' or the 'non-profit sector'. Here professional non-governmental organizations, foundations and philanthropies shoulder welfare and community re-building activities, provide education, health, and community development in a mode that is different from the state. But, once again, this sphere is supposed to function in isolation from, or even counter to, the logic of the market and the state.[12] Indeed, multilateral funding agencies have tried to build up this sphere as an alternative to the state by funding non-governmental agencies and bypassing the 'third world' state in the process. Some groups do not seek to bypass the market, since the rolling back of the state from both civil society and the market forms an integral part of this agenda. Other *avatars* of civil society vigorously promote the activities of non-governmental organizations as providers of services and upholders of democracy, as an alternative to the market. In any case, civil society is definitely de-linked from the state and in some cases from the market.

In sum, whatever we fill civil society with – associations, voluntary agencies, or social movements – it continues to be thought of as the third sphere, neither related to the state and market nor constituted by them. In other words, it emerges in such formulations as something uncontaminated by those impulses that characterize other domains of human interaction. Here people can sort out their problems at the level of the neighbourhood, community, and the workplace with some prospect of reconciliation, for civil society is presumably neither conflictual nor marked with power relations as the other spheres are.

Now by the logic of this argument, collective life, that is the part of life where individuals come into contact with each other outside the household, can be separated into distinct arenas of activity. Each sphere possesses its own logic and its own momentum and no sphere either influences the other or constitutes the other. Collective life can thus be conceptualized as the h.h. (household) + c.s.(civil society) + e (the economy) + p (politics that includes the public sphere as well as the state). The perspective on collective life is – to put it mildly – additive.

But an additive notion of collective life is beset with its own problems. Copernicus once wrote about the astronomers of his day thus: 'With them it is as though an artist were to gather the hands, feet, head, and other members for his images from diverse models, each part excellently drawn, but not related to a single body, and since they in no way match each other, the result would be a monster rather than man.'[13] This illustrates very nicely the problems when we first subdivide collective life into plural and mutually exclusive categories in thought, and then add all the parts we ourselves have crafted with some dexterity, in order to construct a whole. Something of the same kind seems to beset additive social scientists. They first break down human activities into mutually indifferent and exclusive categories and invest each with its own logic, its own range of problems and methods, and then add them together to give us a picture of collective life. In this picture, no one category influences let alone constitutes the other, no category is central to human life, and no category determines how we approach other categories of activity. But – and this is the question – do categories of collective existence *not* constitute each other?

Certainly, we can accept such separation as a heuristic device. We can in effect think of various spheres of human interaction in terms of the *different* ways in which human beings make their own history. So we can, speaking purely theoretically, refer to different sets and kinds of interaction in the household, the economy, in civil society and in politics. What, however, should be resisted is the implication that these sectors of human activity do not constitute each other, or that they are marked by an exclusive and discrete logic that differs from site to site of such interaction. Therefore, whereas we can with some legitimacy conceptualize civil society as a site where people associate in ways that are distinct from the way they associate in the economy or in the political sphere, we can hardly assume that civil society is either emancipated or abstracted from the ethos that permeates these two spheres. There are at least eight reasons for this.

1) State as Enabler of Civil Society

At an obvious level, civil society needs at the least a politico-legal framework that institutionalizes the normative pre-requisites of rights, freedom and the rule of law. Think of constitutions, judiciaries, and even the police, which are required for any meaningful implementation of civil liberties. But this framework, note, is provided by none other than the state. Therefore, ironically, the very state that civil society supposedly positions itself against, *enables* the latter in the sense that it provides the legal and the political settings for the sphere to exist and maintain itself. The shades of the great philosopher Hegel who suggested that the state is a *precondition* for the existence of civil society prove especially strong here.[14] The autonomy of civil society from the state emerges as an optical illusion.

If we accept this point, we cannot help but concede that this power of setting the frame of civil society gives the state immense capacity to define which kinds of civil society organizations are permissible under law. Thus, whereas in India the state can accept organizations of industrialists such as the Federation of Indian Chambers of Commerce or the Confederation of Indian Industries with a great deal of felicity, while it can accept even striking university teacher unions struggling for higher salaries, it has a definite problem in respect of groups that challenge the legitimacy of the system. For unless we subscribe to the liberal fallacy that the state is a disembodied institution abstracted from society, we have to accept – as discussed below – that the state codifies the power relations in society. It is simply a condensate of power, though its identity as a codifier of power gives it a particular status as well as a fair amount of autonomy from the power equations in society. Therefore, it will not axiomatically tolerate any challenge to the structuration of power in society.

It is not surprising that the Indian state has proved notoriously coercive when it comes to, for example, organizations of the landless peasants seeking redistributive justice. It has, for instance, stigmatized Naxalite groups representing the far left, who are fighting for the rights of the landless peasants, as criminal. It has indeed banished them to the utter darkness that constitutes the periphery of civil society. Here, in this unlit and dismal space, groups possessing no rights whatsoever are hounded by the law and the police, killed in police encounters and denied the protection that should in principle be extended to any citizen of the state. True Naxalites use violence to accomplish their objectives. But no one stops to consider *why* they need to use violence. Is it because they have experienced violence as a constitutive element of both state and civil society? Is it because the state simply does not heed the voices of the most under-privileged and disempowered sections of Indian society – the so-called 'low caste' landless peasantry oppressed by the so-called upper castes, on the one hand, and the propertied classes, on the other? [often the two overlap]. But it is a different matter when representatives of the commodified peasantry seek higher procurement prices or cancelling of loans. When it comes to withdrawing the generous subsidies granted to this section of the peasantry, we witness utter furore in Parliament and the press, simply because in today's India it is this group that exercises political influence, even direct political power, at the state level. Towards them, the Indian state is scandalously soft.

This offensive discrimination makes sense only when we comprehend that the domain of civil society is delineated by the state itself. And states simply happen to have their own notions of what is politically permissible, what is culturally permissible and what is socially permissible. And whereas these notions will *enable* some sections of civil society, they will necessarily *disable* others. State action, therefore, possesses momentous consequences for civil society inasmuch as it has the power to lay down the boundaries of what is politically permissible. It simply has the luxury of shaping the structure of civil society organizations to a formidable extent. And civil society may indeed be alarmingly constrained when it comes to ideas of what is politically permissible. What currency can we then give to the idea of a 'third' and presumably autonomous sphere in this context?

2) Limits on Civil Society Autonomy

Of course, actors in civil society have the right under law to challenge state-given notions of what is politically permissible, *provided* that they do so in ways that cohere with the legal limits of political action. They can use the permitted means of opposition, such as moving courts, public action and marches. This is a given under any condition of liberal democracy that is an indispensable pre-requisite of civil society. What, however, civil society actors cannot do is to challenge the state in ways that it does not allow – militancy, for instance, howsoever justified this militancy may be in the face of the brute exercise of state power and that of the privileged groups in civil society itself. Obviously, both discourses and political action in civil society have to function within certain parameters. For the penalties for transgressing these boundaries are far too high. Groups who transgress these boundaries are always likely to be excluded to the space beyond the horizons of civil society. And this space happens to be dark, damp and rather mouldy, much like the medieval dungeons in Europe to which the Catholic Church expelled 'heretics'. Here we find neither rights nor justice, just the naked exercise of brutal police and military power.

Therefore, we can suggest with some justification that the much-vaunted autonomy of civil society is constrained from the word go. Within the frontiers of what is politically permissible, of course, actors in civil society can exercise constant vigilance against arbitrary exercise of power, check and monitor violations of human rights, demand accountability, demand that the state delivers what it promises, and battle unjust policies. They can do all this as long as, recollect, they respect the frontiers laid down by the state – frontiers that may exclude rather than include, disempower rather than empower.

3) Civil Society Needs the State's Support

However, we also need to accept that the relationship between the state and civil society need not be only one of opposition. For actors in civil society *need* the state for various purposes. Or that the relationship between the two can with perfect reason be collaborative and co-operative. This is understandable, for a women's group can hardly demand fresh rights for, say, gender justice, without the corresponding demand for state protection and the setting up of appropriate institutions. Or civil society organizations can scarcely carry out developmental work without the state providing them with resources, personnel and management. Alternatively, civil society groups fighting, say, violations of civil liberties, will *need* the state to punish offenders, need human rights commissions, sympathetic judges and a sensitive police for their objectives. Various groups engaged in providing literacy to the people would of necessity look to the state for both funding as well as institutionalizing their efforts in the form of the right to primary and adult education. A number of other such examples could be cited, but the point is clear enough.

In effect, the argument here is that civil society actors will draw upon the state both to reform state institutions – to redress violation of human rights for instance – and to reform civil society itself, for example, through enacting laws restricting sexual harassment in the work place. This means – and this is a point that is not generally grasped by many advocates of civil society – that the state *frames the limits of civil society, as well as frames social initiatives in civil society.* Even Walzer, with his somewhat romantic view of civil society as 'the setting of settings' and the realm of 'concrete and authentic solidarities' where 'all are excluded and none is preferred', accepts realistically that 'civil society requires political agency'. The state, he agrees, is an indispensable agent, 'Even if', he hastens to add, 'the associational networks also, always, resist the organizing impulses of state bureaucrats'.

4) Civil Society and Nationalism

However, that associational networks always resist the organizing impulses of state bureaucrats is not clear. For one of the uncomfortable realities of political life is that states not only lay down agendas, but that they employ a variety of means to garner and garnish acceptance, and hence legitimacy, for these agendas. Gramsci, recollect, lent the term 'hegemony' to this, in his by now famous formulation. This formulation proves more than apt when we witness the manner in which the current government in India has raised nationalism to a high pitch of hysteria, through the exploitation of first the nuclear explosion at Pokhran 1998 and then the war with Pakistan in Kargil in 1999.

In mid-May 1998, under the Bharatiya Janata Party (BJP)-led government, a nuclear device was exploded in Pokhran. Immediately the country was swept by a powerful storm of 'national pride' at having gatecrashed the exclusive nuclear club. Even as themes relating to the nation, national conceit and jingoistic exuberance reached absurd proportions,[15] all this contributed towards the consolidation of a belligerent culture, initially propelled by the *Sangh Parivar*[16] since the late 1980s. Members of the *parivar,* for instance, wanted to scatter the dust from the site of the explosions all over the country, till someone pointed out to them that the dust was radioactive and bound to harm. In all this euphoria and games of one-up-manship that overtook civil society, reservations expressed by the anti-nuclear movement that the production of weapons of mass destruction was morally, politically and strategically suicidal, were brushed away contemptuously, and dismissed as anti-patriotic. There is, in today's nuclearized India, no room for debate. We witness only the imposition of a particularly mindless nationalistic fervour that has been in major measure propelled both by the state and compliant groups in civil society.[17]

Similarly, the discovery in mid-1999 that Pakistan's armed forces had invaded Kargil in India's northern border, was to reinforce the spirit of assertive nationalism. As the country was invaded by the Kargil fever, with hundreds of young men queuing up to go and fight the invader in the north, even as anger against Pakistan erupted in several unpalatable ways, the rage against our neighbour was displaced to target the Muslim minority in the country.[18] The Kargil incident furthered the already communalized atmosphere in the country to an alarming extent. All this was supremely gainful for the government. For even as discourses in civil society came to be dominated by Kargil, a fertile ground for the BJP to come back to power in the September 1999 election was assiduously prepared. A report on an opinion poll carried in the national weekly *Outlook* was to state before the elections of September 1999 that '[P.M] Vajpayee, fuelled by Kargil, will be the singular engine of the BJP's return … just seven months ago … Vajpayee was widely pitted as a nice man but a poor P.M … Today the nation's collective memory doesn't seem to stretch beyond Kargil; at best, to the bomb'.[19]

The problem is that both the events at Pokhran and Kargil have institutionalized and legitimized a particularly mindless cultural nationalism[20] in India's civil society. Even as this genre of nationalism seeks to cast a strong shadow of suspicion on the minorities within the country, it dismisses those who question the shape of this nationalism as anti-national. Overtaking civil society in India, this nationalism – both exclusive and insular to a frightful degree – strongly bears the imprimatur of the state. Narrow in scope, chauvinistic in content, stereotypical in form, and constructed around the homogenizing impulse, cultural nationalism attempts to accomplish two feats. It seeks to construct majorities and minorities out of a plural, heterogeneous and loosely articulated society, and it seeks to institutionalize fissures between the two constructed groups on the basis of stereotypes and stigmata. Events at Pokhran and Kargil were to consolidate this. In the process, the BJP-led government has managed to legitimize a deep-seated intolerance in India's civil society, as evinced in the fact that criminal and murderous attacks on other minorities such as the Christians have grown.[21] And the tragedy is that with some notable exceptions, the majority of the inhabitants in our civil society seem resigned to the prospect of a majoritarian India, even as the possibility of a meaningful debate on such vital issues is foreclosed. Or at least the pendulum has perceptibly swung in favour of cultural nationalism and against democratic ideologies.

Civil societies we will have to accept, albeit with some amount of discomfort, can be organized in ways that are not healthy for civil society itself. Popular support for state sponsored action in civil society breeds somewhat unfortunate consequences for all those groups who oppose the state or dominant trends within the sphere. But theorizations of civil society as an autonomous sphere, simply neglect to see how the sphere can be colonized by the legitimizing strategies of the state.

5) Politics and Power in Associational Life

Moreover, the idea that associational life is always the source of democratic activism, that can be counterposed to the arbitrary state, is one that is riddled with ambiguity. Should we assume that civil society is not permeated with politics and with power, all of which curtails democratic activity in definite ways? Think of patriarchy that consolidates itself in the sphere of civil society and in the household, or the practices of caste, ethnicity and race that mould inter-personal relationships, or class equations that are always weighted against democratic groups. Or should we assume that politics and power in associational life is not as stultifying as when it is wielded by the state? But as any astute observer will tell us, society itself is riddled with power equations of all kinds – those of patriarchy, class, caste and religion. Surely in a post-Foucauldian age we should be able to accept this. For society, as Michel Foucault argued when directing our attention away from visible and formalized codes of power, is saturated with power, that is ubiquitous and immanent, and that has neither a beginning nor an end. 'The individual is not to be conceived as a sort of elementary nucleus, a primitive atom, a multiple and inert material on which power comes to fasten or against which it happens to strike ... In fact, it is already one of the prime effects of power that certain bodies, certain gestures, certain discourses, certain desires, come to be identified and constituted as individuals.'[22] This individual is not the opposite of power; he is one of its prime effects. The individual whose equality, justice and freedom civil society is supposed to uphold, is already in himself the effect of a subjugation that is much more profound than himself. If this argument makes sense, then civil society as the associational aspect of society cannot be conceptualized as free from or abstracted from power relationships.

6) State, Power and Society

There is more a profound issue at stake here. I suggest we will not be able to understand the complexities of civil society unless we understand what the state is. And the state, as Marx was to tell us a long time ago, is not suspended in mid-air from society, so that other spheres of society can function independently of it. It is neither dis-embodied nor dis-embedded from the power structures of society, for the *state both condenses as well as codifies the power of the social formation.* If this is so, we need to note that *the power codified at the level of the state is gathered up and condensed from society.* State power, in other words, rests on a constellation of power in society.

Certainly, the state cannot be reduced to power structures in society, for it plays a key role in producing, codifying and constructing power. The specificity of the state lies in the fact that it codifies a dominant set of power relations in society, gives to them fixity, and therefore, gives society stability. For instance, in a society marked by proprietors of property, the state will endeavour to secure property rights against those groups who challenge these rights, in the form of, say, laws, or the judicial process that privileges the right to property. The state thus possesses the power to select, categorize, crystallize, and arrange social power in formal codes and institutions. This gives to the state its status specificity and its own distinctive brand of power. In contrast to society where power balances are precarious and unstable, since they are prone to challenges from subordinated groups, the state grants a certain coherence, howsoever minimal, to the power relations of society. As both a concentrate and a codifier of power, the state materializes as a discrete form of power. In effect, since the state through a set of specifically political practices confers fixity to otherwise unstable social blocs in society, society is constituted through the state and exists within the parameters laid down by the state.[23]

However, we also need to remember that this power is not conjured up out of thin air, and that it is always drawn from society, from the nodal points of power relations that define a social order. Any perspective that disregards this is bound to suffer from myopia, for it detaches social and economic from political power. If this is so, then the state as the codified power of the social formation is not detached from civil society where power is expressed and contested, it is the apex organization of power. And if this is so, then civil society cannot be abstracted from the state and defined as a separate sphere. For the two are organically connected through structures of power. The relationship is reciprocal, with the state reflecting the dominant power equation in civil society, and these power equations getting a fresh lease of life through a state that is in complicity with the structuration of power.

7) *The Darker Side of Social Capital*

Therefore, all those theories that tell us that associational life is the answer to state power because associations are democratic *per se* are misplaced because they give us an erroneous picture of civil society. Consider Robert Putnam's celebrated analysis of social capital.[24] Putnam conceives of civil society, in the sense of dense networks of associations, as generating what he calls social capital. Defining social capital as any feature of social relations that contributes to the ability of society to work together and accomplish certain goals, Putnam suggests a correlation between the density of social associations that manage to bridge social cleavages, the creation of civic culture and strong democracy. High levels of civic engagement, argues Putnam, contribute to the sustaining and fostering of democracy.

This is not a new idea. Civic republican thinkers suggested long ago that the vibrancy of any democracy rests on the cultivation of moral virtue, moral commitments, and the fostering of public spiritedness among citizens. But this is not the thrust of Putnam's argument, for he relies solely on the density of associational life as an indicator of high levels of citizen participation in democratic life. Associationalism produces, according to him, habits of co-operation, trust, social networks, and norms: in sum social capital, which is an indispensable pre-requisite for democracy.

Now, the concept of social capital as originally outlined by James Coleman,[25] had suggested that it is a feature not of individuals but of social relations. Coleman had in effect argued that social capital is context-dependent. Professional transactions among bankers, for instance, will be marked by the norms of reciprocity and trust. The existence of these norms constitutes a resource, since it facilitates financial transactions in society. This resource we term social capital. However, and this is a point we need to register, the banker need not carry trust with him to other social contexts, to land transactions with a crafty property dealer, for example. Outside a specific context, norms and values may not translate themselves into social capital, simply because they inhere in particular sets of social relationships. People need not necessarily internalize these values, it is enough that in a given setting they behave according to these values, or behave as they are expected to behave. But, warns Coleman, it is important to note that this capital is unevenly distributed in a society, and not every one has equal access to it.

More importantly, cautioned Coleman, not all forms of social capital are equally valuable as resources to facilitate individual or collective action. The concept, as we can see, becomes a morally neutral category in the hands of Coleman. It can facilitate transactions among a group of fascist organizations as much as it can be employed by a group of human rights activists to the same effect. Further, access to various forms of capital is shaped substantially by inequalities of social location such as race, gender, class or geography. Neither can we aggregate social capital to produce some measure of the resources available in and to a society. Putnam, on the other hand, attaches normative weight to the concept of social capital by abstracting it from social contexts and attributing it to individuals. He not only reduces the concept to associational life *per se*; he concentrates on only that form of life that permits civic engagement. Or he limits his focus to that kind of social capital that produces the civic spirit. He thus moves away from Coleman's formulation that emphasizes socially embedded and context-specific resources.

His theory of social capital in general assumes that the more we *connect* with other people, the more we trust them and vice versa. Generalized social trust in each other, trust in public officials, and tolerance which trust requires as a precondition are integral components of social capital, which has in turn a beneficial effect on citizen participation. Social capital, in other words, is the source of healthy democratic activity that breeds participation.

However, several questions arise at precisely this moment to cast doubts on Putnam's thesis. For one, how do people build trust and reciprocity in associational life in independence from wider contexts? After all, the state can launch projects of political repression, or propel shifting patterns of cultural hegemony, all of which lead to fissures in civil society. Certainly economic disasters can be propelled by the economy. All this can radically alter the balance between groups in civil society even as social conflict over resources can bedevil relations of reciprocity and trust.

Consider for a moment how the politics of 'Mandalization' in India, which by reserving jobs in the public sector for the 'Other Backward Castes' (the OBCs) in addition to the reservations for the scheduled castes, split Indian society irremediably. As the central government headed by Prime Minister V.P Singh in 1990 implemented the recommendations of the Mandal commission for job reservations, civil society in India witnessed the onset of immense rage and *angst*. Young people, most of them students, occupied strategic sites in New Delhi's busy traffic intersection, even as they mounted a diatribe against what they called the sheer incompetence and inefficiency of the OBCs. Several young people died as they set themselves on fire in protest. The country was overcome with the politics of wild, disrespectful and acrimonious protest. Competition for scarce resources had rendered civic life completely uncivil. Rather than trust and reciprocity, we saw nothing but anger and distrust, rendering dreams of social capital into nightmares.

Two years later the Hindu right wing in the country – the complex of organizations known as the *Sangh Parivar* – accomplished their objective of bringing down the Babri mosque in Ayodhaya. The act itself was preceded by large-scale mobilization over a period of at least five years, through the utilization of several means: political theatricals, provocative oratory, and spectacles such as chariot processions – the *rath yatra*. The present home minister L.K Advani journeyed through the country in one such car-turned-chariot making impassioned speeches for recovering history by demolishing the mosque, which it was claimed had been built on a temple of God Ram, by the Mughal Emperor Babar. As Advani commenced the chariot procession young men offered him a cup of blood signifying readiness to achieve martyrdom. The stage was slowly but surely set for the communalization of India's already fragile civil society, a communalization that has unleashed completely when the mosque was brought down in December 1992. Communal riots said to be the worst since the Partition of India in 1947 engulfed the country. We could see no trust here, only the hermeneutics of suspicion and the politics of hate in India's civil society. No civility, but the gradual cleavage of society along religious and caste lines. And all this was brought about through social associations.

Mandalization and Mandirization in India in the 1990s have drastically furthered the fault lines in the country and created cleavages in associational life. Both these events had somewhat disastrous consequences for civil society even as people who had learnt to live together, despite different caste and religious persuasions, were torn apart by the politics of hatred. We can hardly accept Putnam's assumption that social associations function to further civic engagement, just as we cannot agree with the theorists of civil society that civil society as a third sphere is comfortably bounded off from politics and the state.

Moreover, if we confine our attention only to social associations that are beneficial to civic engagement, we not only engage in moral irresponsibility, we also achieve a distorted understanding of civil society. For if civil society consists of associational life *per se*, then we have to accept that associations of every stripe and hue exist in this space. Patriarchal forces exist alongside feminist groups. Religious fascists exist along with movements against communalism. Class oppression exists alongside groups organized to fight for redistributive justice. And pro-state associations that further and strengthen the dominant project of society exist alongside those groups that challenge the legitimacy of the state. Some social groups further civic engagement, others inhibit it, some expand the domain of civil society by bringing in formerly disadvantaged groups, and yet others debar these groups from civic life. For the enemies of democratic life exist in civil society itself, even as groups well organized to make demands and perhaps in a position to have these demands satisfied, strive to impose their mandate upon the sphere.

Let us look briefly at the organization – the Rashtriya Swayam Sevak Sangh (RSS), whose membership, overlapping as it does with the membership of the top leaders of the BJP, currently exercises power in India. The RSS does not tire of telling us that it is not a political but a cultural organization, whose professed aim is to create a Hindu identity that is proudly aware of its cultural heritage. However, the pursuance of this very task makes the RSS the 'fountainhead of aggressive Hindu communalism'.[26] Based upon a firm rejection of the idea that the religious minorities have equal rights as citizens, the RSS and its affiliates subscribe to the views of the founder of modern day *Hindutva* – V.D. Savarkar. In 1923, Savarkar had defined a Hindu as one who regards India as both his Fatherland as well as his Holyland – *pitribhumi* and *punyabhumi*. But this cannot be the case for the Christians and the Muslims, he argues, for their Holy Land is in far away Arabia and Palestine. Therefore, India can never be Fatherland as well as Holy Land for minorities.[27] By this verbal sleight of hand, the minorities are pushed out of the boundaries of the nation. And the nation we have to accept is one of the constitutive ideologies of civil society. Consequently, civil society has either no place or a subordinate place for minorities.

A highly disciplined, closed, and hierarchical organization, the RSS has silently but surely trained its cadres to work for the establishment of a Hindu state, through attempts to forge a regenerated and strong or machismo Hindu culture throughout the country. Using disciplinary modes such as the morning drill,[28] and participating in what is euphemistically called nation building activities, the RSS seeks foremost to subordinate the individual to the collective. 'Physical training in the RSS is only the means to the end of a psychological drill leading to a total surrender of individuality to what the RSS likes to call the "ideal".'[29] In claustrophobic small towns marked by a trade cum professional milieu, the authors of the monograph *Khaki Shorts and Saffron Flags* point out, 'any alternative culture seems, quite simply, non-existent: the young men move from communal minded families to schools and colleges full of RSS teachers, and RSS *shakhas* provide, practically, the only other source of recreation, leisure–time socialization, and intellectual training'.[30] Aimed at effecting a fusion between religion and nationalism, the ideology and the practices of the RSS run completely counter to the values of civil society, values that seek to promote freedom, plurality, dialogue, tolerance, secularism and democracy.

Internally the body is marked by a complete lack of democracy, the command structure is totally centralized, the ethos is militaristic to an alarming degree and unthinking obedience surrounds its activities. Indeed, when it was set up in the 1920s, Hedgewar, the first president or the *sarsanghchalak*, built the internal structure of the RSS along the lines of revolutionary terrorist groups. Externally, the organization concentrating as it does on targeting religious minorities has contributed largely to the communalization of civil society in India. And we cannot regard the RSS as a group which is not of civil society, for this sphere as theorists like Walzer never tire of telling us, excludes no one and includes everyone. If this is so, we are compelled to conclude that civil society organizations need not be democratic at all, need not subscribe to the values of the sphere at all, and need not heed the calls to counter the state at all. For it is precisely organizations such as the RSS that have prepared civil society for the politics of majoritarianism.

Further, if we were to characterize healthy associational life only on the basis of the thickness of bonds within associations, as Putnam suggests, we realize uncomfortably that the most communal of organizations such as the RSS or indeed minority fundamentalist organizations are characterized by thick bonds of social solidarity. Research on the RSS has told us in great detail how the organization functions in a familial like structure, concerned with the most intimate details of its member's existence, and intent on cultivating the ethics of care among the members. And certainly the Ku Klux Klan or the Mafia, as any reader of Mario Puzo's remarkable novel *The Godfather* can tell us, is characterized by strong bonds of caring for and nurturing each other.

In effect, if we take as our referent point the idea that social organizations are the reason for civil society to exist, then we have to accept that the sphere contains every kind of group. We can hardly expel, say, the various chambers of commerce from civil society. They are as much a part of civil society as groups of the working classes fighting for a better living. We can scarcely expel groups of agro-industrialists who benefit from the Narmada dam from civil society and admit the Narmada Bachao Andolan (the NBA).[31] But this will mean that civil society, far from being the realm of solidarity and warm personalized interaction, is itself a fragmented, divided and a hierarchically structured realm. Here we will find organizations of the dominant classes existing alongside organizations of the dominated who are battling for survival, we find patriarchal structures existing alongside women's groups struggling for a place in the sun; we find caste and race based groups along with democratic movements fighting for dignity.

8) Civil Society as Defender of State Power

Civil society emerges in this perspective not the *site of sociability per se*, though this may well be an unintended consequence of associational life. It emerges as a *site for struggle* between the forces that uphold power equations and those that battle these equations in an attempt to further the democratic project. It is important to realize that dominant groups in civil society, far from constituting a sphere that is oppositional to the state, actually defend and extend state power in the domain of civil society.

COMING TO TERMS WITH THE 'CIVIL' IN CIVIL SOCIETY

If the argument made above proves to be at all persuasive, then it follows that civil society must be understood in the following way.

First, civil society as associational life cannot be identified with democracy *per se*. On the other hand, it is a *precondition* for democracy inasmuch as it constitutes both a site for democracy and a cluster of values and institutions that are intrinsic to democracy. Let me put this another way. Democracy requires as a precondition a space where various groups can express their ideas about how society and politics should be organized, where they can articulate both the content as well as the boundaries of what is desirable in a good society. Correspondingly, individuals and groups should possess the right to conceptualize in conditions of relative freedom their notions of the desired and the good society.

The absence of this site would mean the absence of democracy, for it would mean that people do not possess either access to a space, or to the freedom that is necessary for democratic interaction. Imagine a society that calls itself democratic and yet denies to its own people the opportunities to associate in freedom in order to carry out discussions or contestations on what should constitute the good life. That is why in authoritarian states the struggle for civil society primarily demands the consolidation of a space where people in association with others can debate and contest their own versions of the political. It is this dimension of the struggle that is indicated by the phrase civil society 'against the state'.

This achievement is by no measure a mean one. People demand that regimes recognize the competence of the political public to chart out a discourse on the content and the limits of what is politically permissible. Civil society in this instance stakes a claim to autonomy from the state, that people have the right to associate with each other, that this right should be recognized by the state, and that the state should institutionalize this natural right in the form of the legal freedom to associate. Correspondingly, civil societies have demanded the institutionalization of this right in the shape of the rule of law, rights, justiciability. But all this may be sufficient but not enough for democracy.

For one reason, formal democracy as critical theorists have pointed out in great detail can prove an illusion. Freedom and rights can mean the freedom of the propertied classes to carry out their projects of exploitation. Freedom can enable fascist groups to communalize society. The rule of law can be employed by amoral leaderships to debar substantial chunks of the people from the rights of citizenship. And the market, as any critical theorist knows, is supremely insensitive to those who cannot buy or who cannot sell. All this can render civil society supremely uncivil and rotten.

Secondly, this does not mean that we dispense with the argument, it merely means that formal democracy, which the concept is based upon, is supremely insensitive to power equations in civil society. Some groups possess overlapping political, material, and social power; others possess nothing – not even access to the means of subsistence. Civil society, therefore, cannot look only to the state, it needs must look inwards, at the power centres within its domain, which may be in complicity with the state, and battle them.

Therefore, what civil society does afford us is the provision of both a site as well as the values, which can help us to battle with the inequities of the sphere itself. Therefore, if the project of *Hindutva* hegemonized civil society to some extent, civil society also provides a space for anti-communal groups to struggle against this particular formulation, howsoever unequal the battle may seem to be at the present moment.

Thirdly, note that we witness a rather profound transformation in the notion of politics in such and related processes. Politics is not about what the state or the dominant classes do or do not do. In other words, politics is not about the capacity of power to do what it wills with people. Politics is about how ordinary men and women think about, conceptualize, debate, and contest how people belonging to different persuasions, classes, and interests live together in society in conditions of justice and civility.

Let me expand upon this. Politics in one obvious and rather simplistic sense is about competition over state power. Or it is about the decision making process in the state, about the content of these decisions and about the ways the holders of state power decide the fate of entire societies. This notion would restrict the notion of power to the formal and the visible domain of the state. But at a deeper level politics is about the experiences of everyday life. That is, politics is about how people translate their experiences into the expressive, politics is about how the dominant groups seek to retain their power. And politics is about the struggle of the dominated people to live in dignity. Therefore, civil society and its attendant norms of publicity, accountability, rights and rule of law becomes a staging ground for a struggle between democratic and anti-democratic forces. We ignore this aspect of civil society only at the risk of distorting our understanding of the sphere.

But this makes civil society valuable only as a site and as a cluster of values intrinsic to democratic life. For civil societies are what their inhabitants make of them, always keeping in mind that their thoughts and their social practices will be permeated by the logic of both the state and the market. Civil society is constituted by the politics of power as much as it is constituted by the politics of protest. And it is this aspect of civil society that transforms it, in Hegelian terms, into the 'theatre of history'.

CONCLUSION

This article has argued that the idea that civil society constitutes an independent sphere of existence may distort our understanding of the sphere. For though we tend to divide spheres of human interaction into segments, and though we accept that human beings act in different ways in different segments, we need to register that these spheres are mutually constitutive of each other. For this reason it is argued that civil society is only ambiguously the source of democratic activism, for we are likely to discover in this sphere structures of power that tie up with the state. Therefore, civil society emerges as a deeply fractured and hierarchically structured domain of social associations.

However, there is some value to the idea of civil society, because it provides the preconditions of formal democracy. And, though formal democracy is not sufficient for our purposes, it is an essential component of social and political structures. For it provides the space for democratic elements both to challenge power equations in the sphere as well as to transform the sphere itself.

But for this we have to accept that it is not enough that there *be* a civil society, or even a civil society that is independent of the state. Civil society is not an institution it is rather a process whereby the inhabitants of the sphere constantly monitor both the state and the monopoly of power in civil society. Democratic movements have to constantly widen the spaces from where undemocratic practices can be criticized, and for this purpose they have to exercise both vigilance and criticality. They have to be Janus-faced looking to the state and the market as well as inwards. In the process civil society constantly reinvents itself, constantly discovers new projects, discerns new enemies, and makes new friends. It is not something that once constructed can be left to fend for itself because it is a process. And this is important for civil society is an essential precondition for democracy.

NOTES

1. The civil society argument in this part of the world developed fairly rapidly into a polemic slogan that sharply counterposed the sphere of voluntary and purposive collective action based on solidarity and self-help organizations, to dictatorial state power.
2. Z.A. Pelcynzski, 'Solidarity and the "Rebirth of Civil Society"', in John Keane (ed.), *Civil Society and the State* (London: Verso, 1988), pp.361–80.
3. Antonio Gramsci, in Quinton Hoare and G.N. Smith (eds.), *Selections from Prison Notebooks of A. Gramsci* (New York: International Publishers, 1971).
4. Michael Walzer, 'The Concept of Civil Society', in M. Walzer (ed.), *Towards a Global Civil Society* (Providence and Oxford: Berghahn Books, 1998), pp.7 and 16.
5. For Tocqueville, whereas the first sphere is filled in by the state and its institutions, and the second sphere by the economy, in the third sphere, namely civil society, parties, public opinion, churches, moral crusades, literary and scientific societies, professional and recreational groups possess a super abundant force and energy. Through these associations,

the potential excesses of the centralized state can be curtailed. 'An association', wrote Tocqueville, 'unites the efforts of minds which have a tendency to diverge in one single channel, and urges them vigorously towards one single end which it points out'. Alexis de Tocqueville, *Democracy in America, Two Volumes*, trans. Keene (New York: The Colonial Press, 1900, Vol. I first published 1835), Vol. I, p.192.

6. Charles Taylor, 'Civil Society in the Western Tradition', in E. Groffier and M. Paradis (eds.), *The Notion of Tolerance and Human Rights: Essays in Honour of Raymond Klibansky* (Ottawa: University of Carleton Press, 1991), p.117.

7. Axel Honneth, 'Conceptions of "Civil Society"', *Radical Philosophy*, Vol.64 (1993), p.19; Jeffrey Isaac, 'Civil Society and the Spirit of Revolt', *Dissent* (Summer 1993), p.356.

8. Jean Cohen and Andrew Arato, *Political Theory and Civil Society* (Cambridge: MIT Press, 1992), p.18.

9. Ibid., p.346.

10. Adam Seligman, *The Idea of Civil Society* (New York: Free Press, 1992), p.x.

11. Ibid., p.75.

12. For a representative collection of essays on this theme, see Andrew Clayton (ed.), *NGOs, Civil Society and the State. Building Democracy in Transitional Societies* (Oxford: Intrac, 1996).

13. In Thomas Kuhn, *The Structure of Scientific Revolutions* (Chicago, IL: University of Chicago Press, 1992), p.83.

14. This is ironic because for Hegel the state is what it is – the embodiment of universality – because civil society is what it is, namely the domain of particularity containing the seeds of universality. But ultimately it is the state that becomes the condition for civil society. See Neera Chandhoke, *State and Civil Society. Explorations in Political Theory* (Delhi: Sage, 1995), Ch.4.

15. P.M. Vajpayee suggested that we add scientists to the slogan crafted in the mid-1960s of *jai jawan, jai kisan,* which is a slogan that hails the peasant and the soldier. Now it would be *jai jawan, jai kisan,* and *jai vigyan,* the latter being the hindi term for science. It is interesting that the slogan of hailing the soldier had been formulated after the successful war with Pakistan in 1965. That of hailing the peasant was added after the accomplishment of the 'green revolution', which made India self-sufficient in food grains in the same decade.

16. The *Sangh Parivar* refers to the complex of right wing organizations that subscribe to and propagate the idea of *Hindutva* or majority nationalism, and who believe that the rightful inheritor of the nation is the majority community. These organizations – the Rashtriya Swayam Sevak Sangh or the RSS (of which more later), the BJP as the political wing, the Vishwa Hindu Parishad, and the Bajrang Dal – have been involved in a systematic campaign against religious minorities, on the one hand, and the building up of majority sentiments, on the other.

17. See the special issue of the journal *Seminar*, No.468 (Aug. 1998), for a collection of perspectives on Pokhran II.

18. One of the right wing groups who has enjoyed power in Maharashtra – the Shiv Sena – demanded that the noted and respected film actor Dilip Kumar *prove* his loyalty to the country by returning the sign of honour bestowed upon him by the government of Pakistan, the Nishan-e-Pakistan. It is difficult to escape the conclusion that the fact that he is a Muslim was enough to cast suspicion on his credentials as a 'patriotic Indian'.

19. Ishan Joshi, 'A Wee Swing to the Right', *Outlook* (16 Aug. 1999), pp.28–9.

20. This was particularly evident in the complete identification of the BJP with the armed forces, who it was widely perceived had made sacrifices for the sanctity of the borders.

21. A series of attacks on Christian institutions in December 1998, was followed by the burning alive of a missionary, Graham Stewart Staines and his two teenaged sons in Manoharpur in the state of Orissa on the midnight of 22 Jan. 1999, all in the name of *Hindutva*. Whereas the leadership was quick to condemn the brutal killings, they explained them away in terms of resentment against forced conversions. This is laughable when we recollect that despite a long presence in India, Christianity has managed to convert a little over two per cent of the people. It is not mere coincidence that attacks on Christians began to acquire a frequency around the time the BJP settled into power in the central government. In Gujarat, 28 churches

were destroyed in one month and this was accompanied by attacks on the community in other parts of the country. See the cover story by Ishan Joshi, 'Mob Rule', *Outlook* (8 Feb. 1999), pp.12–18.

22. Michel Foucault, 'Body/Power', in Colin Gordon (ed.), *Foucault on Power/Knowledge: Selected Interviews and Other Writings 1972–1977*, trans. Colin Gordon, Leo Marshall, John Mepham and Kate Soper (Brighton: Harvester, 1980), p.98.

23. This has been discussed in some detail in Chandhoke, *State and Civil Society*, Ch.2.

24. Robert. D. Putnam, *Making Democracy Work: Civic Traditions in Modern Italy* (Princeton, NJ: University of Princeton Press, 1993); Robert D. Putnam, 'Bowling Alone: America's Declining Social Capital', *Journal of Democracy*. Vol.6, No.1 (1995), pp.65–78.

25. James Coleman, 'Social Capital in the Creation of Human Capital', *American Journal of Sociology* (1998), pp.95–1120.

26. Tapan Basu, Pradip Dutta, Sumit Sarkar, Tanika Sarkar and Sambuddha Sen, *Khaki Shorts and Saffron Flags. A Critique of the Hindu Right* (Delhi: Orient Longman, 1993), p.2. Also see B.D Graham, *Hindu Nationalism and Indian Politics. The Origins and Development of the Bharatiya Jana Sangh* (Cambridge: Cambridge University Press, 1990); Walter K. Andersen and Shridhar D. Damle, *The Brotherhood in Saffron. The Rashtriya Swayamsevak Sangh and Hindu Revivalism* (Boulder, CO: Westview, 1980).

27. V.D Savarkar, *Hindutva! Who is a Hindu?* (Bombay: Veer Savarkar Prakashan, 1969, first published 1923).

28. This highly ritualized physical training called the *shakha* is performed at identical times by RSS cadres throughout the country. Alongside the enactment of myths glorifying Hindu matyrs who have laid down their life for the country, stories and slogans, the *shakha* trains young men in the art of wielding the lathi or the staff, the sword, the javelin and the dagger. The ultimate aim is to make the Hindu militantly powerful and aggressive.

29. Basu *et al.*, *Khaki Shorts*, p.34.

30. Ibid., p.36.

31. The NBA has launched a massive social movement since the late 1980s in western India, against the complex of dams being built on the river Narmada, which has displaced almost a 100,000 people and that promises to displace many more thousands of tribals residing in the area.

Die Lehrjahre sind vorbei!
Re-Forming Democratic Interest Groups in
the East German Länder

JOYCE MUSHABEN

Between 1972 and 1986, the German Democratic Republic (GDR) witnessed the rise
of an underground civil society which gradually impelled the collapse of the socialist
regime, opening the door to political freedom. Following unification, new elites
eliminated 90 mass organizations that had served as the mainstay of GDR community
interaction, presuming that a common institutional framework would soon allow
Germans 'who belonged together to grow together'. To prove stable in the long run,
however, democratic institutions not only need to be 'representative' in a territorial or
functional sense; they must also prove responsive to more deep-seated citizen needs.
This study posits that citizens who cultivate subjective ties (social capital) in relation
to new institutions will not only internalize democratic values more quickly than those
lacking such ties but will also be more effective in advancing their interests within the
new power structures. It outlines criteria for pinpointing specific associations as
potential social capital 'generators', the foundation of civic culture. It then presents
four case studies, illustrating ways in which East Germans are creating 'space' for
their own norms and associational styles within the new institutional framework. The
cases include: *die Grüne Liga* (Mecklenburg-Vorpommern); the *Volkssolidarität*
(Berlin); Magdeburg's Round-Table against Violence (Sachsen-Anhalt); and the
Gleichstellungsstelle-Erfurt (Thüringen). All are found to be fostering citizen
competence and identification with democratic processes in the young Länder.

> *Eins kann ich Dir sagen:*
> *Die Lehrjahre sind vorbei.*
>
> Mirko Hempel,
> Erfurt (1997)

In the German Democratic Republic (GDR), though not always apparent to
outsiders, the combined influences of generational change, exposure to
West German television, and the chronic deficiencies of a planned economy
provided fertile ground for an underground civil society that blossomed
between 1972 and 1986 (the year Gorbachev introduced 'New Thinking' to
the Soviet Union). Though rudimentary by western standards, a home-
grown network of citizen initiatives – encompassing church groups,
peace/ecology activists, amateur historian clubs, artistic/literary circles and

human rights groups – successfully instigated what 40 years of strategizing
by the North Atlantic Treaty Organization (NATO) could not: the collapse
of an authoritarian, state-socialist regime and the introduction of
fundamental political freedoms as of 1989. Following German unification
in 1990, new elites (mostly western imports) rapidly dismantled virtually all
official GDR administrative, economic and cultural structures, presuming
that a common institutional framework would soon, in Willy Brandt's
words, allow 'that to grow together which belongs together' – a long
divided German nation. They simultaneously eliminated 90 state-directed
mass organizations that had served as the mainstay of eastern social
communication and community interaction for four decades. Even GDR
citizens who had actively mobilized against oppressive state practices by
way of informal, underground groups found their fledgling organizations
(for example, New Forum, Alliance '90, and the Independent Women's
Union) pushed aside in the rush to unity.[1] The paradox of East German
democratization is that an emerging citizen-culture intent on fostering new
forms of grass roots participation was deliberately destroyed, presumably to
warrant its replacement by a civil-society type deemed more compatible
with a western 'free-democratic order'.
    Though countless scholars stress the pivotal role of civil society in
effecting transitions from dictatorship to democracy, few distinguish
between civil society (positing a new delineation of public and private
spheres) and the ideal of a civic culture (evincing a high degree of active
citizen participation in governance). Too many presumed in 1989/90 that
once the structural and procedural parameters of democracy had been
secured, a participatory-democratic culture would naturally follow.[2] While
the delineation of public and private spheres may be a necessary condition
for achieving constitutional qua institutional consolidation, it is not a
sufficient one for integrating non-elites into the governing process,
particularly in an age when even the citizens of long-established
democracies are turned off by politics, in general, and elections, in
particular. The important question here is not how much civil society does
a country need? But, rather, to what extent can new leaders utilize pre-
existing behavioural patterns to foster really democratic ones?[3] Just how
does one reshape a civil society born of authoritarian conditions (hardly
grounded in widespread societal trust) into a self-sustaining network of less-
than-heroic participants willing to contribute their time, energy and money
to securing the common good? How does one construct and consolidate, in
less than a decade, those forms of citizen involvement judged necessary for
deepening democracy? This article contends that civic culture emerges out
of a specific political-cultural context which, in turn, lends a particular
shape and salience to formal democratic institutions and processes over

time – as demonstrated by the experience of the old Federal Republic, 1949–89.[4]

To prove stable in the long run, democratic institutions not only need to represent citizens in a territorial or functional sense; they must also respond to more deep-seated identity needs. I use the German case to argue that citizens who cultivate *subjective* ties to emerging intermediary associations not only internalize democratic values more quickly than persons lacking such ties, but that they will also be more likely to establish effective channels for advancing their own interests. Such ties, alternatively known as social capital, give a democratizing society the coherence it needs, first, to adapt to new institutions and values in the midst of hard transitional times and, second, to create spaces for the initially unorganized interests of average citizens within the new power structures. Social capital nonetheless presupposes the existence of a positive group identity, a subject that has triggered many contentious debates in unified Germany since 1991. Eastern Germany comprises an exception to the rule relative to other Central/East European transformations only insofar as its efforts to reconfigure its own national identity have been repeatedly undermined by a stronger, consolidated, perhaps overly self-righteous western definition of what it means to be a German. Massive financial transfers from West to East (DM 1 trillion by 2000) did little *per se* to promote citizen efficacy and political trust in the new states in the 1990s; indeed, the extraordinary help accorded by way of union with a wealthy, consolidated state has impeded the democratic learning process.

This study comprises the third stage of a project exploring problems of democratic transition in the young Länder.[5] Stage One assessed the role of social capital in the context of democratizing societies, a framework first applied by Alexis de Tocqueville, then revisited by Robert Putnam and Pierre Bourdieu. Stage Two sought to operationalize theoretical and practical linkages between social capital, civic culture and the (re)assertion of *ostdeutsche Identität* as a vehicle for interest-mobilization.[6] It posited that recognition of the socio-psychological conflicts inherent in the transition from the GDR to the Federal Republic of Germany (FRG) offers important lessons for other post-socialist elites trying to build democracy from below as regards the need for positive sub-group identities in those states. The cultivation of a distinctively post-unity East German identity seems to be a very necessary, if not sufficient condition for fostering a reconfiguration of social capital along grass-roots participatory lines.

Stage Three offers an empirical treatment of civic-culture development. It begins with a depiction of the representation gap that is moving increasing numbers of East Germans to (re)align themselves with new or resuscitated intermediary associations. Next, it outlines criteria for recognizing specific organizational configurations as potential generators of social capital, the *sine qua non* of civic culture. Four case studies illustrate ways in which East Germans have begun to create space for their own interests, norms and associational styles within the western-transfer framework. The analysis draws on organizational documents as well as field interviews with key players, conducted over a three-year period, in each of these domains. Though the perception of East Germans as passive, whining second-class citizens still prevails in some quarters – in the old Länder! – it is argued here that a spirit of self-assertion, citizen-competence and 'belonging' has clearly taken root within the region itself.

SUBJECTIVE MOTIVES FOR CIVIC ENGAGEMENT

One school of western analysts insists that official mass organizations in the GDR did little more than forcefully homogenize conflicting identities and interests (for example, in divergent trade unions) into a societal 'one', that one being the Sozialistische Einheitspartei Deutschland, or Socialist Unity Party (SED).[7] Others go so far as to characterize 'Ossis' as 'politically incapable of democracy, believing only in authority and displaying hostility towards foreigners ... (as) provincial, petty-bourgeois, tacky and nerdy, not even very diligent at work, lacking drive and entrepreneurial spirit and, as far as his aesthetic preferences go, (occupying) a totally backwards niveau'.[8] It is simply not true that 'on the basis of many years of dictatorship' GDR residents entered their union with the FRG with 'no experience in self-organisation and voluntaristic engagement', as some maintain.[9] Networking was very dense during GDR times – some of it good, some bad, some forced, but much of it humanly spontaneous. Countless niches and *Notgemeinschaften* operant at workplace or neighbourhood levels arose out of personal, utilitarian reflections: Who can provide me with what, and what can I offer in exchange, once I get it from someone else? Given their ultimate focus on self-defined needs, there is little reason to assume that pre-existing forms of eastern associational life will incontrovertibly impede the process of democratization if resurrected. On the contrary, they can be used like antique bricks to enlarge an older democratic house without disturbing the basic architectural style.

It is highly unlikely that most members of the *Kulturbund*, regional *Fußballvereine*, or the *Volkssolidarität* saw themselves as active accomplices of an authoritarian regime. Although mass organizations were clearly dominated by an oppressive state, 'average citizens' did not wake up every morning thinking deep thoughts about 'political subordination'. They got up went to work, celebrated birthdays with friends (usually at work), went to movies or concerts, engaged in sports, and even took vacations, all of which ultimately involved some formal organization. 'State domination' became relevant when the state tried to push them around in what they construed as 'their' organizations. Yes, they were expected, even required to join the *Freier Deutscher Gewekschaftsbund* (FDGB, or Free German Trade Union Confederation) and the Freie Deutsche Jugend (FDJ) to secure their education and career, but they also learned to use those organizations for their own purposes. This constituted a 'rudimentary civil society' insofar as people *did* learn how to communicate with the state and could even influence its policies; successes ranged from the rescinding of a ban on 'nude beaches' during the height of the Stalinist period, to the creation of 'Construction Soldier' units in the 1970s (for military conscripts seeking exemption from combat weapons and duties), and the promotion of rock music made-in-the-GDR. Ask any former FDJ member who lobbied for the Udo Lindeberg concert and youth radio, DT-64!

Thus, on a day-to-day basis, the millions of GDR citizens who participated in diverse mass organizations were more likely to view their engagement as a normal means of belonging to a larger culture of volunteerism and collective action.[10] This is perfectly rational human behaviour that lends itself well to the embrace of new values once the oppressive institutions themselves are replaced with more open ones. In a 1993 study of 33 clubs, self-help groups and citizen initiatives in Berlin-Hohenschönhausen, for example, only 18.8 per cent of the respondents held that *die Wende* had provided them with their first real opportunity to become active in citizen affairs; 70.3 per cent disagreed.[11]

Drawing on a 1987 study, Eckhard Priller reports that roughly half of all GDR-Germans had exercised diverse volunteer functions under the socialist state (Table 1). Most forms of involvement were tied to the factory or one's occupational field, though 12 per cent polled were directly engaged in communal affairs. The most frequently cited reasons for NOT participating in such functions were a 'lack of time' (34 per cent) or 'family burdens' (31 per cent) – the same excuses offered in the Bundesrepublik, even though GDR women had more children and evinced much higher levels of paid employment (90 per cent) than their FRG counterparts. Despite high levels of engagement, a majority polled before the 1989 upheavals expressed dissatisfaction with state organs, implying that participation was motivated by factors other than positive identification or mere conformity with the regime.[12]

The indigenous if rudimentary civil society rooted in state-socialism had little chance to unfold, given the rapid take-over by well-endowed West German parties. Its agents are now engaging in a natural catch-up process. The clear-cutting of the GDR organizational landscape after 1990 left behind some very fallow ground. Indeed, the first four years of unity were

TABLE 1

EXERCISE OF VOLUNTEER FUNCTIONS IN GDR, 1987 (IN PER CENT)

	Neighbour-hood, Apt. complex	Town, city	County, district	Factory, training site	At least one function	More than one function
Total	11	12	5	28	36	8
Men	12	14	7	31	39	10
Women	9	9	4	26	32	6
Age						
under 25	4	4	2	24	26	3
26–40	12	14	6	33	44	10
41–50	13	17	8	37	46	12
51–60	14	14	8	34	41	11
over 60	12	8	3	8	20	4
Occupational Qualification						
no-skill, semi-skilled labour	4	4	1	17	20	2
skilled labour/master	10	10	3	22	32	5
technical school	19	24	13	51	62	20
university/college	23	19	21	64	77	27

Source: Eckhard Priller, 'Veränderungen in der politischen und sozialen Beteiligung im Ostdeutschland', in Wolfgang Zapf and Roland Habich, *Hg., Wohlfahrtsentwicklung im vereinten Deutschland* (Berlin: Ed. Sigma, 1996), p.290.

marked by a veritable 'founding boom of clubs', though most have been of an apolitical nature (party memberships have also declined in the old states since 1991).[13] A multiplicity of state-directed organizations quickly transformed themselves into registered and/or non-profit associations (Table 2). Ironically, major *western* non-profit organizations attempting to establish a foothold in the East are heavily state-subsidized, while smaller, newly emerging eastern associations – evincing a higher degree of social embeddedness – are expected to compete on the basis of membership dues and private sponsors, especially in the domains of sports, culture, recreation, legal advocacy and environmental protection. The two largest FRG welfare associations, *Diakonie* and *Caritas*, received hefty subsidies for the purpose of extending their services to the new Länder; both are church-affiliated, though three-fourths of the East-residents consider themselves atheists.

National surveys imply that East German rates of participation in associational life lie 'significantly below' West German rates, 26 per cent versus 50 per cent.[14] Drawing on a 1996 sample of 2,000 Westerners and 1,000 Easterners, Zimmer and Priller set the proportion of registered

TABLE 2

NEW ENTRIES IN SELECTED REGISTERS OF ASSOCIATIONS, 1990–96

Register of Associations (Site of County Court)							
	1990	1991	1992	1993	1994	1995	1996
State Capitals							
Berlin	509	1,021	1,566	990	1,112	855	—
Dresden	1,237	102	209	395	495	297	195
Erfurt	536	76	141	233	155	138	127
Magdeburg	554	121	139	165	146	124	91
Potsdam	469	279	248	78	220	148	138
Schwerin	287	128	178	116	76	78	85
Other areas							
(Rural/Industrial Regions)							
Gorlitz	284	70	21	40	44	30	25
Malchin	81	15	22	24	29	14	10
Teterow	54	18	8	18	15	12	13

Source: Helmut K. Anheier, Eckhard Priller and Annette Zimmer, 'Civic Society in Transition: The East German Non-profit Sector Six years after Unification', Working Paper Series No.13 (Baltimore: Johns Hopkins University, Institute for Policy Studies), p.4.

memberships in various organizations at 27 per cent and 16 per cent, respectively. The most frequently cited reason for non-engagement, these scholars found, was that 'no one had personally asked them' to join in specific volunteer events (38 per cent West, 46 per cent East), underlining the importance of face-to-face ties in fostering collective action.[15] It was a striking decline in traditional organizational memberships in the *West* which moved the ruling Conservative government to undertake its own study on 'the significance of volunteer activity for our society' [citation: Helmut Kohl] via a parliamentary inquiry in 1997. Whereas in 1953, 53 per cent of all West German adults aged 18 to 80 were affiliated with one or more organizations, the 1997 figure stood at 12 million, a mere 17 per cent.[16] Church membership fell by 3.7 million between 1963 and 1989, matched by decreases in labour union and party affiliation.

By contrast, 'self-help' or personal development groups, like sports/fitness clubs added 15.9 million registrants from 1960 to 1989.[17] Consonant with this trend, memberships in newly re/created sports-clubs in the East-state of Saxony rose from 358,052 in 1990 to 482,674 in 1996.[18] The extent to which volunteer work in the athletic domain can also foster community identity and democratic learning-experiences is under study in Potsdam. At issue in this project is the extent to which rapidly increasing memberships in non-political associations can ease individual transitions 'from a mono-centrically steered society, completely organised and subject to party-political control, to a polycentrically managed, competitive society' capable of democratic self-organization built upon both collective and individual actors.[19] Of special concern is the potential exclusion of women, the elderly, and the unemployed from such processes, for whom the substantially higher costs of privatized facilities now pose a serious problem.

The East's participation gap in conventional intermediary associations is sooner explained by way of post-unity conditions than via arguments that these citizens have yet to embrace democratic norms. There are still fewer organizational options available to residents in the new states, where communal priorities remain fixated on economic reconstruction. Many would-be activists are still 'sniffing out' various options, now that the spectrum of recreational, cultural and self-help groups has dramatically expanded. Mass unemployment among women in the East means that female trade union and professional-league memberships have plunged, making it impossible for them to engage in volunteer programmes once tied to the workplace. Membership dues and solidarity contributions become luxury items for the long-term unemployed and retirees on fixed incomes, a plight afflicting some three million East citizens. Given the turbulence of the last several years, it is very surprising that so many East Germans are not merely fixated on 'doing their own thing', for example, making up for 40 years of lost time by investing in personal travel or home renovations.

Pollach's study of participatory dynamics in Berlin-Hohenschönhausen found locals active across a broad spectrum of communal services in 1995 (Figures 1 and 2). The pattern here is comparable to western findings: higher educational levels result in higher levels of activism. Many Berlin respondents feel they are directly serving their own needs, as well as contributing to the larger community, especially the unemployed and retired residents; two-thirds nonetheless characterized their activities as having 'political' content.[20] Drawing on what appear to be *pre-unity* participatory leanings, Priller likewise concluded his 1996 study with an optimistic prognosis:

> a dynamic and multifaceted yet structured organisational landscape has been established in the East German transformational society. The impression that people are generally tired of organisations, which could arise *inter alia* by looking at the widespread decline in [traditional] memberships, is consequently not accurate. The engaged intervention of a significant part of the East German citizenry finds its expression by way of the creation and activities of associations.[21]

Older East Germans who helped to build the GDR may be motivated to engage in volunteer work as a function of a deeply rooted collective identity.

FIGURE 1

PREVIOUS PARTICIPATION IN SPECIFIC ACTION MODES (N=128)

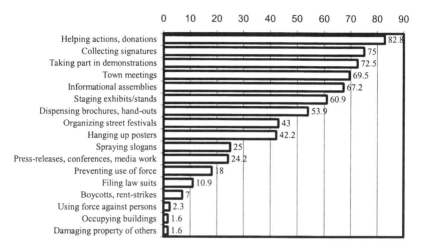

Source: Günther Pollach, *Unabhängige Bürgerbeteiligung in Berlin-Hohenschönhausen*
(Berlin: Berlin Institut für Sozialwissenschaftliche Studien-BISS, 1993), pp.50–51.

FIGURE 2

ACTIVIST INVOLVEMENT ACCORDING TO SECTORS (N=128)

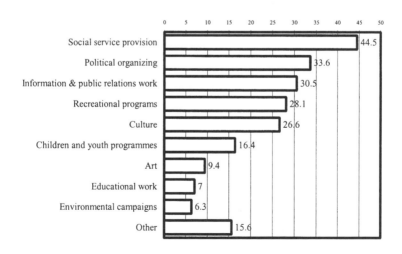

Source: Günther Pollach, *Unabhängige Bürgerbeteiligung in Berlin-Hohenschönhausen*
(Berlin: Berlin Institut für Sozialwissenschaftliche Studien-BISS, 1993), pp.50–51.

The rest, however, find grounds for mobilization largely in *post-unity* developments; millions over the age of 55 have lots of time on their hands, having been forced into early retirement since 1990. Federally subsidized privatization deals have produced major real-estate windfall and production booms for the old FRG: 85 to 90 per cent of all GDR-state property sold off by the *Treuhand* now lies in western hands.[22] Eastern unemployment in 1997 surpassed the 1991–96 figures. Millions of women have been not-so-randomly de-selected by the (paid) labour market, precluding their ability to engage in political-economic communication and to build new reserves of social capital through familiar workplace channels. What piques eastern citizens the most, however, is the Bonn government's long-standing premise that West German political culture comprised an unalterable mainstream, and that East German political culture ought to be driven to extinction precisely because it has been defined, from above, as 'marginal'. The reassertion of *Ost-identität*, especially since 1995, 'does not entail wayward erring but rather sober recognition, normalisation and differentiation ... the basis for a real unification instead of only accession' – that is, unification from below.[23]

OBJECTIVE MOTIVATIONS FOR MOBILIZATION FROM BELOW

East Germans may emerge as the real experts in times of ongoing economic crisis, Reinhard Höppner [SPD Minister-President, Sachsen-Anhalt] stresses, 'because we – in contrast to the old Federal Republic – have not been blinded by 40 years of economic growth, through which politics could again legitimise itself simply by way of the distribution of the increases in economic growth'.[24] Prior to 1998, Bonn's politicians ignored eastern rumblings that the Republic as a whole is ripe for change, causing complaints to increase in volume as well as in scope. Höppner's 1997 critique of the FRG's lack of 'readiness to reform' led to consternation among insiders but made perfect sense to outsiders following its higher educational and structural unemployment crises for over a decade:

> countless breakdowns came to pass because conditions just weren't so, the way they really should have been according to West German legal requirements ... I had to stand by and observe for years, how a system totally fell apart, based on its inability to implement future oriented reforms. I do not want to stand around watching this new, victorious system experience the same destiny.[25]

East Germans have distanced themselves from western parties, as a post-1992 plunge in membership levels testifies; only 9 per cent deemed life in a *pluralistic party system* 'very important', 32 per cent 'important' for their own well-being in 1997.[26] Two factors have contributed to this decline, the first being a mounting irritation over the personality-centred, confrontational style of western party politics. Prior to 1989, GDR activists learned they could be more effective in wrangling concessions from the regime when they mobilized in small but very committed private circles, found prominent mediators able to negotiate for them behind closed doors, and presented their cases in terms of a common cause, for example, the Church *in* socialism, and creating peace with ever fewer (NATO) weapons.

GDR protest likewise assumed a different form, for example, silent, candle lit-vigils and 'library' visitation in local churches (in contrast to mass FRG demonstrations featuring a host of prominent speakers). As Christiane Lemke observes, non-violent protest levels – a tried-and-true vehicle for articulating citizen interests in the old FRG – remained 'surprisingly high' in the young Länder (or what used to be known as the *Fünf Neue Länder*), in 1990 to 1994. Protest serves multiple social-capital functions, creating and strengthening social identities, at the same time it helps to solidify group structures.[27] Sustained over a long period, protest activity fosters the rise of lasting, non-state institutional networks. West German experiences 1968–84 confirm that protest mobilization can result in 'a great leap forward' for democracy by expanding the grass roots base of civic culture.[28]

On a different but related track, James Coleman has argued that an organization initiated to serve one set of social-capital needs 'is available for appropriation for other purposes'.[29] The reassertion of regional identities [the Brandenburger Way, the Magdeburger Model] for *Land*-political purposes, coupled with the cultivation (or at least the *toleration*) of non-traditional inter-party alliances at state and local levels, for example, Christian Democratic Union (CDU)/Greens, Social Democratic Party (SDP)/Party of Democratic Socialism (PDS), are two strategies for re-creating modes of social capital in the East that will, eventually, command the recognition of policy communities in the West. What's good for Bavaria, namely, a regional party of its own making, could also be good for *Neufünfland*. The 1998 SPD-Green coalition agreement accorded Cabinet status to Rolf Schwanitz as State Minister for East-Reconstruction, a move paralleling Adenauer's Cabinet-level embrace of the *Block der Heimatvertriebenen und Entrechteten* (BHE, or Association of Persons Expelled and Disenfranchised from the Eastern Territories), the organizational voice of 8 to 10 million East German refugees, through the 1950s.[30]

One force driving the PDS-comeback of 1994 (when it captured three direct mandates and 19.8 per cent of the regional vote) and its 1998 consolidation (four direct mandates, 5.1 per cent nationally, and *Land* tallies ranging from 13.5 per cent to 23.6 per cent) is the fact that East Germans have grasped the need for self-propelled vehicles of interest-representation at both formal and informal levels.[31] The new Germans are doomed to permanent minority status, not only on the basis of their numbers (constituting less than a fourth of the population) but also as a result of their minimal economic importance to the FRG. The East German Gross Domestic Product returned to 1990 levels in 1994, hardly compensating for a 40 per cent decline between 1989 and 1990; still, GDP-East amounted to less than ten per cent of the western GDP in 1994 (DM 256.7 billion and DM 2,709.6 billion, respectively).[32]

In formal-constitutional terms, the *Beitrittsgebiet* enjoys no special representational rights in the governing organs, despite the extraordinary problems it faces. The two East Germans who served in the cabinet through September 1998 – Claudia Nolte and Angelika Merkel – possessed none of the political clout exercised by eastern/BHE spokespersons under Adenauer. The five young states face eleven old ones in the Bundesrat; yet the four biggest West-Länder were accorded a veto-vote or *Sperrminorität* (24 out of 68 votes) deliberately denied the East-Länder as of 1990.[33] Not a single Justice from the East graces the benches of the *Bundesverfassungsgericht* [Constitutional Court], a sore point with respect to the controversial 1993 abortion verdict.[34]

Outnumbered in the *Bundestag* by 523 to 139, eastern lawmakers are further reined in by party-discipline; pressure to toe the party line often evokes polarization among East-MPs where no substantive policy differences exist, though the latter formed their own parliamentary group in 1997. East-members enjoy token representation in the top executive organs of the major parties and occupy 20 per cent of the seats in larger delegate bodies. As Heidrun Abromeit attested prior to 1998, 'in *none* of the relevant interest mediation organisations do eastern interests have even the slightest internal chance of being carried out. The representational gap could hardly be greater'.[35] The prevailing notion (at least until the 1998 election in Sachsen-Anhalt) that only party-bosses in Bonn were qualified to determine electoral themes and strategies for the East is reminiscent of the FRG's long-standing *Alleinvertretungsanspruch vis-à-vis* the GDR. Ironically, *Politikverdrossenheit* was a heavily debated problem in the West well prior to unification. The one thing East and West voters share is their annoyance over the self-serving machinations of 'the party state'.

Back in their home states, eastern constituents still find their cabinets, administrative agencies and party headquarters dominated by western 'imports' ten years into unity. In a major study of FRG elite composition, Willy Bürklin found 41 per cent of the 402 leadership positions in the new states occupied by Westerners, 59 per cent by East Germans. Comprising 20 per cent of the total population, East Germans account nationally for only

2.5 per cent of higher administrative posts, 4 per cent of the economic leaders, 12.4 per cent of union officials, 11.7 per cent of the media executives, 7.4 per cent of the academic/scientific elites, and virtually none of the military brass. Some 56 to 69 per cent of all indigenous managerial positions disappeared with the downsizing or closing of major GDR processing industries.[36]

Where they might have felt irritated by the 'extreme asymmetry of the starting conditions' implicit in the structural representation gap in the years immediately following unity, the focus has now shifted to a responsiveness gap in relation to policy outcomes, a gap only the PDS saw fit to address prior to 1995. Not surprisingly, East-residents are seeking opportunities for public engagement in other places, at the informal or non-institutional level. The original promoters of East German civil society have yet to recover from having been rapidly pushed aside by the people they helped to liberate.[37] Paralysis among once prominent civil-society activists is now being offset by new forms/old forms/synthesized forms of civic engagement among actors who once occupied 'the second row' but are now moving forward in intermediary organizations.

CIVIC CULTURE: SYNTHESIZING AND NEW ASSOCIATIONAL PATTERNS

Emerging out of the private space set free by civil society, social capital is the keystone of civic culture, in essence holding it together. Civic culture, in turn, is what enables citizens to mediate directly between three sets of public functions: the political function of interest-aggregation, the economic function of fulfilling perceived needs for goods and services, and the national *qua* cultural function of social integration.

Like Larry Diamond, Hans-Joachim Lauth and Wolfgang Merkel construe civil society as an historical entity, subject to changes in form and function depending on the amount of democratic consolidation that has already taken place. They distinguish between associational forms which help to consolidate civil society (en route to a civic culture) and those which do not. Such distinctions can be expanded to provide a set of operational standards for investigating specific organizations as potential generators of social capital of the democratic sort. Elaborating on their terms, we posit that associations lending themselves to such purposes should evince the following properties:

1. They should involve pre-statal or *non-state* spheres of operation, meaning they occupy spaces somewhere between the purely private and strictly state realms.

2. They should reflect a *plurality* of (sometimes competitive) groupings in society, based on specific normative and/or material interests, articulated and aggregated on an autonomous basis.

3. The objectives such associations pursue should be connected to *res publica*, meaning that they seek something larger than strictly personal benefit or individual gain. The focus on public issues does not boil down to the pursuit of political office.

4. There should be an element of *heterogeneity* in the group's composition; this differentiated group of actors should nonetheless share a degree of normative consensus.

5. All members are expected to display *tolerance* and *fairness* with regard to in-group differences, abjuring the use of physical force in resolving differences inside and outside the organization.

6. Each association must be capable of some measure of *collective-strategic action*, oriented toward public cooperation and/or communicative behaviour.

7. The group engages in *self-regulated, collective-action* processes, including but not limited to information gathering, communication, networking, and resource mobilization.

8. Collective activity can be expected, in the longer run, to lead to the development of *citizen consciousness* among the individual participants.[38]

I argued previously that those forms of social capital which have proved effective vehicles for interest aggregation in the past will be the first to resurface under the new institutional order, other new systemic conditions permitting. While 44 per cent claim the old regime offered average citizens diverse opportunities for 'co-determination', only 25 per cent feel that the new system affords comparable chances; 57 per cent hold that under the current FRG, citizens 'have nothing to say'.[39] There is growing evidence that a conscious disassociation from western ways is engendering feelings of citizen-competence at the state and local levels, marked by at least a partial return to pre-unity mobilization channels. One municipal official in Magdeburg noted in June 1997 that his *Referat* receives many personal letters requesting his unit to 'fix things', a practice stemming from the *Eingabe*-petitions of old (last-resort appeals addressed to high-ranking SED leaders).

Naturally conditions must ripen a bit for this resurfacing to occur. Lauth and Merkel are correct to say that the temporary weakening of civil society (implying a stronger mobilizational role for the state, or at least for officials like Höppner, Stolpe, and Ringstorff) which often follows the overthrow of an authoritarian regime, contributes in paradoxical fashion 'to the stabilisation of young democracies. Only in the course of further stabilisation does a new revitalisation of civil society become important for the deepening of democracy.'[40] Instead of discrediting calls for Republic-wide reform as the work of whining ingrates (*'Jammer-Ossis'*), national politicians need to value these appeals for what they are: eastern steps in the direction of *national* identification. The newcomers increasingly feel they have mastered the basics of 'the rule of law', giving them the right to engage henceforth in policy debates beyond their own state lines.

To illustrate this, four case studies are offered involving old and new forms of associational life, all of them meeting the preliminary civil-society-turned-civic culture criteria outlined above. The larger pool of cases focuses on regional, single-state or communal issues, at least one for each state, covering a wide range of policy concerns. Two not covered here (*Forum Ostdeutschland* and *Aufbau Ost*) involve initiatives seeking to carve out meaningful space for East-interests within West-dominated party structures in ways that go beyond the 'ossification' of specific personalities like Kurt Biedenkopf (the western CDU Union Minister-President of Saxony).[41] The writer's field work centred on three associational types: first, organizations once operating within the GDR which have democratized themselves and taken on new purposes; secondly, groups or organizational modes emerging out of the 1989 'turn-around' period which are also pursuing new causes and membership bases; and thirdly, West German organizations taking root in the East that are being 'reshaped' to fit local or regional conditions. The following sketches include at least one from each category.

DIE GRÜNE LIGA (GREEN LEAGUE) OF MECKLENBURG-VORPOMMERN

One particularly successful interest organization that has deliberately employed GDR experiences in its pursuit of democratization from below is the Green League, a *Wende*-era environmental group with increasingly entrepreneurial branches operating in all five East-states (Table 3). The League's roots lie in the underground ecology movement that initially took refuge in the Lutheran Church during the late 1970s. Hoping to compel state recognition of a looming environmental crisis after three decades of total neglect (GDR environmental data were legally classified as 'state secrets'), concerned citizens began to build a broader constituency by way of the state-sanctioned Society for Nature and the Environment (GNU) in 1980. Initial SED-tolerance owed to its own desire not to leave this topic up to the churches, which were starting to harbour a plethora of opposition groups.

TABLE 3

GRÜNE LIGA: REGIONAL AND STATE-LEVEL MEMBERSHIPS (1995)

Berlin	about 40 co-workers 50 member-groups 42 individual members 4 districts: Friedrichshain, Hellersdorf, Köpenick, Pankow 5 project groups
Brandenburg	6 co-workers 14 member-groups (about 400 persons) 20 individual members 3 regional bureaus: Potsdam, Finsterwalde, Brandenburg
Mecklenburg Vorpommern	20 co-workers 12 member-groups 120 individual members 3 district bureaus: Rostock, Schwerin, Neubrandenburg
Sachsen	90 co-workers 50 member-groups 2000 individual members 5 districts: Dresden, Chemnitz, Leipzig, Bautzen, Dippoldswalde
Sachsen-Anhalt	about 30 co-workers 170 members (group and individual) 6 regional bureaus: Magdeburg, Halle, Salzwedel, Zörbig, Wolfen, Förderstedt
Thüringen	16 co-workers about 70 members 20 projects/themes 5 district bureaus: Weimar, Erfurt, Sudthüringen, Arnstadt, Jena

Source: Grüne Liga, e.V. (Bundesverband), *Die Landesverbände und ihre Projekte,* Berlin
(Nov. 1995).

By 1987 an increasingly critical Interest Community for Urban Ecology boasted 380 groups with 7,000 members. The latter staged its own forum with delegates from 26 'urban-ecology task forces' in conjunction with the GDR's 40th anniversary (7/8 October, 1989), even calling for democratic reforms. The latter position enabled the group to seat its own representative at the Central Round Table under the interim Modrow Government as of December 1989. On 24 November 1989, participants issued a 'founding document', agreed upon at the *Bekenntniskirche* in Berlin-Friedrichsfelde under the name *Grüne Liga*. Its first official congress took place on 3 February 1990 in the 'ecological catastrophe regions of Halle/Bitterfeld', located in the heart of the GDR's chemical production zone.

The Green League (GL) is not immune to many developmental paradoxes afflicting the eastern region. Despite the extraordinary environmental degradation which stands as the legacy of GDR 'industrialisation at any price' policies over a span of four decades, most East-residents accord very low priority to such issues in the face of more pressing unemployment concerns (ranging from 14 to 40 per cent in various locales).[42] The Bündnis '90/Green Party, which merged with its western counterpart in 1993, has failed to attain a stable block in any of the eastern state legislatures; it lost its only seats in the Sachsen-Anhalt assembly as a result of the April 1998 elections.

The period following the 1989/90 'turn around' witnessed a rapid differentiation among environmental initiatives. The GL itself withdrew from parliamentary processes after the first democratic communal elections of May 1990. The decision not to merge with either the Green Party or other ecology groups was part of a conscious effort to maintain its own image, work-style and name even before unification was in full swing. Autonomy was perceived as 'an identity question, to be sure' (interview with Matthias Baerens, GL-Schwerin) and an attempt 'really to make use of a little bit of what was good about the GDR'.[43] Members established a quasi-federative NGO structure warranting the legal autonomy of the five state organs (*Landesverbände*), codified in 1992. Its Central Speakers' Council and Executive Committee are located in Berlin, supplemented by regional Contact Bureaus, a National Members Assembly and semi-annual regional meetings focusing on specific themes. Executive officers responsible for routine coordination tasks [*Geschäftsführung*] have been serving on an unpaid/volunteer basis since 1996.

The League has been quite successful at holding its own against much older, larger West German organizations (for example, the *Naturschutzbund Deutschland*, the *Bund für Umwelt und Naturschutz*, the BBU) on eastern turf. GL organs were officially recognized in 1991 as 'bearers of public concerns' under the Federal Nature Protection Law, entitling them to deliver impact statements and participate in hearings on plans for public development. It sustains 'political visibility' through high rates of member activism: at least 50 per cent are directly engaged in project work, in contrast to the 'cheque-book memberships' of many larger organizations. Individual and group memberships are integrated into non-hierarchical networks whose 'anti-institutional' thrust is maintained through an emphasis on self-organized initiatives. The Mecklenburg-Vorpommern bureau will only agree to co-operate in securing funding, for example, when interested parties provide evidence of having formed a grass-roots group capable of sustained action; they must secure their own sponsors in order to make use of the GL label. This logic pervades the organization as a whole: 'The people who come to us are the ones who want to do something themselves. We don't just represent them. We give advice that promotes self-organisation, action on site.' They claim further, '[we are] working on ourselves', not only to acquire democratic participatory skills but also to advance personal lifestyle changes. The Green League 'wants to be a subversive element in a system that is generally considered 'the victor of history', in view of the fact that 'the western economic system based on private ownership of the land, the means of production and resources serves the privatisation of profits but socialises the resulting damages to water, air and soil'.[44]

The spectrum of GL projects ranges from campaigns to block expansions of the Autobahn (21/241 A), the ICE and the Transrapide (super-speed trains) through sensitive areas, to actions against brown coal strip-mining and damming projects along the Saale, Elbe and Havel rivers. Others work to promote nature preserves along formerly undeveloped border zones (*Mauerstreifen Berlin*), as well as nature-friendly sanitation/waste disposal systems, and 'skill sharing' though city-partnerships with other East European groups. Not averse to new technologies *per se*, it has established multiple e-mail and web-page sites, in addition to publishing its own ecological telephone/marketing directory. GL efforts to educate youth by way of eco-tours and eco-vacation camps are so popular in Mecklenburg-Vorpommern that coordinators can hardly meet the demand!

The League currently derives its financial resources from a combination of membership dues, charitable contributions, and project grants secured through state or federal ministries; it received DM 230,000 from the Federal Ministry of the Environment for its 1994 Trans-regional Initiative for Public Education, for example.[45] Its latest entrepreneurial ventures (organic 'bio-farms', beach-hikes, self-financing kindergartens) are at least partially grounded in the belief that the GL must 'expand or stagnate', suggesting that activists are also cultivating free market skills. Members are simultaneously learning how to 'use the system' in other ways, such as by tapping into federal structural funds linked to unification processes. Though it actively encourages volunteer work, the GL has utilized federally funded *ABM-Stellen* (temporary job creation programmes) to establish projects at local levels. The Schwerin office reported it had six to seven such workers 1992–94 (before funding ran out), and that it has become 'interesting as a job-providing model' for West Germans (Baerens). In addition to supplying recognized 'alternative service' workplaces for conscientious objectors ('green helmets'), the League participates in the *Freiwilliges Ökologisches Jahr* (FÖJ, a year-long ecology-volunteer programme for youths aged 17 to 26) which enrolled 60 to 70 adolescents in Mecklenburg-Vorpommern. Costs are borne by the Ministry for Family, Elderly, Women and Youth, supplemented by the state ministries; the national budgetary allocation for FÖJ totalled DM 4.5 million in 1996. This programme, in turn, procures monies through the European Union Social Fund.[46] Five Polish youth acquired eco-experience as Mecklenburg interns in 1997, affirming the GL's interest in international cooperation beyond the 'earth summit' in Rio de Janeiro. Thus *die Grüne Liga* not only embodies 'a bit of successful self-assertion' as far as the reconfiguration of *ostdeutsche Identität* goes. It concurrently promotes the kind of practical skills and community orientation that are essential to the internalization of democratic values and to participation in broader political processes in the young Länder.

VOLKSSOLIDARITÄT – LANDESVERBAND BERLIN

Created in 1945, the People's Solidarity preceded the GDR's founding but nonetheless became the national provider of a wide array of volunteer support services to the elderly and the disabled between 1949 and 1989. Registering nearly 500,000 dues-paying subscribers, 40,000 paid employees and 4,000 volunteers in 1996, this association 'which had a good reputation' in GDR times has overtaken its western competitor, the *Arbeiterwohlfahrt* in Berlin and Brandenburg.

Volkssolidarität (VS) was formerly a mass organization of two million members tied together by common life conditions, since most eastern social capital ties evolved via the workplace. Although GDR citizens were usually permitted to travel to the West upon reaching retirement age (assuming that their permanent departure would save on pension costs), limits on currency-exchange meant that most could not go very far. The network of VS clubs, situated in neighbourhoods and factories, blanketed the country until 1989; individual branches scheduled social events, ensured house-cleaning assistance, warm meals and select health services for citizens no longer able to care for themselves. The organization lost many members after *die Wende*, experiencing its most dramatic decline in 1990/91 (down to 852,083) – not as a result of mass resignations but because executive offices stopped functioning and/or collecting dues, once orders were no longer issued 'from above'.

Despite an overall loss of 30 per cent (the largest decline occurred in Saxony), the VS deserves credit for having retained half a million members as a traditional association whose primary purpose is ministering to the needs of others, not promoting self-interest and individual advancement (Table 4).[47] By contrast, no political party has managed to *attract*, much less keep at least 100,000 eastern members – except for the PDS; the number of all dues-paying party members in the young states was 225,000 in 1996.[48] The VS remains the largest senior-organization in the East; Brandenburg, Sachsen-Anhalt and Mecklenburg-Vorpommern registered modest membership increases as of 1996. While the number of unpaid VS volunteers dropped from 45,097 in 1991 to a low of 27,046 in 1993, it rose again to 36,528 in 1996.[49]

Those who struggled to preserve the association had to adapt to radically new conditions virtually overnight. Dues were raised from the standard 50 pfennigs to 1 Ost-Mark to DM 10–15, while most state subsidies disappeared. Despite its limited revenue base, the VS suddenly had to create a chain of 'social stations' for home-/health care formerly assumed by publicly financed community nurses. Unlike the *Grüne Liga* which was free to build new sites on uncharted territory after 1990, People's Solidarity faced direct competition from big, well-entrenched western welfare organizations (*Caritas, Diakonie*) which immediately sought to divide up Berlin into distinct service-provider areas.

Though 'not initially understood by the panel of western evaluators' sent in to decide its fate in 1991 (interview with Director Norbert Clemenz, Landesverband Berlin), the VS did receive strong support from the national umbrella-organization of welfare providers, the *Paritätische Wohlfahrsverband*, in which it now enjoys formal standing as the seventh member. The review amounted to a learning experience for both sides. Westerners were surprised by the large contingent of volunteers whose point of affiliation was the workplace, in contrast to their own networks of career-tracked social service suppliers. Easterners (including the then probational director, Clemenz) had to develop a certain amount of 'backbone', such as in not allowing themselves to be put in same corner with the PDS because of the VS's deep system-roots. Western directors seem not to comprehend that their organizations are more directly shaped by ideological factors, conditioned by their obvious religious affiliations. Individual East Germans have also had to learn not to talk publicly about the size of their pension checks, something that is 'not done' in the West where earnings-differentials tend to be much larger than was true in the GDR.

Having democratized its operational statutes and having shifted to a market- (albeit non-profit) based accounting system, the *Volkssolidarität* now rests on three functional pillars. First, it remains a mass membership

TABLE 4

VOLKSSOLIDARITÄT: MEMBERS AND VOLUNTEERS, 1997

Landesverband	Members	Members as % of population	% of population 60 years or older
Berlin	37,853	2.92	14.5
Brandenburg	89,522	3.50	14.9
Mecklenburg-Vorpommern	82,223	4.52	20.3
Sachsen	120,840	2.66	9.7
Sachsen-Anhalt	78,570	2.88	11.2
Thüringen	69,049	2.77	11.1
Total	478,057	3.10	12.5

Landesverband:	number of Active Volunteers
Berlin	3,958
Brandenburg	6,376
Mecklenburg-Vorpommern	5,868
Sachsen	7,973
Sachsen-Anhalt	4,963
Thüringen	5,734
Total	34,872

Source: *Die Volkssolidarität im Jahr* 1997, Info-Blatt 2 (Berlin: Bundesverband e V., 1998), 2A.

organization. The East has witnessed a dramatic breakdown in familiar forms of solidarity, due to the inequities produced by mass unemployment as well as to a reconfiguration of the social opportunity structure. Though West German pension rules have benefited many, the elderly feel particularly overwhelmed by 'the extraordinary amount of bureaucracy' they must now master to access their entitlements. The VS assists members (75 to 80 per cent of whom are aged over 60) with applications for housing subsidies and the like, having cut back on administrative staff in order to put more people directly into care-work. It has designated five target groups for future recruitment and publicity campaigns. Officials admit they face real difficulty in trying to secure the long-term involvement of younger citizens, too busy with their own problems (like unemployment) at time of rapidly increasing need: One-third of all Germans are already older than 60, though the ageing of the East German population is not as extreme as in the western states. Still, by 2010 the number of citizens over the age of 80 will almost equal those under 18 years.

Secondly, People's Solidarity offers a wide array of social services, professional care services and cultural activities. It manages 24 old-age homes with 616 places, as well as adult day-care facilities, self-help stations, and in-home services. The western legal requirement that persons with disabilities be divided up into degrees of 'need' (criteria for determining the amount of subsidization they 'deserve') initially proved problematic for eastern seniors, women and men, who viewed care as 'an equal right' after decades of participation in the paid labour force. Many were too proud to admit actual need, leading to a deterioration in their condition. Thanks to VS intervention, Berlin is no longer subject to functional/territorial divisions; since 1996, most processing has taken place through the health insurance system rather than through 'welfare' offices.

Against complaints that the New Germany is an alienating, selfish, overly individualistic place, the VS has worked to avoid isolation of the elderly by orchestrating more than 42,759 interactive events last year, attracting some 1,200,000 participants; it also maintains 506 social centres. One of its most popular causes is making it possible for senior citizens to share in a long-coveted freedom to travel: the Berlin branch arranged 38,000 visits to the Matterhorn in 1995, and 30,000 senior vacations to Mallorca (practically a German vacation-colony) in 1996. It also carries weight as a potential future employer, having accounted for 12,553 jobs in 1997: 8,561 were regular, paid-positions, 1,350 involved *ABM-Stellen*, and 1,110 were 'alternative service' jobs.

The third pillar of VS activity centres on political interest representation for seniors. *Volkssolidarität* hopes to establish itself as 'a value community with economic clout'. On 8 June 1997 it staged a theatre 'happening' at the Berlin Schauspielhaus around the motto, 'Hot Hearts against Societal Coldness'; the first 2,000 tickets sold out within hours, compelling coordinators to schedule a second performance for the same day. The enthusiasm generated by this event was not only cultural (since the price of privatized theatre and concert tickets has become prohibitive for many on fixed incomes). It also constituted a protest action against the conservative government's 1996 and 1997 welfare-state cuts. The association's political thrust was more explicit in the '31 Theses – On the Future Development of the State Pension System' issued by VS President Jost Biedermann two days earlier and formally presented to the Berlin Assembly. The organization engages in the political education of its members, describing relevant legal developments by way of a quarterly magazine, *Volkssolidarität heute*. The Federal Executive moreover issued a platform statement in preparation for the national election, titled *Wahlprüfstein der Volkssolidarität – 1998*.

In sum, People's Solidarity also offers clear evidence of organizational sustainability under the new democratic requirements. Like the GL, it has begun to expand its range of direct services, offering child-care, youth homes and services for persons with disabilities (the latter have also developed a very effective interest organization since 1991). It has assumed a kind of 'model' character, having established its first western branch in Berlin Spandau in 1997 with the support of all political parties; it is also creating a social-station in co-operation with Turkish community activists in Berlin-Kreuzberg. Efforts to institute a door-to-door contribution drive have also paid off: its 1994 recruitment marked a 120 per cent increase over the previous year. Having brought in a total of DM 504,000 in 1995, volunteers collected DM 560,264 during the first ten days of its February 1997 fund-drive.

During the week in 1997 when the author carried out the interviews, the VS-Berlin staff was heavily involved in crisis management: a West-German catering company which functioned as the contractual provider for its meals-on-wheels programme went bankrupt in June 1997 – and simply stopped delivering meals without prior notification. This placed the elderly at risk to a degree 'inconceivable in the GDR'. Director Clemenz revealed that he 'didn't bother to call a second West Berlin business' for an estimate; the East German firm that came to the rescue was given an immediate contract. *Wir kaufen Ost* is a slogan making the rounds throughout the young states.

RUNDER TISCHE GEGEN GEWALT
(MAGDEBURG, SACHSEN-ANHALT)

The city administration in Magdeburg offers a concrete example of a western organizational transplant being partially reshaped by eastern problems, norms and interactive styles. Magdeburg has been rocked with sensational incidents of skinhead violence since unification, targeted against foreigners in particular. The first four years of democratic governance in Sachsen-Anhalt were plagued by scandals at the highest levels, compelling the resignation of three (West) CDU governors, 18 ministers and 21 state-secretaries by 1994! Opposition leader Reinhard Hoeppner (SPD) formed a minority government after the 1994 elections, 'tolerated' by the Greens and the PDS; he was reelected in 1998 (with PDS toleration), though an extreme-right party, the German People's Union, scored a shocking 12.9 per cent. Joblessness throughout the Land hovers between 20 and 30 per cent, although it has begun to attract significant foreign investment (interview with State-Secretary Matthias Gabriel, 14 July 1998).

The active catalyst for the creation of Magdeburg's Round Table against Violence, which convened for the first time on 11 September 1995, was the death of a young punk rocker murdered by skinheads in the dismal Plattenbau neighbourhood of Olvenstedt. It was nonetheless conceived as a forum for engaging party delegates, bureaucratic experts, social agencies, and quasi-private field-workers in discussion over 'the entire spectrum' of violence issues affecting city residents. Public solicitation of participants resulted in a roster of 44 voting members and some 30 'permanent guests'; as of 1998, the RT moved to 'clear the corpses from its membership file', that is, voting out delegates who fail to attend faithfully. Initially adopting a three-month cycle, the group now meets on average for two to three hours every two months, its deliberations resting on a set of formal by-laws, a pre-circulated agenda and voting rules. Though some participants are tied to public agencies, representation takes place 'after work' (four to seven o'clock in the afternoon) on an unpaid, volunteer basis. The RT elects its own Chair, though responsibility for technical coordination (issuing invitations, producing minutes, advising on legal issues) rests with Dr. Hans-Heinrich Tabke and Christiane von Wagner, who work in the *Dezernat für Kommunal- und Ordnungsangelegenheiten*, directly subordinate to the Mayor.

The Round Table was a participatory model utilized in the GDR during the heady transitional period of December 1989 to March 1990, drawing on the experiences of the Polish *Solidarnosc*. Spokespersons for various opposition groups were accorded equal standing with official members of the interim Modrow Government, not only in the hopes of ensuring stability and non-violence but also in an effort to quickly turn around a sclerotic ship of state with grass-roots representation and input. Since 1990, many elected politicians, with little grass-roots experience of their own, have used the term indiscriminately to indicate their 'closeness to citizens', leading Leo Jansen to specify seven objective criteria for recognizing 'the real thing'. Democratically constituted Round Tables (a) undertake an objective/substantive treatment of a clearly determined problem; (b) make use of self-organization to strengthen personal responsibility among groups and individuals; (c) strive to maintain an unbureaucratic character, enabling them to take up work on short notice through special linkages to politicians and administrators; (d) emphasise transparency and foster public access during early stages of decision making, in an effort to accelerate the political process; (e) attempt to forge trust among groups affected by conflict, especially among the most polarized interests; (f) set out to establish common interests (and set criteria for defining them as such) through an open presentation of competing interests. Last but not least, the primary goal of Round Tables is to build consensus as the key to problem resolution.[50]

The *Runder Tisch gegen Gewalt* (RT) in Magdeburg has experienced none of the high drama typical of the Central Round Table immediately prior to the SED's collapse in 1989/90, though some of the violence to which it owes its existence has been sensational. The 'table' the writer experienced in the old City Hall was not round but rather an inverted U (its predecessor in Berlin also had 'square edges'). According to the author's interviews, the municipal constellation was initially framed by a cultural clash of a different sort, not between 'the Party, which always was right' and an ever more self-assertive *Volk* nor between East and West; rather, city administrators were caught between 'bureaucratic perfectionism' imported from the West and ingrained eastern habits of trying to circumvent the system through personal appeals (*Eingaben*) to select officials.

The Round Table's accomplishments over a two-and-a-half year period do suggest that it qualifies as 'the real thing'. Given the scandal-ridden beginnings of democratic governance in the state capital through 1994, it is conceivable that the RT initially provided a source of moral support for fledgling organs or groups which had long been part of the state apparatus but were compelled to become 'free agents' lobbying on their own behalf under new institutional imperatives. The GDR had invested heavily in youth clubs and culture centres as vehicles for collective socialization, accounting for their earlier political and financial dependency. The RT format afforded a unique opportunity for participants to acquaint themselves with new projects and actors throughout the area, expediting the networking process. Blessed by substantial continuity of personnel (even when individuals' day-jobs and titles changed), as well as by a few very committed personalities, the group managed during its first year of operation to generate a shared understanding as to the multifaceted nature of violence (*Gewalt*).

By the spring of 1997 the Round Table had formulated a catalogue of 15 broadly defined measures against youth criminality that are preventative as well as reactive in nature. Proposals range from the creation of local urban-district conferences and coordination offices (linking neighbourhood resources available to families, children and schools), to the adoption of anti-violence curricular modules, to changes in court proceedings against young offenders, police training for handling sexual abuse, to direct discussions between neighbourhood officers and troublesome youth groups. The RT thus provides concrete recommendations for the Mayor, with whom the ultimate power of decision rests. Insofar as its proposals are the outcome of non-partisan, expert deliberations, the group helps to diffuse controversy over especially sensitive proposals, like the one to open youth club facilities to skinheads to prevent them from aligning themselves with explicitly political, professionally organized neo-Nazi organs.

Its ability to generate an expert, non-partisan consensus has induced the city to allocate more funds for youth programmes, despite its dire financial straits; by 1997 Magdeburg had more youth club facilities (44) than the wealthier West-city of Braunschweig (33) with an equivalent population. Communal allocations rose from DM 3.96 million in 1991 to DM 4.53 million in 1995, to DM 6.78 million in 1997, subsidizing 70 local organizations and projects (data graciously provided by Dr Tabke). In addition to shoring up multiple project workers after *ABM* funding ran out (continuity of personnel being absolutely essential to building youth trust), Magdeburg succeeded in providing every local applicant with an apprenticeship in 1997/98. It is increasingly difficult to add new projects, however, since allocations tend to come at expense of those already up and running.

The Round Table's relative effectiveness has ironically given birth to a potential competitor at the formal-administrative level, the Council for Crime-Prevention (*Kriminalpräventiver Beirat*). Though initially proposed by the CDU Interior Ministry in 1994, the Council was actually established under SPD auspices in 1997; its Steering Group consists of the Mayor, two administrators (Communal Order and Social/Youth Affairs) and three top-ranking police officials. They are supplemented by five Work Groups with a focus on preventing addiction, city planning/housing, school violence, youth-recreation, and technical-prevention/shop-lifting. Troubling to RT activists is the *Beirat's* drain on resources that might have otherwise gone to its own affiliates: DM 2 million (US $1.2 million) went directly to the police for programmes along the lines of 'midnight basketball', enabling them to hire trainers and referees unavailable (or unaffordable) for comparable RT-approved programmes. The interview partners expressed further concern over the enhanced power of the police 'to make youth policy' independently of substantive-expert actors, including the official *Jugendamt* (Office of Youth Affairs). Relying on direct ties between the Mayor's office and Police Directorates, the Council's very composition means less decision-making transparency (though Dr Tabke is in the steering group, due to his position as *Beigeordneter*) – and certainly fewer input opportunities for affected citizen groups.

The Round Table's most notable achievement in relation to my core thesis is undoubtedly its contribution to building 'transparency, tolerance and trust'. Attempts to instrumentalize the RT for any one group's own political goals seem to be rare (two examples mentioned involved the PDS and the Women's Round Table). The actual votes cast are more moderate than the rhetoric employed on occasion, suggesting that no single organizational actor wants to fracture the work of the whole. Three participants interviewed at length in June 1998 held that East-West differences do not play a role in group deliberations (though the two lead-figures are West-imports). More important is the need to clarify differences which exist as a function of each group's involvement with separate dimensions of the problem (for example, street-worker/state prosecutor).

The writer recalls how Ms von Wagner (a brand new law graduate from Bonn) had insisted in 1997 that 'no Easterners had the legal qualifications necessary' for the post for which she had been recruited. By 1998 she openly admitted that as a jurist, she initially had trouble digesting the idea that such a *Quasselgremium* (translation: a motley crew of random chatterers) could accomplish anything. Having been brought together with people from Baha'i (a transcendentalist religious movement), soccer fan clubs, advocates for the sexually abused, drug counsellors, *inter alia*, she has 'personally developed more tolerance for other approaches'. The mix is multicultural and colourful, she went on; people can clarify 'fronts', work in small groups, bundle their issues and still draw common conclusions. In her own words, 'they have to grasp this as valuable in and of itself … There is no other place where these people would come together to discuss with each other; there is no substitute for the kind of network(s) developed here'.

In short, the Municipal Round Table comprises a prime example of what Jansen labels 'the rediscovery of the political through problem-oriented learning'.[51] It has afforded a sobering but real-democratic experience for the residents of this eastern city as to the inherent limits of 'the state of law' and its corollary institutions. Participants stress the need to secure a more binding character for the RT's 'engaged citizen' resolutions; volunteer efforts have generated 'a flood of information' not matched by an equivalent ability to turn data around into practical solutions. There is also a need for more effective feedback loops among party-political factions. Equally pressing is the need to find ways of directly engaging youth in its deliberations (an early effort to invite school-representatives fizzled out). The Round Table must develop better channels for communicating with the public, having intentionally banned the media from its regular sessions to ensure candid discussion. In addition to these constraints, RT delegates have been confronted with the ultimate free-market paradox: There is a real public demand for effective programmes against violence, as well as a more than adequate supply of citizens willing to develop such programmes; yet there is little money to pay for them in a profit-driven economy

The associational mix found in Magdeburg once again offers a model for deepening democracy in relation to stagnating western policy-making structures, though it is certainly not the only one of its kind. A few Round Tables were established in the FRG prior to 1989, to deal with problems of structural adjustment in coal-mining Aachen, for instance. Other Round Table experiments have actually failed in their efforts to preserve and democratize pre-existing institutions.[52] Especially important in the unification context is the fact that Magdeburg participants are given a chance to view themselves and their contributions to the system as essentially equal, a welcome antidote to the 'second-class citizenship' perception of many East residents to date.

GLEICHSTELLUNGSSTELLE-ERFURT (THÜRINGEN)[53]

Formal legal equality, economic opportunity, full reproductive rights and infrastructural support for women as paid workers-and-mothers counted among the socialist achievements of the GDR to a degree not realized in united Germany. The SED's practice of *Gleichberechtigung* often deviated from the theory, however, especially with regard to the unequal division of household labour its policies took as a given, as well in relation to darker issues of domestic violence and child abuse under real-existing socialism. Nor did women necessarily enjoy 'a room of their own', given the subordination of all women's organizations and needs to Party-defined priorities.

Erfurt saw the creation of the first GDR Women's Centre in February 1990, called to life by a *Wende*-era group known as Women for Change. Situated in a villa formerly used by the Stasi to wire-tap local residents, the Centre offers a cafe, drop-in child-care, meeting rooms for self-help groups and instructional programmes, along with three on-site counsellors (a former western owner filed a property restitution claim immediately after it opened, but the site has been retained). Shortly thereafter, the city named Sabine Fabian as the first Director of the Office for Equalisation of the Sexes (hereafter Equality Office or GSS). She assumed her post, together with three co-workers, on 15 March 1990, three days prior to the free *Volkskammer* elections. This office quickly moved to establish a number of 'safe' apartments for victims of domestic violence (no easy task in a country plagued by a continuous housing shortage) and began reaching out to rapidly proliferating initiatives covering a wide array of women's issues. The current GSS Director, Birgit Adamek, appointed in April 1993, espouses a 'co-operative leadership style'. The Women's Centre and the GSS engage in 'coordination discussions' every two weeks; 'team meetings' between the co-workers of both entities take place every eight to ten weeks. By 1997, the Centre enjoyed the services of five regular employees and six co-workers hired under ABM contracts; from 1991 to 1997, the Centre and GSS provided ABM places for a total of 47 women.

To borrow a European Union formula, the *Gleichstellungsstelle* (GSS) appears to be following a strategy of 'completion, deepening, and enlargement'. By institutional completion is meant here the recognition and formalization of its functions and competencies relative to 'real' decision-making entities. Despite a few shifts in leadership and a redefinition of its 'location' in the official power structure, the GSS has succeeded in cultivating a positive working relationship with City Hall. The symbiosis is particularly noteworthy insofar as both the state and local governments have been dominated by the CDU since unification – a party which has proved quite resistant to active *Frauenförderung* at the national level (a CDU majority replaced the tension-ridden Grand Coalition in 1998). The Equality Office has enjoyed the support and cooperation of CDU Mayor Manfred Ruge from the start (he included Fabian in City Council meetings) and allows the GSS to review pending legislation for its women-specific impact. Thüringen's dire financial straits notwithstanding, the city has provided regular public funding for GSS initiatives, especially for its extended campaign against domestic violence. In 1991, Mayor Ruge allocated DM 400,000 to renovate a four-story shelter in the city centre, with places for 25 women and children (increased to 44 places in 1994). The state has allocated another DM 1 million for shelters and initiatives.

The GSS prides itself on a 'high measure of professionality' in its dealings with the bureaucracy and in the wider execution of its functions. Public funding has not deterred women's advocates from speaking out against certain equal opportunity violations on the part of 'city fathers' themselves. It protested the actions of one key official who fired City Hall's in-house staff of 130 cleaning women and replaced them with a mostly male, private janitorial service (*'Jetzt wird im Rathaus nicht mehr nach Hausfrauenart geputzt sondern professionell'*). It has called for a modernization of municipal administration (*Projektgruppe 'Optimiertes Personalmanagement'*), in light of the fact that women occupy 68.7 per cent of the City's lower/mid-range positions. Its aim is to improve the working conditions of government employees by way of flexible hours, as well as to preserve jobs of 'endangered' groups like pre-school teachers, in the face of declining birth rates and budget deficits.

The GSS has engaged in formal networking with various municipal and state agencies (for example, with the *Ausländerbeirat*), as well as with counterpart offices at different levels. By 1993, some 420 Equal Opportunity Offices had been established throughout the new states, the year Erfurt hosted the Commission of Women's Affairs Officers for the German Conference of Cities. Its Director participates in both the national roof organization for *Frauenbeauftragte* (1,125 throughout the FRG), as well as in the *Landesarbeitsgemeinschaft* for Women's Affairs officials (56 in Thüringen). It issued its First Women's Report of the City of Erfurt in June 1995, a vehicle for documenting the life-conditions of the city's female and male residents on an ongoing basis. It added data-collection to its core tasks in 1996. The Office further cultivates formal co-operative or advisory relationships with some 55 local and regional clubs, associations and autonomous groups.

As to functional enlargement, the projects supported by the GSS mushroomed rapidly under the sudden crush of mass unemployment; women accounted for 58 per cent of the jobless in 1991, up to 61.2 per cent by 1993. The latter has ostensibly contributed to increasing domestic violence (or at least in women's willingness to flee abusive situations): 48 women made use of the new shelter facility in January 1991 alone. The GSS/Centre sponsors seminars on alcoholism, drug addiction (leading to the *Modellprojekt 'Haus Drehtür'*), eating disorders (a post-unity phenomenon), and divorce law; 3,580 woman and children enrolled in its 32 'creative classes' in 1997.

The GSS conducted its own mail survey in 1992 on 'the life situation of women and men', which led it to explore women's mounting concerns with personal safety in Erfurt, especially after nightfall (resulting, at least in part, from the rise of pornography/sex shops, thanks to 'the free market'). There are now night taxis, women's parking places, and a new focus on women's experiences in urban planning processes (for example, improved street lighting). It has also addressed the issue of homelessness stemming from higher addiction/joblessness rates. Erfurt's equality activists have moreover taken up the cause of female unemployment in more direct ways, featuring seminars on job application processes, advising women on their legal rights, for example not to reveal child-bearing plans during interviews, and arranging training courses.

The Equality Office has likewise expanded its capacity for public relations and consciousness-raising, despite its underdeveloped info-technology infrastructure (four co-workers were still sharing one phone line and one computer in 1997). In 1999 the GSS issued 120 press releases, 35 'statements', moderated 18 public fora, and distributed over 80 different brochures; it saw a ten per cent increase in the number of written inquiries it received (processing 1,900 in total). First staged in May 1992 with booths representing 48 organizations, its *Info-Börse* has become an annual event. According to official visitor statistics, 18,885 Erfurt residents attended its various events in 1997, suggesting that women's rights are a matter of 'legitimated' public concern.

Despite its established *Querschnittfunktion*, that is, its ability to cut across functional domains and establish ties among diverse initiatives and agencies, at least one participant-observer believes that co-operation among different groups 'could be more intense'. Dagmar Grüner (a founding member still at the GSS) pointed to a well coordinated and highly publicized campaign, Violence against Women has Many Faces, the local version of a 1996 national campaign that drew on the energies of 'ten municipal agencies, eleven women's projects, all factions of the Erfurt City Parliament, the autonomous welfare-service providers, 20 associations and organizations, representatives of individual unions and city councils, the Justice Ministry, the Police Presidium, the State Criminal Office and local police directors' (internal document). The group involved 70 actors in putting together a programme encompassing nearly 100 activities spread over the first half of 1996.

Despite the event's public resonance, Ms Grüner voiced muted disappointment during a June 1997 interview that rather than building on their own momentum and new-found contacts, most groups continued to look to the GSS, expecting it to 'organize' a top-down, sequel event. Grüner and her colleagues had hoped that co-operation would become a self-sustaining activity. By the summer of 1998, she seemed to feel that local activists were about to enter a new stage: She is waiting for a broad spectrum of exchanges and cooperative ventures to spring up from below, 'now that participants know each other and can communicate directly'. They are better positioned to undertake *rege Prävention in der Frauenarbeit*, that is, to block policy initiatives deleterious to women before they become the law of the land.

The *Gleichstellungsstelle* provides an example of significant democratic deepening as regards lawmakers' incorporation of the interests/needs articulated by this traditionally 'excluded' group into the public agenda. In November 1997, the GSS was forced to seek a new legal foundation for its affirmative actions plans, when its project funding expired after four years. Hearings on the proposed legislation [249 HAFG] were held in January 1998, encompassing representatives from diverse Family, Health, Welfare and Equality projects. Participants sought agreement on a common understanding of 'women's projects', in the hopes of creating new lines of responsibility among public agencies and administrative departments (Children, Youth, Health). They issued a Common Paper (approved in April) delineating which agencies should be held responsible for financing particular applications. The GSS has been accorded 'hard-money' financing for another half-time position, which was increased to three and a half positions in 1999 (partially funded by the state of Thüringen). The understanding reached in 1999 helps to establish priorities for future projects (half-funded by the state). It provides a permanent legislative basis for equality politics, giving the Office 'roots' in the city's larger administrative structure, even though it must also secure a degree of private or supplementary financing for its activities.

The Erfurt *Gleichstellungsstelle* entails the more or less successful adoption of a western model rapidly confronted and reshaped by the specific problems of the East. The Office's effectiveness derives from its willingness to respond pragmatically, first, to women's material needs (devoid of a feminist *Gesamtkonzept,* typical of the old FRG at the onset of the Second Wave of the movement) and, secondly, to activists' inclination to work with 'the state'. The *1997 Jahresbericht* further affirms women's learning experiences *vis-à-vis* democracy since unification. The GSS serves 'as form

of interest representation within the framework of the established system ...
By bringing in women's interests, the Equal Opportunity Commissioner
helps to influence communal-political consensus building, exercises
internal administrative control and initiative functions and delivers external,
innovative impulses for changing consciousness' as to women's needs. It
notes further, 'our work is accompanied by ever more conflicts of interest',
linked to the deeper sources of female disadvantage and preordained by
attempts 'to integrate equality-relevant concepts into general political plans
and decision-making'. Its task is no less than to challenge traditional power
structures and policy arenas: 'Interest representation necessarily means
becoming engaged in conflicts of interest conflicts'. Though 'feminist'
initiatives still meet with a degree of public scepticism in the East, women
directly involved in equality causes in Erfurt have come of political age in
that they have learned to view conflict as a normal feature of pluralistic
society.

As to further 'eastern' dimensions of its organizational identity, Grüner
holds that the Erfurt Office was never strongly oriented towards its more
established western counterparts responsible for Women's Affairs
(*Frauenbeauftragte*). She and her colleagues have 'occasionally checked
out the activities' of the Equal Opportunity Offices in Munich and Mainz
(Erfurt's Sister-City) to see if their projects or tactics might lend themselves
to use on the homefront. For the most part, however, they look to Leipzig
for ideas and experiences, though the Munich office did organize a major
fund-raising campaign in 1991 to help with Centre start-up costs. GSS co-
workers also take cues from other East-models, for example, Saxony's
Round Table: Women and Employment, which foresees grants of DM 5,000
to 20,000 to help women establish their own businesses.

Despite a recent 'separation of functions', activists still attempt to
influence formal decision-making through conventional party channels (the
Frauenbeauftragte now treats internal problems, the Equal Opportunity
Office deals with external sources of female disadvantage). According to
Grüner, eastern women 'have not yet learned to follow the kind of career
profiles *qua* managerial specialisation common among women in the
western states'; instead, they all try 'to follow through on all of the details
to the end'. She sees the latter as evidence that 'something remains' of a pre-
unity East German work-style, grounded in an effort to cultivate existing
personal contacts, as a vehicle for trusting one another, and 'then being able
to rely on one another'.

In summary, the *Gleichstellungsstelle-Erfurt* has come a long way in its
ability to expand the set of women's services now deemed legitimate public
tasks by democratically elected authorities. Though quite small, under-
equipped, short on womanpower and facing a 'growing paper flood' *vis-à-*

vis the bureaucratic forces of City Hall – located right across the town square, the *Fischmarkt* – the Equality Office has performed effectively, given women a sense that gender-specific interests are reviewed in official circles, and scored critical successes in institutionalizing anti-discrimination policies (substantiated by its press reviews). In September 1997 Erfurt was singled out as one of 15 winners of a national competition in search of Children- and Family-Friendly Communities, out of a pool of 364 applicants. It still has a way to go in rendering diverse groups capable of self-mobilization within a broader policy-making framework. As Grüner admitted in June 1998, 'there is too little political work going on', though Erfurt did see the creation of a Free Women's List in time for the 1994 elections (a strategy that produced positive results in Coburg but fizzled out locally). Women's political theme for the 1999 state/communal elections was *Macht was!* (Do Something!). The 1998 incorporation of four self-avowed feminists into the Federal Cabinet under SPD/Green auspices provided new impetus for their campaign.

CONCLUSION: THE END OF APPRENTICESHIP

As posited at the outset, democratic institutions can only prove stable in the long run if they do more than represent citizen interests in a territorial/legislative/administrative sense. Democratic theory presumes that all citizens are unique and thus entitled to make their own 'rational choices'. As an *institutional process*, democratization requires that all members of a society be willing to ascribe to a single constitution, one which accords them fundamental civil liberties, grants them access to free elections, and ensures a separation of public and private spheres. Democratization as a *political-cultural process* requires no such standardization or levelling; indeed, it mandates a sensitivity to difference which cannot be achieved through formal institutional and procedural channels alone. The case studies profiled here show that citizens who cultivate subjective ties to emerging intermediary associations not only internalize democratic values more quickly than non-active individuals but are also more likely to establish effective channels for advancing their own interests within the new power structures. A spirit of political *Ost-trotz* ('not with me you don't!') is giving rise to a new sense of civic nationalism in the eastern states.

The image of 'underdeveloped' East Germans initially proved useful not only for newcomers who wanted to forget the GDR past and assume the FRG *habitus* as quickly as possible; it also held heuristic value for Westerners hoping not to be troubled further by questions about their own national identity and reform needs. Whether or not they are grounded in reality, these images highlight the necessarily reciprocal nature of the

German democratization process: The larger system needs to open itself to at least a partial recycling of eastern practices and value orientations. Prior to 1998, the Kohl Government's approach tended to substantiate the Lauth/Merkel hypothesis that a strategy limited to elite-driven consolidation at the institutional level has the unsalutary effect of impeding normative consolidation at the grass-roots level. Westerners involved with eastern actors and problems 'below' stress the need for a dramatic overhaul of administrative structures and practices 'up there'. Werner Jann asserts, 'without a doubt, the head-over-heels and all-encompassing transfer of the western administrative model has led to major distortions and reconstruction problems'. He urges the government to utilize its relocation to Berlin as a genuine 'fitness cure', shaking off the fat and rigidity it has accumulated over the last two decades.[54]

Though still in the process of consolidation, intermediary associations in the East are less tightly bound to centralized umbrella-organizations than western entities. This quality applies not only to groups pursuing sports, culture and recreation but even to 'carriers' in the heavily regulated welfare domain.[55] This might be interpreted as a logical response to four decades of over-centralization, coupled with a willingness to circumvent problems of West-dominance already witnessed in the formal-democratic realm. Eastern networks moreover 'tend to be apolitical, promoting an image of purely private rather than political or ideological associations', in the eyes of some analysts. But this presumes that East Germans share the same notion of what is political as their western counterparts – a debatable proposition at best, among citizens raised under a system in which all forms of human activity (even reproduction) were configured, supported, or otherwise undermined in the name of centralized political goals. To pursue 'private' interests in the GDR was a highly political act.

The comparative lesson derived here is that a transfer of legal-constitutional structures does not automatically trigger the participatory norms and behaviours that western analysts insist will consolidate democracy in transitional states. The ability to articulate and aggregate interests from below, *in one's own terms*, is just as critical to democratic consolidation as legal competence cultivated above, leading average citizens to recognize their own stake in the system. Though no doubt a welcome change after years of state domination, the privatization of associational activities does not mean that East Germans have also abandoned other, deep-seated collectivist values and behaviours. In short, most East Germans are unlikely to enjoy 'bowling alone' for years to come.

Civic culture can assume many different forms, as Almond and Verba 'revisited' have shown. Citizens at home in pluralist democracies should not have to draw on the same wellsprings of social capital, nor even on the same types of associational structures, in order to have their needs or interests recognized as legitimate ones. As regards the creation of new intermediary organizations, a certain amount of 'small is beautiful' thinking can prove more cost-effective in resource-strapped economies than a rush to build major interest group structures from scratch. It may also counteract negative historical experiences with mass organizations and ease the problem of insufficient social trust by allowing citizens to draw on the familiar. As Richard Rose notes, 'the construction of trustworthy institutions is more likely to happen from the bottom up than from the top down. East Europeans know those whom they trust, and trust those whom they know. Their customary practice is to make inquiries among friends or friends-of-friends in order to find out whether strangers can be trusted.'[56]

These cases deliver substantive proof that democratic apprenticeship has come to an end in the eastern Länder, a point West German *Politmeisters* would do well to recognize. By displaying the courage to mix old and new modes of social capital, established political elites may serve their own purposes, both mitigating citizen vexation over do-nothing electoral campaigns and administering small but regular doses of do-it-yourself consciousness so essential to a truly civic culture.

NOTES

1. Though the distinction between 'official GDR-organizations' and the oft-persecuted 'opposition groups' is a crucial one, the argument here is that independent 'citizen movement' groups were not the only ones capable of providing important learning experiences for East German citizens in their dealings with the state before or after 1989. The former were eliminated outright under the terms of the Unity Treaty; the latter largely 'faded away' insofar as they could not compete with larger, wealthier, more professionalized West German entities, especially the political parties that came to dominate the transformation processes. For a detailed analysis of how the citizen movements were displaced, see Christiane Olivo, *Creating a Democratic Civil Society in Eastern Germany: The Case of Citizen Movements and Alliance 90* (New York: Palgrave, 2001).

2. The civic culture construct, as popularized by Almond and Verba in the early 1960s, was itself grounded in a similar 'universally applicable' assumption, which blurred the lines between the normative, empirical and day-to-day-practice aspects of democracy. The original study posited the US as a working model of the civic culture, *inter alia,* leading the authors to find other states lacking in the cultural prerequisites inherent in that model. See Carole Pateman, 'The Civic Culture: A Philosophical Critique', in Gabriel A. Almond and Sidney Verba (eds.), *The Civic Culture Revisited* (Boston/Toronto: Little, Brown, 1980), pp.57–102.

3. Wolfgang Merkel and Hans-Joachim Lauth, 'Systemwechsel und Zivilgesellschaft: Welche Zivilgesellschaft braucht die Demokratie', *Aus Politik und Zeitgeschichte,* B 6-7/1998, pp.3–12.

4. David P. Conradt, 'Changing German Political Culture', in Almond and Verba, op. cit., pp.212–72.

5. The writer's forthcoming book, *What Remains? The Dialectical Identity of Eastern Germans Before and After Unity.* Sources treated in that work include: Alexis de Tocqueville, *Democracy in America* (New York: Doubleday, 1969 edn.); Robert D. Putnam, 'Bowling

Alone: America's Declining Social Capital', *Journal of Democracy*, Vol.6, No.1 (1995), pp.65–78; and Pierre Bourdieu, 'Ökonomisches Kapital, kulturelles Kapital, soziales Kapital', in Reinhard Kreckel (ed.), *Soziale Ungleichheiten* (Göttingen: Otto Schwarz, 1983), pp.183–98. Tocqueville focused on the elements necessary for building a democratic culture, as opposed to Putnam's concern over the deterioration of a participatory culture. Given the GDR's brief history, 1949–89, Bourdieu offers a more manageable case study of social capital than Putnam's 500-year sweep of Italian democratization processes. Putnam defines *social capital* as a broad assortment of interpersonal networks embodying organized reciprocity and civic solidarity which renders a democracy both stable and responsive to citizen needs. Social capital is posited to foster sturdy norms of generalized reciprocity, leading citizens to undertake rational and purposive action on behalf of others. For Bourdieu, social capital is the sum of resources, actual or virtual, that accrue to an individual or group by virtue of possessing a durable network of more or less institutionalized relationships of mutual acquaintance and recognition. Pierre Bourdieu and Loic Wacquant, *Invitation to Reflexive Sociology* (Chicago: University of Chicago Press, 1992), p.119.

6. Joyce Marie Mushaben, *'Auferstanden aus Ruinen*: Social Capital and Democratic Identity in the New Länder', *German Politics and Society*, Vol.14, No.4 (1997), pp.79–101. Three further approaches reviewed in the larger work centre on: (a) milieu theory (studies by Vester, Michael and Zierke), focusing on worker responses to changes in the industrial landscape; (b) the (re)discovery of cultural capital, an interpretative framework espoused by Pierre Bourdieu (1982); and (c) 'civilizational gaps' (Engler's *zivilisatorische Lücke*), accounting for East-West asymmetries. See Michael Vester, Michael Hofmann and Irene Zierke (eds.), *Soziale Milieus in Ostdeutschland. Gesellschaftliche Strukturen zwischen Zerfall und Neubildung* (Köln: Bund Verlag, 1995); M. Vester, 'Deutschlands feine Unterschiede. Mentalitäten und Modernisierung in ost- und Westdeutschland', *Aus Politik und Zeitgeschichte* B-20, pp.16–30. Further Pierre Bourdieu, *Die feinen Unterschiede* (Frankfurt/M: Suhrkamp, 1982); and Wolfgang Engler, *Die zivilisatorische Lücke. Versuche über den Staatssozialismus* (Frankfurt/M: Suhrkamp, 1992).

7. Rainer Weinert, 'Intermediäre Institutionen oder die Konstruktion des "Einen". Das Beispiel der DDR', in Birgitta Nedelmann (ed.), *Politische Institutionen im Wandel, Kölner Zeitschrift für Soziologie und Sozialpsychologie*, Sonderheft 35/1995, pp.237–53.

8. Thomas Ahbe, 'Ostalgie oder die Fähigkeit zu trauern', *Freitag*, 23 May 1997, p.17.

9. This view is cited by, but not subscribed to by Annette Zimmer, Eckhard Priller and Helmut Anheier in 'Der Nonprofit-Sektor in den neuen Bundesländern: Kontinuität, Neuanfang oder Kopie?', *Zeitschrift für öffentliche und gemeinwirtschaftliche Unternehmen*, Heft 1 (1997), p.59 ff.

10. Among the largest membership organizations were the SED (2.3 million), the Free Democratic Youth (FDJ, 2.3 million), the *Demokratischer Frauenbund* (1.5 million), and the FDGB (9.6 million) which clearly had 'system maintenance' functions but which also provided a wide array of social services, ranging from rock-concerts and discos to family-vacation packages. The *Verband der Kleingärtner, Siedler und Kleintierzüchter*, the *Volkssolidarität*, and the *Deutsche Turn- und Sportbund* had several million members each; the *Kulturbund* drew upon 260,000 dues paying members; all of these relied heavily on volunteer work. See Eckhard Priller, 'Veränderungen in der politischen und sozialen Beteiligung in Ostdeutschland', in Wolfgang Zapf and Roland Habich (eds.), *Wohlfahrtsentwicklung im vereinten Deutschland* (Berlin: Ed. Sigma, 1996), p.285ff.

11. Günther Pollach, *Unabhängige Bürgerbeteiligung in Berlin-Hohenschönhausen* (Berlin: Berlin Institut für Sozialwissenschaftliche Studien – BISS, 1993), p.33. This neighbourhood is reputedly a *Hochburg* of PDS support; only 47 per cent of those sampled supported the PDS without reservation, however, and the overwhelming majority claimed they were not active in any political party, a claim substantiated by low party membership rates.

12. Priller, op. cit., pp.289–99.

13. Zimmer, Priller and Anheier, op. cit., p.59.

14. Statistisches Bundesamt, *Datenreport* (München: Olzog Verlag, 1994), p.560.

15. Still, nearly a third of the East-respondents would consider donating part of their estates to community causes after death, in contrast to 17 per cent of their western peers. Eckhard

Priller and Annette Zimmer, 'Ende der Mitgliederorganisationen?', paper presented at the 20th Congress of the German Political Science Association (DVPW), Bamberg, 13–17 Oct. 1997, p.9.

16. *Das Ehrenamt: Verantwortung übernehmen – Zukunft gestalten.* CDU/CSU Fraktion in Deutschen Bundestag: Bonn, 1997, p.56. Women (less likely to be in paid employment in the West) provide 75 per cent of all volunteer services in 'social' arenas. Claudia Nolte, (then) Federal Minister of Families initiated a Stiftung Bürger für Bürger, with 16 regional Volunteer Centres.

17. Priller and Zimmer, 'Ende der Mitgliederorganisationen?'.

18. *Das Ehrenamt*, pp.45, 77 and 85.

19. Given the brutal acts of hooligan violence that accompanied the World Cup football games in France in 1998, and bearing in mind that convicted Oklahoma City bomber Timothy McVeigh was, in fact, a bowling league member, these groups do merit explicit political attention. Jürgen Baur, 'Die Rolle der Sportvereine im sozialen und politischen Transformationsprozess der neuen Länder', p.5, unpublished manuscript graciously provided by Eckhard Priller.

20. Their personal motives involve a blend of old and new concerns, as a few comments illustrate:

> Those weren't only [acts of participation] that you would just check off somewhere because you were supposed to, but rather it was also something that was important to me. Because I thought, you just can't let things run along the way they have been going. You have to try to help shape things yourself, and to somehow co-determine the direction things are going.

> I feel really satisfied with this activity. Satisfied insofar as: … I really didn't do anything evil during GDR times. But, how should I say this, I would also like to try somehow to make up for things …

> That one just sits here so totally powerless, and despite finding this and that not so good, well even then, can't do anything more. Besides being asked to vote every four years and then always voting for the party, that won't be elected. I told myself, there must be some way through which one can become engaged in society again without having to join a political party und [through which one] can try to influence societal developments with the rest.

See Pollach, op. cit., pp.34–9.

21. Priller, op. cit., p.296.

22. See Daniela Dahn, *Westwärts und nicht vergessen*, op.cit.; and Hans J. Misselwitz, *Nicht länger mit dem Gesicht nach Westen. Der neue Selbstbewußtsein der Ostdeutschen* (Bonn: Dietz, 1996). Also, Peter Merkl, 'An Impossible Dream? Privatizing Collective Property in Eastern Germany', in P. Merkl (ed.), *The Federal Republic of Germany at Forty-Five* (New York: New York University Press, 1995), pp.199–221; and Daniela Dahn, *Wir bleiben hier oder Wem gehört der Osten. Vom Kampf um Häuser und Wohnungen in den neuen Bundesländern* (Reinbek: Rowohlt, 1994).

23. Ahbe, op. cit.

24. Dr Reinhard Höppner, 'Menschenrecht auf Arbeit', Rede auf dem Forum Ostdeutschland in Leipzig, 8 June 1996, provided by press speaker Hans-Ulrich Fink.

25. Dr Reinhard Höppner, Rede auf dem Rechtspolitischen Kongreß der Friedrich Ebert Stiftung am 20 April 1997, Rheingoldhalle-Mainz.

26. Eckhard Priller, *Ein Suchen und Sichfinden im Gestern und Heute. Verändern die Ostdeutschen ihre Einstellungen und Haltungen zur Demokratie und gesellschaftlichen Mitwirkung?*, Working Paper FS III 97–411, Wissenschaftszentrum Berlin (Dec. 1997), p.8.

27. Christiane Lemke, 'Protestverhalten in Transformationsgesellschaften', *Politische Vierteljahresschrift*, H. 1 (März 1997), p.55. Further, Bert Klandermanns, 'Identität und Protest. Ein sozialpsychologischer Ansatz', *Forschungsjournal Neue Soziale Bewegungen*, Jg.10, H.3 (1997), pp.41–51.

28. Joyce Marie Mushaben, *From Post-War to Post-Wall Generations. Changing Attitudes*

towards the National Question and NATO in the Federal Republic of Germany (Boulder, CO: Westview, 1998), Ch.5.

29 James Coleman, 'Social Capital in the Creation of Human Capital', *American Journal of Sociology*, Vol.94 (1988, supplement), p.98.

30. The Ost-Länder meet several criteria some analysts find essential for creating and sustaining a new party base. Unity has initiated a new regional conflict along multiple axes which shows little sign of abating soon. Secondly, it has brought in a new group of voters who have yet to solidify their partisan-political identification. Thirdly, there is no credible opposition party with enough clout to render eastern interests a regular feature of major policy decisions. Last but not least, the newly enfranchized Germans constitute a majority within their own region.

31. Heidrun Abromeit, 'Zum Für und Wider einer Ost-Partei', *Gegenwartskunde*, No.4 (1992), p.445; further, 'Die "Vertretungslücke". Probleme im neuen deutschen Bundesstaat', *Gegenwartskunde*, No. 3 (1993), pp.281–92. For a study of how East Germans are adapting to new political roles, see Jennifer Yoder, *From East Germans to Germans? The New Postcommunist Elites* (Durham, NC: Duke University Press, 1999).

32 DIW data, reported by Thomas Kuczinski, 'Wirtschaftlich wurde Ostdeutschland um zehn Jahre zurückgeworfen', *Neues Deutschland*, 1 Sept., 1995.

33. Abromeit, op. cit., p.442 ff.

34. The Court invalidated a reform law ensuring women's freedom of choice, coupled with mandatory counselling, which had passed with strong cross-party support. The decision recriminalized what had been a free/legal procedure for Eastern women since 1972. Joyce Marie Mushaben, 'Concession or Compromise? The Politics of Abortion in United Germany', *German Politics*, Vol.6, No.3 (1997), pp.69–87.

35. Abromeit, 'Für und Wider', p.443; further, Helmut Wiesenthal, 'Interessenreprasentation im Transformationsprozess. Probleme und Irritationen', in Hans J. Misselwitz (ed.), *Die real-existierende postsozialistische Gesellschaft* (Potsdam: Landeszentrale für Politische Bildung, 1996).

36. Wilhelm Bürklin, 'Einstellungen und Wertorientierungen ost- und westdeutscher Eliten 1995. Gesellschaftliches Zusammenwachsen durch Integration der Elite?', in Oskar Gabriel (ed.), *Politische Orientierungen und Verhaltensweisen im vereinigten Deutschland* (Opladen: Leske & Budrich, 1997), pp.235–62. Also, Markus C. Pohlmann and Hans-Joachim Gergs, 'Manager in Deutschland – Reproduktion oder Zirkulation einer Elite?', *Kölner Zeitschrift für Soziologie und Sozialpsychologie*, Jg.49, H.3 (1997), pp.540–62.

37. Relentless attempts to relegitimize their own role and that of other albeit selected 'victims of the old regime' have delegitimized many once prominent civil rights activists in the eyes of other would-be reformers; there is also mounting intolerance among the competing victim-factions themselves. A few have found a hearing in Alliance '90 (born of New Forum and local Round Tables), while others have allied themselves with the conservative powers-that-be in conjunction with 'the working through of the SED-dictatorship'. The question of how to process the socialist past has generated deep cleavages among East Germans themselves.

38. Lauth and Merkel, op. cit. The conditions these authors establish correspond to those advanced by Diamond though they do not specifically cite Diamond. See Larry Diamond, 'Towards Democratic Consolidation', *Journal of Democracy*, Vol.5, No.3 (1994), pp.4–17.

39. Priller, *Ein Suchen und Sichfinden*, p.11.

40. Lauth and Merkel, op. cit., p.31.

41. For background, see Gudrun Heinrich, 'Von Einheit keine Spur? Bündnis '90/Die Grünen', *Berliner Debatte INITIAL* 8 (1997), pp.40–48.

42. This unnamed activist cited in Anne Hampele, 'Dem Aufschwung Ost ökologisch auf die Beine helfen. Die Grüne Liga e.V. Ein Beispiel erfolgreicher ostdeutscher Selbstbehauptung', *Deutschland Archiv* (1996), p.243.

43. Cited in Hampele, ibid., pp.247–9.

44. Reported by Hampele, ibid., p.247.

45. *Das Ehrenamt*, p.29.

46. It is worth noting that Saxony introduced its own programme, Action 55, to encourage volunteerism and otherwise cover persons (55–60) forced into early retirement; 45 persons

are directly involved with the *Grüne Liga* through this programme. It also includes a Senior-Expert Service and consulting initiatives.

47. Priller, *Ein Suchen und Sichfinden*, pp.38–9.
48. *Volkssolidarität* (ed.), *Info-Blatt* 1 (Berlin: Bundesverband, 1998), p.8.
49. One former participant described the Central Round table phenomenon in almost euphoric terms: 'It was a really unique experience for me, that all were present in equal measure at the table, that all had the same rights and that suddenly one would discover that the truth usually comes out of a very different corner than one would have suspected. That was the deeper, most important sense of the Round Table, this democratic experience: We all have responsibility together'. Cited in Lothar Probst, 'Das Modell Runder Tische. Befunde eines politischen Experiments an Hand einer Regionalstudie', in Misselwitz, *Die real-existierende post-sozialistische Gesellschaft*, pp.90–91.
50. Leo Jansen, 'Die Wiederentdeckung des Politischen durch problemorientiertes Lernen. Regionale Runde Tische und Politische Netzwerke', *Forschungsjournal Neue Soziale Bewegungen*, Jg.9, H.3 (1996), p.44.
51. Jansen, ibid., pp.40–56.
52. Isolde Stark, 'Der Runde Tische der Akademie und die Reform der Akademie der Wissenschaften der DDR nach der Herbstrevolution 1989. Ein gescheiterter Versuch der Selbsterneuerung', *Geschichte und Gesellschaft*, 23 (1997), pp.423–45.
53. The writer extends her deep, personal thanks to Dagmar Grüner at the GSS-Erfurt for her consistent willingness to serve as an in-depth interview partner on short notice three summers in a row. Ms Gruner also provided important documentation for this analysis, including but not limited to the *Pressespiegel der Gleichstellungsstelle, 15. Marz 1990 bis 15. Marz 1995,* reports on the Campaign *'Gewalt gegen Frauen hat viele Gesichter'* and the annual *Informationsbörse*, as well as the Office's 1997 annual report.
54. Werner Jann, 'Die Transformation der politischen Institutionen und des Verwaltungssystems in Ostdeutschland', p.19, manuscript provided by the author; and 'Zeit zum Entrümpeln', *Die Zeit*, 25 Aug. 1995.
55. Anheier and colleagues conclude in this context, 'We are witnessing the emergence of an East German non-profit sector whose organisations are more dynamic, more modern than their West German counterparts, which remain entrenched in an increasingly outdated policy formulation'. Helmut K. Anheier, Eckhard Priller and Annette Zimmer, *Civic Society in Transition: The East German Non-Profit Sector Six Years after Unification*, Working Paper Series No.13 (Baltimore, MD: Johns Hopkins University, Institute for Policy Studies), p.4.
56. Richard Rose, 'The Problem of Trust in Post-Communist Societies', *Journal of Democracy*, Vol.5, No.3 (July 1994), p.29.

Civil Society and Transnational Non-Governmental Organizations in the Euro-Mediterranean Partnership

ANNETTE JÜNEMANN

The Euro-Mediterranean Partnership (EMP) is based on the assumption that the deepening of interregional relations cannot be achieved through governmental agreements alone, but requires popular participation. Against the background of mutual prejudices and misperceptions between the South and the North, co-operation at the level of civil society contributes to intercultural understanding. Furthermore, as the lines of conflict run not only between North and South, but exist also within each of the two regions – between Israelis and Palestinians, Greeks and Turks, Turks and Kurds – civil society co-operation can be particularly important in facilitating the reconciliation of conflict. This positive potential of civil society is recognized by all members of the EMP, and the Barcelona Declaration (1995) stresses 'the essential contribution civil society can make in the process of development of the Euro-Mediterranean Partnership and as an essential factor for greater understanding and closeness between the people'.[1]

The EU, however, also adheres to a less consensual goal in supporting civil society initiatives within the EMP, namely the promotion of democratization in the Mediterranean Partner Countries (MPC). The EU's post-cold war focus on democracy includes the promotion of institutional reform, the rule of law and good governance, but also complements this classical top-down approach to democratization with a bottom-up strategy, based on the assumption that democratization is inseparable from greater respect for human rights and a strong civil society.

Authoritarian regimes in the southern Mediterranean are aware of this hidden agenda. To the extent that civil engagement can undermine authoritarian structures, these governments feel threatened by European support for civil society actors. Beneath the superficial consensus concerning civil society's importance to the EMP, as laid out in the Barcelona Declaration, there exist strong reservations amongst MPCs. The latter accepted the civil society dimension only because it was essentially imposed upon them by the EU, in exchange for the promise of deeper economic co-operation and enhanced financial assistance. To reduce the risk that civil society might endanger present power structures, some authoritarian MPCs insisted on the insertion of a formula into the Barcelona Declaration specifying that civil society projects must be 'within the framework of national law'.[2]

Civil society not only challenges authoritarian regimes in the South. Respected human rights non-governmental organizations (NGOs) like Amnesty International also criticize the EU and its member states, for example over European migration and political asylum policies.[3] Furthermore, representatives of civil society have also criticized the lack of a social dimension and the neglect of environmental considerations within the EMP. The major reproach against the EU concerns the unbalanced commercial interdependence between the MPCs and the EU, developed strongly to the latter's advantage. As the concept of the EMP was elaborated predominantly by the European side, these criticisms are directed mainly against the EU.[4] For the EU itself, civil engagement is, in sum, a double-edged sword.

Authoritarian MPCs openly oppose civil society co-operation and/or try to undermine it through various hidden strategies. While the EU is more generally supportive towards the role of civil society, it has been ambivalent over the extent of its support for civil society initiatives. The reason for the EU's ambivalence is less the fear of being challenged by European civil society actors than concern over the potentially destabilizing effects of civil society support within the MPCs. The EU's goal of promoting democratization can, at least during periods of transition, conflict with the EU's predominant goal of stabilization. In most of the MPCs, processes of democratization will most probably lead to extremely unstable transition periods, with the risk of violent upheavals or even civil wars.[5] Consequently, the EU aims to promote only a gradual process of democratization under the strict control of ruling elites. This caution is advocated especially strongly by France and Spain, owing to these states' special relations with their respective former colonies and protectorates in North Africa. In contrast, the Commission, with no direct interests in the region, has been more ambitious in its attempts to encourage democratization in co-operation with civil society. The strongest supporter of civil society in the Mediterranean has been the European Parliament (EP), but the EP is a relatively weak player within the predominantly intergovernmental EMP.[6]

This account analyses civil society work undertaken within the framework of the EMP. It begins with some basic reflections on the theoretical conceptualization of civil society. The second section outlines and evaluates the various instruments and programmes set up by the EU to support Euro-Mediterranean civil society co-operation within the EMP. The account then analyses the political impact of transnational NGOs, in particular by examining the work of the Euro-Mediterranean Human Rights Network. Finally, a brief assessment is offered of the future prospects of the EU's bottom-up approach to democratization.

CONTRASTING VIEWS OF CIVIL SOCIETY

Civil society is a European concept based on Enlightenment concepts of reason and rationality, and supposing there to be a basic separation and tension between (civil) society, economy and the state.[7] There has never been a universally accepted definition of civil society, even within the western world. Civil society has remained a normative and value-laden concept:

> The values involved are those relating to liberty, to civilized or civilizing behaviour, and to a set of ethics relating to work, social relationships, respect for human rights and so on. The emphasis on one or another aspect may vary from definition to definition, yet liberty must always be at the centre. Descriptive definitions which focus on pluralism or on a realm that is simply distinct from the state miss the point. There are pluralistic societies in which civil society does not exist; they are little more than fragmented societies if liberty does not transcend the various groups.[8]

There is general agreement that civil society organizations should properly exhibit a number of characteristics, and that these help to describe – rather than define – civil society:[9] participation in the political and social development of the country; tolerance and a rejection of violence; democratic internal structures.[10] Beyond this, however, there is a wide range of different forms of civil society, depending on the historical, cultural and religious background of a society and also on the nature of the political system.[11] Consequently, other criteria often seen as central to civil society organizations are highly controversial: independence from the state; independence from private business; independence from primordial structures.

Independence from the State

The most controversial aspect of defining civil society concerns the relationship between civil society and the state. In this respect there have been two competing perspectives: a 'dichotomous' view, going back to the English philosopher John Locke (1632–1704); and an 'integrative' definition going back to the French thinker Montesquieu (1689–1755).[12] According to the dichotomous concept, civil society is completely independent of the state and its primary function is to control the latter. The relationship between civil society and the state is thus conflictive and polarized, and civil society is legitimately concerned with undermining authoritarian regimes. In contrast, the integrative concept sees civil society as part of a political system, with no clear-cut divisions existing between the state and civil society. According to the integrative concept, civil society's function is both to control the state and to enhance the latter's legitimacy through civic participation.

The European Commission has not favoured co-operation with representatives of the dichotomous concept of civil society such as would bring the EU into conflict with southern Mediterranean governments. Clear preference has been given to representatives of the integrative concept, in accordance with the EU's long-term interest of supporting no more than a carefully controlled process of gradual political reform. From a theoretical perspective, the preference given to the integrative concept of civil society is problematic in the context of the Mediterranean basin, given that this concept presumes the existence of a *democratic* political system. In practice, the difference between the dichotomous and integrative concepts is not as clear-cut as the theoretical model implies. In most contexts, civil society's relations with the state are in practice situated somewhere between the two poles of (dichotomous) anti-system opposition and (integrative) mediation. Civil society actors can fluctuate between these two poles. This complicates the EU's selection of essentially integrative civil society partners and, as examined below, affects the composition of transnational NGOs.

The classification of an NGO in the wide spectrum between dichotomous and integrative civic engagement depends very much on the issue it addresses. Human rights NGOs have a mainly conflictive, dichotomous relationship with regimes in the Mediterranean. Their antagonism towards these regimes is so strong that it leaves little room for mediation. In contrast, environmental NGOs and trade unions have slightly more room for manoeuvre: as long as they do not openly question the political system as such, they can function as both critical watchdogs and integrative mediators. They can push political reforms forward within the confines of an autocratic system, using a mixed strategy of political pressure and professional consultancy. Regimes have an incentive to work with such actors, as a means of enhancing their own domestic legitimacy. However, the experience of eastern European states demonstrated that these seemingly less political actors can help 'open the doors' to democratization.

Authoritarian regimes in the Mediterranean have been sensitive to this and have sought to suppress, infiltrate or co-opt trade unions and integrative NGOs. From the point of view of EU strategy, this has made the support of civil society a difficult and risky task in all spheres.

Independence from Private Business

Another debate concerns the question of whether private business is part of civil society or whether it should be regarded as a separate sphere.[13] While trade unions are widely accepted to be part of civil society, the classification of private entrepreneurship is less clear. Having set up the MED-Invest programme to promote exchanges between small- and medium-sized enterprises within the framework of the EMP, the EU clearly sees private entrepreneurs as being part of civil society. Indeed, there are two reasons why their inclusion is seen as important in the context of the EMP. First, private trade accelerates interregional and intraregional *rapprochement*; second, private entrepreneurs are seen as reducing the dominant role of the state sector and thereby undermining the structure of authoritarian regimes.

Nevertheless, the EU's inclusion of the business sector within its conceptualization of civil society is not without its problems. This is so in particular with regard to the high priority that the EU attaches to privatization processes within the economic basket of the EMP. Some theorists warn that Europe's focus on privatization 'may increase the power of groups in society that are connected to the political establishment',[14] and thus actually undermine the cause of democratization in authoritarian countries. As entrepreneurs depend on stable political structures to run their business, they have no interest in directly challenging the state. Thus, entrepreneurs often tend to side with the state, even if it is authoritarian, rather than with the democratic forces of civil society:

> If we wish to treat civil society as that realm which stands against the political despotism of the state, then we should ... leave the economy out, because entrepreneurs, merchants and firms will not fight the state politically but only in defence of their economic interests, and the pursuit of these interests may well lead to alliances with the state that reinforce its political authority and its despotic tendencies.[15]

Hence, entrepreneurs should be acknowledged as part of civil society only if they stand for political and social goals that go beyond their private economic interests. Thus, in contrast to the apparent belief of many officials – in Brussels and national capitals – the encouragement of privatization is not on its own sufficient to promote political change in the MPCs. Privatization might be important for economic development, but does not necessarily constitute a positive contribution in support of democratization.

Independence from Primordial Structures

Likewise it is difficult to answer the question of whether groups that are organized according to primordial structures of society such as the family, clan or tribe should be seen as being part of civil society. As religious institutions also belong to the category of primordialism, the political sensitivity of this question concerns the problem of how to deal with Islamist associations. Do Islamist associations meet the theoretical categories defining civil society?

> Some Islamist thinkers reject the concept of *civil society (al-mutjama al-madani)* because of its western roots. They argue that the acceptance of the term already implies the acceptance of a western model of society. So they developed the alternative concept of *citizen society (al-mutjama al-ahli)*, meaning primordial structures of society such as the family, clan and especially the religious institutions. These are not seen as (second best) equivalents to civil society, but as authentic structures in the context of a Muslim state.[16] [original emphasis]

The values of citizen society do not necessarily contradict the values that constitute civil society. Yet many intellectuals in Europe and the Arab world, especially those within the secular sphere of society, refuse to accept citizen society as an equivalent to civil society, as their understanding of civil society is based on individual rights and freedoms, not those of groups or clans. It is argued that primordial institutions should not be accepted as parts of civil society as they are not based on the free and rational will of their individual participants. Some also reject the idea that political Islam is capable of tolerance. Against the background of Algeria's civil war, some analysts draw the decisive line not between society and the state, but between secularism and Islam.[17]

The European Commission has not included primordial associations in its civil society projects, in order to avoid conflict with both secular NGOs and MPC governments (especially in Tunisia, Algeria and Turkey). MPC governments fear that Islamist groups persecuted in their home countries might gain international recognition in the framework of religious dialogue projects initiated by the Europeans. Due to these reservations of the MPCs, the EU has reduced its support for religious dialogue projects to a minimum and the few projects that are organized involve only those representatives of Islam that are loyal to their governments. Many governments in the southern Mediterranean have co-opted sectors of political Islam to counterbalance the growing popularity of anti-system political Islam. Algeria and Egypt, for example, made far-reaching concessions to political Islam in the realm of civil law – concessions that are passionately combated by women's rights activists.

The vast majority of participants in civil society programmes are secular intellectuals, many with a western-influenced education and socialization. Although it is much easier for Europeans to co-operate with partners who share a similar political background, there is a growing awareness that the problem of how to integrate Islamists has to be addressed, as the secular segments of civil society taken alone are not fully representative of societies in the MPCs.[18] Most Islamist associations have deep roots in society, not least because of their charitable engagement that has compensated for incompetent or corrupt government. The difficulty for the EU in choosing dialogue partners within the heterogenous spectrum of political Islam lies in the inscrutable links that often exist between radical and moderate groups.[19] It would, however, be a severe misperception to reduce Islamism to its radical segments and ignore its manifold non-violent components.

> So long as religious based parties and associations accept the principle of pluralism and observe a modicum of civility in behaviour toward the different 'other', then they can expect to be integral parts of civil society. In this respect, even the Islamists may evolve into something akin to the Christian Democrats in the West or the religious parties in Israel. There is nothing intrinsically Islamic that contradicts with the codes of civil society or democratic principles.[20]

The integration of non-violent Islamist associations into Euro-Mediterranean civil society networks would help generate a better understanding between Muslims and non-Muslims both within Europe and across the Mediterranean. It would also make these networks more representative and thus enhance their legitimacy.

EU SUPPORT FOR CIVIL SOCIETY CO-OPERATION

Basket III of the EMP – the Partnership in Social, Cultural and Human Affairs – comprises a variety of civil society initiatives. The MED programmes were the first to be launched, promoting Euro-Mediterranean dialogue at the level of universities, the media and local authorities.[21] The distinctive feature of the MED programmes was that European organizations could choose their partners without consulting the government of the country concerned, this being seen as key to the strengthening of genuinely independent civil society structures. The MED programmes were taken up very positively by associations in the MPCs. Many significant projects were initiated – in fact, so many that these initiatives overstretched the capabilities of the Commission's administration, which had not anticipated such a strong interest. For the first year of the EMP it seemed, therefore, that the MED programmes were highly successful. Unfortunately, an inspection of the MED programmes by the Court of Auditors in 1996 revealed significant funding abuses in the period between 1992 and 1994.[22] European participants had benefited far more from many projects than their Mediterranean partners. Other projects were criticized because they had failed to respect co-financing rules. The Commission accepted mismanagement in the MED programmes but also complained that the Court had overstretched its competences, evaluating not only the management of funds, but also the political content of the programmes.[23] Indeed, the Court evaluated only the financial administration procedures and was not able to judge the undoubtedly positive effects of the MED programmes. The Court's report led to the suspension of all MED programmes in September 1996. The Commission tried for several years to reinstall these programmes, before these again became an issue within the corruption scandal at the Commission in 1999.

Unsatisfied with the limited approach of the MED programmes – which did not offer support for NGOs – the EP pushed in 1996 for an additional instrument to support democratization at the level of civil society. Threatening the Commission and the Council that it would refuse approval of the EMP's financial protocol (MEDA), the European Parliament secured the establishment of MEDA Democracy. This was to be a programme that:

> grants subsidies to non-profit-making associations, universities, centres of research and to public bodies to implement projects which aim to promote democracy, the rule of law, freedom of expression, of meeting and of association, to protect target groups (women, youth, minorities) and to increase the awareness of socio-economic rights.[24]

MEDA Democracy[25] was more challenging for the governments of the MPCs, as it potentially covered groups representing the dichotomous concept of civil society, such as human rights NGOs. From the perspective of southern NGOs, it was the most important instrument in the framework of the EMP. Participation in MEDA Democracy projects has, however, been criticized by civil society representatives as being unduly complicated by an extremely slow flow of funds and opaque application and selection procedures.[26] This helps explain how it was possible for the Tunisian government to block the funding of projects that were eligible and already approved within the framework of the MEDA Democracy programme.[27] The severest setback for MEDA Democracy was in June 1998, when the Commission froze all projects following a ruling of the European Court of Justice. This ruling concerned the lack of a legal basis for a relatively minor budget line dealing with an anti-poverty programme, but its consequence was the freezing of all projects within the European Initiative for Democracy and Human Rights (EIDHR), including MEDA Democracy projects.[28] There followed a period of considerable uncertainty for civil society activists, until later in 1999 the Council adopted two regulations providing the missing legal basis.[29] Uncertainty has since returned as the administration of democracy projects in the Mediterranean was in 2000 transferred to a new Democracy and Human Rights Department in the Commission and has been subject to an unsettling ongoing process of reform.

The abolition of the MED programmes and the temporary freezing of MEDA Democracy projects added up to a severe setback for the EU's bottom-up approach to democratization. The programmes within the third 'basket' that have proceeded less problematically, such as Euromed Heritage[30] and Euromed Audiovisual,[31] are valuable in their own field and generate transnational contacts between the North and the South, but are politically less ambitious. In contrast to the MED Programmes and MEDA Democracy, these do not exclusively target civil society, but also include the public sector and require projects to be approved by recipient governments. Only the Euromed Youth Action Programme[32] is clearly and explicitly oriented to EU democratization policy in the region.

Against the background of these limitations to EU co-operation programmes, civil society actors have attached more importance to the Civil Forum, which has met alongside ministerial conferences. Meetings of the Civil Forum are part-financed by the Commission and organized in co-operation with the country hosting the official Euro-Mediterranean conference. The incorporation of the Forum into EMP events has had ambivalent effects. The Forum is too far away from the decision-making process to be effective in influencing EMP policies, but too exposed to the political influence of the member states hosting its meetings to fulfil an external, critical 'watchdog function'.[33] Governmental interference was especially strong during the Civil Forums in Barcelona in 1995 and in Marseille in 2000, because the Spanish and French governments wanted to protect the North African participants of the ministerial conference from too much embarrassment through the civil society activists.[34]

Only once, at Stuttgart in 1999, did the Forum manage to show its teeth, by organizing a conference dedicated exclusively to human rights, a taboo at all previous Forums.[35] Some of the MPCs tried to block this conference, but, having adopted the Barcelona Declaration and thus a commitment to the principles of human rights, could not openly do so. Behind the scenes, however, they put considerable pressure on the organizers, trying to influence the agenda and the list of participants. Germany's Friedrich Ebert Stiftung, hosting the conference, did everything to protect the participants from the pressure of their governments and invited only genuine and trustworthy NGOs.[36] This could not prevent the appearance of some North African 'GONGOs', organizations parading as NGOs but in reality linked to and controlled by governments. Despite this, the human rights conference at Stuttgart gained considerable public interest and media attention, indeed almost as much as the Euro-Mediterranean ministerial conference.[37]

One year later at the Marseille Civil Forum there was also a human rights workshop, but it was downgraded at the behest of the French government. A lot of lobbying was necessary in the run-up to the workshop and many compromises had to be accepted. For example, at the request of the French government, the human rights workshop had to be held under the less challenging title of *État de droit et démocracie*. Although there is common agreement that human rights are inseparable from the rule of law and democracy, the avoidance of the term 'human rights' reflected the lack of political will to strengthen this issue on the agenda of Euro-Mediterranean relations. In addition, in Marseille human rights were dealt with only in one workshop among many others, rather than being the subject of a whole conference. This reduced the media attention given to human rights.[38]

A NEW START FOR EUROPEAN DEMOCRATIZATION POLICY?

As a consequence of the corruption scandal involving the MED programmes, growing pressure from repressive MPCs and the ambivalent position of southern member states, the Commission has become increasingly careful, even restrictive, in its dealing with civil society. For example, it proposed to give preference to big projects of at least €500,000, instead of splintering the funds between many small grass-root projects. This step was severely criticized by civil society representatives during the EU human rights discussion forum in November 1999. They warned the Commission that this size of project was far beyond the capacity of most southern NGOs and would therefore favour larger European groups.[39] Such big projects in the Mediterranean have invariably attracted more government attention and interference, and are therefore a completely inadequate and inappropriate approach to strengthening genuinely *independent* sectors of civil society. It remains to be seen how the Europe Aid Co-operation Office, established in 2001, will deal with these problems. It is too early to assess the Office's performance comprehensively, but there have been some positive signals for civil society work: the proposal to delegate more competences to EU delegations in partner countries;[40] and the lowering of the minimum for projects to €300,000.

The Commission's communication on 'The European Union's role in promoting human rights and democratization in third countries' of May 2001 seems to indicate a new start for the EU's democratization policy, based on improved strategies and instruments.[41] According to this document, higher priority will be placed on human rights and democratization objectives in the EU's relations with third countries. So-called Country Strategy Papers, assessing the performance of each partner country in the sphere of human rights, democratization, the rule of law and good governance, are to become decisive instruments for the creation of more coherence in external relations and for the mainstreaming of human rights as a cross-cutting category. The document also emphasizes that the EIDHR is to be carried out primarily in partnership with NGOs and international organizations. The proposed guidelines acknowledge the importance of ensuring that civil society projects include micro-projects and are run independently of governmental consent.[42] Most civil society representatives are still sceptical, however, over the prospects for a reinvigoration of the bottom-up approach. Southern member states are likely to remain hesitant and administrative improvements cannot overcome their politically-motivated reservation against a reinforced EU democratization policy in the region.

THE SPECIAL ROLE OF TRANSNATIONAL NGOS: THE CASE OF THE EURO-MEDITERRANEAN HUMAN RIGHTS NETWORK

European support for civil society in the framework of the EMP has led to various forms of transnational co-operation at the level of civil society, including among NGOs. These projects have not always been unproblematic, however. Southern NGOs complain that co-operation with European partner organizations often turns out to be to their own disadvantage, especially if the European partners are to a greater or lesser extent imposed on them. Being more experienced in co-operating with the

Commission, some European NGOs have taken the bigger share of funds for themselves, actually undermining the aim of supporting civil society development in the MPCs rather than in Europe.

Transnational NGOs offer a means of mitigating such imbalance. Instead of working together in temporary projects with changing (and often unwanted) partners, transnational NGOs are able to pursue long-term, co-operative interests within the framework of stable institutional structures. Transnational NGOs can combine the capacities of all their member organizations, creating positive effects of synergy. They have more power in their struggle against repressive regimes than individual national NGOs could ever accumulate. Transnational NGOs could become the backbone of civil society co-operation in the EMP, a development that would reflect a general trend in international relations since the end of the cold war. Transnational NGOs are helped by the increasingly binding character of international norms and the increasing support offered to them by international organizations.

One of the most notable transnational NGO networks that has evolved in the context of the Barcelona Process is the Euro-Mediterranean Human Rights Network (EMHRN). This was set up in 1997 on the initiative of both northern and southern human rights organizations. Today it has more than 60 members representing human rights organizations and institutions, as well as individuals, from over 20 countries. The network's overall objectives are to support the development of democratic institutions and the promotion of the rule of law, human rights principles and human rights education in the Euro-Mediterranean region. It recognizes that the Barcelona Process has provided important instruments for the promotion and protection of human rights, but that its success is dependent on the active participation of civil society. The network defines itself as a constructive interface between the EMP institutions, human rights organizations in the region and other relevant agents involved in the Barcelona Process.[43]

The EMHRN is engaged in three interlinked and interrelated activities: the documentation and dissemination of information; dialogue, advocacy and campaigning; and capacity building and education. At its last general assembly in November 2000 in Marseille, the network adopted a plan of action that, apart from seeking to monitor the EMP and human rights developments, stressed the need to enhance human rights organizations' capacity to work on the ground through a synergistic process of exchange of experience and knowledge between different organizations.[44] Reports on human rights conditions in the Euro-Mediterranean region, the general activities of the EMHRN and the provisions of the EMP are disseminated to the MPCs, EU institutions, EU member states and the public on both sides of the Mediterranean. A computerized information service has been established, including a web site[45] and an electronic mailing list. The EMHRN is engaged in campaigns to raise human rights awareness, for example offering legal advice to immigrants and promoting seminars on gender equality. The network provides education and capacity-building programmes for human rights defenders, to strengthen the professionalism of the network itself. The EMHRN is also engaged in fund-raising and co-operates closely with major international human rights NGOs working in the region and with international organizations.

The EMHRN links its programme of activities to the official agenda of the EMP. It has set up an office in Brussels to follow and influence more effectively developments within the EMP. The office will help to maintain close contacts with the Commission, the EP,[46] the Council of Ministers, international human rights NGOs and international organizations based in Brussels. The EMHRN confronts authoritarian governments permanently with the discrepancies between their declared position on human rights, in particular as enshrined within the Barcelona Declaration, and their actual political performance. By doing so, it puts these governments under growing pressure to defend their repressive behaviour: the loss of control over political discourse is a severe setback for any authoritarian regime, forcing it gradually onto the defensive.

The EMHRN also presses the EU to stick to the commitments it made in the framework of the EMP. As the EU has linked its economic and financial co-operation to the precondition of democratic reform and respect for human rights, the EMHRN puts pressure on the Europeans to transform this principle into political practice. It recommends the use of positive conditionality, pressing the EU to offer stronger incentives for governments engaged in political reforms.[47] The EMHRN has focused on the Commission's 2000 document advocating a higher priority to be attached to the promotion of human rights and democratization, pressing the Council of Ministers to show the political will to act on this recommendation.[48]

In Brussels and EU member states the EMHRN has gained respect as an integrative, professional and politically credible consultant, and has benefited from stable financial EU support.[49] In contrast, the relationship between the network and repressive governments in the South is much more complicated. While dialogue and professional consultation has been a successful lobbying tool in the EU, southern NGOs are inevitably more cautious when addressing their governments. Southern human rights NGOs have to protect themselves against prosecution, but also against governmental co-option. The EMHRN is able to combat this problem, by taking on dialogue with Mediterranean governments as a transnational actor in a way that domestic NGOs would not be able to do on their own.[50]

As an umbrella organization, the EMHRN is open to any independent national or regional organization, or individual, that is active in the struggle for human rights in any of the 27 member countries of the EMP. Due to the politically sensitive issue of human rights, however, strict requirements have to be fulfilled to acquire membership. Application candidates need the support of two regular members and are carefully screened before being accepted. After having proved their active commitment to the struggle for democracy and human rights and their full independence from government authorities, they obtain membership if they gain the unanimous approval of the network's general assembly.[51] Such safety measures are necessary to protect the network from governmental infiltration.

The network tries to balance the interests of northern and southern NGOs, to avoid the dominance of single countries or (sub)-regions, and to reflect the functional diversity of human rights work. An effort is made to reach decisions on the basis of consensus, in order to strengthen confidence and mutual respect. The search for consensus is sometimes a difficult task owing to the extreme heterogeneity of the network. The spectrum extends from large, well-established NGOs through to micro-NGOs comprising only a handful of people. Some of the southern NGO activists have themselves been victims of human rights violations, while northern human rights activists lack this personal experience. Some NGOs are supported by their government, while others are repressed. Furthermore, cultural gaps within the network have to be bridged, not only between North and South but also within these two regions. It has often been difficult to reconcile the variety of interests and needs that exist under the common umbrella of the network. The biggest challenge arises from the fact that member NGOs are in competition with each other for resources. Moreover, all member NGOs are committed primarily to their work at home and have attached only a secondary importance to the interests and needs of the network.

An example of the tensions within the EMHRN was witnessed after the outbreak of the Al-Aqsa *intifada* in autumn 2000. Palestinian NGOs expected their partners in the network to support their fight against Israel's increasingly brutal oppression, not least since the right of self-determination is an essential human right and mentioned as such in the statutes of the network. The Palestinians did indeed gain overwhelming support for their cause. A fact-finding mission was sent to Palestine, reports and open letters were written, and the *intifada* was discussed intensely in meetings.

However, the request for solidarity started to incur displeasure from some member NGOs as the ongoing debate on the Middle East conflict started to marginalize other tasks of the network. This internal conflict came to the surface during the Civil Forum in Marseille, when Palestinian NGOs called for a boycott of the Forum in protest against Israeli participation. While most Arab NGOs supported the boycott, members of several European NGOs complained that the Palestinians had exploited the Forum too much for their own interest, neglecting the equally important interests of other NGOs. The EMHRN solved the problem by putting the Palestinian issue at the top of the agenda of the *État de droit et démocracie* workshop. After firmly condemning Israeli human rights violations in the context of the *intifada* and Israel's ongoing neglect for the Palestinian right of self-determination, the workshop was able to give other NGOs room to present their reports on other subjects. This demonstrates how, despite the heterogeneity of its members, the network is held together by the strong commitment of all its members to defend human rights and by the many modest achievements the network has already made, especially as a consultant to the Commission. All members of the network are well aware that it needs the joint effort of a transnational organization to have any impact on the political development of the EMP.

CONCLUSION

In discussing the role of civil society in the EMP, this study has looked both at the EU's bottom-up approach to democratization and civil society's attempts to make use of this approach. The EU's bottom-up approach has not been implemented with great success. Problems related to the administering of grass-roots projects seem to have been mitigated by an institutional renewal within the Commission. A more serious problem is still unresolved, however: some member states, particularly France and Spain, have political objections to a strengthening of the EU's democratization policy in the Mediterranean and would actually prefer to see it downgraded even further. Against this background, civil society activists in the region, among them the EMHRN, welcomed the Commission's 2001 communication on democracy and human rights, which indicated a desire to attach greater priority to democracy and human rights. According to the Commission, the promotion of democracy and human rights should no longer be neglected in favour of security and trade interests, but instead become a pivotal objective, cross-cutting all areas of EU foreign relations. It remains to be seen if the pressure of the

Commission, the EP and some northern member states will be strong enough to persuade the Council of Ministers to follow suit, especially in the context of the EMP. If this support were forthcoming, this would improve the working conditions for transnational NGOs like the EMHRN and help them to carry out their difficult yet indispensable contribution to the promotion of democracy and human rights in the Euro-Mediterranean region.

NOTES

The author is grateful for the editorial input of Richard Gillespie and Richard Youngs.

1. See the Barcelona Declaration adopted at the Euro-Mediterranean Conference (27–28 Nov. 1995), Final Version, *Agence Europe*, 6 Dec. 1996.
2. Ibid.
3. For an evaluation of the EU's asylum policy, see Wolfgang Genz, *Menschenrechte und internationaler Flüchtlingsschutz – Wohin geht die europäische Harmonisierung?*, Amnesty International, Sektion der Bundesrepublik Deutschland, Asylpolitik-Stellungnahme, 20 Jan. 2000. For a critical discussion of Europe's migration policy, see Annette Jünemann, 'Europas Migrationspolitik im Mittelmeerraum – Strategien im Spannungsfeld zwischen Festungsmentalität und neuem Partnerschaftsgeist', in Axel Schulte and Dieter Thränhardt (eds.), *International Migration and Liberal Democracies, Yearbook Migration 1999/2000* (Münster: Lit. Verlag, 1999), pp.185–211.
4. The Barcelona Conference that established the EMP in 1995 was accompanied by two conferences at the level of civil society, the Euromed Civil Forum, discussed later on, and the smaller Alternative Mediterranean Conference (AMC). The AMC was more critical of the EMP.
5. Annette Jünemann, 'Democratization – Reflections on the Political Dimension of the Euro-Mediterranean Partnership', in Peter G. Xuereb (ed.), *The Mediterranean's European Challenge* (Msida: European Documentation and Research Centre, University of Malta, 1998), p.92.
6. The strongest weapon of the EP is the assent procedure. Yet, this instrument is rather blunt and allows no gradual or modified response. Activities in the framework of the newly established Euro-Mediterranean Parliamentarian Forum have comparatively little influence. For details concerning the decision-making procedures in the EMP, see Annette Jünemann, 'Auswärtige Politikgestaltung im EU-Mehrebenensystem. Eine Analyse der strukturellen Probleme am Beispiel der Euro-Mediterranen Partnerschaft', in Gisela Müller-Brandeck-Bocquet and Klaus Schubert (eds.), *Die Europäische Union als Akteur der Weltpolitik* (Opladen: Leske und Budrich, 2000), pp.65–80.
7. For an in-depth reflection on civil society in European thought, see Charles Taylor, 'Die Beschwörung der Civil-Society', in Michalski von Krzysztof (ed.), *Europa und die Civil Society* (Stuttgart: Castelgandolfo-Gespräche, 1989), pp.52–81.
8. R. Mabro, 'Civil Society in the History of Ideas in European History', in Arab Thought Forum and Bruno Kreisky Forum (eds.), *The Role of NGOs in the Development of Civil Society – Europe and the Arab Countries* (Amman and Vienna: Arab Thought Forum, 1999), p.46.
9. For the problem of defining civil society, see Jean L. Cohen and Andrew Arato, *Civil Society and Political Theory* (Cambridge, MA: MIT, 1995).
10. This can be problematic: in the Mediterranean efficient NGO structures are needed to resist repression and persecution. The internal organization of NGOs therefore often reflects the authoritarian structures of the regime they oppose. European standards of internal democracy can thus not simply be transferred to the MPCs. On the sometimes problematic internal structure of civil society associations, see Wolfgang Merkel and Hans-Joachim Lauth,

'Systemwechsel und Zivilgesellschaft – Welche Zivilgesellschaft braucht die Demokratie?', *Aus Politik und Zeitgeschichte*, B No.6–7 (1998), pp.3–12.

11. For the contemporary discussion of civil society in the Arab world, see Ibrahim Ferhad and Heidi Wedel (eds.), *Probleme der Zivilgesellschaft im Vorderen Orient* (Opladen: Leske und Budrich, 1995).

12. Emmanuel Richter, 'Die europäische Zivilgesellschaft', in Klaus Dieter Wolf (ed.), *Projekt Europa im Übergang?* (Baden Baden: Nomos Verlag, 1997).

13. For the role of private business, see Jillan Schwedler, 'Introduction', in Jillan Schwedler (ed.), *Civil Society and the Study of Middle East Politics* (London, 1995), pp.1–32.

14. Mabro, op. cit., p.47.

15. Ibid., p.39.

16. Ibrahim Ferhad, 'Die arabische Debatte über Zivilgesellschaft', in Ferhad and Wedel, op. cit., p.39.

17. Ibid., p.28.

18. The need to integrate political Islam into Euro–Arab intercultural relations was one of the results of the Third German–Arab Media Dialogue. See Institut für Auslandskunde (ed.), *Deutsch-arabischer Mediendialog* (Stuttgart, dokumente No.3, 1999).

19. Radical groups are also often engaged in social welfare, so that charitable activities are not a sufficient criteria for choosing a partner organization.

20. Saad Eddin Ibrahim, 'Democratization in the Arab World', in Schwedler, op. cit., p.38.

21. See European Commission, DG I, *Manuel des Programmes MED. Votre Guide pour le Partenariat Euro-Méditerranéen* (Brussels: European Commission, 1996).

22. See Court of Auditors, *Special Report* (Brussels: Court of Auditors, 1996).

23. Author interviews, Directorates General (DG) IB, Brussels, Sept. 1996.

24. MEDA Democracy, Euro-Mediterranean Partnership, Information Note No.2, European Commission, Unit IB/A.1, Sept. 1997.

25. See MEDA Democracy Programme, Budget Line B7-705N, Criteria and Conditions of Eligibility, DG IB/A2, Brussels, 25 April 1996. MEDA Democracy was part of the European Initiative for Democracy and Human Rights, launched by the EP in 1994 to bring a series of budget headings specifically dealing with the promotion of democracy and human rights together in a single chapter (B7-70).

26. See Euro-Mediterranean Human Rights Network, *The MEDA Democracy Programme, Recommendations by the Euro-Mediterranean Human Rights Network (EMHRN) to the European Commission, the European Parliament and the EU Member States regarding the MEDA Democracy Programme* (Copenhagen: EMHRN, May 2000), p.4f.

27. Ibid., p.4. To avoid further political conflict between the governments of the MPCs and the EU in the context of MEDA Democracy, the Commission avoided co-operation with NGOs promoting the interests of ethnic minorities (for example, the Kurds in Turkey) and NGOs belonging to the Islamist spectrum.

28. See Khémais Chammari and Caroline Stainer, *Guide to Human Rights in the Barcelona Process* (Copenhagen: EMHRN, 2000), p.108.

29. See Council Regulation (EC) No.975/1999 and Council Regulation No.976/1999, which came into effect on 11 May 1999.

30. For further information on the Euromed Heritage Programme, see 'The Euromed Heritage Programme – Cultural Heritage at the Heart of the Euro-Mediterranean Partnership', *Euromed Special Feature*, No.7, 29 Sept. 2000.

31. For more on Euromed Audiovisual, see http://europa.eu.int/comm/avpolicy/extern/coop_ de. htm.

32. For further information on the Euromed Youth Action Programme, see http://europa.eu.int/comm/education/youth/youthprogram.html.

33. For an analysis of the Euromed Civil Forum, see Annette Jünemann, 'The Forum Civil Euromed. Critical Watchdog and Intercultural Mediator', in Stefania Panebianco (ed.), *The Euro-Mediterranean Partnership in Social, Cultural and Human Affairs – The Human Dimension of Security as the Key to Stability and Prosperity* (London: Frank Cass, forthcoming).

34. For the results of the Forum in Barcelona 1995, see Institut Català Mediterrània, *Towards a*

New Scenario of Partnership in the Euro-Mediterranean Area, Forum Civil Euromed (Barcelona: Institut Català Mediterrània, 1996). For the results of the Forum in Marseille 2000, see http://www.euromed_ong.org/decla_finales/decla_ong.htm. The Forum in Malta 1997 was comparatively small and restricted to a politically less challenging cultural dialogue. See Foundation for International Studies at the University of Malta (ed.), *Intercultural Dialogue in the Mediterranean. Civil Forum Euromed in Malta* (Valletta: Foundation, 1997).

35. Civil society's room for manoeuvre was wider in Stuttgart because Germany has no priority national interests in the region that could be challenged through a civil society conference. Furthermore, a new government had just come to power.

36. The Friedrich Ebert Stiftung functioned as host and co-ordinator, delegating the task of choosing the participants to two trustworthy partner organizations, the Euro-Mediterranean Human Rights Network and the Forum des Citoyens de la Méditerranée.

37. The human rights conference of Stuttgart is documented in Friedrich Ebert Foundation (ed.), *Human Rights and Civil Society in the Mediterranean, Stuttgart 15–16 Apr 1999* (Bonn: FES, 1999).

38. Marseille hosted one conference for the trade unions, a second one for local authorities and a third for NGOs.

39. These complaints are documented in Commission of the European Communities, *Report from the Commission on the implementation of measures intended to promote observance of human rights and democratic principles in external relations for 1996 – 1999* (Brussels: European Commission, 2000), p.86.

40. *Euromed Special Feature*, No.10, 10 April 2001.

41. See Communication of the Commission to the Council and the European Parliament, *The European Union's role in promoting human rights and democratisation in third countries*, Brussels, 8 May 2001, COM(2001) 252 final.

42. Ibid., p.13f.

43. According to its statutes, it is a 'non-partisan and non-profit membership organization dedicated to the welfare of the community'. Statutes of the Euro-Mediterranean Human Rights Network (EMHRN), approved by the Second General Assembly of the EMHRN at its meeting in Copenhagen, 12–13 Dec. 1997, p.1.

44. See Euro-Mediterranean Human Rights Network, 'Plan of Action', adopted at the Fourth General Assembly, Nov. 2000.

45. http://www.euromedrights.net.

46. The EMHRN advocates the establishment of a human rights committee within the framework of the Euro-Mediterranean Interparliamentary Forum, having the mandate to address human rights issues, including individual cases and country issues. See Euro-Mediterranean Human Rights Network, 'Plan of Action', p.7f.

47. See Euro-Mediterranean Human Rights Network, 'The Role of Human Rights in the EU's Mediterranean Policy. Setting Article 2 in Motion', European Parliament, Brussels, 9 Nov. 1999.

48. See Euro-Mediterranean Human Rights Network, 70th Information letter, Copenhagen, 7 June 2001. Another document of importance in this context is European Commission, 'Reinvigorating the Barcelona Process', *Agence Europe*, 14 Sept. 2000, a working document of the European Commission Services prepared for the 'think tank' meeting of Euro-Mediterranean Foreign Ministers, Lisbon, 25–26 May 2000. In this document the Commission proposes that preferential aid should be given to countries that engage in human rights and democratization reforms.

49. Funding an umbrella organization instead of single NGOs is in line with the Commission's new strategy to fund big rather than small projects. In June 1999, the EMHRN submitted a €2.5m project to the Commission covering the period 1 Jan. 2000 to 31 Dec. 2003. The project was finally approved at the end of 1999 and the contract was signed in late May 2000. See EMHRN Annual Report of Activities, http://www.euromedrights.net.

50. Regarding the dialogue conducted by members of the network with their respective governments, the EMHRN is in the process of designing a toolbox with good examples and methodologies, taking into consideration the different cultural and religious traditions and

approaches to dialogues. See Euro-Mediterranean Human Rights Network, 'Plan of Action'.
51. The question of whether or not affiliation with political Islam is compatible with the statutes of the network has not been an issue of discussion until now, because no Islamist NGO or individual has ever shown interest in membership.

Democratization in Bosnia:
The Limits of Civil Society
Building Strategies

DAVID CHANDLER

For many commentators, the construction of civil society in East European states is considered a precondition for the development of consolidated democratic institutions. Nowhere is this more the case than within Bosnia-Herzegovina, where ethnic and nationalist identification indicate a deeply politically segmented society. To challenge this segmentation international institutions are providing financial and technical support to a growing civil society sector based on non-governmental organizations. Research into the civil society support work of the Democratization Branch of the Organization for Security and Co-operation in Europe indicates that the predominantly middle-class constituency of these groups reflects the extensive external international regulation of the new state under the Dayton Peace Agreement. However, the extension of autonomy and self-government may well create more fruitful conditions for the growth of civil society alternatives.

Since the signing of the Dayton Accords in December 1995, the international community has been involved in the management of the democratization process in Bosnia-Herzegovina. As the United Nations (UN) Secretary-General has noted 'democratization is predominantly a new area' for the UN, nevertheless it is already seen as 'a key component of peace-building' addressing the 'economic, social, cultural, humanitarian and political roots of conflict'.[1] Democratization is broadly defined by the UN to constitute a 'comprehensive approach' covering the broad range of new peace-building priorities: 'top-down' international regulation of elections, institutional development and economic management, accompanied by 'bottom-up' assistance to develop a democratic political culture through civil society-building.[2]

Civil society development is generally viewed to involve support for the associational sphere of interest groups which stand between the private sphere of the family and market economy and the public sphere of the state and government. A richly pluralistic civil society, generating a wide range of interests, is held to mitigate polarities of political conflict and develop a democratic culture of tolerance, moderation and compromise.[3] The main focus of civil society-building has often been local non-governmental organizations (NGOs) seen as capable of articulating needs independently of vested political interests and involving grassroots community 'voices'. The UN's internet web-site incorporates nearly 2,000 documents referring to 'civil society',[4] while the Secretary-General's *Agenda for Development* Report explains that:

> A vigorous civil society is indispensable to creating lasting and successful development ... Locally based NGOs, in particular, can serve as intermediaries and give people a voice and an opportunity to articulate their needs, preferences and vision of a better society ... in countries where civil society is weak, strengthening civil society should be a major purpose of public policy.[5]

The discussion of civil society-building as a priority for democratic consolidation has been sharply focused by the democratic transitions of eastern Europe and the conflict in former Yugoslavia.[6] It has often been viewed that the wars of Yugoslavia's dissolution were the product of ethnic segmentation, reflecting a lack of civil society and leading to a failed transition to democracy.[7] In Bosnia-Herzegovina, war resulted in thousands of casualties and nearly half the population becoming displaced or refugees, and was only brought to an end by forceful United States (US)-led international intervention. In December 1995, the Dayton Peace Agreement was signed. This created an independent Bosnian state divided between two separate entities, the Muslim (Bosniak)-Croat Federation, occupying 51 per cent of the territory, and the Serb-held area, Republika Srpska (RS), occupying 49 per cent.

For the Dayton Peace Agreement to hold, many commentators argue that civil society development should be central to the democratization and peace-building process. Without civil society, economic reconstruction aid is said to have little impact on political and social division within Bosnia. Leading analysts have argued that European Union funding of over US$2,500 per head to residents of Muslim and Croat-divided Mostar has done little to reduce tensions and that US aid to Bosnia, amounting to US$1,200 per head in fiscal year 1998, is creating dependency and acting as a disincentive for Bosnians to resolve problems.[8] There is similar disillusionment with the political sphere. Influential commentators have stated that 'elections without civil society will not produce democracy', and that elections in Bosnia are 'deeply flawed', legitimizing nationalist elites responsible for the war and division.[9]

While top-down economic and political interventions are often seen to perpetuate social segmentation and ethnic nationalism, bottom-up support for the sphere of civil society is held to have an empowering and transformative content. For example, Ian Smillie, author of an influential

CARE Canada report on non-governmental organizations (NGOs) and civil society building in Bosnia, argues:

> Rebuilding tolerance and pluralism in Bosnia and Herzegovina is perhaps more important than anywhere else in the former Yugoslavia. It is important because without it, the Dayton Accord … and the hope of a united Bosnia and Herzegovina will be lost … Accountability, legitimacy and competence in public life are the key, and these can only be achieved through the active participation of the electorate, buoyed by a strong, plural, associational base, by a web of social, cultural and functional relationships which can act as a 'societal glue' and as counterbalance to the market and the state. The alternative for Bosnia and Herzegovina … is paternalism, exploitation, corruption, and war.[10]

Dialogue Development, preparing the 1998 European Union PHARE Civil Society Development Programme for Bosnia, state:

> The strong emergence of a Third Sector in the form of civil society in Bosnia will be instrumental in the gradual emergence of a pluralistic and democratic society … NGOs are … destined to play an important role in this post-conflict situation as they have a vast potential for transcending the faultlines of society through the creation of new partnerships and alliances. They can moderate and mediate in addressing the relevant needs of society, not always within the realm of the state.[11]

The Organization for Security and Co-operation in Europe (OSCE) Mission in Bosnia was restructured at the end of 1996 to enable it to carry out a more long-term approach to democratization, focusing on the challenges of creating or restoring civil society in the region. This perspective was informed by the consensus that peace and stability in Bosnia was 'still very much dependent on the development of a democratic civil society'.[12] The first monthly report of the OSCE Mission's Democratization Branch outlined the institution's view of the obstacles to civil society development. The obstacles listed were all connected to the incapacity of the Bosnian people in general, or specific sections of them, to act and think in a manner suited to meet the 'challenges' of democratization. For the Bosnian elites, the problem was seen to be a lack of technical and organizational abilities. These incapacities were highlighted by the people involved in building local NGOs in Republika Srpska, who 'continue to struggle for funding, programme ideas and the acquisition of administrative skills', and in leaders of opposition parties more broadly, because 'even though the number of political parties is increasing, they are only now beginning to receive training on how to enlarge their popular appeal'.[13]

While the skill-shortages of the elites could be overcome by training and aid, the other obstacles, located at the level of Bosnian society in general, were seen to be more long-term. First, the problem of an ethnic mentality: 'the passive acceptance of prejudices [which] must be overcome for real and psychological barriers to inter-ethnic reconciliation to be dismantled'. Secondly, the problems stemming from a lack of awareness of the workings of a democratic society, which meant that it was difficult to make informed choices at elections: 'The elections served as the basis for the establishment of democratic institutions, yet more efforts are required to increase citizen's awareness of the working and roles of their authorities, the rule of law, and democratic rule and procedures.'[14]

The barriers to local NGOs and civic groups empowering communities are either viewed as technical problems which the Bosnian elites are seemingly unable to grasp or as deeper problems of Bosnian culture. This approach sidelines the fact that the citizens of Bosnia and the former Yugoslavia had extensive higher education provision, an historical record of inter-ethnic tolerance and understanding and a relatively high level of involvement in local political and civic life.[15] This article investigates the possibility that paying attention solely to the incapacities of Bosnian citizens may result in a lack of attention to failings within international democratization practice itself. Experience on the ground in Bosnia indicates that the top-down approach of international regulation and the bottom-up approach of empowerment and civil society development may have conflicting impacts on Bosnian society, rather than the complementary one assumed by the proponents of extended internationally-led peace-building. If it is the case that the comprehensive nature of international mandates does act to constrain the emergence of civil society initiatives, then the extension of external regulation could make international withdrawal problematic and lead towards the development of an international protectorate, rather than facilitate the creation of a stable self-governing democracy.

BUILDING CIVIL SOCIETY

The focus on civil society, going beyond the governing institutions of the country, gave the international community a much broader remit of involvement in Bosnian affairs by extending the role of the OSCE under Dayton. Annex 3 of the Dayton Peace Agreement, the *Agreement on Elections*, gave the OSCE the authority to 'lay the foundation for representative government and ensure the progressive achievement of democratic goals throughout Bosnia and Herzegovina'.[16] Under the broader interpretation of the 'spirit of Dayton' this was now seen to include the promotion of civil society through support for the work of Bosnian NGOs and civic groups.[17]

This wider remit facilitated the development of a separate Democratization Branch, a unique step for an international institution. The OSCE Democratization Programme for 1997 was designed to bring the international community into a closer relationship with grass-roots groups and associations which could provide a counterpoint to the politics of the governing authorities and nationalist parties; through this, opening political debate and creating new opportunities for alternative voices to be heard.[18] As Jasna Malkoc, the Senior Co-ordinator for Democratization/ NGO Development explained: 'Establishing NGOs is a first principle for democratization. NGOs are vital for the reconstruction of civil society. Political parties deal with majorities. It is important to address issues without thinking about minorities and majorities.'[19]

The OSCE strategy for encouraging political participation is a three stage process: first, identifying targeted individuals or groups who are open to external support and influence; secondly, providing training and building a civil society agenda within these groups; and thirdly, mobilizing active NGOs as political voices in the domestic and international environment.

Targeting

The Democratization Branch works through the extensive OSCE field presence covering the whole of Bosnia, and co-ordinated through five regional centres of operation, based in Mostar, Tuzla, Bihac, Banja Luka and Sokolac. This means that they are strategically placed to play a key role in identifying individuals and groups for democratization initiatives.[20] Based in the field, the Democratization Officers have the role of assessing which groups are most open to OSCE influence and to develop strategies in relation to them.

OSCE strategy has a regional approach because the receptiveness to external intervention and support is dependent on the local political situation. In the Federation there are many active NGOs, partly because of the influx of foreign donors and partly because the political climate is more receptive to external influence. The OSCE feels that in many urban areas in the Federation there is a 'diverse and vibrant NGO community'.[21] The climate has been less receptive in RS, with the Banja Luka area being the centre for NGO activities and parts of Eastern RS having virtually no NGOs.

The strategy is to integrate the 'more developed', politically active NGOs into the broader OSCE perspective, and under OSCE 'facilitation' for them to link up with groups and individuals in areas with 'less developed' NGOs and a low NGO presence. In the Tuzla region experienced local NGOs are encouraged to expand their networks to give the OSCE new areas of influence.[22] In areas with little organized NGO presence the OSCE has to trawl for prospective partners. Staff in Banja Luka, for example, created a workshop on proposal drafting for NGOs with plans to travel outside the city to the surrounding areas. In Velika Kladusa, a targeted area where the OSCE was concerned about the 'clear dearth of local initiatives', the OSCE organized a one-day seminar *How to Establish an NGO*, which targeted teachers, students, political party representatives, women, intellectuals and local journalists, to enable them to 'form a clearer idea of what fields NGOs work in, their legal status, and funding possibilities'.[23]

The target groups for developing networking and community-building initiatives are essentially those that the OSCE feels it can influence. Within this, the more social weight a group has, the better is its perceived qualification. Elite groups, such as lawyers, journalists, religious leaders, teachers, academics and intellectuals are therefore of great importance. Outside this, the OSCE has been able to establish links with groups that are either excluded from the mainstream political processes, in need of funding and resources, or unhappy with their current situation, such as self-help initiatives including women's groups, youth associations, and displaced persons' associations.

Any activity that can be undertaken in a cross-entity form, and thereby become a potential challenge to ethnic segmentation and division, is likely to be supported. The OSCE's interest is not so much in the activity itself but in locating people who are willing to organize around alternative political focus points to the majority parties. However, the OSCE fears that being up-front about its aims may put off potential supporters: 'When groups focus on non-political matters they have an optimal chance of making gains.'[24] The Democratization Branch monthly report for March 1997 demonstrates this in relation to sponsorship and other information: 'While promoting inter-ethnic tolerance and responsibility is the main goal of confidence building, events this month show how this is sometimes easiest done when it is not an activity's explicit goal.'[25]

Developing a Civil Society Agenda

Regardless of the humanitarian aid or information needs which an NGO was initially established to meet, it will be expected to participate in cross-entity forums and training and to become part of the NGO lobbying network dominated by the more openly political 'civic groups'. The OSCE involvement with local NGOs (LNGOs) has a directly political goal:

> The goal of the NGO development work is to assist LNGOs [to] become self-sufficient, participatory, and actively involved in working on behalf of their communities. The kind of LNGO projects which most closely reach this aim, offering a new political voice to

citizens, are those which focus on advocacy and are willing to tackle actual political or social issues. As more and more LNGOs accept the responsibility of implementing these kinds of programmes, they gradually strengthen Bosnia's civil society.[26]

There is no hiding the feelings of frustration that the officers of the OSCE have for the local NGOs which they see as 'less developed' because they are concentrating on needs, as opposed to becoming part of a political opposition. Their willingness to use their influence to alter the approaches and goals of local NGOs also cannot be denied. The following extract from a Democratization Branch monthly report is worth quoting at length to illustrate the support and guidance available from the OSCE:

> In areas where LNGOs are barely developed, as a start they implement humanitarian-type programmes which seek to satisfy basic needs. Over the past month, local groups identified in Eastern Republika Srpska (excluding Bijeljina) correspond to this. As true civil actors however, LNGOs must do more; otherwise they will be providing temporary solutions to what remains long term problems. An early step was taken [when] the Helsinki Committee Bijeljina started monitoring and investigating human rights abuses in mid-1996 … In the Bihac area [of operations], the Centre for Civic Co-operation (CCC) in Livno has gradually gone with OSCE support from a humanitarian LNGO working with children to one which seeks to increase awareness about human rights and democracy.[27]

The OSCE women's development work demonstrates how this process works. Reporting on the OSCE-organized Mostar Women's Conference, in March 1997, it is noted that nine women currently living as displaced persons in Republika Srpska attended. The OSCE was disappointed that while the Federation women were willing to organize politically, the women from RS clearly had not grasped the OSCE's agenda:

> while the Federation women appeared poised to work on joint activities, those from the RS seemed more keen on fulfilling their immediate personal wish of visiting Mostar. Whether the RS participants recognize that working with other Mostar women they have a chance of addressing some of the deeper underlining obstacles to freedom of movement and return, is thus likely to determine future conferences' success.[28]

The work with women's organizations seems to be having some success as the OSCE has noted that 'women are increasingly finding ways to take on political roles, even though frequently outside of political parties'.[29] The report notes that in Bihac a women's NGO is reportedly keen to organize a radio broadcast on elections related issues with OSCE support and that women's groups in Mostar are considering a similar initiative. The women's groups most active in political activity have so impressed the OSCE that: 'In the coming months OSCE staff may consider encouraging these women to become electoral monitors ... This is a step towards preparing civic groups to take on bigger responsibilities in the political process.'[30]

The OSCE also runs the election process and the regulations of the OSCE chaired Provisional Election Commission allow for citizens' organizations as well as political party representatives to monitor the electoral process, after receiving accreditation from a Local Election Committee. From the OSCE's perspective this is 'an important chance to involve a greater number of actors in the political process'.[31] Of course, the new actors involved in this process are those that have already been carefully hand-picked by the OSCE itself. As the Mostar strategy report advises: 'Field Officers and the Regional Centre should begin identifying local partners who could benefit from poll watching training.'[32] Democratization Officers have been instructed by the OSCE Democratization Branch to facilitate training for these groups, with the assistance of the US-funded National Democratic Initiative and the Council of Europe.[33]

For the OSCE, the sign of successful civil society building is when the new local NGOs begin to act as political actors in their own right. The third monthly report of the Democratization Branch celebrates the success of their work in northern Republika Srpska, where 'local NGOs are independently addressing more and more sensitive political subjects'.[34] Examples include an internationally-financed inter-entity roundtable, initiated by the Forum of Citizens of Banja Luka, entitled *The Legal Aspects of Return for Refugees and Displaced Persons* and the establishment of preliminary contacts between a new Doboj NGO and displaced persons in Zenica. The OSCE is full of praise for the two NGOs which are raising an issue that it sees as a major part of its own agenda: 'The fact that the two groups are addressing the politically sensitive issue of return points to their ability to take on the kind of independent stance necessary in any democratic society.'[35]

The Voice of Civil Society

The directly political impact of this NGO work can be seen in initiatives like the Citizens' Alternative Parliament and the Coalition for Return, actively supported by the OSCE-backed NGOs. The Citizens' Alternative Parliament (CAP) is a network of Bosnian NGOs which the OSCE sees as strengthening and co-ordinating the work of NGOs in Bosnia. To strengthen the impact of the CAP the OSCE intends to focus on developing the 'member organizations' commitment and capabilities of taking action in their regions'.[36] The OSCE's work with displaced persons' groups is designed to feed in with the activities of the Coalition for Return (CFR). The CFR is an association of more than 40 refugee and displaced persons groups from Bosnia, Croatia, Serbia and Germany.

In advance of the September 1996 elections, Deputy High Representative Steiner had already raised the prospect of refugee associations being used to put pressure on political parties 'from below'. In July he promised that: 'In the future we will aim to include representatives of refugee associations in our meetings in order to speed up the work of the authorities on both sides which has so far been very slow.'[37] The decision to form the CFR was taken at the Office of the High Representative (OHR), following the nationalist parties' success in the September 1996 polls.[38] The Deputy High Representative discussed plans to establish the association with representatives from associations of displaced persons and refugees and gave full support for the formation of a strategy planning group to liaise directly with international organizations and the relevant authorities. The CFR, meeting under the chair of the Office of the High Representative then worked to encourage return and to raise the profile of the issue with international organizations. In December 1996, the CFR decided to extend its remit to the directly political questions related to the issue of return and to develop an integrated approach to reconstruction and economic recovery.

By February 1997 this political role had extended to developing information and aid networks calling on displaced persons and refugees to vote for candidates committed to the issue of return in the forthcoming municipal elections. The Deputy High Representative then sought to promote the CFR as a popular 'grass-roots movement' and, in July 1997 at its first meeting not organized and chaired by the OHR, the CFR finally came of age as an independent organ of civil society.[39] It then requested observer status for the municipal elections and equal partnership with elected political representatives in negotiations on donations and reconstruction implementation projects.

THE LIMITS OF CIVIL SOCIETY DEVELOPMENT

International attempts to ensure that the 'different voices' in Bosnia are heard by the outside world have involved giving support to a variety of groups and organizations within Bosnia which attempt to challenge the political domination of the main political parties. Groups such as Circle 99, the Tuzla Citizens' Forum, the Citizens' Alternative Parliament and the

Coalition for Return have been actively supported by many international funders and have logistical and training support from the OSCE Democratization Branch.

However, as the OSCE Reporting Officer, Sabine Freizer, explained: 'The central problem we have is how to encourage participation.'[40] It may seem surprising that these groups with an international reputation should have problems involving Bosnian people in their work, especially as they represent a grass-roots movement for a different voice to be heard. Adrien Marti, the Co-ordinator for Political Party Development, explained the problem of the lack of popular support for the citizens' groups:

> The Citizens' Alternative Parliament, the Shadow Government and the Coalition for Return are basically the same 20 people when you scratch the surface a little. There is really no depth to this. The nationalist parties have a lot of good and respected people, they play on people's fears but also deliver security and a feeling that you can live normally. They are also much closer to the average person than the elitist Sarajevans. The overqualified Yugoslavs are seen as elitist, whereas the HDZ, SDS and the SDA [the leading political parties] have members and supporters on the ground facing the same problems as you.[41]

When asked why, if there was so little support within Bosnia for the approach of these groups, the OSCE considered it a priority to assist their development, Marti's response was: 'They need the money to make them more efficient. But it should be up to the public at the end of the day. I think there is a balance, the public wants the nationalist parties for security, but they also want an opposition.'[42]

The problem with this approach is that the opposition is in this case one that has not been chosen by the electorate but by the OSCE and other international agencies. Jens Sorenson notes that:

> The local NGO sector is primarily the creation of an urban middle class, which has been squeezed in the social transformation in the new republics. With polarization increasing … as the ethnic states reward supporters of the ruling party, what remains of the politicized middle class can find a new niche in NGOs. Here the distinction between NGOs as social movements or as service providers becomes unclear.[43]

Zoran Jorgakieski, the OSCE Democratization Branch Co-ordinator for Dialogue and Reconciliation, expanded on the problem:

> These groups are all run by intellectuals but they have very little influence. During the war they stayed aside and withdrew from politics. These are the people we have to focus upon. They are a minority, but the best, the cream of Bosnian intellectual society. They

have good relations with their colleagues across the Inter-Entity Boundary Line. They are top intellectuals, you can't expect ordinary people to understand them. The language they use is too complicated. People doubt they are good patriots.[44]

There seems to be a large gap between the civil society associations funded and supported by the OSCE, and other international institutions, and Bosnian people. For the OSCE and the international community, this gap demonstrates the lack of a democratic culture in Bosnia. While few people are actively involved in civil society associations, leaving them predominantly middle-class based, the main nationalist parties still easily attain the majority of the votes in elections. In response to this gap Adrien Marti is advising some of the new civil society groups which became established as political parties before the September 1997 municipal elections, to abandon electoral competition after the local polls and become NGOs instead: 'They have no chance as political parties', he said, these 'groups would have much more influence as NGOs and lobby groups than as political parties with 0.001 per cent of the vote'.[45]

There is little evidence that this civil society strategy is helping to challenge support for the nationalist parties or to overcome ethnic segmentation and division in Bosnia. The OSCE Democratization Branch, in its attempts to celebrate cross-community co-operation and turn this into an alternative political voice, unfortunately tends to politicize, and consequently problematize, everyday activity which organically contributes to confidence-building. While thousands of people cross the Inter-Entity Boundary Line every day, to work, shop, see relatives, or go to school, this is seen as everyday life going on and making the best of the situation.[46] The people whose lives involve cross-entity co-operation do not necessarily want to turn everyday survival into a political movement. The moment these actions become politicized they become an implicit threat to the *status quo* and create a backlash to a perceived threat that did not exist previously. As an experienced Senior Democratization Officer related: 'I'm surprised they tell us anything anymore. Inter-entity contacts are very common with businesses etc. If I was a businessman I wouldn't report it, not just for tax reasons – no one pays tax anyway – but because it just creates problems.'[47] The OSCE Youth and Education Co-ordinator explained that the teachers she worked with had not wanted attention to be drawn to them and had told her not to park her OSCE car near to their houses.[48] Similarly, people were much more willing to use the cross-entity bus-line once the OSCE licence plates were removed.[49] People want to cross the Inter-Entity Boundary Line, and in some cases to return to their pre-war homes, but without drawing attention to themselves and without their actions being seen as threatening the security of others. Returns that have been organized spontaneously have had much more success than internationally enforced return under the threat of sanctions which have both angered and raised the fears of current residents.[50]

Ironically the more support given to the 'grass-roots' civil associations by the OSCE, the less effective they tend to be. The unintended consequence of creating civil society NGOs which are reliant on external support has been that they are never forced to build their own base of popular support or take on the arguments or political programmes of the nationalists. Guaranteed funding and the ear of international policy-makers, the Citizens' Parliament and other favoured groups are in fact more likely to prevent or impede the development of an opposition with roots in society. As Jens Sorensen notes, the reliance on external funders can tend to fragment society rather than create a pluralistic exchange of political opinions.[51] Because the funding of civil society NGOs is portrayed as apolitical assistance to democratization, this has led to a variety of projects and NGOs being funded with no overall strategy. Instead of building bridges within a society as political parties would have to, in order to aggregate support around a political programme, these NGOs relying on outside funding have no need to engage in discussion or create broader links to society.

INTERNATIONAL REGULATION AND CIVIL SOCIETY DEVELOPMENT

The points raised above about the democratic status of raising unelected minority groups over political parties elected by majorities, and the dangers of downplaying the electoral process of discussion and debate, highlight general questions over the democratic deficit created by international regulation which attempts to shape the political process. However, consideration of the specific context in which civil society building is being promoted in Bosnia demands a further clarification of these questions. While commentators often write of the need to develop Bosnia-specific programmes of civic capacity-building, they rarely consider the broader context of their work. Discussion tends to focus on the problems faced by local civic groups without consideration of the impact of the post-Dayton international administration, nor of its legitimation through a denial of Bosnian people's capacity for self-rule.

The advocates of civil society democratization strategies are undoubtedly correct in their assertions that democracy is about more than holding elections every few years, and in their emphasis on the need for the consent of the governed, the accountability of policies to the electorate, the opportunity for participation in decision-making, and for the decision-making process to be transparent.[52] In Bosnia there are elections but Bosnian society lacks all the above factors. However, before greater international attention to the promotion of NGOs is called for, it is worth taking a step back to consider the democratic framework in Bosnia.

Since the 1995 Dayton Peace Agreement, Bosnia has been undergoing a process of internationally imposed democratization. This process has been implemented by the major international powers, including the US, Britain, France, Germany and Russia, under the co-ordination of the Peace Implementation Council. The plans drawn up by this body have then been implemented by leading international institutions, such as the UN, North Atlantic Treaty Organization, OSCE, Council of Europe, International Monetary Fund, World Bank and the European Bank for Reconstruction and Development, under their own mandates, creating a network of regulating and policy-making bodies.[53] Co-ordinating the civilian side of this project has been the UN's High Representative for Bosnia, the state's chief administrator with the authority to make and enforce law at both state and entity levels and dismiss obstructive Bosnian officials.

Dayton initially established this interlocking network of international policy-making forums as part of a one year transition to limited Bosnian self-government. The Dayton Agreement assumed that with state and entity elections, run under OSCE auspices in September 1996, the external international administration of the state would come to an end. Guarantees of long-term stability were built in to the Bosnian constitution which gave key regulating powers to an IMF-appointed director of the Central Bank and to European Union-appointed judges as final arbiters of law through the Constitutional Court. Other Dayton annexes gave the international community further regulating powers through the establishment of key commissions run by international appointees from the UN, OSCE, Council of Europe and European Bank for Reconstruction and Development.[54]

Within a few months of the Dayton settlement the Peace Implementation Council (PIC) began to consider the prospects of extending the international peacekeeping process and, by June 1996, was already discussing a two-year 'consolidation period', duely ratified by the PIC in December 1996. The UN High Representative was mandated to draw up two 12-month policy 'action plans' to be ratified and reviewed at six-monthly PIC meetings. This meant that the newly-elected state and entity governments were reduced to little more than rubber-stamps for predetermined international policies. There was little opportunity for the elected politicians to negotiate their own compromises on issues. Any opposition was met with the threat to cancel donors meetings and the World Bank and IMF refusal to release reconstruction aid. In December 1997, just one year into this extended consolidation period, the international administration of Bosnia became an open-ended international commitment, with no clearly defined point at which even the limited Bosnian self-government, promised by Dayton, could be realized.

This extended process of international regulation has involved a 'top-down' approach to democratization. Governing representatives at municipal, canton, entity and state levels have little choice but to follow international policy at the threat of being dismissed from their posts or having sanctions imposed. This process extends from the tripartite Presidency, from which the Serb member, Momcilo Krajisnik, was threatened with dismissal in October 1997, to the municipal level where the September 1997 election results were only ratified *post festum* by the OSCE, not in relation to any electoral irregularities but on the basis of policies pursued by elected representatives once in post. This level of external regulation has even extended to the international take-over of the state-run television station in Republika Srpska and the High Representative deciding the national flag of the new country.

While the Bosnian politicians are fully accountable to the international community, there are no mechanisms making international policy-making accountable to the Bosnian people. The International Crisis Group (ICG) acknowledges this 'credibility gap', and their response to it serves to highlight the diminished nature of democracy in Bosnia under Dayton. The ICG argue that:

> Respect for Bosnian authorities and basic notions of reciprocity argue for at least the degree of transparency necessary for the Bosnian authorities and people to understand the basis for decisions, and the decision-making processes, that so affect them. If the point of the international encampment in Bosnia is to 'teach' democracy, tolerance and good governance to the Bosnians then there is no better way to start than by example.[55]

In this case democratic accountability is reduced to 'transparency'. 'Teaching democracy' ends up as a call for international institutions to make widely available their future plans and policy goals for the region. This does little to alter the fact that the Bosnian people have no active role in decision-making, and are instead reduced to the role of passive onlookers. This level of international regulation has given little opportunity for elected representatives, let alone the general public, to voice their concerns or make any input into policy-making. In a society where even elected officials and judges have to be instructed in what the laws of their own country are, and are compelled to rely on international institutions to provide translations and guidance for them, it is unsurprising that people outside the political elites feel excluded and marginalized from the policy-making process.[56]

The guarantee of a measure of autonomy and political self-government for the three ethnic constituencies, all of whom are minorities in the new state, promised by Dayton, was never delivered. Far from international policy rebuilding links between communities, the division between the two entities has been increased through differential international treatment. For example, the US has re-trained and re-equipped a separate Federation army, and turned down RS calls for military integration. At the same time, economic aid and reconstruction projects have been concentrated narrowly within the Federation, with the weaker RS economy receiving less than two per cent of the reconstruction aid in 1996 and less than five per cent in 1997.

Limited political autonomy for the two entities, promised by Dayton to grant security to minorities fearful of domination in the new state, has been similarly undermined by international regulation. Within the Federation the formal divisions of power at cantonal and entity level have not facilitated self-government, instead policy at all levels is imposed from the top down through the US and UN co-chaired Federation Forum. Concerns of the Bosnian Serbs for equal treatment have been little assuaged by international policy: including what is generally perceived as a selective anti-Serb bias in The Hague war crimes tribunal; international community prevention of links with Serbia, allowed under Dayton; the extension of direct international rule over Serb-claimed Brcko; the overruling of the RS Constitutional Court and imposition of new Assembly elections; the international take-over of entity media prior to the 1997 elections; and a new government established through international intervention, which excludes the party which gained the most votes.[57]

The lack of security caused by the still-born nature of the self-government proposed under Dayton would appear to be the major barrier for the cross-entity civil society groups funded by the international community. As long as basic political security is lacking from the Dayton framework, and there is no guarantee that entity borders or rights to land, housing or work can be assured, opposition parties and civic groups are seen by many as a potential threat to the *status quo* which is guaranteeing peaceful coexistence. The OSCE Democratization Branch has no mandate to question Dayton, or the tensions resulting from this lack of autonomy, and therefore deals with symptoms rather than the underlying problems. This has led to seeing the problems as lying with Bosnian people rather than the framework imposed by external powers. Once the Dayton framework is taken out of the picture, Bosnian concerns about security are interpreted by OSCE officers as either a result of nationalist propaganda, war trauma, or ethnic prejudice against other Bosnian groups.

CIVIL SOCIETY AND DEMOCRACY

The impetus behind the reorganization of the OSCE Bosnia Mission and the establishment of the OSCE Democratization Branch was the international community's decision to extend the peacekeeping mandates of the international institutions. It was only after this decision, in December 1996, that the creation of civil society became a central issue in Bosnia.[58] The focus on civil society legitimated a unique situation. The September 1996 elections were held to have been democratic, and to have met the standards set by the OSCE for the recognition of the results, yet they were also declared to be not democratic enough to allow self-rule. A Democratization Branch information document explains this apparent contradiction:

> In the biggest event since the signing of the Dayton Accords, Bosnia's citizens chose for themselves a legitimate democratically elected system of government in September, 1996 … Accordingly the first foundations have been laid for Bosnia to become a democracy. Yet even though elections are essential for the creation of a legitimate democratic state, they are not enough to ensure that democracy in Bosnia prevails. It is a mistake to see elections as the endpoint of democratization. They are in fact an early stage of what remains by definition a long term process.[59]

Many commentators would agree that elections can only be part of the broader democratization process, however there would appear to be a problem in asserting that democracy must be consolidated or democratization completed *before* self-government and electoral accountability are permitted. The focus on civil society development has avoided confronting this problem by moving the focus away from the fact that internationally-made policy is being externally imposed on Bosnian institutions. This new grass-roots approach has been welcomed as a long-term international commitment to democratic transition, but it could also be seen as expressing a more disillusioned approach to the prospects of democracy in Bosnia.

The success of the nationalist parties came as a shock to international agencies which had assumed, prior to the September 1996 elections, that tighter international regulation over the political process would enable popular opposition groups to gain a hold on power. Their universally poor showing created a strong air of pessimism about the future of a united Bosnia.[60] This disillusionment with the choice expressed through the ballot box, resulted in a much more negative view of the capacities of the Bosnian people themselves.

For example, Duncan Bullivant, Spokesman for the High Representative, has argued that 'Bosnia is a deeply sick society, ill at ease with even the most basic principles of democracy'.[61] For Christian Ahlund, the OSCE Director General for Human Rights: 'Elections are just the first primitive stage of democracy. Political parties are still a pretty blunt form.'

He saw the OSCE's role as a 'pedagogic' one of informing Bosnian people about international standards and 'telling them what democratization is all about'.[62] This view was supported by a Senior Democratization Co-ordinator: 'Political parties are a new appearance. People don't know how to cope and neither do their leaders, they have no political programme. People just follow the flock. It is the same with the independent parties, people vote for them just because they are the alternative.'[63]

The disparaging attitude towards ordinary people, 'the flock', was not even diminished when they voted for opposition parties because it was assumed that they were not capable of making an independent judgement. The widespread acceptance of this perspective amongst the NGO-building community was illustrated by the Helsinki Citizens' Assembly organizer in Sarajevo, who explained that the people had no democratic experience and were used to 'living under a strong hand', and that this lack of democratic education had to be challenged through NGOs 'teaching people how to behave and to know right from wrong'. She told a joke to illustrate the problem her NGO faced: 'The opposition party leader asks the peasant why he is not going to vote for him. The peasant says that he will vote for him. The opposition leader asks "when?". The peasant says "when you get in power".'[64]

Often the analogies about democracy tend to involve uneducated peasants as the symbol of ordinary people. One of the leading officers of the Democratization Branch went further, to the extent of seeing Bosnian people not supportive of civil society initiatives as caught up in the backward ideology of feudalism. At the OSCE in Sarajevo, Jasna Malkoc, one of the activists whose ideas lay behind the initiation of the Democratization Branch, openly explained that democratization would be a long process of changing the culture of the majority of the Bosnian people in order to 'implement the concept of individualism':

> The lack of democratic values stems from the divisions of the Austro-Hungarian Empire which instilled individualistic ideas. Areas outside the Empire had feudalist systems which continued as communist structures. Serbia is feudalist, Croatia is individualist. Bosnia is in-between and the division is between urban, individualist areas and peasant, feudal areas. For example, Banja Luka [in Republika Srpska] is urban and is influenced by the West and Croatia.[65]

A similar perspective which emphasizes the long-term problems of civil society construction is the psycho-social approach, also pursued by the Democratization Branch. Using this framework, one of the main barriers to building civil society in Bosnia is seen to be psycho-social problems. Much or even most of the population is adjudged by many democratizers to be unable to see the gains of a civil society approach, due to the impact of their part as victims or as passive supporters of human rights violations during the war.[66] This approach puts psycho-social work at the centre of strategies for democratization because: 'These persons may offer special resistance to confidence-building, dialogue and reconciliation efforts due to the victims' mistrust, isolation, demoralization and anger. Due to symptoms of victimization, they are also less likely to be willing to take on new responsibilities as active members of civil society.'[67]

Even its advocates admit that this work is 'entering new territory' where 'not much theory exists' in relation to psycho-social projects.[68] However, these doubts do not figure highly for the Democratization Branch, their Semi-Annual Report states categorically that 'trauma symptoms have become an obstacle to the implementation of the General Framework Agreement for Peace and the development of pluralistic society in Bosnia'.[69]

Central to the OSCE Democratization Branch's approach is the understanding that the Bosnian people, 'damaged' or 'traumatized' by the war and the transition from one-party state regulation, are not capable of acting independently or making choices between 'right and wrong'. This approach was not universally popular with the OSCE Democratization Officers, some of whom mentioned in confidence the dangers of a gap between democratization in theory and in practice: 'It is easy to get patronizing. Bosnian society pre-war was highly developed, it was not the civil society of the West, but these people were not illiterate, or not cultured, or not developed, just different'; 'Democratization is not a good term – it is like teaching them how to behave – naturally people are sensitive to this. A lot of people are educated, they know theory, and they know right and wrong'; 'Civil society and democratic values existed – Bosnia had a multi-cultural society, good nationalities policy and progressive policies regarding women'.[70] However, those that felt awkward with the approach of their superiors did not feel it was possible to express this easily within the organization: 'There is no discussion about what democracy is'; 'big principled questions you have to leave out and try to find a corner, an area where you can do good work'.[71]

Taking over the language of empowerment from the psycho-social counselling work being developed in the war, the new focus of the senior officials within the Democratization Branch is on the capacity of individuals for democracy as opposed to that of governments. This means that the broader framework of political and economic regulation is ignored. If anything, the Democratization Branch work of civil society building from the bottom-up is perhaps more invidious to democracy than the enforced international administration, because it implicitly assumes that Bosnian people are 'damaged' and incapable of rational choice. Once the capacity of Bosnian people as rational political actors is negated, whether this is understood as due to feudalism, to ethnic identity or to war trauma, there is little reason for the international administration of the new state to be seen as temporary or 'transitional' in the short-term, or for self-government and democracy to be seen as preferable.

At the end of the day, the civil society approach not only fails to build support for political alternatives, it also provides *carte blanche* for the international administrators to override democratic processes, on the grounds that Bosnian voters are not responsible enough to have the rights granted to citizens in Western states. As Klaus Kinkel openly confirmed, in December 1997, the international community has little hesitation in moving to make decisions contrary to the will of the Bosnian people.[72] The implication of this approach is the end of formal democracy, of legitimacy through accountability to the electorate. Democracy is redefined as its opposite, adherence to outside standards not autonomy and accountability. High Representative Carlos Westendorp illustrated the new logic of this reversal of democratic accountability when overruling elected Bosnian representatives on the grounds that in his opinion: 'They have a wrong perspective. They are not serving their population properly'.[73]

CONCLUSIONS

This article has suggested that there is a link between the low level of support for civil society alternatives to the leading political parties and a lack of democracy in Bosnia. However the relationship between civil society and democracy seems to be very different from the one suggested by the advocates of greater international support for NGO-led civil society building strategies.

There is little disagreement that the lack of security is the main political resource of the leading nationalist parties.[74] It seems entirely possible that the extent of international regulation over Bosnian life, the denial of self-government at local and state level, and the inability of Bosnian political actors to negotiate their own solutions, and thereby give their constituents a level of accountability for policy-making, is perpetuating a political climate unconducive to the development of political alternatives. For civil society to have the space to develop, and for alternative opinions to gain a broader audience, the basic questions of political self-government and security for entity borders would have to be settled. As long as there is no assurance that existing rights to land, homes and employment will not be put to question through international administrative decisions, taken above the heads of

Bosnian people, the leading nationalist parties seem secure and civil society alternatives will remain marginalized.[75]

With the indefinite extension of international mandates over Bosnia there seems to be little prioritization of self-government. The OSCE's Democratization Branch has no way of assessing whether their civil society development strategy has had only limited success due to the impact of extended international regulation or because of purely local factors which have so far been immune to international democratization initiatives. According to Siri Rustad, Deputy to the Head of Mission for Democratization:

> It is difficult through the [OSCE] activities to measure the overall democratic level of the country. We can't say for definite that any particular activity in itself has changed anything. We propose a set of different activities but then measure them on other levels – the running of institutions, the role of NGOs, the views of the Peace Implementation Conference etc. We don't have a broader theoretical approach at all. That's how the Mission works – its concerned with practical results.[76]

The lack of any way of accounting for the success or failure of civil society-building projects means that the assumption of leading OSCE officers that there are long-term cultural barriers to democracy is never an issue. Once extended democratization mandates ignore political power and relations between political elites and the international community and instead focus on ethnic segmentation and civil society, assessment becomes a subjective exercise in the measurement of attitudes and culture. The lack of progress only reinforces the idea that the people are too backward or traumatized to be able to cope with political choices. The solution then is not to question the theoretical framework which informs the approach of top-down imposition and bottom-up empowerment, but to tinker with the programmes and call for more resources. As the process continues a vicious circle is created in which the Bosnian people are seen to be less capable of political autonomy and the international community appears ever more necessary to guarantee peaceful and democratic development.

NOTES

1. UN Secretary-General Report, *Agenda for Democratization*, A/51/761 (Dec. 1996), pars.13 & 46.
2. Ibid., par.124. See also the UN Secretary-General Report, *Support by the UN System of the Efforts of Governments to Promote and Consolidate New or Restored Democracies*, A/50/332 (Aug. 1995), par.13.
3. L. Diamond, 'Rethinking Civil Society: Toward Democratic Consolidation', *Journal of Democracy*, Vol.5, No.3 (1994), pp.4–17. See also: A.B. Seligman, *The Idea of Civil Society* (New York: Free Press, 1992); J. L. Cohen and A. Arato, *Civil Society and Political Theory* (Cambridge, MA: MIT Press, 1992); and J. Keane, *Democracy and Civil Society* (London: Verso, 1988).
4. Available from: <http://un.org>.
5. UN Secretary-General Report, *Agenda for Development*, A/48/935 (May 1994), par.107.
6. See, for example, T. Gallagher, 'Democratization in the Balkans: Challenges and Prospects', *Democratization*, Vol.2, No.3 (1995), pp.337–61; K.S. Fine, 'Fragile Stability and Change: Understanding Conflict during the Transitions in East Central Europe', in A. Chayes and A.H. Chayes (eds.), *Preventing Conflict in the Post-Communist World* (Washington, DC: Brookings Institution, 1996), pp.541–81; P. Sztompka, 'Looking Back: The Year 1989 as a Cultural and Civilizational Break', *Communist and Post-Communist Studies* Vol.29, No.2 (1996), pp.115–29; Z. Rau (ed.), *The Reemergence of Civil Society in Eastern Europe and the Soviet Union* (Oxford: Westview Press, 1991); and E. Gellner, *Conditions of Liberty: Civil Society and its Rivals* (London: Hamish Hamilton, 1994).
7. For example, S.L. Burg, 'Bosnia Herzegovina: a Case of Failed Democratization', in K. Dawisha and B. Parrot (eds.), *Politics, Power, and the Struggle for Democracy in South-East Europe* (Cambridge: Cambridge University Press, 1997), pp.122–45; B. Denitch, *Ethnic Nationalism: The Tragic Death of Yugoslavia* (revised edition, London: University of Minnesota Press, 1996); P. Ferdinand, 'Nationalism, Community and Democratic Transition in Czechoslovakia and Yugoslavia', in D. Potter *et al.* (eds.), *Democratization* (Cambridge: Open University, 1997), pp.466–89; *Unfinished Peace: Report of the International Commission on the Balkans* (Washington, DC: Carnegie Endowment for International Peace/Aspen Institute Berlin, 1996); and S.L. Woodward, *Balkan Tragedy: Chaos and Dissolution After the Cold War* (Washington, DC: Brookings Institution, 1995), Ch.5.
8. B. Deacon and P. Stubbs, 'International Actors and Social Policy Development in Bosnia-Herzegovina: Globalism and the "New Feudalism"', *Journal of European Social Policy* (1998); G. Kenney, '"New Imperialism" of Bosnia Mission', *The Times* (20 Dec. 1997: Letters).
9. See, for example, Denitch, op. cit., p.210; T. Gallagher, 'A Culture of Fatalism Towards the Balkans: Long-Term Western Attitudes and Approaches', paper presented at the British International Studies Association, 22nd Annual Conference, Leeds, 15–17 Dec. 1997; S. Woodward, 'Implementing Peace in Bosnia and Herzegovina: A Post-Dayton Primer and Memorandum of Warning', Brookings Discussion Papers (Washington, DC: Brookings Institution), 1996, p.35; and M. Kaplan, 'Was Democracy Just a Moment?', *Atlantic Monthly* (Dec. 1997), p.58.
10. I. Smillie, *Service Delivery or Civil Society? Non-Governmental Organizations in Bosnia and Herzegovina* (CARE, Canada, 1996), p.13.
11. Dialogue Development, *Survey of Bosnian Civil Society Organizations: Mapping, Characteristics, and Strategy* (Copenhagen: Dialogue Development, 1997), Annex 1, p.1.
12. OSCE Democratization Branch, *Monthly Report*, 1 (Feb. 1997), p.3.
13. Ibid.
14. Ibid.
15. In the mid-1970s a third of all secondary school graduates entered 'higher schools', comparable to US community colleges, figures from the United Nations Educational, Scientific and Cultural Organization for the same period place Yugoslavia highest among East European states for student enrolment in higher education and in university institutions, see R.E. Heath, 'Education', in S. Fischer-Galati (ed.), *Eastern Europe in the 1980s*

(London: Croom Helm, 1981), pp.225–55. On inter-ethnic tolerance, see for example: G.K. Bertsch , 'The Revival of Nationalisms', *Problems of Communism*, Vol. XXII, No.6 (1973), pp.1–15; and X. Bougarel, 'Bosnia and Herzegovina – State and Communitarianism', in D.A. Dyker and I. Vejvoda (eds.), *Yugoslavia and After: A Study in Fragmentation, Despair and Rebirth* (London: Longman, 1996), pp.87–115. On political participation, see B. McFarlane, *Yugoslavia: Politics, Economics and Society* (London: Pinter, 1988), pp.45–54; J. Seroka, 'The Interdependence of Institutional Revitalization and Intra-Party Reform in Yugoslavia', *Soviet Studies*, Vol.XL, No.1 (1988), pp.84–99; and J. Seroka 'Economic Stabilization and Communal Politics in Yugoslavia', *Journal of Communist Studies*, Vol.5, No.2 (1989), pp.125–47.

16. *General Framework Agreement for Peace in Bosnia and Herzegovina*, available from: <http://www.state.gov/www/current/bosnia/dayton>.

17. W. Woodger, *The Letter of Democracy and the Spirit of Censorship: The West Runs the Media in Bosnia*, unpublished paper (1997).

18. OSCE Democratization Branch, *Democratization Programme: Strategies and Activities for 1997*.

19. Interview by the author with Jasna Malkoc, the Senior Co-ordinator for Democratization/ NGO Development, Sarajevo, 16 June 1997.

20. Interview by the author with Sabine Freizer, OSCE Democratization Branch Reporting Officer, Sarajevo, 16 June 1997.

21. OSCE Democratization Branch, *Monthly Report*, 1, p.5.

22. OSCE Democratization Branch, 'Regional Centre Tuzla Priority and Strategy Paper: Summary, Planned Activities, Head Office Suggestions', unpublished paper (1997), p.4.

23. OSCE Democratization Branch, *Monthly Report, 3* (April 1997), p.6.

24. OSCE Democratization Branch, *Monthly Report*, 1, p.4.

25. OSCE Democratization Branch, *Monthly Report*, 2 (March 1997), p.4.

26. OSCE Democratization Branch, *Monthly Report*, 1, p.5.

27. Ibid., p.6.

28. OSCE Democratization Branch, *Monthly Report*, 2, p.3.

29. Ibid., p.5.

30. Ibid.

31. OSCE Democratization Branch, *Regional Centre Sokolac priority and strategy paper: summary, planned activities, Head Office suggestions*, unpublished paper (1997), p.3.

32. OSCE Democratization Branch, *Regional Centre Mostar priority and strategy paper: summary, planned activities, Head Office suggestions (first draft)*, unpublished paper (1997), s.IIb.

33. OSCE Democratization Branch, *Regional Centre Sokolac*, p.3.

34. OSCE Democratization Branch, *Monthly Report*, 3, p.6.

35. Ibid.

36. OSCE Democratization Branch, *Monthly Report*, 1, p.6.

37. *Office of the High Representative Bulletin*, 8 (23 June 1996), available from: <http://www.ohr.int/ bulletins/b960623.htm>.

38. International Crisis Group Report, *Going Nowhere Fast: Refugees and Internally Displaced Persons in Bosnia and Herzegovina* (Sarajevo: International Crisis Group, 30 April 1997), p.9.

39. *Office of the High Representative Bulletin*, 40 (13 March 1997), available from: <http://www.ohr.int/bulletins/b970313.htm>; *Office of the High Representative Bulletin*, 49 (28 May 1997), available from: <http://www.ohr.int/bulletins/b970528.htm>.

40. Interview by the author with Sabine Freizer, OSCE Democratization Branch Reporting Officer, Sarajevo, 16 June 1997.

41. Interview by the author with Adrien Marti, OSCE Co-ordinator for Political Party Development, Sarajevo, 14 June 1997.

42. Ibid.

43. J.S. Sorenson, 'Pluralism or Fragmentation?' *War Report* (May 1997), p.35.

44. Interview by the author with Zoran Jorgakieski, OSCE Democratization Branch Co-ordinator for Dialogue and Reconciliation, Sarajevo, 16 June 1997.

45. Interview by the author with Adrien Marti, OSCE Co-ordinator for Political Party Development, Sarajevo, 14 June 1997.
46. *Bosnia and Herzegovina Country Report on Human Rights Practices for 1996*, released by the Bureau of Democracy, Human Rights, and Labour (30 Jan. 1997), US Department of State, s.2d, available from: <www.state.gov/www/issues/ human_rights/1996_hrp_ eport/ bosniahe.html>.
47. Confidential interview with the author, Sarajevo, 14 June 1997.
48. Interview by the author with Rannveig Rajendram, OSCE Democratization Branch Youth and Education Co-ordinator. Sarajevo, 14 June 1997.
49 *Bosnia and Herzegovina Country Report on Human Rights Practices for 1997*, released by the Bureau of Democracy, Human Rights, and Labour (30 Jan. 1998), US Department of State, s.2d, available from: <www.state.gov/www/global/ human_rights/1997_hrp_report/ bosniahe.html>.
50 *Bosnia – The International Community's Responsibility to Ensure Human Rights*, Amnesty International Report, 1996, s.V.A, available from: <http://www.io.org/amnesty/ailib/aipub/ 1996/ EUR/46301496.htm>; ICG, *Going Nowhere Fast*, p.13.
51. Sorensen, op. cit., p.35.
52. For example, Smillie, op. cit., p.10.
53. P. Szasz, 'Current Developments: The Protection of Human Rights Through the Dayton/Paris Peace Agreement on Bosnia', *American Journal of International Law*, Vol. 90 (1996), p.304.
54. *General Framework Agreement*; see also D. Chandler, 'A New Look at the Democratization Process: The Case Study of Bosnia-Herzegovina Post-Dayton', in Z. Sevic and G. Wright (eds.), *Transition in Central and Eastern Europe*, Vol.2 (Belgrade: Yugoslav Association of Sasakawa Fellows, 1997), pp.217–41.
55. *Aid and Accountability: Dayton Implementation*. ICG Bosnia Report No.17, Sarajevo: International Crisis Group (1996), p.17.
56. *Rule of Law Analysis Report* (Feb. 1997), OSCE Democratization Branch, p.3; *Rule of Law Analysis Report* (March 1997), OSCE Democratization Branch, p.2.
57. Prior to the November 1997 RS Assembly elections NATO troops seized four Republika Srpska TV transmitters, this ended the system of shared broadcast control between Pale and Banja Luka, and gave control to the pro-Dayton opposition party led by RS President Biljana Plavsic, see *Office of the High Representative Bulletin*, Vol.61, No.1 (1 Oct. 1997), available from: <http://www.ohr.int/bulletins /b971001.htm>. There were prolonged negotiations to form a new government. The deadlock was broken after a parliamentary session was adjourned and many delegates had gone home, UN Deputy High Representative Jacques Klein asked NATO troops to intercept an opposition deputy to return him to parliament to give the opposition coalition a majority. A new government was elected which excluded the SDS which had obtained the most seats. See: M. Kelly, 'Step by Step, Preventing the Destruction of Bosnia', *International Herald Tribune* (22 Jan. 1998); M. O'Connor, 'West sees Payoff from Backing Flexible Leaders in Bosnia', *New York Times* (24 Jan. 1998); and see Table 1:

TABLE 1

PARTY COMPOSITION OF THE NATIONAL ASSEMBLY OF REPUBLIKA SRPSKA (NOVEMBER 1997)

Party	Seats	%
Serb Democratic Party (SDS)	24	28.8
SDA-led Coalition	16	19.2
Serb Radical Party	15	18.0
Serb People's Alliance (SNS)	15	18.0
RS branch of Milosevic's Socialists	9	10.8
Independent Social Democrats	2	2.4
Bosnian Social Democratic Party	2	2.4

Source: OSCE Bosnia Mission, '1997 Election Results National Assembly of Republika Srpska', available from web site <http://www.oscebih.org/RSresults.htm>.

58. During 1996 many international officials were still referring to the establishment of joint institutions with the elections as the birth of Bosnian democracy. See, for example: 'Statement by Secretary of State Warren Christopher on the Bosnian Elections', released by the Office of the Spokesman 18 Sept. 1996, US Department of State, available from: <www.state.gov/www/regions/eur/bosnia/1996_bosnia_speeches.html>; and 'Chairman's Conclusions of the Peace Implementation Council. Florence, 13–14 June, 1996', Office of the High Representative, par.27, available from: <http://www.ohr.int/ docu/ d960613a.htm>.
59. OSCE Democratization Branch, untitled information document (26 Feb. 1997), p.1.
60. Despite the large number of parties and large turn-out, the election results gave a substantial popular mandate to the three main pre-war nationalist parties, the Muslim Party of Democratic Action (SDA), the Serbian Democratic Party (SDS) and the Croatian Democratic Union (HDZ). The three main nationalist parties won about 86 per cent of the seats and, including the Muslim Party for Bosnia and Herzegovina and Serbian Party for Peace and Progress, the ethnic political blocks accounted for about 95 percent of the seats. See M. Kasapovic, '1996 Parliamentary Elections in Bosnia and Herzegovina', *Electoral Studies,* Vol. 16, No. 1 (1997), p.120, and see Table 2.

TABLE 2

PARTY COMPOSITION OF THE BOSNIAN PARLIAMENT (SEPTEMBER 1996)

Party	Seats	%
Party of Democratic Action (SDA)	19	45.2
Serb Democratic Party (SDS)	9	21.4
Croatian Democratic Union (HDZ)	8	19.0
Party for Bosnia and Herzegovina	2	4.8
Joint List	2	4.8
Party for Peace and Progress	2	4.8

Source: Mirajana Kaspovic, '1996 Parliamentary Elections in Bosnia and Herzegovina', *Electoral Studies*, Vol.16, No.1 (1997), p.119.

61. 'Clearing the Bosnian Air', *Washington Post* (6 Oct. 1997: Editorial).
62. Interview by the author with Christian Ahlund, OSCE Director General for Human Rights, Sarajevo, 16 June 1997.
63. Interview by the author with Jasna Malkoc, OSCE Senior Co-ordinator for Democratization/NGO Development, Sarajevo, 16 June 1997.
64. Interview by the author with Mirjana Malic, HCA, Sarajevo, 16 June 1997.
65. Interview by the author with Jasna Malkoc, OSCE Senior Co-ordinator for Democratization/NGO Development, Sarajevo, 16 June 1997.
66. J. Mimica, 'Ethnically Mixed Marriages from the Perspective of the Universal Declaration of Human Rights', in I. Agger (ed.), *Mixed Marriages: Voices from a Psycho-Social Workshop held in Zagreb, Croatia* (European Community Humanitarian Office, 1995), p.22.
67. OSCE Democratization Branch, *Monthly Report* 1, pp.7–8.
68. I. Agger, and J. Mimica, *Psycho-social Assistance to Victims of War: An Evaluation* (European Community Humanitarian Office, 1996), pp.27–8.
69. OSCE Democratization Branch, *Semi-Annual Report* (1997), p.15.
70. Interviews by the author with OSCE Democratization Branch Officers, Sarajevo, June 1997.
71. Ibid.
72. *SRT Banja Luka News Summary*, 10 Dec. 1997. Office of the High Representative, e-mail list available from: <LISTSERV@CC1.KULEUVEN.AC. BE>.
73. K. Coleman, 'Sceptic Serbs Doubt the Plavsic Revolution', *The Guardian* (22 Nov. 1997).
74. *Office of the High Representative Bulletin*, No.50 (4 June 1997), available from: <http://www.ohr.int/bulletins/b970604.htm>;International Crisis Group Project, *Changing the Logic of Bosnian Politics: ICG Discussion Paper on Electoral Reform* (Sarajevo:

International Crisis Group, 1998), p.2.
75. For further views of the possibility of civil society emerging once this uncertainty is removed see: Woodward, 'Implementing Peace in Bosnia and Herzegovina', p.83; and C.G. Boyd, 'Making Bosnia Work', *Foreign Affairs*, Vol.77, No.1 (1998), pp.42–55.
76. Interview by the author with Siri Rustad, OSCE Deputy to Head of Mission for Democratization, Sarajevo, 14 June 1997.

Building Civil Societies in East Central Europe: The Effect of American Non-governmental Organizations on Women's Groups

PATRICE C. McMAHON

Since the collapse of communism, East Central Europe has been a laboratory for democratic experimentation. On several fronts, the experiment appears to have been a great success. While many have described this historical transformation, too little has been written about the role of international actors in this process. This is surprising given the number of external actors, particularly American non-governmental organizations (NGOs). The article examines the relationship between American NGOs and women's groups in Hungary, Poland and Russia. It argues that although American NGOs have had discrete positive effects on certain groups and individuals, the strategies employed by these groups may have actually hindered the success of the very goals they pursued. Employing the concept of a domestic advocacy network, the article explains the importance of elite support, contextually rooted organizations and ideas that resonate with local conditions and culture.

INTRODUCTION

As the iron curtain came down, Western governments, intergovernmental organizations, and international non-governmental organizations (NGOs)[1] made their way to the former Warsaw Pact countries. Whether they were interested in political party development or cleaning up the environment, they assumed that democratic consolidation depended on the existence of vibrant civil societies.[2] Believing that money, advice and good intentions could fill the gap created by the retrenching state, members of the international community, almost exclusively from North America and Western Europe, invested in local NGOs, particularly public advocacy groups.[3] The recipe was simple. Advocacy groups would broaden public participation, promote institutional pluralism, and instil democratic values. In record time, it was hoped, this investment would produce civil societies in East Central Europe that would perform the same functions as civil societies in the West.[4]

International assistance has undeniably contributed to the rapid pace of change in this region. At the same time, the strategies used by these international actors may have actually hindered the success of the very goals they pursued.[5] The problem with the strategies adopted by international actors is their failure to help foster a domestic advocacy network. A domestic advocacy network consists of support among local elites, autonomous, contextually rooted organizations,[6] as well as the employment of ideas that resonate with societal conditions and local culture. By supporting and even creating organizations that modelled themselves on those in the West, well-intentioned international actors have overlooked the fact that civil society is inherently about 'things domestic', about citizens' interests, domestic politics and local culture. As the voluntary, self-generating realm that lies between the state and the individual citizen,[7] organizations found in civil society are traditionally created from the bottom up, rather than the top down. Thus, the success of international efforts depends on their ability to cultivate what needs to become an organic relationship between public advocacy groups, citizens and the state. These ties are only possible when local NGOs seek to influence government policies on behalf of citizens they genuinely represent.

The goal of this article is to circumscribe what is a broad and complex topic in an effort to understand the impact of civil society initiatives on East Central Europe. It does so by focusing on the relationship between certain international groups in one narrowly defined sector. This research focuses on the relationship between American NGOs and women's groups in three post-communist countries – Hungary, Poland and Russia. Although the focus is on American non-governmental actors involved in women's issues, these strategies, and the problems encountered as a result, do not appear to be unique to women's issues, American groups, or even NGOs.[8] Nevertheless, it only discusses and evaluates the strategies of American private foundations, including the network of Soros foundations, the Ford Foundation, the German Marshall Fund, the MacArthur Foundation, and the Global Fund for Women, and American women's organizations like the Network for East-West Women, Women's World Banking, and the League of Women Voters.[9] Despite important differences among these post-communist countries, American NGOs interested in this aspect of civil society development have adopted similar strategies and instruments to assist the female population and promote gender equality.

Under the rubric of civil society development, some 60 international groups focused their attention on helping women respond to the challenges posed by the move to democracy and a market economy.[10] For some, this assistance was meant to provide immediate help to women threatened by unemployment, domestic violence and the reduction of state benefits. Others aspired to create independent women's movements, ensuring the female population a voice in the democratic process and thereby strengthening civil society. Among these international actors, American

NGOs were important and generous supporters of gender initiatives, particularly women's advocacy groups. After a decade of involvement, tentative conclusions about the impact of this assistance on women's groups and post-communist society are possible.

Evaluating international assistance initiatives has become a topic of immense interest for policy-makers and academics alike.[11] Democracy promotion or assistance[12] and civil society development have become cottage industries, particularly with the collapse of communism in East Central Europe.[13] In the last decade, the United States government has spent close to '$1 billion on democracy programmes for post-communist countries'.[14] Yet, national governments are hardly alone. The democracy assistance industry now includes 'a growing number of privately formed groups that are international in scope and membership'.[15] It is, thus, not surprising that governments, foundations, boards of various non-profits, and even development banks, want to know more about the efficacy of these programmes. Despite practitioners' obvious interest in evaluating these programmes, those involved in day-to-day issues of democracy making have neither the time nor tolerance for academic debates, and they tend to focus on the future rather than the past.[16] What this has meant is that the questions regarding the impact of democracy assistance efforts too often go unanswered or are asked and answered by citizens of the donor countries.[17]

Understanding the effects of international assistance is also of interest to political scientists studying transnationalism,[18] democratization,[19] international civil society,[20] as well as the diffusion of international norms.[21] Even though, or perhaps because, democracy assistance relates to such a variety of issues, scholars have only started to come to terms with these questions.[22] There are many other reasons for the paucity of research on this topic. In short, political scientists are challenged conceptually, methodologically and even empirically. Terms like *democracy, civil society,* and *NGOs* are often used, but all suffer from definitional or conceptual ambiguity.[23] Methodologically, it is difficult to evaluate international assistance programmes because one must establish somewhat objective criteria for success and demonstrate the causal links between these programmes and domestic outcomes.[24] While some outcomes are quantifiable, this is generally an inadequate way to measure the effect of external actors on domestic outcomes.[25] Finally, while the plethora of actors, projects and countries offer numerous possible case studies, it is not surprising that scholars feel overwhelmed by the thousands of international programmes currently underway around the world.

Without resolving these challenges entirely, primary and secondary research on this sector from 1989 to 1998 explains how assistance by these international actors has contributed to the marginalization and even 'ghettoization' of women's groups in post-communist society. The argument proceeds in four parts. The brief discussion that follows identifies the strategies American NGOs have used to support gender initiatives in the region. It is important for understanding the different ways in which American groups have approached civil society development in this sector. The second part describes some of the positive effects of American involvement. As indicated, however, this assistance has hardly fulfilled initial expectations. The third part of the article initially explains the importance of a domestic advocacy network to the advancement of women's issues and civil society development. It then describes some of the unintended, and certainly undesired, effects of foreign involvement. To summarize, while numerous women's groups currently exist, many more have fallen by the wayside. Moreover, the ones that remain have few members and remain isolated from mainstream politics. While disheartening to admit, ten years of investment and activism have neither improved the status of women nor produced discernible women's movements in any post-communist state. Ironically, American NGOs have discouraged, rather than encouraged, women's groups in East Central Europe from becoming the voice of the female population or an integral part of civil society. Yet, even these conclusions, made at the end of 1999, are still tentative. Rather than asserting that this is the final chapter in the assessment of external actors on women's groups in East Central Europe, the conclusion acknowledges emerging trends that might help reverse some of the detrimental effects identified here.

SUPPORTING GENDER INITIATIVES

Gender equality was one of the myths propagated by communist governments, and the political and economic reforms that took place in the early 1990s only intensified the discrimination women faced.[26] Within a few years, scholars began to document women's disproportionately high unemployment, declining political participation and the effects of conservative backlash.[27] For some politicians, the dawn of a new era meant that women should return home to their 'rightful place' in society.[28] Post-communist governments occasionally acknowledged the disproportionate burden women faced. Yet, socialist principles, which had officially supported gender equality, were so completely discredited that most post-communist governments showed little interest in what were patronizingly referred to as 'women's concerns'.[29] In response to ongoing changes and governments' apathy, numerous independent social organizations began to emerge. In the last decade, these groups have spearheaded efforts to improve the status of women.

The inability or unwillingness of post-communist governments to support gender initiatives forced women's groups to look to the international community for assistance. American NGOs were among the most numerous and eager to lend their support to this cause. Women's groups clearly satisfied American expectations of the organizations that should be found in a strong civil society. While few of these groups enunciate clearly specified strategies toward this sector, it is possible to categorize the similar approaches they have used to promote gender equality in this region: *infrastructural assistance, human capital development* and *project-specific support.*[30]

American groups have focused the lion's share of their energies on infrastructural assistance, which includes financial and in-kind support to establish or support women's groups. For better or worse, the strength of civil society is often measured in terms of the number of local non-governmental groups that comprise civil society.[31] What better way to promote gender equality and a strong civil society than through support for social organizations working on behalf of the female population? At first, American NGOs were largely *reactive*; that is, they provided monies to help develop the infrastructures for institutions that had already formed.[32] Having an office, modern equipment, and a paid staff undeniably helps a group get its message out and make a presence in the community. Within a short time, many of these international groups become more *proactive*, making their own interests and priorities for the region explicit. Requests for proposals and grant solicitations, which often translated into seed money to start new organizations, encouraged the development of numerous groups that would not have formed otherwise.

Human capital development, or the training and education of individuals, has also figured prominently in the strategies of American actors. As in other sectors, the 'reasons for this strategy are both principled and practical'.[33] Well-trained, knowledgeable individuals are crucial for creating strong social organizations.[34] The success of women's groups and ultimately a women's movement depends on capable leaders but also on a critical mass of individuals devoted to gender equality and the advancement of women's rights. Human capital development is also a relatively inexpensive way to promote new ideas and norms. Conferences, fellowships and workshops remain the most obvious manifestations of this approach, but in most cases the content as well as personnel have changed.

Like many other international actors involved in East Central Europe, American NGOs initially targeted small groups of elites who they believed would become future leaders of the women's movement. What this essentially meant was one- or two-day seminars held in the capitals and led by western trainers. By 1993, women in the region had made their dissatisfaction with such techniques known. While few imagined that their American trainers would speak the local language, most assumed that they would have some knowledge of the region. Instead, trainers often preached to participants on how they should 'fight back' and combat inequality, with little regard for historical conditions or local needs. Disappointment with these tactics persuaded American NGOs to modify this strategy. Today, training seminars are more likely to focus on grass-roots organizations in smaller cities and rely on local trainers.

A third, far less coherent strategy used to promote gender initiatives is support for specific projects or research.[35] Throughout the region and in every sector, American groups are increasingly eager to become involved in product-oriented projects, which lend themselves to short-term, identifiable objectives. Involvement in specific projects suggests a beginning, end, and, thus, definitive amounts (if not less) investment. This strategy also allows American groups to be more strategic with their support, providing assistance to the projects they believe are likely to have the most impact. A representative of the Center for the Advancement for Women admitted that it was relatively easy to get foreign support for the Center's *Directory of Women's Organizations*.[36] Yet, these same groups never assisted her organization directly or supported the Center's workshops for unemployed women.

THE MAKING OF WOMEN'S MOVEMENTS

Ten years ago, there were no independent women's groups in any country in East Central Europe. Today, it is not unusual to find legal centres, advocacy groups, or research institutes devoted to gender issues, even in smaller cities and towns. Further evidence of the evolution of this sector comes from interviewing women who are running or closely involved in women's organizations. Such samples are indeed incomplete, but they do provide a more nuanced picture of the changes some women have experienced in the last decade. In examining the landscape of groups and interviewing their representatives, there is little doubt that American NGOs have played an important role in creating and sustaining scores of women's organizations, empowering individuals and supporting countless projects.

In Poland, support from abroad has had a tremendous impact on the number and diversity of women's organizations established in the last ten years. In 1998, more than 90 Polish organizations, foundations, or research institutions claimed to be focused on gender or associated with the women's movement.[37] In contrast to other East Central European countries, a variety of women's advocacy groups have emerged, each one with a specific area of expertise.[38] A glance at the *Directory of Women's Groups* as well as interviews with representatives of women's organizations confirms the important role of external actors, particularly private American foundations. As more than one activist from Poland admitted, it is hard to imagine women's groups in Poland without the support of American NGOs.

Hungary has attracted fewer international donors to the plight of women's rights. Other than the Soros foundations, there are no other major foundations focusing on women's issues. With that said, several American NGOs have been active in this country, including the League of Women Voters, the Global Fund for Women and the Network for East-West Women. Although individuals in both Hungary and the US estimated that somewhere between 100 and 200 women's organizations existed, one would be hard pressed to generate a list of more than 30 organizations actively involved in women's issues.[39] The absence of big American foundations has not prevented activists in Hungary from claiming that they have benefited enormously from the involvement of American groups, particularly the Soros foundations network. The question on the minds of many, however, is what will become of women's advocacy in Hungary once the Soros network begins to withdraw its support for the region, which is set to begin in 2010?[40]

American NGOs and other international actors have also supported the proliferation of women's groups that currently dot the Russian landscape. The MacArthur Foundation, for example, was one of the first international groups to support gender initiatives as early as 1993 when the *Initiative in the Former Soviet Union* was established.[41] The Initiative focused on four priority areas, one of which was human rights and specifically targeted the rights of women and ethnic minorities. This assistance was crucial for making the Centre for Gender Studies in Moscow the hub of independent activism in Russia.[42] With the help of other major American donors, such as the Ford Foundation, the Eurasia Foundation and the Soros foundations network, women's groups have become almost commonplace in larger cities, such as Moscow, St. Petersburg and Yekaterinburg.[43] The Ministry of Justice of the Russian Federation has some 600 women's organizations registered, though some claim that the number of unofficial women's groups exceeds 2000.[44] According to one survey of over 100 women's organizations in Russia, almost half stated that they had received assistance from foreign donors.[45]

While less obvious, American NGOs have been instrumental in educating and empowering women through human capital initiatives and project support. Determining the impact of these strategies is far more difficult than counting the number of groups and discerning their source of support. Nonetheless, interviews with activists from the region and with representatives of American NGOs suggest that the latter have been crucial to skill development for particular individuals and members of certain groups, such as unemployed women. A representative of the League of Women's Voters claims that its projects in Hungary and Poland have positively affected women and men alike.[46] In a couple of cases, women have even indicated that their participation in League-sponsored projects encouraged them to run for parliament. As initially intended, human capital development appears to have influenced the leaders of women's organizations the most. The skills these women learned from foreign-supported workshops, fellowships and international conferences have directly affected the forms of activism that have emerged in East Central Europe. For example, the Director of the Women's Rights Centre credits much of her organization's success, in terms of longevity and growth, to the tactics she learned while on a fellowship in the United States.[47] Since returning to Poland, she has started a Women's 'hotline', lobbied parliament, and written to senators on behalf of women's rights. While hardly novel by Western standards, such practices were unheard of in the region in the early 1990s.

The Network of East-West Women is probably the best example of how an American NGO has empowered individuals and helped promote new ideas associated with women's rights. The Network is involved with numerous projects that either are inspired by experiences in the West or apply to the unique circumstances of women in East Central Europe.[48] However, the most important function the Network provides is 'the voice' it gives to women's groups and individuals from the former Soviet bloc by providing them with computers, training and access to the Internet.[49] The Network currently links over 2000 advocates in more than 40 countries. Since 1990, it has been the primary facilitator of information on and for women in the region.

GOOD INTENTIONS GONE AWRY

For women's groups in East Central Europe with few places to turn, foreign assistance has provided a tremendous financial and moral boost. Along with other international actors, American NGOs have helped establish numerous advocacy groups, brought a level of respect to women's concerns, and sped up the process of building a feminist consciousness among elites and society. In a few notable cases, international interest in women's issues has even encouraged post-communist governments to create offices that acknowledge the unique problems facing women. As one official in Budapest admitted, without pressure from the international community, the Hungarian government would have little interest in women's concerns.[50] The Ministry of Labour's decision to establish an Office on the Status of

Women in 1996 was due largely to Hungary's desire to become a member of the European Union. Without such an office, it was believed, the Europeans would not even consider Hungary's future membership.

While the positive effects of international involvement cannot be ignored, too often this is the only side of the story that is told. As indicated, there are many reasons for the lack of more sophisticated evaluations, including the difficulties involved in isolating the effects of international actors and measuring change.[51] Nonetheless, periodic visits to the region and interviews with individuals closely involved in this sector, as well as other sectors of civil society allow a more complete picture to emerge. Despite the involvement of American NGOs and the flurry of local activities, the past ten years have not culminated in a significant improvement in the status of women, and no discernible women's movements exist in any of the country's studied.

The limited success of women's groups in this region could be the result of history, culture, or poor leadership. It may be just a matter of time, and at present, it is still premature to speculate on the future status of women's movements in East Central Europe. Differences among countries in the region suggest that there are many possible reasons for the success, failure and direction of women's advocacy in these countries.[52] Without ignoring other possibilities, an important reason for this sector's arrested development is international involvement itself. Research on the relationship between American NGOs and women's groups in East Central Europe revealed important similarities, and shortcomings, in the strategies American groups adopted toward gender initiatives in the region.

Cultivating a Domestic Advocacy Network

Indeed, there is a certain paradox in outsiders seeking to build or strengthen civil society in East Central Europe.[53] As the *voluntary* associational realm that lies between the family and the state, civil society organizations, by definition, are created and sustained because of citizens' interests and support.[54] Given the traditional grass-roots trajectory of civil society, external actors must take great care to ensure that a domestic advocacy network is created. This network includes three main components: support among local elites, autonomous, contextually rooted organizations, and culturally specific ideas.

Several literatures are replete with references to the importance of individuals as the intermediaries between the international system and domestic outcomes.[55] Whether one is looking at the effectiveness of transnational actors, the role of ideas in shaping foreign policy, or the adoption of international norms, agency is central to the analysis. Moreover, in all cases, the support of elites or 'important decision-makers' is essential to domestic policy changes. Although advocacy groups are outside mainstream politics and activists are the political entrepreneurs pushing for change, shifts in domestic policy are most likely when activists create political opportunities for elites to support their cause.[56] A domestic advocacy network, at the least, requires attempts by political entrepreneurs to create incentives for decision-makers to proclaim themselves supporters of women's issues and elevate this issue on the domestic agenda.

Creating the necessary links with citizens and the state depends on more than just activists trying to persuade elites to support their cause. Formal and informal institutions are also necessary to ensure contact and interaction among its constituents, with other social groups, and with the state.[57] If nothing else, theoretical and empirical research has concluded that institutions matter; they not only affect outcomes, but they also structure individuals' preferences and behaviour.[58] The advancement of women's issues, as well as civil society development in general, depends on organizations that are formal and robust in order to make claims on the state. At the same time, women's organizations must be flexible and informal enough to represent and co-ordinate grass-roots activities.

International actors did not conceal their belief that local NGOs, particularly ones that modelled themselves on those in the West, were essential to improving the position of women and key to civil society development. What they failed to resolve was how these organizations would become 'contextually rooted'? In other words, how would women's groups sustain local support, develop the necessary links with less formal social groups and retain their autonomy? Although numerous women's organizations continue to exist in East Central Europe, they tend to be small, have paid staffs, and focus on organizational and communications skills. This is not surprising; in fact, it reflects the trend toward the professionalization of social movements and non-profit organizations.[59] The structure and focus of these organizations is perhaps unavoidable, as they need hierarchy and professionalism to develop sustained and legitimate contacts with the state. Nonetheless, they must balance this reality with their need for informal contacts with other social groups and grass-roots ties to the local population. In other words, a domestic advocacy network requires women's organizations to engage and involve their local communities, not just seek to advocate on their behalf.

Involving citizens inherently says something about the ideas that are used, both by international and local groups, to motivate and mobilize citizens.[60] Just as new international norms are more likely to take root when they coincide with domestic norms, support for local advocacy groups is more likely if local groups employ ideas that fit with existing belief systems and culture. How issues are 'framed' is the essentially the glue that links activists and organizations with their constituents and the decision-making elite. Ironically, these ideas must be both familiar and original. They must nurture pre-existing feelings and concerns while they encourage new interests and identities to be forged. To foster grass-roots support and challenge established beliefs, a domestic advocacy network requires language, ideas and myths that exploit but also work with shared understandings and culturally specific discourse.

Taken together, the components of a domestic advocacy network are a way to conceptualize the connective ties that must be established between public advocacy groups, citizens and the state. While important for understanding civil society development in general, this concept helps us understand the multifaceted impact, as well as the shortcomings, of international assistance in this sector. Although American NGOs have had discrete positive effects on the capacities of some women's groups, particular individuals, and isolated projects, these efforts have not produced a net positive effect because of their failure to foster a domestic advocacy network. In other words, how American NGOs have gone about their business of promoting gender issues is essential to understanding why women's groups have yet to become the voice of the female population or an integral part of post-communist society. The unfortunate reality is that while numerous women's groups continue to exist, they are often too consumed by infighting and the need to maintain international support to focus on domestic needs or contribute to civil society. Moreover, these groups are ideologically adrift as they seek to define women's rights or 'their movement' in the post-communist context.

De-politicizing Women's Groups

The strategies adopted by American NGOs have not encouraged women's groups to seek the support of domestic political elites or become involved in mainstream politics. Despite the genuine desire of American NGOs to influence, if not substantially alter, the political environment in these countries they are often unable to pursue these objectives directly because of tax laws in the US that circumscribe their behaviour.[61] Consequently, American NGOs interested in 'supporting the equal participation in society of women and minorities' are prohibited from assisting political organizations.[62] Foundations and other non-profit organizations can make grants for charitable, scientific, literary, or educational purposes only. Thus, although groups are interested in altering the political environment to ensure that women's interests are better represented, their support cannot be used to influence legislation or support groups with a political agenda.

Some American NGOs have been able to side step such regulations. Nonetheless, these restrictions have affected their work and left an ambiguous legacy for women's groups in their relations with domestic actors. In fact, international assistance, which is often not linked to outcomes or grass-roots support, provides disincentives for domestic groups to work with local politicians or other groups in society. Women's groups were either aware of these official stipulations or felt that they would be punished if they adopted an agenda that was deemed too political. For example, women's groups in Russia that had received grants from an American NGO had to write letters to their benefactor testifying that they were not *primarily* lobbying groups.[63]

Restrictions on American non-profit groups did not prevent some international groups from conducting political training workshops for women's groups. In fact, the League of Women Voters conducted workshops throughout Poland and Hungary. Thus, it is possible to encourage groups to be more active in domestic affairs without necessarily breaking any laws. The de-politicization of certain women's groups also does not mean that all women's groups in East Central Europe opt to stay on the margins of political life. A Hungarian government representative noted that while the groups funded by American NGOs tended to be feminist groups which were not active in political affairs, this was not true of Hungary's largest women's groups.[64] In fact, several groups represent women's interests in political parties, trade unions and professional organizations. Despite the numerical strength of these organizations and their popularity with Hungarian women, they receive scant international support. This representative believed these organizations were not supported because their structure and agenda did not coincide with the American vision of 'feminist advocacy groups'. In Russia, there is also some evidence to suggest that there is an inverse relationship between foreign support for women's groups and the latter's interest in working with political elites or becoming involved in mainstream politics. Women's groups that received funding from abroad were less likely to work with political parties as a means to achieve their goals. 'Unfunded groups', or those not supported by Western groups, reported that they were more likely to campaign for politicians sympathetic to their goals more often than funded groups.[65]

Perhaps the de-politicization of women's groups has little to do with the restrictions imposed on American groups working abroad. The de-politicization of women's groups may have more to do with the incentive structure created by American groups themselves, which makes domestic actors, whether they are political or not, irrelevant. When local activists were asked to imagine what this sector would look like if international actors had not become involved in women's issues, most responded that few women's groups would currently exist. Looking at things very differently, an activist from Warsaw speculated that women's groups would continue to exist, but those that did would be far more involved in political and social life.[66] Put plainly, without international support, women's groups would have to get more involved in the 'dirty business' of politics. In mentioning this conversation to an activist in Budapest, she added that at present, there were few advantages for women's groups to tie themselves to particular elites or political groups.[67] If they did, and in the process ignored foreign groups, they would be paid less, travel little, and have no standing outside their country. The outcome, unfortunately, is that women's groups in East Central Europe have become narrow, single-issue groups with little interest in domestic politics.

Discouraging Grass-roots Support

It is perhaps understandable why political leaders themselves have not shown greater interest in women's groups: there are too few incentives for them to do so. Most women's groups have not only failed to become involved in mainstream politics, but a number of factors have prevented them from becoming influential social groups. While independent of the state, they remain extremely dependent on the international community. This predicament has affected the issues they take on, as well as the type of activism they use to respond to inequality and existing political conditions. The bottom line is that this dependence on the international community has translated into a lack of accountability, if not interest, in grass-roots constituency building.

While women's groups cannot depend on their own governments or other domestic sources for funding, American groups (and other international actors) have supported gender initiatives rather half-heartedly, providing some, but only a limited amount of financial support.[68] Being unable to secure a stable source of funding has had two immediate effects on women's groups. First, they must give priority to financial matters over programmatic activities. The feverish efforts to keep their organization afloat and secure funding for the next year means that fund-raising and proposal writing are an organization's main concern, while proposed activities and outreach must be secondary. Ironically, but not surprisingly, groups have to focus on keeping their organization going rather than undertaking programmes to help women or increase their domestic following.

Dependence on the international community also means that the activities of women's groups are often shaped by what the international community determines is worthy of support rather than by what their domestic constituency needs or wants. For example, a few American NGOs have made violence against women and the trafficking of women 'regional priorities'. What this means is that money, in-kind assistance, and invitations to conferences are available for those who take on these issues. As Hungarian activists noted, women in Hungary simply do not see these issues as priorities. Yet, although local groups would prefer to conduct workshops on small business development, which would attract much more grass-roots support, women's groups cannot afford to pass up international assistance, even if it does limit their effectiveness and influence at home.

Ignoring Sustainability and Solidarity

International actors have not always been able to direct or limit their influence. Foreign interest in helping women has thus unintentionally contributed to the high attrition rate among women's groups as well as intense competition among groups with similar goals. The lure of foreign money and attention makes it difficult to forego the advantages of creating a new organization, instead of working with a group that already exists. For example, in the early 1990s when Poland was flush with foreign support for groups that focused on reproductive rights, several such organizations emerged. Although it was hard to distinguish any differences between them, and they seemed to have many of the same members, they remained separate organizations, largely because of the existence of foreign funds. A few of these organizations still exist, but there remains the hope that international support, rather than domestic interest, will breathe new life into these largely defunct organizations.

In the last few years, declining international support for the region has contributed to substantial problems among women's groups. While infighting might have occurred anyway, many activists admitted that the tension was due primarily to the involvement of international groups.[69] In a few notable cases, rifts could be traced to the funding decisions of American foundations. In Poland, women's groups have started to join forces, but resentment still lingers among activists whose organizations were overlooked when an American foundation invested heavily in the creation of a new woman's group in Warsaw. In Hungary and Russia, similar stories abound. Since women's groups do not know how much money other groups receive, there is a tendency to exaggerate the amount of foreign support. Groups and individuals with similar objectives and even a common vision of gender equality are unwilling to share information or work together to build an effective women's lobby because of the obvious benefits of 'going at it alone'. In Hungary, the lack of contact among women's groups was astonishing; more than one activist in Budapest indicated that they were eager to know more about the activities of other Budapest-based women's groups.

Promoting a Western Agenda

By identifying 'areas of interest' or regional priorities, American NGOs are able to 'set the agenda' for women's groups in the region. This second face of power is perhaps as insidious as the grip of the communist party because it too limits choices and shapes the way individuals perceive and respond to their environment, albeit in more subtle ways.[70] As indicated, foreign assistance is difficult to come by, but not all organizations suffer from this problem. American NGOs have supported some women's groups regularly and even generously while others have difficulty getting a computer or an invitation to a conference. While one would hope that only strongly supported, effective organizations are able to enlist foreign support, this is not the case at all. Who gets what is often determined by the grant-writing abilities of the groups' representatives. One might be surprised to learn that many of the women's groups that currently exist have impressive offices and modern equipment but lack a significant following. Support for such groups often continues because the American NGO does not want to lose its investment or acknowledge that it has made a poor funding decision. A final, though important reason why certain women's groups are supported over others is that American NGOs naturally choose groups that reinforce their assumptions and priorities for gender equality.

Human capital initiatives are also guilty of agenda setting, attempting to shape individuals' perception of gender equality based on American values and norms. Instead of providing individuals with general skills, perhaps in community outreach or organizational development, human capital initiatives have focused narrowly on issues associated with gender and equal rights. Too many of the seminars and workshops supported by American NGOs were akin to what could be considered 'feminist training' rather than education meant to empower individuals or become active members of civil society. Consequently, many women's groups in East Central Europe have merely adopted feminist ideas from the United States and tried to replicate American styles of activism. As a consultant to the Ford Foundation noted, the wholesale adoption of American ideas and strategies has backfired on women's groups in Poland.[71] The women's groups that currently exist do not appeal to, nor represent, the average Polish woman.

Simply put, the benefits of ensuring that your organization's objectives fit within the parameters of what international groups are interested in are too great to ignore. Furthermore, international involvement has discouraged women's groups from developing their own ideas on equality and women's rights in the post-communist context. Without realizing it, American NGOs were merely replacing the communist model of equality with an equally foreign, Western model. Attempts to encourage activism with calls for women to 'fight back' and participate in public life have engendered amusement, if not hostility. Such phrases indicate a lack of understanding of recent history as well as ignorance of the accomplishments of women in socialist countries.

CONCLUSION: MAKING INTERNATIONAL ASSISTANCE MORE EFFECTIVE

The abundance of information on American NGOs as well as their high profile in this sector, rather than any presupposition about their behaviour determined the parameters of this research. Studies that evaluated Western governmental and non-governmental assistance to women's groups in Russia, international assistance toward media development in the Czech Republic and Slovakia, and US government programmes in Romania, note similar outcomes and unintended consequences.[72] Yet, they address different sectors and examine a broad array of external actors. It is, thus, fair to conclude that these observations are somewhat representative of international actors involved in civil society development in East Central Europe.

To recap, American NGOs have been crucial to the development of women's groups in Hungary, Poland and Russia. They even shaped the strategies and agendas pursued by these groups because of their ability to reach individuals through human capital initiatives and project specific support. No longer are politicians in these countries wholly dismissive of the problems facing the female population, and the media has become genuinely interested in covering the activities of women's groups. In the process, however, American NGOs have hindered the effectiveness of women's groups and perhaps retarded the development of women's movements. The strategies used by international groups to support gender initiatives failed to create a domestic advocacy network in these countries. Lack of political support, institutional autonomy, and the creation of domestically supported organizations have together resulted in the marginalization of women's groups, which neither depend on nor seek to cultivate domestic support.

These outcomes are indeed disappointing, but it would be wrong to suggest that the international community should merely withdraw its support for women's groups in East Central Europe. If gender equality and human rights are still worthy goals, the response should be, and has indeed become, a modification of the strategies used by international groups. Early assessments of democracy assistance programmes were short-term, administrative evaluations that provided information on specific organizations or projects. In the last five years, scholars and practitioners have started to consider the bigger picture. From this growing literature, a common theme has emerged: how the international community goes about its business of promoting democracy and strengthening civil society makes a difference.

In terms of women's groups and the development of this sector, there are several ways international assistance could be more effective. The three recommendations that follow are not unique to this sector; others involved in similar evaluations have made comparable suggestions.[73] At the risk of stating the obvious, international groups cannot forget the importance of domestic context. Trying to develop a uniform approach to support gender initiatives throughout East Central Europe will ultimately fail because of the distinctiveness of each country. Women in Russia and Poland may face some similar challenges, but their perception of these challenges and likely response to them are mediated by different histories, cultures and political conditions. This may imply the use of totally different strategies for each country. Alternatively, it might mean that international actors must merely consider sequencing their support for gender initiatives. For example, while Poland was ready for a long-term investment in a new woman's organization with extensive outreach capability, a similar enterprise in Hungary would fail miserably because of the lack of nation-wide activity.

Domestic politics determines what is both desirable and possible. Thus, the international community must discourage women's groups from becoming overly dependent on them for support and direction. To ensure that women's groups remain close to the people they claim to represent, assistance should be contingent upon a group's domestic following or its ability to forge ties with other social and political groups. This would not only encourage women's groups to pay more attention to the average citizen but also to collaborate with other social and political groups. It also suggests that members of the international community might think about targeting other groups in society in an effort to have these issues defined as social, rather than women's concerns.

Finally, promoting civil society should mean encouraging indigenous ideas and strategies. While international groups must have their own agenda, they cannot ignore different definitions of equality or innovative ways of promoting women's rights. Sensitivity to local culture means that international groups should provide support for a broader variety of gender initiatives and not focus so heavily on groups which model themselves after those in the West. Similarly, educational initiatives should emphasize civic skills and broad-based training rather than feminist ideology or American activism. The goal should be training groups and individuals in the art of becoming more effective in their unique domestic environments rather than indoctrinating them on how they should define and respond to inequality.

International groups must adopt strategies that seek out the concerns and ideas of women within these countries. Assistance should target gender initiatives that are sensitive to domestic context, political constraints and local culture. In total, these recommendations suggest that international actors must be more bottom-up rather than top down in their support for gender initiatives. International groups need to promote the organic relationship between women's groups, citizens in these countries, and the state by cultivating a domestic advocacy network, rather than merely supporting groups that look and act those in their own countries.

What the Future Holds

With this said, the process is hardly over. A combination of international and domestic factors may lead to significant changes in this sector and a strengthening of women's groups; perhaps the development of women's movements will just take longer than expected. More important than modifications in the behaviour of the international community are the domestic changes that are currently underfoot, which suggest a somewhat brighter future for women's groups in these countries. The glaring inadequacies of current advocacy groups have generated a great deal of criticism from within these countries. Women in the region have started to challenge, reject and adapt feminist concepts; many are eager to replace American or Western European feminism with Hungarian or Russian feminism.[74] In the long-term, in light of declining international support for the region, anti-Western sentiment, and the rise of East Central European feminism, notions of equality are more likely to rely on and respond to domestic input. This region's definition of liberation may mean the development of an array of locally specific women's movements, such as movements that focus on reproductive rights in Poland, unemployment issues in Hungary and political marginalization in Russia.

American NGOs and other international actors have indeed shaped the institutions, individuals, and ideas that currently comprise this aspect of post-communist society. However, large doses of international support cannot inherently or magically strengthen civil society, nor can it define its parameters. Like other aspects of the transition of this region, the future of gender equality and women's groups hinges not on international assistance but on the behaviour, skills and ideas of East Central Europeans themselves.

NOTES

The research on which this essay is based was supported by The Open Society Institute of New York and The Carnegie Corporation of New York. It was undertaken in conjunction with a two-year project entitled 'Democracy Assistance and NGO Strategies in Post-Communist Societies'. For more on this project, see The Carnegie Endowment for International Peace website, http://www.ceip.org. This essay benefited significantly from the comments of Fiona Adamson, Jeff Cole, Larry Diamond, David Forsythe, Rajan Menon, David Rapkin and Jack Snyder.

 1. This term was chosen over possible alternatives because it includes only institutionalized forms of transnational relations. These permanent organizations, which work in more than one country and do not represent a government, have bureaucratic structures with explicit rules and roles assigned to individuals and groups working inside the organization. See Kjell Skjelsbaek, 'The Growth of International Nongovernmental Organizations in the Twentieth Century', *International Organization*, Vol.25, No.3 (1971), pp.420–42.
 2. On the importance of civil society, see Larry Diamond, 'Rethinking Civil Society: Toward Democratic Consolidation', *Journal of Democracy*, Vol.5, No.3 (1994), pp.4–17; Axel Hadenius and Fredrik Uggla, 'Making Civil Society Work, Promoting Democratic Development: What Can States and Donors Do?', *World Development*, Vol.24, No.10 (1996), pp.1621–39; and Michael Bernhard, 'Civil Society and Democratic Transition in East Central Europe', *Political Science Quarterly*,Vol.108, No.2 (1993), pp.307–26.
 3. Advocacy groups are believed to be essential for democracy because unlike professional associations or cultural groups, they seek to influence government on some specific issue. The groups usually included in this category include human rights groups, environmental organizations and feminist groups. See Thomas Carothers, *Assessing Democracy Assistance* (Washington, DC: Carnegie Endowment for International Peace, 1996) p.113.
 4. While rarely enumerated, strong civil societies are believed to encourage institutional diversity while they propagate democratic values. In explaining the functions of civil society in democracies, Robert Putnam distinguishes the 'external' from the 'internal' functions of this independent public space. See Putnam, *Making Democracy Work: Civic Traditions in Modern Italy* (Princeton, NJ: Princeton University Press, 1993) pp.89–90.
 5. While scholars discuss the actors, issues and challenges associated with democracy assistance, they give little or no mention of the strategies used to promote democracy abroad. For example, see Larry Diamond, *Promoting Democracy in the 1990s: Actors and Instruments, Issues and Imperatives* (New York: Carnegie Corporation of New York, 1995).
 6. This term is taken from Sidney Tarrow, *Power in Movement. Social Movements and Contentious Politics* (Cambridge: Cambridge University Press, 1998).
 7. While slightly modified, this is the definition provided by Marina Ottaway and Theresa Chung in 'Toward a New Paradigm', *Journal of Democracy,* Vol.10, No.4 (1999) p.106. Yet, there is no dearth of debates over its definition. See Alison Van Rooy (ed.), *Civil Society and the Aid Industry* (London: Earthscan Publications, 1998); David Rieff, 'Civil Society and the Future of the Nation-State', *The Nation*, 23 Feb. 1999, pp.11–16; and Sheri Berman, 'Civil Society and the Collapse of the Weimar Republic', *World Politics*, Vol.49 (1997), pp.401–29.
 8. The similarities of the strategies used by western non-governmental organizations in various sectors of civil society, including civic education, the media, human rights and the environment, in East Central Europe and Central Asia, are discussed in John Glenn and Sarah Mendelson (eds.), *Evaluating the Role of Western NGOs in Post-Communist Transition* (Washington, DC: Carnegie Endowment for International Peace, 2000). Some of the same strategies and problems are discussed by Marina Ottaway and Theresa Chung, though the international actors they address are both governmental aid agencies and non-governmental organizations. See their 'Toward a New Paradigm', pp.99–113.
 9. The writer did not initially intend to focus exclusively on American NGOs. However, as interviews in the region progressed, it was apparent that women's groups in the region had

the most contact with American NGOs. In fact, many individuals claimed that American groups, particularly private foundations, offered the greatest hope for women's groups in their countries.

10. Since 1991, the writer has followed women's politics in East Central Europe, maintained regular contact with advocacy groups, and conducted approximately 70 interviews in the region in 1993 and 1998. While in Hungary, Poland and Russia, the author interviewed donors, grant recipients, government officials, NGO leaders and academics. The author also conducted over 40 interviews in the US during 1997–98 with programme officers from various American foundations, representatives of government agencies, and individuals involved in women's issues and NGO development in this region. Furthermore, this research was informed by secondary literature on women's politics in East Central Europe. See Tanya Renne (ed.), *Ana's Land* (Boulder, CO: Westview Press, 1997); Barbara Einhorn, *Cinderella Goes to Market* (London: Verso, 1993); and Nannette Funk and Magda Mueller (eds.), *Gender Politics and Post-Communism* (New York: Routledge, 1993).

11. For this reason, Columbia University's Institute of War and Peace Studies sponsored a conference in May 1997 to bring together academics and NGO practitioners. Supported by the Carnegie Corporation of New York, the conference was an important component of the three-year project 'Evaluating NGO Strategies for Democratization and Conflict Prevention in the Formerly Communist States'. Reports from this project are available on the Carnegie Endowment for International Peace's website. See http://www.ceip.org/programmes/democr/NGOs/index.html.

12. Although these terms are used interchangeably by most and are here, Kevin Quigley argues that there is an important difference. Quigley argues that 'assisting democracy' is a better term because it places the impetus of development more squarely on the countries themselves rather than the external actor. See *For Democracy's Sake: Foundations and Democracy Assistance in Central Europe* (Washington, DC: The Woodrow Wilson Press, 1997) pp.8–10.

13. This is not to say that democracy promotion is new. As Tony Smith notes, promoting democracy abroad as a way of enhancing national security was America's mission throughout most of the twentieth century. See *America's Mission* (Princeton, NJ: Princeton University Press, 1994), pp.1–33.

14. Carothers, *Aiding Democracy Abroad* (Washington, DC: Carnegie Endowment for International Peace, 1999), p.41.

15. Chiang Pei-heng. *NGOs at the UN* (New York: Praeger Publishing, 1981) p.11.

16. Thomas Carothers, 'Democracy Assistance: The Question of Strategy', *Democratization*, Vol.4, No.3 (1997) pp.117–19.

17. Kevin F.F. Quigley, 'Political Scientists and Assisting Democracy: Too Tenuous Links', *PS: Political Science and Politics* (Sept. 1997) p.566.

18. In the US, Joseph S. Nye and Robert Keohane are often cited as the intellectual fathers of this tradition. See *Transnational Relations and World Politics* (Cambridge, MA: Harvard University Press, 1971). For recent writings, see Thomas Risse-Kappen (ed.), *Bringing Transnational Relations Back In. Non-state Actors, Domestic Structures and International Institutions* (Cambridge: Cambridge University Press, 1995).

19. The democratization literature is enormous, but only recently have scholars emphasized the role of international actors in the democratization process. See Lawrence Whitehead (ed.), *The International Dimensions of Democracy* (Oxford: Oxford University Press, 1996).

20. The classic piece on international society is Hedley Bull's *The Anarchical Society: A Study of Order in World Politics,* 2nd edn. (New York: Columbia University Press, 1995). For recent discussions of global civil society, see Anne Marie Clark, 'Non-Governmental Organizations and their Influence on International Society', *Journal of International Affairs,* Vol.48, No.2 (1995), pp.507–25.

21. The literature on international norms is growing rapidly. See Jeffrey Checkel, 'The Constructivist Turn in International Relations Theory', *World Politics,* Vol.50 (1998),

pp.324–48; Martha Finnemore, *National Interest in International Society* (Ithaca, NY: Cornell University Press, 1996); and Peter Katzenstein, *The Culture of National Security: Norms and Identity in World Politics* (New York: Columbia University Press, 1996).

22. For example, Thomas Carothers has written a good deal on this subject. While his writings assess only US government democracy assistance programmes, his insights and conclusions are relevant to other international actors. See Carothers' *Aiding Democracy Abroad*; *Assessing Democracy Assistance*; and 'Democracy Assistance'. Also, Ann L. Phillips, 'Exporting Democracy: German Political Foundations in Central-East Europe', *Democratization*, Vol.6, No.2 (1999), pp.70–98; David Chandler, 'Democratization in Bosnia: The Limits of Civil Society Building Strategies', *Democratization*, Vol.5, No.4 (1998), pp.78–102; Joanna Regulska, 'Building Local Democracy in Poland: The Role of Western Assistance', *Voluntas*, Vol.9, No.1 (1998), pp.39–57; and Glenn and Mendelson op. cit.

23. For authors who discuss the conceptual problems associated with democracy and civil society, see Diamond, 'Rethinking Civil Society', pp.5–17, and Quigley, 'Political Scientists and Assisting Democracy', pp.564–5. For a discussion of NGOs, see P.J. Simmons, 'Learning to Live with NGOs', *Foreign Policy* (Fall 1998) p.85.

24. For a brief discussion of these challenges, see Carothers, *Aiding Democracy Abroad*, pp.281–302.

25. Ibid., pp.291–7 and Quigley, 'Political Scientists and Assisting Democracy', p.566.

26. On the status of women during the communist period, see Chris Corrin (eds.), *Superwomen and the Double Burden: Women's Experience of Change in Central and Eastern Europe and the former Soviet Union* (London: Scarlet Press, 1992); Sharon L. Wolchik and Afred G. Meyer (eds.), *Women, State, and Party in Eastern Europe* (Durham, NC: Duke University Press, 1985); and Sharon L. Wolchik, 'Ideology and Equality: The Status of Women in Eastern and Western Europe', *Comparative Political Studies*, Vol.13, No.4 (1981) pp.445–78.

27. There are now numerous accounts of the effects of transition on women in post-communist countries. See Barbara Lobodzinska (ed.), *Family, Women, and Employment in Central-Eastern Europe* (Westport, CT: Greenwood Press, 1995); Marilyn Rueschemeyer (ed.), *Women in the Politics of Postcommunist Eastern Europe* (Armonk, NY: M.E. Sharpe, 1994); Bozen Levin, 'The Status of Women and Poland's Transition to a Market Economy' and Patrice C. McMahon, 'The Effect of Economic and Political Reform on Soviet/Russian Women', both in N. Aslanbeigui, S. Pressman and G. Summerfield (eds.), *Women in the Age of Economic Transformation* (New York: Routledge, 1993).

28. Jacqueline Heinen, 'Polish Democracy is a Masculine Democracy', *Women's Studies International Forum*, Vol.15, No.1 (1992) pp.129–38.

29. This is not so say that there was no reaction by national governments or government leaders. In Hungary, the Ombudswoman Programme Office was created in 1992 and the Ministry of Labour established an Office on the Status of Women in 1996. In Poland in the early 1990s, both the Parliamentary Group of Women and the Plenipotentiary for Family and Women's Affairs were active in ensuring that women's issues were represented in parliament. In Russia, the Commission for Questions concerning Women, Families and Democracy, attached to the President's Office, was established in 1992 and the Women of Russia party managed to secure between 24 and 26 seats during the Russian legislative elections in December 1993. See Wendy Slater, 'Female Representation in Russian Politics', *RFE/RL Research Report*, Vol.3, No.22 (3 June 1994) pp.27–33.

30. These terms were adapted from Kevin Quigley's writings. See 'For Democracy's Sake. How Funder's Fail ... and Succeed', *The World Policy Journal*, Vol.13 (Spring 1996) pp.109–118.

31. In fact, the number of groups in civil society tells us little about the strength of civil society. The Philippines, for example, has over 20,000 registered NGOs, which suggest that a vibrant civil society exists in this country. Yet, the NGO sector is highly fragmented, and given their numbers, they are 'especially unable to advance a progressive social agenda'. See Hadenius and Uggla, 'Making Civil Society Work', p.1627.

32. The terms *reactive, proactive* and interactive, though used somewhat differently, are borrowed from Quigley. See his 'For Democracy's Sake', pp.109–18.
33. Karen Ballantine, 'International Assistance and the Development of Independent Mass Media in the Czech and Slovak Republics', Report prepared for the Carnegie Project on 'Evaluating NGO Strategies for Democratization and Conflict Prevention in the Formerly Communist States', Oct. 1998, p.21.
34. According to Julie Fisher, an institution's autonomy and strength are correlated with the knowledge and expertise of its staff. See *Nongovernments. NGOs and the Political Development of the Third World* (West Hartford: Kumarian Press, 1998), pp.76–182.
35. This is a simplification of the strategies used by international actors. For an elaboration of these strategies, see Patrice McMahon, 'What a *difference* they have made: International actors and women's NGOs in Poland and Hungary', Report prepared for the Carnegie Project on 'Evaluating NGO Strategies for Democratization and Conflict Prevention in the formerly communist States', June 1998.
36. Interview with the Director, the Center for the Advancement of Women, Warsaw, Poland, March 1998.
37. *Directory of Women's Organizations and Initiatives in Poland (Informator o Organizacjach I Inicjatywach Kobiecych w Polsce)* (Warszawa: Fundacja Centrum Promocji Kobiet, 1997).
38. According to Joanna Regulska, Director, Center for Russian, Central and East European Studies at Rutgers University, there are both more and a broader variety of women's groups in Poland. Telephone conversation 18 May 2000.
39. The author obtained a list from the Programme on Gender and Culture at the Central European University in Budapest.
40. Interview with the Director, MONA – The Hungarian Women's Foundation, Budapest, April 1998.
41. Telephone interview with Andrew Kuchins, Center for International Security and Arms Control (formerly programme officer at the MacArthur Foundation), July 1997. Correspondence with Katy Hart, programme assistant, The John D. and Catherine T. MacArthur Foundation, Aug. 1999.
42. Interviews with Anastasia Podsaskaya-Vanderbeck, Director, the Women's Programme, The Open Society Institute-New York, formerly Director, The Center for Gender Studies in Moscow. Interviews in July 1993, Moscow, and June 1997, New York.
43. For more on Western assistance to women's groups in Russia specifically, see James Richter, 'Citizens or Professionals: Evaluating Western Assistance to Russian Women's Organizations', Report prepared for the Carnegie Project on 'Evaluating NGO Strategies for Democratization and Conflict Prevention in the Formerly Communist States', Oct. 1998; and Sarah Henderson, 'Importing Civil Society: Western Funding and the Women's Movement in Russia', Paper presented at the American Political Science Association Annual Meeting, Boston, MA, Sept. 1998.
44. Henderson, p.5.
45. Ibid. p.6.
46. These projects are 'Building Political Participation in Poland', and 'Project Demokracia' in Hungary. Telephone interview with Orna Tamches, emerging democracies programme manager with the League of Women Voters Education Fund, June 1998.
47. Interview with the Executive Director, the Women's Rights Centre, Warsaw, Poland, March 1998.
48. Interview with the Director, Network for East-West Women, Washington, DC, Sept. 1997.
49. NEWW's website is: http://www.neww.org.
50. Interview with a representative from the Women's Section, Hungarian Ministry of Labour, Budapest, April 1998.
51. Several political scientists discuss the methodological problems associated with studying transnational actors, which includes international NGOs. See Thomas Risse-Kappen (ed.), *Bringing Transnational Actors Back In* (Cambridge: Cambridge University

Press, 1995), Ch.1; and Margaret Keck and Kathryn Sikkink, *Activists beyond Borders. Advocacy Networks in International Politics* (Ithaca, NY: Cornell University Press, 1998) Ch.1.

52. For differences between Poland and Hungary, see McMahon, 'What a *difference* they have made'.

53. This echoes a comment made by Irena Lasota in 'Sometimes Less is More', *Journal of Democracy*, Vol.10, No.4 (1999), pp.125–8.

54. Ottaway and Chung, p.106.

55. For perspectives from the transnationalism literature, see Matthew Evangelista, 'The Paradox of State Strength: Transnational Relations, Domestic Structures and Security Policy in Russia and the Soviet Union', *International Organization*, Vol.49, No.1 (1995), pp.1–38 and Thomas Risse-Kappen, 'Ideas do not Float Freely: Transnational Coalitions, Domestic Structures, and the End of the Cold War', *International Organization*, Vol.48, No.2 (1994), pp.185–214. On the importance of individuals to democratic transitions, see Guillermo O'Donnell and Philippe C. Schmitter, *Transitions from Authoritarian Rule: Tentative Conclusions about Uncertain Democracies*. Note: this is the fourth and final volume published by G. O'Donnell, Philippe C. Schmitter and Laurence Whitehead (eds.), *Transitions from Authoritarian Rule* (Baltimore, NJ: The Johns Hopkins University Press, 1986). From the literature on international norms, see Richard Price, 'Reversing the Gun Sights: Transnational Civil Society Targets Land Mines', *International Organization*, Vol.52, No.3 (1998), pp.613–44.

56. Tarrow, pp.71–90.

57. For more on the definition and importance of institutions, see Samuel Huntington *Political Order in Changing Societies* (New Haven, CT: Yale University Press, 1971). More recently, and in terms of foreign assistance to civil society, Julie Fisher also talks about the importance of institutional autonomy and the need to be integrated into civil society. See Fisher, *Nongovernments*.

58. Theory-oriented research on institutions includes James G. March and Johan P. Olsen, 'The New Institutionalism: Organizational Factors in Political Life', *The American Political Science Review*, Vol.78 (1984), pp.734–47. For an empirical example of how institutions matter to domestic policy changes, see Jeff Checkel, 'Ideas, Institutions, and the Gorbachev Foreign Policy Revolution', *World Politics*, Vol.45, No.2 (Jan. 1993), pp.271–300.

59. Tarrow, pp.123–38. For a discussion of the professionalization of women's groups in Russia, see Richter.

60. The role transnational actors' play as 'conveyor belts' which carry western liberal ideas throughout the world has been the subject of recent debate among scholars. While international ideas do affect domestic policy and take hold in certain countries, we have no definitive answer as to why certain ideas 'win out' or take hold and others do not. As Keck and Sikkink note, it is not easy for transnational actors to frame issues successfully because the ideas need to fit with domestic conditions See Keck and Sikkink, p.204.

61. Correspondence with Katherine Hart, Programme Assistant, The MacArthur Foundation, Aug. 1999.

62. 'Initiative in the Independent States of the Former Soviet Union', The MacArthur Foundation document, 1992.

63. Correspondence with Sarah Henderson, based on evaluations for The Ford Foundation, Aug. 1999.

64. Interview with a representative from the Women's Section, Hungarian Ministry of Labour, Budapest, April 1998.

65. Henderson, op. cit., p.6.

66. Interview with the Director, The Women's Information Centre, Warsaw, March 1998.

67. Interview with the Director, MONA – The Hungarian Women's Foundation, Budapest, April 1998.

68. This point is also made by Carothers, *Aiding Democracy Abroad*, p.345.

69. James Richter argues that infighting among women's groups in Russia also occurred between

groups that lacked substantial foreign contacts and, thus, concludes that infighting is not necessarily associated with international actors.

70. For an explanation of the faces of power, see Peter Bachrach and Morton S. Baratz, 'Two Faces of Power', *The American Political Science Review*, Vol.56 (1962), pp.947–52.

71. Interview with local consultant, The Ford Foundation, Warsaw, March 1998.

72. For information on western assistance to Russia, see Henderson, and Richter; Ballantine's report discusses media development in the Czech Republic and Slovakia, and all of Carothers' writings deal with US government programmes.

73. See Glenn and Mendelson; Carothers, *Aiding Democracy Abroad*; Ottaway and Chung, op. cit.; and Lasota, op. cit.

74. Renne's book and Ellen E. Berry's book, *Postcommunism and the Body Politic* (New York: New York University Press, 1995) both discuss the relationship and tensions between western and eastern feminism.

Index